FAMILY THERAPY AND
MAJOR PSYCHOPATHOLOGY

SEMINARS IN PSYCHIATRY

Series Editor

Milton Greenblatt, M.D.

Director, Neuropsychiatric Institute Hospital and Clinics
Professor and Executive Vice Chairman
Department of Psychiatry and Biobehavioral Sciences
University of California at Los Angeles
Los Angeles, California

Other Books in Series:

Psychiatric Aspects of Neurologic Disease, edited by
    D. Frank Benson, M.D., and Dietrich Blumer, M.D.
Borderline States in Psychiatry, edited by John E. Mack, M.D.
Topics in Psychoendocrinology, edited by Edward J. Sachar, M.D.
Consultation-Liaison Psychiatry, edited by Robert O. Pasnau, M.D.
Drugs in Combination with Other Therapies, edited by
    Milton Greenblatt, M.D.
Suicidology: Contemporary Developments, edited by
    Edwin S. Shneidman, Ph.D.
Alcoholism Problems in Women and Children, edited by
    Milton Greenblatt, M.D., and Marc A. Schuckit, M.D.
Ethological Psychiatry: Psychopathology in the Context of
    Evolutionary Biology, edited by Michael T. McGuire, M.D.,
    and Lynn A. Fairbanks, Ph.D.
The Family in Mourning: A Guide for Health Professionals, edited by
    Charles E. Hollingsworth, M.D., and Robert O. Pasnau, M.D.
Clinical Aspects of the Rapist, edited by Richard T. Rada, M.D.
Sex Education for the Professional: A Curriculum Guide, edited by
    Norman Rosenzweig, M.D., and F. Paul Pearsall, Ph.D.
Psychopharmacology Update: New and Neglected Areas, edited by
    John M. Davis, M.D., and David Greenblatt, M.D.
Methods of Behavioral Research, edited by
    E. A. Serafetinides, M.D., Ph.D.
Alcohol and Old Age, by Brian L. Mishara, Ph.D., and
    Robert Kastenbaum, Ph.D.
Psychiatric Research in Practice: Biobehavioral Themes, edited by
    E. A. Serafetinides, M.D., Ph.D.
The Assessment and Treatment of Afro-American Families, edited by
    Barbara Bass, M.S.W., Gail Wyatt, Ph.D., and Gloria Powell, M.D.

FAMILY THERAPY AND MAJOR PSYCHOPATHOLOGY

Edited by

Melvin R. Lansky, M.D.

Adjunct Associate Professor of Psychiatry
University of California at Los Angeles
School of Medicine
Staff Psychiatrist and Chief
Family Treatment Program
Brentwood VA Medical Center
Los Angeles, California

GRUNE & STRATTON
A Subsidiary of Harcourt Brace Jovanovich, Publishers
New York   London   Toronto   Sydney   San Francisco

Library of Congress Cataloging in Publication Data
Main entry under title:

Family therapy and major psychopathology.

(Seminars in psychiatry)   Allen County Public Library
Includes index.   Ft Wayne, Indiana
    Contents: Introduction/Melvin R. Lansky—Family therapy during the
aftercare treatment of acute schizophrenia/Michael J. Goldstein—Communication
and problem-solving skills training with relapsing schizophrenics and their
families—[etc.]
    1. Family psychotherapy. I. Lansky, Melvin R. II. Series: Seminars in
psychiatry (Grune & Stratton) [DNLM: 1. Family therapy. 2. Mental disorders—
Therapy. WM 430.5 F2 F1986]
RC488.5.F335   616.89'156   81-4641
ISBN 0-8089-1360-3   AACR2

Grune & Stratton, Inc.
111 Fifth Avenue
New York, New York 10003

Distributed in the United Kingdom by
Academic Press Inc. (London) Ltd.
24/28 Oval Road, London NW 1

Library of Congress Catalog Number 81-4641
International Standard Book Number 0-8089-1360-3

Printed in the United States of America

To Karen, Madeleine, and Joshua

Contents

Acknowledgments   *ix*

Foreword   *x*

Preface   *xii*

Contributors   *xiv*

Part I   Introduction

1   Major Psychopathology and Family Therapy   *3*
    Melvin R. Lansky

Part II   Schizophrenia

2   Family Therapy During the Aftercare Treatment of Acute
Schizophrenia   *19*
    Michael J. Goldstein

3   Communication and Problem-Solving Skills Training with
Relapsing Schizophrenics and Their Families   *35*
    Ian R. H. Falloon

4   Multiple Family Therapy   *57*
    H. Peter Laqueur

5   Multiple Family Therapy with Schizophrenics:
Experiences with Single Males and Their Families of Origin   *71*
    Carol R. Bley

Part III   The Affective Disorders and Suicide

6   Posthospital Treatment for Psychotic Depressed Mothers and
Their Young Children   *91*
    Judith S. Musick, Frances M. Stott, Bertram J. Cohler,
    and Jerry Dincin

7   Treatment of the Married Bipolar Patient in Conjoint Couples
Psychotherapy Groups   *123*
    Yolande B. Davenport

8   Suicide and the Family: Affective Disturbances and Their
Implications for Understanding, Diagnosis, and Treatment   *145*
    Joseph Richman

Part IV   Character, System, and Symptom in the Personality Disorders

9 Treatment of the Narcissistically Vulnerable Marriage   *163*
     Melvin R. Lansky

10 The Borderline Adolescent and the Family   *183*
     David A. Berkowitz

11 Family Therapy in the Treatment of Alcoholism   *203*
     E. Mansell Pattison and Edward Kaufman

12 Special Problems in Family Therapy Posed by Alcohol Abuse   *231*
     Donald I. Davis

Part V   Special Problems in Family Therapy

13 Anorexia Nervosa and the Family   *249*
     Joel Yager

14 On Stabilizing Families with an Unstable Illness:
     Helping Disturbed Families Cope with Cancer   *281*
     David K. Wellisch

15 Organic Brain Syndrome and the Family   *301*
     *Robert O. Pasnau, Fawzy I. Fawzy, and
     Melvin R. Lansky*

Part VI   Assessment and Treatment

16 The Assessment and Treatment of Disturbed Adolescents
     and Their Families: A Clinical Research Perspective   *327*
     Kathryn L. West

17 Combining Family Therapy and Pharmacotherapy:
     Literature Review and Methodologic Issues   *359*
     Stephen Marder

18 Medication and Family Process   *375*
     Melvin R. Lansky

19 Family Psychotherapy in the Hospital   *395*
     Melvin R. Lansky

Index   *415*

Acknowledgments

My special thanks and gratitude go to colleagues, past and present, in the Family Treatment Program: Vernice Ashley, Carol Bley, Archie Carter, Bonnie Brotman Comfort, Sylvia Douglas, Eugenia Elliott, Revere Forbis, Robin Frasier, Michael Gales, Tara Hicks, Betty Hodges, Adeline James, Jolinda Jose, Victoria Keyes, Geneva McVey, Ellen Simenstad, Albert Sutton, Nina Wendahl, Kathryn West, and Hazel Williams. I am also greatly indebted to Mrs. Robbie Surrence and to Milton Greenblatt, the Series Editor.

Foreword

There was a time when many psychotherapists totally excluded the family from the patient–therapist dyadic relationship. The family was seen as a seriously complicating factor and a force difficult to contend with as it pressured the patient to return to his or her pathologic role within the family—a role that may have led to the illness in the first place.

In hospital practice, visiting hours for relatives used to be severely restricted. Often, family members were specifically enjoined from visiting the sick relative at all; this was especially true when previous visits appeared to have exacerbated the patient's disturbed behavior.

Needless to say, family members were greatly frustrated by their inability to participate in the therapeutic process, and frustrated as well by their inability to obtain information about their sick relative. Often, little was done to allay their curiosity or to help them understand and better tolerate their anxieties, fears, guilt, and depression. Especially disappointing to family members was the lack of guidance on how to help the patient when the therapist was not at hand.

As family process has come under intensive scrutiny, it has become apparent that family dynamics are surpassingly complicated. Early pioneers emphasized one or another core psychopathologic element, but they also recognized what a finely tuned, multifaceted system was the family constellation. Interactions between that system and the outside world raised still other puzzling problems about social networks and support systems. The etiology and treatment of a given individual's disorder appeared to be resting upon an ever-widening base.

In the last few decades, a pronounced change has taken place. Some very good research and a great deal of experience have accumulated regarding the use and practical value of family therapy for a wide variety of psychopathologic disorders. The enormous potential of the family for assisting therapeutic progress is now recognized, and much effort is being directed toward harnessing its energies. The family has become part of the therapeutic process in almost every conceivable medical and emotional situation. The successful combination of family therapy and other effective modalities has come to be viewed as the great challenge by many members of the new generation of family therapists, and it is from the large body of experience and knowledge possessed by this group that Dr. Melvin Lansky has assembled this volume.

Melvin Lansky was the logical choice for the formidable editorial job of bringing out this collection, not only by right of his enormous energy and erudition, but by virtue of his reputation as a teacher, lecturer, researcher, and theoretician. Over the years he has become thoroughly grounded in the day-to-day practical use of family therapy for a great variety of serious psychopathologic disorders. His family therapy program at the Brentwood VA Medical Center has specialized in the use of family therapy for each and every admission, combined wherever indicated with other effective treatments. In addition, during his years of professional activity, Dr. Lansky has become intimately acquainted with most of the thoughtful, enterprising people working at the growing edge of this field. This book, the result of much experience and research, and expressing many differing viewpoints and insights, is herewith commended to the reader.

Milton Greenblatt, M.D.
Series Editor
Seminars in Psychiatry

Preface

So many books on family therapy have been written in recent years that the appearance of a new one requires justification. This book is meant to correct a deficit in the literature on major psychopathology and family therapy. Shortcomings in the literature on this important area of synthesis came to my attention increasingly during the course of my work in family psychiatry, done since 1973 in a general psychiatric setting—the Family Treatment Program at the Brentwood VA Medical Center in Los Angeles. The program is located on a general psychiatric ward that specializes in family treatment and sees families in virtually every case. The criteria for admission are the need to be hospitalized and the presence of a family. Suitability for family psychotherapy as it is usually conceptualized is unimportant. Many of our patients are transferred from other psychiatric settings, and many of them were treatment failures prior to treatment involving the family. It is the primary intent of this book to increase the chances for improvement of seriously disturbed patients who would be at high risk of becoming treatment failures without the use of treatment strategies involving the family.

From the vantage point of a general psychiatric service, the lack of overlap between family psychotherapy and general psychiatry, as they are commonly practiced, is striking. General psychiatry—especially hospital psychiatry—has become increasingly biologic since the advent of effective psychopharmacologic agents; and practice tends to be oblivious to psychosocial factors, especially the family. Family therapists, since the optimism for a reversal of psychotic processes by family therapy alone has waned, have largely abandoned general psychiatric settings and tend to be found in special programs that often do not treat the most disturbed patients in the most disturbed families. The split between family therapy and general psychiatry is, at times, almost complete. Splitting always comes at the cost of integration, and the split between family therapy and general psychiatry is no exception. Many patients most in need of family treatment do not get it. Dynamic issues concerned with management and aftercare are largely neglected by both hospital psychiatrists and family therapists, as are the dynamic and systems significance of the medication process and the hospitalization process—at great cost to the overall effectiveness of treatment.

Until recently, the psychiatric literature has reflected the same type of splitting, with general psychiatric literature often oblivious to family dynamics and family therapy literature often ignoring psychotic or hospitalized patients. The chapters in this book, all but two of which were written expressly for this volume, are organized around problems commonly seen on general psychiatric wards: schizophrenia; affective disorders; organic brain syndrome; and personality disorders and their manifestations in suicidality, marital disharmony, substance abuse, and behavior disorders. Family dynamics, as they interact with the processes of medication and hospitalization, are emphasized heavily. In each chapter, the point of view emanates from the author's clinical setting, case material, and personal conceptualization of the problem. Great pains have been taken to present the context as well as the clinical data, so that the reader can independently estimate the generalizability to other settings of the authors' conclusions. Although there are many common themes in applying family therapy principles and the family systems emphasis to the problems posed by major psychopathology, no attempt has been made here to force a premature consensus on issues that are far from settled.

Melvin R. Lansky, M.D.

Contributors

David A. Berkowitz, M.D.
Director of Family Therapy Training
Clinical Director
Tufts Family Institute
Associate Professor of Psychiatry
School of Medicine
Tufts University
Boston, Massachusetts

Carol R. Bley, M.S.W.
Program Coordinator
Family Treatment Program
Brentwood VA Medical Center
Los Angeles, California

Bertram J. Cohler, Ph.D.
William Raney Harper Associate Professor of Social Sciences
The College
Associate Professor
Departments of Education and Behavioral Sciences
University of Chicago
Consultant to Thresholds
Chicago, Illinois

Yolande B. Davenport, M.S.W.
Chief, Unit of Family Studies
Clinical Psychobiology Branch
National Institute of Mental Health
Bethesda, Maryland

Donald I. Davis, M.D.
Director, Family Therapy Institute of Alexandria
Clinical Associate Professor of Psychiatry
School of Medicine
George Washington University
Washington, D.C.

Jerry Dincin, M.S.W., Ph.D.
Executive Director
Thresholds
Chicago, Illinois

Ian R. H. Falloon, M.B., M.R.C.Psych.
Director, Family Aftercare Program
Assistant Professor of Psychiatry
School of Medicine
University of Southern California
Los Angeles, California

Fawzy I. Fawzy, M.D.
Chief, Consultation Liaison Service
Assistant Professor of Psychiatry
School of Medicine
University of California at Los Angeles
Los Angeles, California

Michael J. Goldstein, Ph.D.
Professor of Psychology
University of California at Los Angeles
Los Angeles, California

Edward Kaufman, M.D.
Associate Clinical Professor of Psychiatry
University of California at Irvine
Irvine, California

Melvin R. Lansky, M.D.
Chief, Family Treatment Program
Adjunct Associate Professor of Psychiatry
Brentwood VA Medical Center
School of Medicine
University of California at Los Angeles
Los Angeles, California

H. Peter Laqueur, M.D. (deceased)
Associate Professor of Psychiatry
School of Medicine
University of Vermont
Burlington, Vermont

Stephen Marder, M.D.
Staff Psychiatrist
Brentwood VA Medical Center
Assistant Professor of Psychiatry
School of Medicine
University of California at Los Angeles
Los Angeles, California

Judith S. Musick, Ph.D.
Director, Thresholds Mothers' Project
Faculty, Erickson Institute for Early Childhood Development
Chicago, Illinois

Robert O. Pasnau, M.D.
Chief, Adult Psychiatry Program
Professor of Psychiatry
School of Medicine
University of California at Los Angeles
Los Angeles, California

E. Mansell Pattison, M.D.
Professor and Chairman
Department of Psychiatry and Health Behavior
Medical College of Georgia
Augusta, Georgia

Joseph Richman, Ph.D.
Associate Professor of Psychiatry
Albert Einstein College of Medicine
Bronx, New York

Frances M. Stott, Ph.D.
Senior Psychologist, Thresholds
Faculty, Erikson Institute for Early Childhood Development
Chicago, Illinois

David K. Wellisch, Ph.D.
Assistant Professor of Medical Psychology
Department of Psychiatry
School of Medicine
University of California at Los Angeles
Los Angeles, California

Kathryn L. West, Ph.D.
Clinical Psychologist
Family Treatment Program
Brentwood VA Medical Center
Assistant Clinical Professor
Department of Psychology
University of California at Los Angeles
Los Angeles, California

Joel Yager, M.D.
Associate Professor
Director of Residency Education
Neuropsychiatric Institute and Brentwood VA Medical Center
University of California at Los Angeles
Los Angeles, California

P A R T I

Introduction

Melvin R. Lansky

1

Introduction: Major Psychopathology and Family Therapy

THE DIVERGENCE OF DISEASE AND SYSTEMS MODELS

The study and treatment of the family are relevant to the treatment of major psychopathology, but the task of applying our insights is not as simple as it might appear. Family therapy grew from the work of those in psychiatry who sought the psychosocial origins of schizophrenia, so initially the movement was closely related to problems of major pathology. Subsequently the two fields diverged widely.[1] Family therapy and that part of clinical psychiatry concerned with major pathology are now distinct disciplines, each with its own methodologies, attitudes toward professional affiliations, standards of competence, views of disease, and attitudes toward reliance on research studies. Family therapy has become interactional, dynamic, intuitive, interpersonal, and dialectical. The trend in clinical psychiatry (with regard to major psychopathology) is Kraepelinian—oriented toward classification and observation, with observables defined apart from interpersonal situations. These differences make it difficult to relate the two disciplines.

For both the clinician and the researcher, integrating family therapy into the study and treatment of major psychopathology requires a change of focus. In seeking greater mastery and knowledge, one cannot remain wedded to a single treatment method. Rather, one must blend methods to prevent treatment failures. Over the past 30 years, much has been learned about psychopathology; so many varieties of treatment have been developed that defining what is most feasible in any given case has become an exceedingly difficult task.

In order to understand the requirements for a rapprochement between the fields of major psychopathology and family therapy, it is helpful to understand their historic divergence. Family therapy arose approximately 30 years ago in the context of the study of major pathology. Major psychopharmacologic agents had not yet appeared. There was little psychiatric treatment other than custodial care in large psychiatric hospitals, or psychoanalysis and forms of psychoanalytic psychotherapy. The family therapy movement stemmed from research efforts to investigate the etiology of schizophrenia within the context of the family. This was at a point in the history of psychoanalysis when ego psychology was dominant and the adaptational dimension of symptoms was of paramount interest. Researchers of different persuasions investigated the hypothesis that the symptoms of schizophrenia could be explained in terms of adaptation, i.e., that schizophrenic symptoms occur as an adaptation to family processes. It was thought possible by some (and presumed by others) that the disorder could be reversed by reversing the family processes that were felt to be causative.

In the early 1950s, consistent psychiatric diagnosis based on the phenomenology and expected course of an illness was rare. There was virtually no drug treatment, and psychotherapeutic circles were dominated by a purism that stressed the advantages of psychoanalytic treatment without modifications. The emphasis on ego psychology generated the notion that all kinds of symptoms could be observed to fill the needs of persons other than the patient, people in the patient's immediate interpersonal surround, and especially those in the family. Homeostatic mechanisms within the family, including interlocking pathologic symptoms, were described in detail by Bateson and co-workers in Palo Alto, by Lidz and Fleck and their co-workers at Yale, and by Murray Bowen and Lyman Wynne in Washington, D.C.

Bateson, Jackson, Weakland, and Haley formulated the "double bind" theory from Bateson's observations of animal play, providing a model for the genesis of the thinking disturbance in schizophrenia.[2] Briefly stated, the theory postulated the programming of the patient with two conflicting injunctions, one at a higher level of abstraction than the other, and a third injunction that precludes the patient's leaving the emotional field. The concept of a "double bind" is commonly mistaken to refer simply to the presence of conflicting injunctions, but the authors were indicating something more complex—that, as a result of conflicting injunctions at different levels of logical types, there would be a learned inability to metacommunicate, that is, to give and receive communications about the kind of communication that is taking place. This would render the individual unable to interpret correctly the messages received. Bateson drew attention to such metacommunication animals, who are able to discern the difference between play, courtship, and attack, even though the actual behavior that makes up these three types of activity may resemble each other. He reasoned that disordered thought and communication in schizophrenics might be understood as a defect in metacommunication.

Lidz and Fleck, from a more psychoanalytic standpoint, reported a number of studies that pointed to the violation of sexual and generational boundaries in the families of schizophrenics, and to the prohibition of extrafamilial socialization.[3] Their observations of the families of schizophrenic patients led them to describe "marital schism," an open rift in the marriage of the parents, which they found to be more prevalent in the families of female schizophrenics, and "marital skew," a deep disturbance in one parent masked by compensatory functioning and distorted communication in the other, more prominent among the families of male schizophrenics.

Murray Bowen, starting from a study of entire families hospitalized for a lengthy period, proposed the hypothesis that schizophrenia developed as the result of immaturity compounded and projected through marriages over at least three generations.[4] In Bowen's opinion, the most vulnerable child in a family is the one most likely to absorb some of the immaturity present, even in a relatively normal marriage. This child, now more dysfunctional than either parent, tends to marry someone with a similar degree of dysfunction, thus forming a union of even greater immaturity, which is absorbed in turn by its most vulnerable offspring. Through such a declension of immaturity, a schizophrenic patient eventually develops.

Wynne, in collaboration with Singer and others, described in detail disordered patterns of communication in the families of psychiatrically disturbed patients, and described the communication deviance that particularly characterized the parents of schizophrenics.[5] He coined the terms "pseudomutuality" and "pseudohostility" to refer to the peculiar patterns of relatedness found in such families, and he developed "rubber fence" metaphor to describe the manner in which a family system holds onto its sick member and the impulsive quality of the patient's return to that system.

All of these early studies posed a hypothetical question: What must be the nature of an intrafamilial situation in order for it to transmit schizophrenia on an entirely interpersonal basis? Disclaimers notwithstanding, these investigations were efforts to determine etiology. Unfortunately, they suffered from a variety of methodologic flaws. For example, none dealt adequately with the issue of diagnosis. One[5] even included patients with actue reactive schizophrenia, a clinical entity which today is considered more a schizophreniform condition than a true schizophrenia. In all, these early investigations yielded no convincing evidence that family processes in and of themselves can cause schizophrenia. Furthermore, family therapy was designed as a technique for altering pathologic family systems; the hope was that this would suffice to reverse the schizophrenic process. At best, it has served to modify the course of the disease, rather than effect a cure.

Many family therapists have dealt with disappointment in the treatment of schizophrenia by confining their efforts to treating conditions more easily reversed by family therapy alone. The family therapy movement has grown enormously, but in directions that isolate it from the mainstream of psychiatry and general mental health care.

This isolation of family therapy is more significant as monumental advances in the fields of general psychiatry and psychoanalysis have occurred since about 1950. The advent of neuroleptics, tricyclic antidepressants, monoamine oxidase (MAO) inhibitors, and lithium carbonate have made effective treatment possible for many psychotic disorders. Much knowledge on the classification and treatment of such disorders has been accumulated.[6,7] In many cases, diagnosis is indicative of an expected course of illness and response to treatment. Patient follow-up and outcome research are used increasingly to select rational treatment strategies. General psychiatry has proceeded in the exact opposite direction to that of the family therapy movement; that is, toward the medical model, and toward classification, phenomenology, natural history and specific treatment of the individual.

Psychoanalysis has also evolved since family therapy arose as an offshoot of the adaptational point of view.[8] The last several decades in particular have witnessed attention to patients previously thought to be untreatable through psychoanalysis, or untreatable altogether, including borderline patients, patients with narcissistic personality disturbances, and, in some case, psychotics.

Drawing from earlier works by Melanie Klein[9] and her co-workers,[10] the object relations theorists[11-14] have elaborated conceptualizations of character structure, clinical phenomenology, and modifications of psychoanalytic technique to treat patients previously thought to be too deeply disturbed to profit from psychotherapy. Klein drew attention to defects of self-regulation manifested by ego splitting together with the phantasy of fusion (projective identification), for the purpose of controlling or being controlled, and of avoiding the experience of separateness. Klein's conceptual apparatus, confusing as it may seem at first, provides a major bridge between psychoanalysis and systems thinking. The patient's attempts to deal with difficulty by inviting or provoking a relationship based on fusion phantasies and mutual control is often detected only by the therapist's emotional response to the patient, i.e., by awareness of the countertransference. Elaboration of the concepts of splitting, projective identification, and countertransference-derived interpretation (in intensive psychotherapy or for larger social units, such as families and institutions) has grealy enlarged our capacity to treat very disturbed patients.

Since about 1970, much attention has been paid to narcissistic personality organization, to the specific mirror and idealizing transferences found in such patients, and to the central defensive activity of preventing fragmentation experiences and humiliation. Heinz Kohut, has drawn particular attention to the disorganizing effect of interpretation that points abruptly to what the patient does, rather than one beginning with an empathic grasp of the patient's experience.[15] Kohut has delineated specific transferences of narcissistic patients in analysis and stressed the importance of forming a relationship that will allow for cohesiveness of self-structure so that development can continue. Kohut's line of thinking[9] implies that many heretofore "untreatable" patients may have been mortified by narcissistically wounding features of treatment technique, rather than by an inherent untreatability in their condition. The psychology of the self holds out new hope, especially for patients with personality disorders—narcissistic and otherwise. These advances have made psychoanalytic treatment more powerful and broader in scope. There is also greater potential for the application of psychoanalytic insights to other treatment modalities in patients previously thought to be untreatable.

Systems of health care delivery have evolved so that mental health services no longer consist of analysts and asylums with very little in between. There now exist feasible public resources and insurance programs to definitively treat many more people than decades ago.

In contrast, the family therapy movement has grown in a different direction. Its basic orientation has been that of the family system: how it functions internally, and how it interlocks with other systems in the environment. The relevance of systems factors is not in question. For anyone willing to observe families carefully, the malignant effects of blaming, scapegoating, and other processes of disowned delegation are obvious. The point to stress is that the family therapy movement has focused on systems factors to the virtual exclusion of all others. Family therapists pay little, if any, attention to individual assessment and diagnosis or to the specific phenomenology of mental illness. They rarely employ either psychotherapy or pharmacotherapy as adjuncts to their treatment of the family as a group. The specific family therapy techniques they practice often derive from one school of thought and are thus strategically limited. The mode of psychopathology most often considered is that of conflict alone, leaving little room for addressing problems due to deficits.

Perhaps the most serious result of the narrow focus that much of the family therapy field reflects is the limitation it places on the problems it *can* address. This is particularly unfortunate when it serves to neglect the use of family therapy in the treatment of patients with major psychiatric disorders. Attempts to use family therapy in the treatment of schizophrenia and other severe psychiatric illnesses have met with discouraging results. Consequently, many family therapists have abandoned attempts to treat severely disturbed patients and concentrate instead on psychiatric conditions that respond to this particular form of treatment. An alternative response to discouraging results in the past would be to examine ways in which techniques of family therapy might be modified in order to be appropriate and effective in treating cases involving major psychopathology. It is the intent of this volume to explore such alternatives.

THE NECESSITY OF RAPPROCHEMENT

Early in the development of a discipline, it is justifiable to engage in therapeutic purism and the exclusive development of one method only. But psychiatry, psychoanalysis, and family therapy are now beyond their adolescence, and there is a necessity for rapprochement in these fields. Indeed, therapeutic purism in all three fields has resulted in a constriction of the therapeutic range so that treatment tends to be offered to the kind of patient that the therapist is comfortable treating. In family therapy, this has sometimes resulted in an abandonment of the patient with major psychopathology. For psychoanalysis, Eissler proposed that specific modifications in technique be devised for specific modifications in the ego.[16] This proposal resulted, in the main, in a constriction of psychoanalysis justified by the notion that any so-called parameter of technique was to be avoided. Psychopharmacologic research, with its heavy emphasis on well-designed and controlled studies, has tended to steer away from, or at least mistrust, any methodology employing treatment modalities that cannot be studied in the same way that drugs are evaluated.

Nonetheless, these areas are interdependent and should all be considered in the treatment of major psychopathology. A knowledge of systems, especially the family system, is necessary, not only for psychoanalysis but for competent psychopharmacologic treatment. Major forces that oppose both forms of treatment come from unrecognized and unresolved difficulties in the family. Psychopharmacologic treatment may unwittingly recapitulate family processes that the patient sees as dominating, controlling, rejecting, rendering asexual, or humiliating him. Furthermore, the patient's drug lapses may be related to the family's need to label the patient the crazy, dysfunctional member. The family may, in fact, engage in maneuvers that ultimately sabotage drug treatment. Then, too, the patient's remission on medication may come at the cost of losing a sort of power that symptoms granted. If so, the patient may *invite* interference by the family, or may resist or confound treatment in ways that require dynamic understanding in order to minimize medication lapse, treatment refusals, or rehospitalizations.[17]

The dynamic therapist dealing with families or individuals must understand that major psychopathology involves not only internal and interpersonal conflicts, but also outright deficits.[18] Deficits, whether they derive from faulty nurturance or from basically genetic ego impairments, find their way into the attachment behavior of the person with the disorder, and manifest themselves in overattachments, erratic detachments, and difficulties differentiating himself within the family or elsewhere. Deficits can be so intertwined in the family process that they become part of the family homeostasis, in terms of collusive transpersonal defensive operations, provocations or invitations to external control on the part of the patient, or symptomatic flare-up at times that deflect attention from other trouble spots in the family. The hope that major psychopathology would be completely reversible by psychotherapy (either psychoanalysis or family therapy) has not been borne out. There always remains the problem of deficits and a course of residual illness even after the best and most successful of treatments.

Treatment predicaments vary not only from family to family but also from disorder to disorder. When major psychopathology is involved, family therapy should be designed to meet specific psychopathologic predicaments found in that disorder. In schizophrenics, this includes the use of symptoms to control the family, the exacerbation of symptoms in response to conflict in those on whom the patient depends, post-psychotic depressions, and residual psychotic pheonmena during remissions. In manic-depressives, typical predicaments include contentiousness of the manic phase, the vulnerability to separations, and rapidity of onset of a potentially disastrous manic episode. In personality disorders, narcissistic vulnerability may take the form of destructive symptoms (suicidal, alcoholic, acting out), chronic conflict (blame), or dysfunction in one member of the family system. A chaotic family homeostasis is maintained by collusive defenses, humiliation proneness, and terror of separations.

Furthermore, family therapy must include not only immediate care of major symptomatology, but aftercare for a lengthy or indefinite course of illness, where the expected course of that illness can be significantly altered.

There is a striking shift in emphasis from family therapy that purports to discover the etiology of a disorder to family therapy that purports to avoid treatment failures, no matter what the cause of the disorder. The justification for family psychotherapy does not depend on the supposition that the family *causes* psychiatric illness in any way. The only assumptions necessary are that the vicissitudes of family process can alter the course of a disorder, for better or for worse, and that the family process is modifiable by therapy.

The task of adapting family therapy to difficulties posed by a disorder differs greatly, depending upon whether one's goal is to avoid treatment failures or to ascertain how much can be accomplished by family therapy alone. Emphasis on the reduction of treatment failures often calls for the use of more than one kind of treatment. The study and evaluation of combinations of treatment modalities raise questions different from those raised by the study of one modality alone. Studying a particular medication, one might worry about absorption, dosage, timing, specific indications, measurements of outcome, correct diagnosis, etc. The same drug, as it is considered from the point of view of the interplay of pharmacology and family dynamics, may raise additional questions, such as: What was the pressure to give the drug in the first place? Was the judgment made because of the therapist's feeling of futility or because of a correctly discerned indication for the drug? Was the move by the therapist to take over (by medicating) helpful or harmful in terms of the maximum feasible return of responsibility to the patient? Especially from the aspect of personal responsibility, the very act of medicating has enormous implications. At times, medicating may work synergistically and, at times, antagonistically with the overall project of helping the patient to be as self-regulating and responsible as possible.

An appreciation of the practical limits of combined biologic and psychotherapeutic methodology depends on an intimate knowledge of all the components and their interaction. The blend of modalities per se—the specific components, and the timing of their use—is never as isolatable for study from the style of the person or persons doing it than is any one of the methods alone. Accordingly, a blend is much more difficult to scrutinize, and the results of such scrutiny are more context-dependent and tentative than are the results of examining a single method. It is with these difficulties in mind that the following chapters put special emphasis on clinical context and on the specifics of the conduct of treatment.

A NEW ECLECTICISM

An application of family therapy principles to the predicaments posed by major psychiatric illness must consider the overall goal of coping with the illness and minimizing its effects. It is not sufficient to treat the family in isolation with the sole aim of reducing conflict. A new eclecticism is required, based on rational strategies designed to overcome specific psycho-pathologic obstacles appearing as specific treatment difficulties. Such obstacles include pathologic features found in schizophrenia, affective disorders, personality disorders and symptomatic manifestations thereof, and organic brain syndromes, as well as the problems of narcissistic vulnerability, medication discontinuance, and family psychotherapy in the hospital. Adaptations of family therapy for specific problems have been developed and are the subject of the ensuing chapters. Each account deals with the family system and uses family psychotherapy as one major modality of treatment. All but two of the chapters were written especially for this volume.

Recent research on schizophrenia and the family has yielded studies free of etiologic presuppositions that emphasize the role of the family in affecting the course of schizophrenia. In a carefully designed study, Brown[23] and co-workers have identified within the families of schizophrenics a type of transaction—negative expressed emotion—that adversely affects the course of illness. Altering either the quantity or quality of family transactions has been found, on this study and in replications, to decrease the incidence of rehospitalizations.

Knowledge of the specifics of schizophrenic disorders and the effects of the illness can be helpful to the family. Professionals have often been reluctant to tell patients or their families that the patient has schizophrenia. This hesitance is understandable, given the social stigma that remains attached to the disease, and it is certainly justified if the diagnosis of schizophrenia is not made precisely and consistently. Nonetheless, there are enormous disadvantages in having the patient and family not know what is wrong with the patient. There are well-understood features of the illness that they can master if they are able to anticipate and understand them as part of the disorder. If treatment is properly handled, this knowledge does not remove the patient's sense of responsibility, but rather, promotes agreement within the family about the needs of each member and the extent to which each is capable of assuming specific responsibilities.

The chapters on schizophrenia, the disorder of original interest to pioneers in the study of the family, include one by Michael J. Goldstein that is unique in its consideration of the relationship between family therapy and medication. The chapter by Ian R. H. Falloon outlines a behavioral approach to the treatment of schizophrenics in the family setting. The late H. Peter Laqueur was among the first to appreciate the significance of multiple family group therapy and was the foremost theoretician on multiple family groups. Unfortunately, he died before he was able to complete his chapter on multiple family therapy in the treatment of schizophrenics; one of his most recent papers is reprinted here instead. Carol R. Bley gives a detailed account of the use of multiple family group therapy with a hospitalized schizophrenic population, and deals with the application of multiple family group therapy principles to the long-term treatment of schizophrenics.

There has been a dearth of published work on the family treatment of the affective disorders. Much is known about the course of manic-depressive psychosis: exacerbations at times of separations, the difficulties managing the acute manic patient, and the urgency in dealing with emerging illness rapidly. Outright didactic sessions are helpful, if not mandatory, in managing mania, especially outside the hospital. Major contributions to the literature on the family treatment of manic depressives have come from Yolande Davenport and her colleagues at the National Institute of Mental Health. Davenport's chapter on the treatment of bipolar patients in homogeneous couples groups draws on her extensive previous work and presents an up-to-date statement of this major treatment and research effort. The chapter by Judith Musick and her co-workers outlines the innovative Thresholds Project, a model treatment program for depressed and economically disadvantaged women and their children that draws upon a variety of disciplines, theories, and research studies in order to intervene effectively in a particularly difficult clinical situation. Joseph Richman's chapter on suicide and the family draws special attention to the problem of affect in the family; his contribution is a unique statement on suicide in the context of the family.

With personality disorders that manifest in antisocial actions, substance abuse, suicidality, or in chronically conflictual relationship systems, one faces the choice of treating a symptom, a family system, or a personality system. It is difficult to make substantial changes in the patient's personality system if the family system is undermining the treatment or if the patient's symptomatology is so rampant as to be life-threatening. In general, destructive symptomatology of this sort must be brought under control before systems can be expected to change. Furthermore, collusive and sabotaging family systems must be dealt with before personality changes can occur in the patient. Such considerations are very important in treatment strategies for specific cases, such as the suicidal patient, the alcoholic patient, the acting-out adolescent, the person with sexual dysfunction, and the couple in a chronically conflictual marriage.[24]

My conceptualization of the psychopathology in the narcissistically vulnerable marriage tries to provide bridges between personality organization, family system, and symptoms, in order to discuss the rationale for treatment strategies specific to problems posed by the personality organization of narcissistically vulnerable spouses. Treatment strategies aimed at narcissistic vulnerability address overreactivity, humiliation proneness, and failure of repression (blame, acting out) rather than the inability to react directly, excessive guilt, and excessive repression found in less severe disturbances. The technique of having all transactions in conjoint sessions go through the therapist may be effective in dealing with overreactivity, at least in the therapy session.[4] The use of intergenerational reconstructions to make pathologic preoccupations intelligible and more acceptable to the family may help deal with humiliation proneness. So may an interpretive style that begins with empathic contact with the patient's and family's experiences, rather than by attention to their behavior. The latter should be addressed only after empathic contact has been made.

Specific adaptations of family psychotherapy, individual psychotherapy, and even pharmacotherapy to aspects of narcissistic vulnerability are necessary because narcissistic vulnerability seems to be a common concomitant of personality disorders and the psychoses. The specific forms of splitting and projective identification noticeable in the families of patients with severe personality disorders are usually repeated in hospital settings. Splitting must be dealt with in ways that expand therapeutic possibilities, rather than in ways that recapitulate pathologic cycles of interaction.

David A. Berkowitz, writing on the treatment of borderline adolescents, places heavy emphasis on the family system in the treatment of personality disorders. A psychodynamic understanding of vicariousness is necessary to explain the investment that people in the immediate surround have in perpetrating someone else's pathology. In families and in treatment situations, such patients have the capacity to invoke or exploit preexisting tensions so that they reappear with the patient at the center of them, and in a situation where learning from experience is impossible unless the provocation to collude is resisted.

The chapters by Davis and by Pattison and Kaufman dwell on many theoretical and practical aspects of treating alcohol abuse in the family system. Yager, in a scholarly chapter on anorexia nervosa and the family,

presents a carefully documented skepticism regarding premature conclusions about this enigmatic condition, together with specific treatment
recommendations.

There remain many disorders for which family treatment is usually
neglected, including organic brain disease and cancer. This neglect may be
due to a sense of hopelessness about the patient's condition, or out of the
conviction that the disorder is entirely biologic and needs supportive
treatment only. The organic etiology of the disorder and the irreversibility
of the process so dominate the clinical picture that the psychotherapist
may forget the possibility of working through in the family system and in
the personality system without changing the organic disorder, whether it
be somatic or psychiatric. Robert O. Pasnau, Fawzy I. Fawzy, and I
discuss the clinical phenomenology or organic brain syndrome, point out
difficulties commonly found within the family system, and describe a type
of family psychotherapy designed specifically for the treatment of this
large, neglected group of patients. David Wellisch considers issues
relevant to the treatment of a family when one of its members has cancer.

The section on evaluation and treatment begins with a study by
Kathryn West that forms a pathway toward systematic consideration of
treatment strategies originated by the renowned UCLA Family Project in
their treatment of families who are also studied by the project researchers.

The dynamics of the process of medication must be enriched by a
knowledge of the specific effects of medication that either confirm or
confront various family myths.[19] Such myths may have a destructive effect
on treatment. One such idea is that all the badness in the family resides in
the behavior of a volatile member and must be eradicated. Another is the
notion that the patient is not sexually fit or competent; therefore, there is
no harm done if he or she is deprived of libido or of the capacity to
function sexually through use of neuroleptics. Also, a myth may exist that
an individual's psychosis justifies domination and control by others who
are responsible for the patient.

Properly applied, a knowledge of the dynamics of medication may
enhance treatment; if neglected, large numbers of treatment failures are
likely to ensue. For example, medication discontinuance is a major
problem in purely biologic approaches to psychiatric disorders. An
understanding of the factors that affect drug compliance is, therefore, a
crucial part of the pharmacologist's armamentarium.[20] Stephen Marder's
careful review highlights theoretical issues and summarizes recent studies
on the combination of medication and family therapy. My clinical article
on the same subject emphasizes the effects of family process on
medication and the effect of medication on the family process, hopefully
highlighting common difficulties that lead to treatment failures.

The applicability of family psychotherapy for the hospitalized patient needs clarification.[21,22] That the patient requires hospitalization to contain chaos that cannot be contained by the personality system or the family system cannot be incidental in the psychotherapy. The therapist's awareness of the significance of hospitalization—settling into the hospital, using the hospital, and finally leaving the hospital—must be employed in all phases of the family treatment process. It is usually a costly error to conduct family therapy without an awareness of the effects of hospitalization as a containment process for the patient. Unmanageable splitting often confounds the family treatment when (1) the sensitivity of the family to blame and demands is not anticipated early in treatment; (2) management issues arising in the hospital are settled outside of the family sessions; or (3) the significance of disowned but deep nurturant ties to the family and hospital system are not dealt with prior to discharge from the hospital. These issues are addressed clinically and theoretically in my chapter on family psychotherapy in the hospital.

With the adaptation of family treatment to major psychopathology in the specific psychiatric disorders, many common themes emerge. Multiple family group therapy, for example, pioneered by H. Peter Laqueur,[25] has been found useful in treating many disorders. The fact that families come together facing a shared problem, and that ego strength may be shared by identification with people in similar parts of another family, make for enormous therapeutic possibilities resulting in treatment that is more supportive and confrontative, and simultaneously more sustaining and explorative. Multiple family groups consisting of families homogeneous for predicament (this may include diagnosis of the index patient[20]) have been advocated for narcissistically vulnerable couples, for manic-depressive patients and their spouses, for schizophrenics in their families of origin, and for alcoholics and their families, to name several of the homogeneous groups.

The role of instruction in the process of family therapy has considerable value, but has been either neglected or relegated to a minor role in most family therapy literature to date. It may be important to teach a depressed mother to nurture her children, or to teach the family of a schizophrenic about the nature of the illness, as well as to work on pathologic aspects of the family's transactions. Hopefully, previously neglected educational strategies can in the future be developed to the point of being fruitful.

In general, an approach for almost any type of major psychopathology might include multiple family group therapy: attention to features of narcissistic vulnerability; awareness of family processes that affect medication; handling of splitting (especially as it shows up in countertransference phenomena); and proper instruction about the specific difficulty being treated. These have to be blended with specific biologic and psychotherapeutic approaches to the disorder. Anecdotal and systematic study of treatment combinations is vital, but the task of studying combined therapies is much more difficult than studying the effects of the component treatments themselves.

There are topics worthy of inclusion that are not represented for reasons of limited availability and space, among them sexual dysfunction, neurosis, child abuse, unipolar depression, perversions, and the abuse of substances other than alcohol. I hope that these and other areas of pathology in which family therapy can contribute to treatment will be addressed in subsequent works.

REFERENCES

1.   Lansky MR: Research in family therapy, in Serafetinides EA (ed): Methods of Biobehavioral Research. New York, Grune & Stratton, 1979
2.   Bateson G, et al: Toward a theory of schizophrenia. Behav Sci 1:251–264, 1956
3.   Lidz, T, et al: Schizophrenia and the Family. New York, International Universities Press, 1965
4.   Bowen M: The use of family theory in clinical practice. Compr Psychiatry 7:345–374, 1966
5.   Wynne, L, et al: Pseudomutuality in the family relations of schizophrenics. Psychiatry 21:205–220, 1958.
6.   Feighner J, Robbins E, Guze S, et al: Diagnostic criteria for use in psychiatric research. Arch Gen Psychiatry 26:57–63, 1972
7.   DSM III, American Psychiatric Association, 1980
8.   Hartmenn H: Ego Psychology and the Problem of Adaptation, New York, International Universities Press, 1958
9.   Klein M: Notes on Some Schizoid Mechanisms (1946), in Riviere J (ed): Developments in Psychoanalysis. London, Hogarth, 1952
10. Bion WR: Seven Servants. New York, Jason Aronson, 1977
11. Fairbairn WRD: Psychoanalytic Studies in the Personality. London, Tavistock, 1952
12. Winnicott D: Playing and Reality. New York, Basic Books, 1971
13. Dicks HV: Marital Tensions. New York, Basic Books, 1967
14   Kernberg O: Borderline Conditions and Pathological Narcissism. New York, Jason Aronson, 1975
15. Kohut H: The Analysis of the Self. New York, International Universities Press, 1971
16. Eissler KR: The effect of the structure of the ego on psychoanalytic technique. J Am Psychoanal Assoc 1:104, 1953

17. Lansky MR: Establishing a family-oriented inpatient unit. J Operational Psychiatry 8:66–74, 1977
18. Grotstein J: The psychoanalytic concept of schizophrenia: I. The dilemma. Int J Psychoanal 58:403–425, 1977
19. Stierlin H: Group fantasies and family myths. Family Process 12:111–127, 1973
20. Lansky MR, Bley, CR, McVey, GG, et al: Multiple family groups as aftercare. Int J Grp Psychother 28:211–224, 1978
21. Lansky MR: On the idea of a termination phase for family psychotherapy in the hospital, in Wolberg L, Aronson M (eds): Group and Family Therapy 1980—An Overview. New York: Brunner Mazel, 1980, 323–334
22. Lansky MR: The initial phase of family therapy in the hospital. Int J Family Psychiatry (in press)
23. Brown B, Birley JLT, Wing JK: The influence of family life on the course of schizophrenic disorders. Br J Psychiatry 121:241–258, 1972
24. Lansky MR: On blame. Int J Psychoanal Psychother 8:429–456, 1980
25. Laqueur HP: Mechanisms of change in multiple family therapy, in Sager & Kaplan (eds): Progress in Group and Family Therapy. New York, Brunner Mazel, 1972

PART II

Schizophrenia

Michael J. Goldstein

2

Family Therapy During the Aftercare Treatment of Acute Schizophrenia*

With the last few years, the thrust of the community mental health center movement at the national and local levels has generated a treatment model for acute schizophrenia composed of two phases—a brief inpatient phase, measured in days, followed by an extended period of aftercare in the community. In the old system, relatively complete remission of schizophrenic symptoms was the goal, whereas minimal remission of only the most acute and disorganizing symptoms is the goal of inpatient treatment in the new system. The balance of the recovery process, it is believed, can be more effectively achieved once the patient has been returned to community life.

Although this new model emphasized aftercare in the community, it was far from certain what this meant, particularly for the acute, young, first-admission schizophrenic. A number of key questions still remain to be answered concerning effective modes of treatment in community settings. First, what role should antipsychotic drugs play in the aftercare program? We know well the impact and significance of these drugs during extended inpatient treatment of schizophrenics.[1] But, given our knowledge of the difficulties involved in continued acceptance by patients of these drugs following discharge, how can they be utilized in community-based treatment of acute schizophrenics, and for how long?

*Reprinted with permission from Goldstein MJ: Family therapy during the aftercare treatment of acute schizophrenia, in Strauss J et al (eds): The Psychotherapy of Schizophrenia. New York, Plenum Press, 1981

Second, many patients released from community mental health centers still manifest residual symptoms and adjustment difficulties. What models of social therapies are appropriate to deal with the reintegration of such patients into the community, and perhaps prevent future psychotic breakdowns? The issue of psychotherapeutic approaches to schizophrenia has moved to a new arena and deals with a different stage of the illness. No longer do we ask whether psychotherapy is effective in aiding the patient to reconstitute from psychotic confusion. Now we ask whether, once some partial restitution has been effected, social therapies can play a significant role in the treatment of schizophrenia.[2,3] Can the interacting roles of drugs and social therapies be utilized to maximize the effects of each? The research project described in this paper represents an attempt to attend to these issues.

METHOD

Design of Study

The study conducted with my colleagues, Eliot Rodnick and Phillip May, was carried out at the Ventura (Calif.) Mental Health Center. In this center, schizophrenic patients are released to the community after an average of 14 days' hospitaliztion. A previous study,[4] on a sample of all consecutive schizophrenic admissions over an 18-month period in that center, found that 45 percent were readmitted for substantial periods within six months of discharge. Further, the majority of readmissions (31 percent) occurred within three to four weeks. Two other facts were noted: first, patients simply did not take the oral dose of phenothiazines prescribed on discharge; second, they rarely used the outpatient supportive social therapy that was provided. Therefore, we developed an experimental design that focused on the first six weeks after discharge (a critical period, according to the above data), and then studied the relative significance of depot phenothiazine treatment and crisis-oriented family therapy carried out during that critical period. This study involved almost all first-admission schizophrenics in a county of half a million people. The 2×2 factorial design of the study had two levels of maintenance phenothiazine (high and low dose), and two social therapy conditions (present or absent).

Selection of Patients

All consecutive first and second inpatient admissions to the Ventura Mental Health Center were screened for the presence of schizophrenic symptoms. Independently interviewed by the project psychiatrist and psychologist, each patient was rated on a five-point scale on the probability that he was schizophrenic.[5] Each patient who passed this initial screening was studied for another two to three days, and then rated on the New Haven Schizophrenia Index.[6] Those who received a score of 4 or higher (a cutting score found by Astrachan et al.[6] to correlate highly with a clinical diagnosis of schizophrenia) were entered into the study. Of the 104 patients selected for the study, 69 percent were first life-time admissions, and the balance recent second admissions (during the same calendar year). They were young (mean age 23.36 years; SD, 4.21), and predominantly white (79 percent, with 14 percent of Hispanic origin, and 7 percent black. Forty percent had not graduated from high school, 35 percent were high school graduates, and 25 percent had some college. Sixty-two percent were single, 15 percent previously married, and 23 percent currently married. They were hospitalized only briefly (mean 14.24 days; SD, 5.97) before discharge to the aftercare program.

After a patient was selected, he or she and a relative were interviewed separately, and informed of the nature of the study. Both the patient's and the relative's consent were required for the patient to participate. The patient was informed that he or she could withdraw from the study at any time.

The Phenothiazine Drug Condition

It was decided to compare a relatively high therapeutic dose level of phenothiazine with a therapeutically marginal or lower dose level of the the same drug. The original intent was to use orally administered phenothiazines, but this was not feasible because of a low rate of compliance. Accordingly, we shifted to a longer-acting injectable phenothiazine, fluphenazine (Prolixin) enanthate, which solved the problem of medication delivery successfully.

Fluphenazine therapy was started within a day after the patients had been admitted to the center. A test dose of 0.25 ml was given; if no sensitivity was noted, the patient was then assigned by a random method to one of two conditions: high or low dose. Originally we had intended that the high dose should be 1.5 ml, and the low dose 0.5 ml, but pilot data suggested that the side effects of the higher dose were too severe, dosages were therefore reduced in the actual experiment to 1 ml for the high-dose condition, and 0.25 ml for the low-dose condition, and were kept fixed throughout the study. (Although we use the term "high dose" for the 1-ml condition, it is clear that, in contrast to other studies using this same drug with acute schizophrenic patients,[7] a more appropriate term would be "moderate dose.") Prophylactic antiparkinsonian medication was provided routinely: benztropine mesylate, 2 mg intramuscularly with each injection of fluphenazine; and trihexyphenidyl, 5 mg/day orally during both the inpatient and aftercare phases of the study. The study period was typically one to two weeks as an inpatient, and a six-week after care period as an outpatient. During the inpatient period, if the treating psychiatrist thought that more medication was needed, he was permitted to administer phenothiazine orally. During the aftercare period, three injections were administered at 14-day intervals, the first on the day of discharge. The study was single-blind, as the patient was blind to dose level but the treating psychiatrist was not. However, all ratings of clinical behavior were carried out by raters blind to drug and family therapy status.

Crisis-Oriented Family Therapy

The social therapy used was family oriented. Here, our original desires or goals were modified by experience. It was our hope, based on other work, that we could move into some kind of relationally oriented family therapy. However, it became obvious that this was not feasible for such disorganized patients. Instead, a crisis-oriented six-session family therapy was devised, directed at the following sequence of objectives: (1) the patient and his family are able to accept the fact that he has had a psychosis; (2) they are willing to identify some of the probable precipitating stresses in his life at the time the psychosis occurred; (3) they attempt to generalize from that to identification of future stresses to which the patient and his family are likely to be vulnerable; and (4) they attempt to do some planning on how to minimize or avoid these future stresses. We find that this concrete form of family therapy can be meaningfully carried out with schizophrenics and their families during this phase of treatment. The primary goal in this therapy is to help the patient and significant others use the events of the psychosis, rather than sealing it over and deflecting attention away from the psychotic episode.

RESULTS

Deliverability and Compliance

Of the 104 patients who agreed to participate in the program, eight withdrew after release from the hospital. Three of these left the area immediately; five remained in the area, but rejected compliance with their assigned treatment program. Thus, 92 percent participated in the aftercare program. The treatment refusers came from three groups: high-dose therapy (two), low-dose therapy (three), and low-dose no-therapy (three).

Figure 1 presents the rate of relapse within each treatment condition at the end of the six-week controlled trial and at the time of the six-month follow-up contact. During the six-week controlled treatment period, 10 patients deteriorated clinically, such that either they had to be rehospitalized or their medication had to be altered substantially—a relapse rate for treatment acceptors of 10.4 percent. This is substantially less than the 31 percent rate for the comparable six-week postdischarge period found for a very similar consecutive admission cohort at this same facility.[7] Relapses were ordinarily not the decision of the research team, as they usually involved action by the center's emergency psychiatric team, carried out independently of the project team. In cases where the decision to hospitalize was made by the research staff, a consensus of staff—both blind and nonblind to treatment status—was necessary.

Although this is a small number of relapses to search for differential trends across treatment conditions or patient's attributes, some suggestive findings do appear. These data indicate that there are two extreme groups in the sample, the high-dose therapy group, with not a single relapse, and the low-dose no-therapy group, with 24-percent relapse. The other two conditions fell between these two, and do not differ significantly. Only the

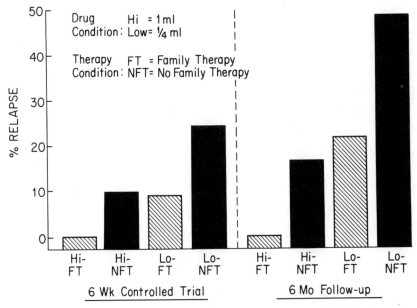

Fig. 1. Relapse rate within each treatment condition at the end of the six-week controlled trial and at the time of the six-month follow-up contact.

extreme groups differ at a statistically significant level. The trends in the marginal totals for dose level and therapy effects, though suggestive, are not statistically significant for either factor. Thus, despite the small number of relapsing patients, they are concentrated largely in the group with minimal medication and an absence of family-oriented intervention.

The number of breakdowns following the completion of the controlled period parallels the pattern for the first six weeks. There was not a single relapse in the high-dose therapy group, whereas by the six-month point nearly 50 percent of the low-dose no-therapy group had had some sort of clinical regression. The other two conditions had more breakdowns than the high-dose therapy group, but less than the low-dose no-therapy group. Thus, even though the high-dose therapy patients were no longer receiving therapy, and were no longer rigorously assigned to a maintenance medication condition, they continued to remain outside of a hospital for a six-month period.

If we add together the relapses during the controlled period with those that followed into an overall cumulative six-month relapse figure, a significant drug effect ($p < .01$) and a near-significant therapy effect ($p < .10$) are found.

Symptomatic Status at End of Aftercare Period

Patients were rated four times (at admission, at discharge, at six weeks, and at six-month follow-up), using the Brief Psychiatric Rating Scale (BPRS).[8] The rater was a research psychologist who remained blind to drug and therapy status throughout the six-month period. Factor analysis of admission BPRS ratings was carried out to reduce the 16 scales to a smaller set of dimensions. Fourteen of the scales loaded on four factors, *anxious depression, hostility, emotional withdrawal, and schizophrenic thought.* Data were analyzed in two ways, with relapsed patients deleted (all completers), and with last contact ratings used to include all starters in the sample.

Family Therapy Effects

The strongest effects are noted when the endpoint ratings for the relapsers are included in the analysis. Significant effects were found for the family therapy variable on: total BPRS score ($p < .01$); *withdrawal* ($p < .02$); and *anxious depression* ($p < .05$), for all patients who began the therapy (all starters). In all instances, there was evidence of less residual psychopathology in the samples that received family therapy.

The magnitude of the therapy effect on *withdrawal* is as significant for all completers as for all starters. Therefore, the impact of the family therapy on *withdrawal* applies to all cases in the sample. The mean scores on the *withdrawal* factor are presented separately below for all starters and all completers:

All Starters ($p < .02$)		All Completers ($p < .03$)	
Therapy	No Therapy	Therapy	No Therapy
2.41	3.65	2.39	3.72

If we examine, for the completers, the individual BPRS scales constituting the *withdrawal* factor, one stands out particularly, *blunted affect* ($p < .005$), in which the therapy cases manifested significantly less flattening of affect at six weeks than the no-therapy cases.

Analyses of BPRS data at the time of six-month follow-up was only significant for the *withdrawal* factor, but only in the group that originally received the high phenothiazine dose. As before, family therapy cases on high dose showed less residual psychopathology than comparable no-therapy cases ($p < .05$). However, the therapy advantage, previously observed with low-dose patients, was no longer observable at six-month follow-up. Note that the sustained effect on the high-dose group persisted long after those patients were systematically receiving the drug. It suggests a prophylactic effect of the adequate dose upon the retention of family therapy effects over the more extended time period.

Further Analyses of the Family Therapy Process

Up to this point, we have been treating the psychotherapeutic intervention as a homogenous process applied equally to all patients. However, we recognize that there is considerable variation in styles of therapy and the ability of patients and therapists to utilize each other's resources.

An analogy may be drawn with a similar issue in pharmacotherapy, when patients are assigned medication but often fail to comply. Thus, it has been necessary for researchers to devise methods to assure delivery, or at the very least monitor compliance. We felt that a comparable index of the deliverability of a psychotherapeutic intervention would permit a more accurate appraisal of its effects, as well as greater insight into the process of change.

Previously we indicated that the crisis-oriented therapy had relatively specific objectives. Four specific sequential objectives were designated:

1. Acceptance by patient and family that he has had a psychotic episode, and achieving consensus concerning the important precipitating stresses at the time the psychosis occurred.

2. Development of strategies to prevent the occurrence of identified stresses and for coping when stress occurs.
3. Evaluation of progress in implementation of prevention and coping strategies.
4. Anticipatory planning to prevent future stresses and to cope with those which arise.

In this study, therapists rated the extent to which the patient and participating family members achieved each of the four objectives.

A graduate student, Charles King, and myself[9] hypothesized that the greater the number of therapy objectives attained, the greater the sustained benefit by patient and significant others.

Measures

ACHIEVEMENT OF OBJECTIVES IN THERAPY

At the completion of therapy, therapists rated each patient on a five-point scale of the extent to which he was successful in achieving each of the four therapy objectives. The scale included descriptions of typical patient achievements for each point on the scale for each objective. For the purposes of analysis, the four objectives were treated as a Guttman Scale, with the assumption that achievement of a given objective implied achievement of all of the lower objectives. A patient was considered to have achieved an objective if he was rated 3 (moderately successful) or above. The highest objective achieved by each patient became his single score for the achievement of objectives in therapy. These scores range from 0 to 4, distributed as follows: 0, 20.5 percent; 1, 20.5 percent; 2, 9 percent; 3, 9 percent; 4, 41 percent. For some analyses, subjects were categorized as "achievers" or "nonachievers" of therapy objectives, employing a median split on highest objective achieved. Thus, subjects who achieved objectives 3 or 4 were classified as "achievers"; those who achieved no higher than objective 2 are referred to as "nonachievers."

Achievers and nonachievers did not differ significantly on the demographic variables of age, marital status, race, education, or father's education. In addition, there was no significant difference between achiever groups in the number of family members participating in therapy sessions.

RATINGS OF ACHIEVEMENT OF THERAPY OBJECTIVES AS A DEPENDENT VARIABLE

First, we examined whether factors observed prior to the initiation of the aftercare family therapy could predict therapists' perceptions of the level of objectives achieved. The variables used were the individual difference measures of sex, premorbid status, paranoid status, Global Assessment Scale, GAS[10] level ratings at admission, and BPRS factor scores at admission and discharge. For the quantitative variables, a median split was used to subdivide groups. In addition, we examined whether assigned drug level (high versus low) was associated with greater success in delivering the therapy model.

None of the individual difference variables or drug levels were found related to therapist ratings of patients' achievement of objectives in therapy.

Next, interactions between individual difference variables and drug level were examined to determine whether the combination of certain patient attributes and assigned drug level could predict the therapists' perceived success in attaining the four levels of therapy objectives.

Hostility and suspiciousness are important barriers to the development of therapeutic trust. Therefore, we examined the relationships among ratings on the BPRS factor *hostility*, rated at discharge (the period immediately before the initiation of family therapy), drug level, and the level of therapy objectives attained. For this analysis, patients were classified as high or low on *hostility*, based on a median split. The interaction between drug level and *hostility* at discharge, depicted in Figure 2, was highly significant, $F(1,36) = 9.25$, $p < .005$. This figure indicates that when a patient showed considerable *hostility*, *suspiciousness*, and *uncooperativeness* at discharge, therapists indicated that they could achieve the majority of their therapy objectives only when the patient was on the *high* dose. However, an inverse effect was noted for patients below the median on BPRS *hostility* at discharge. Attainment of therapy objectives was more likely for patients assigned to the low-dose condition. No other BPRS factor score interacted with drug level in predicting level of therapy objective attained.

RATINGS OF ACHIEVEMENT OF OBJECTIVES
AS A PREDICTOR VARIABLE

After examining some of the variables that affect ratings of patients' achievement of objectives in therapy, we next determined whether the variance in these ratings related to clinical status at six-week and at the six-month follow-up period. For these analyses, patients were divided on the basis of a median split on the Guttman scaling of the ratings of achievement of objectives. Patients below the median achieve no higher than objective 2, and are referred to as "nonachievers." Patients above the median achieved objective 3 or 4, and are referred to as "achievers."

A repeated measure ANOVA using GAS[10] ratings at admission, six weeks, and six months indicates a large improvement for both groups $F(1,36)$ for linear trend $= 201.5$, $p < .005$. However, a significant

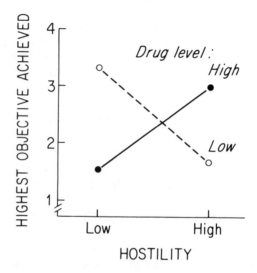

Fig. 2. Mean ratings of highest object achieved in therapy. The interaction of drug level and BPRS factor *hostility* rated at time of discharge from inpatient treatment is illustrated.

difference in the slope of the GAS scores was found for achievers and nonachievers of therapy objectives $F(2,42) = 5.10, p < .01$. As Figure 3 indicates, patients who were rated as achieving therapy objectives showed greater improvement than patients who did not achieve objectives. GAS scores were also analyzed separately for each period. There were no significant differences between these groups at admission or at the end of the six weeks, but patients who achieved therapy objectives were rated significantly higher at six-months follow-up, $F(1,36) = 4.65, p < .04$. It appears that the two groups were similar at admission and at the end of treatment. Between the end of the controlled period treatment and the six-month follow-up, patients who were rated as having achieved therapy objectives continued to improve markedly on independent ratings of functioning, whereas patients who did not achieve higher therapy objectives improved little during this period.

Analyses of the BPRS factor ratings at six weeks and six months were conducted in order to identify the specific symptom clusters which contributed to the greater improvement of patients rated as having achieved therapy objectives. Of the four factors, only *thought disorder* revealed clear differences between achievers and nonachievers. There was no difference between these groups at six weeks, but achievers displayed significantly less thought disorder at six months, $F(1,36) = 8.13, p < .01$.

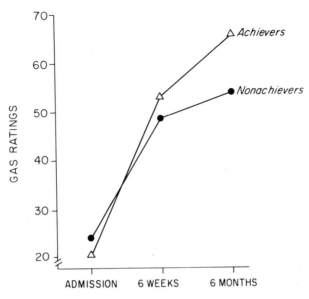

Fig. 3. Mean Global Assessment Scale (GAS) Ratings. Ratings were made at admission, six weeks, and six months for achievers and nonachievers of therapy objectives.

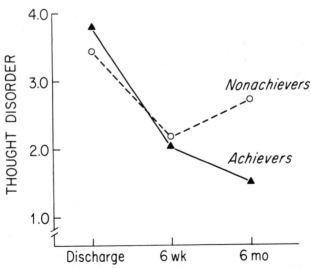

Fig. 4. Mean *thought disorder* factor scores. The Brief Psychiatric Rating Scale was administered at discharge, six weeks, and six months, for achievers and nonachievers of therapy objectives.

Figure 4 indicates that patients who were rated as achieving therapy objectives continued to show decreases in thought disorder, whereas patients who did not achieve therapy objectives displayed a tendency for thought disorder to return to prior levels.

BEHAVIORAL CORRELATES OF THERAPIST RATINGS OF OBJECTIVES

The previous analyses indicated that therapist's perceptions of the degree to which they could deliver the objectives of the crisis model significantly predicted the longer term course of the patient's disorder, particularly on key symptoms of the schizophrenic process. But, what were therapists reacting to in their ongoing contacts? Evidently, it was something other than classic symptoms of psychopathology. In an effort to get a clearer idea of therapeutic behavior that differentiated achievers from nonachievers, Dennis Schorr, currently a graduate student in psychology at Yale, coded the audiotapes of the therapy sessions. He coded them blind as to therapist rating of objectives.

Schorr's coding system drew from many sources, but most interestingly from the work of Vaughn and Leff[11] on a concept they termed *expressed emotion* (EE), which has been reported to predict relapse in schizophrenics. EE refers to familial attitudes of criticism, hostility, and overinvolvement specifically directed at the identified patient. Schizophrenics returned to high-EE homes have been found to have very high rates of relapse. Schorr developed codes to mirror the EE components of hostility, criticism, and overinvolvement as they might be expressed in actual family interaction in the therapy tapes. Using tapes from the latter part of the six-session crisis-oriented series, he found that higher levels of EE-type behaviors were observed in nonachiever-rated family units ($p < .002$) Interestingly, the criticism, hostility, and overinvolvement was as likely to be manifested by the patient as the family member. While this is a gross oversimplification of Schorr's data, it does indicate clearly that there are clear behavioral differences observable between families rated as achievers or nonachievers. The differences observed indicate that, late in the course of therapy, high-EE type behaviors are still occurring in the nonachiever group, providing a link between the Vaughn-Leff literature on relapse and the current intervention study. Currently, we are investigating whether these high-EE behaviors are present in different degrees in early therapy sessions in achiever and nonachiever samples. If they are, then clearly there are systematic differences between these two types of families that persist throughout six weeks of therapy. If they are not present initially, then it tells us something about possible failures in the application of the crisis model which are potentially correctable.

COMMENT

The present study indicates clearly that both phenothiazine medication and a form of family therapy play a very significant role in decreasing relapse in acute, young schizophrenics after discharge into the community. In the short run, all therapy cases showed less residual symptomotology than cases who did not receive therapy, with the most notable effects on *emotional blunting* and *withdrawal*. Over the longer follow-up period, only the therapy cases who had originally been maintained at the higher dose level sustained their earlier gains. We do not know at this point how this delayed effect was achieved—whether high-dose patients were more likely to follow subsequent treatment recommendations, or whether this is a genuine delayed effect of a short-term intervention remains to be established.

Although all therapy patients showed positive results on *emotional withdrawal*, impact on other components of the core schizophrenic symptoms were dependent upon the degree of therapist success in delivering the full model of the crisis therapy. These date suggest that there may be two levels of therapy effects, nonspecific and specific. Nonspecific effects are the consequence of maintaining a relationship with patient and significant others, but do not require attainment of all therapy objectives. Such a family support system appears to reduce the affective symptoms associated with the postacute phase of a schizophrenic episode such as *emotional withdrawal*, *blunted affect*, and to a lesser degree *anxiety* and *deression*.

Specific therapy effects, on the other hand, require achievement of discrete therapeutic objectives, such as those identified by the current crisis model. Achievement of these specific objectives is not necessary for improvement in affective symptoms, but is critical for sustained improvement in a core symptom of schizophrenia—*thought disorder*. Signs of the return of thought disorder are evident in cases who did not move beyond step 2 of the crisis model, whereas continued attenuation is noted for those who were rated as attaining steps 3 or 4. If we examine the difference between steps 1 and 2, and 3 and 4, it delineates a shift between a past and future time perspective. Patients who are rated as 3 or 4 can extrapolate from a look at the immediate, crisis-laden past to develop strategies for dealing with future stresses. When that shift in time orientation is noted, there is sustained improvement for the next six months not only in the affective symptoms, but in thinking as well. These data support the position that, when the schizophrenic individual can integrate the psychotic experience into his life and use this integration in dealing with subsequent life events, a more positive outcome can be anticipated.

REFERENCES

1. May PRA: Treatment of Schizophrenia. New York, Science House Inc, 1968
2. May PRA: The implications of psychopharmacological research for the treatment of schizophrenia, in West L, Flinn D (eds): Treatment of Schizophrenia: Progress and Prospects. New York, Grune & Stratton, 1976, pp 61–77
3. Schooler NR: Antipsychotic drugs and psychological treatment in schizophrenia, in Lipton MA, DiMascio A, Killam KF (eds): Psychopharmacology—A Generation of Progress. New York, Raven Press, 1978
4. Evans JR, Goldstein MJ, Rodnick EH: Premorbid adjustment, paranoid diagnosis and remission in acute schizophrenics treated in a community mental health center. Arch Gen Psychiatry 28:666–672, 1973
5. Mosher LR, Pollin W, Stabenau JR: Families with identical twins discordant for schizophrenia: Some relationships between identification, thinking styles, psychopathology and dominance-submissiveness. Br J Psychiatry 118:29–42, 1971
6. Astrachan BM, Harrow D, Adler D, et al: A checklist for the diagnosis of schizophrenia. Br J Psychiatry 121:529–539, 1972
7. Chien C, Cole JO: Depot phenothiazine treatment in acute psychosis: A sequential comparative clinic study. Am J Psychiatry 130:13–18, 1973
8. Overall JE, Gorham DR: The brief psychiatric rating scale. Psychological Report 10:799, 1962
9. King C, Goldstein MJ: Therapists ratings of achievement of therapy objectives: An aid to research on psychotherapy with acute schizophrenics. Schizophrenia Bull 5:118–129, 1979
10. Endicott J, Spitzer RL, Fleiss JF, et al: The global assessment procedure for measuring the overall severity of psychiatric disturbance. Arch Gen Psychiatry 33:766–771, 1976
11. Vaughn CE, Leff JP: The measurement of expressed emotion in families of psychiatric patients. Br J Social and Clinical Psychology 15:157–165, 1976

Ian R. H. Falloon

3

Communication and Problem-Solving Skills Training with Relapsing Schizophrenics and Their Families

Eighty years after Emil Kraepelin first described a mental disturbance characterized by delusions, hallucinations, illogical thought patterns, inappropriate affect, and a generally unfavorable prognosis, schizophrenia remains a disorder of huge economic and social proportions. However, from those beginnings to the present it has been noted that not all individuals who show the florid signs of this condition remain handicapped; a substantial proportion recover completely and do not suffer further relapse even when treatment is not sustained. While Kraepelin reported a 13-percent recovery rate, studies in more recent years have revealed even larger percentages of fully recovered schizophrenics.[1]

In an attempt to seek explanation for the differences in the course of schizophrenia in different individuals, studies in recent years have attempted examination of the association between psychosocial stress factors and florid symptomatic relapse. Two such factors that have been clearly implicated in the relapse process are disturbed family relationships and stressful life events. Although disturbed family relationships have been linked to subsequent schizophrenic illness for 50 years,[2] the hypothesized mechanisms for this effect have seldom withstood objective evaluations. Most studies have examined the impact of interpersonal communication deficits in the parents on the etiology of schizophrenia in their offspring. The methodology of these studies has been complex, and the interpretation of results has remained on the speculative level. Several excellent reviews of these studies have been published.[3-6]

Two well-designed studies completed a decade apart by research workers at the Institute of Psychiatry in London examined the impact of family relationships on the course of an established schizophrenic illness. Brown, et al found that the best single predictor of subsequent relapse in a patient discharged from the hospital after treatment of a florid schizophrenic illness was the emotional atmosphere of the family environment.[7] This was determined by an extensive interview with each member of the household concerning the patient's behavior and the patient's emotional and behavioral responses in the period prior to hospitalization for a relapse of florid symptoms. When a relative with whom the patient was living made frequent critical comments, showed hostility and overinvolved emotional attachment, the patient had a high risk of relapsing during the subsequent nine months after discharge from the hospital, despite other factors considered to predict a good prognosis, eg, good premorbid adjustment, and acute onset, with the index episode being the first.

This finding was almost exactly replicated in a more recent study.[8] A striking 92 percent of patients in both studies relapsed when living with high expressed emotion (EE) relatives, compared to 15 percent who returned to low-EE relatives. Two protective factors appeared to modify this result. First, regular phenothiazine continuation medication halved the relapse rate in high-EE families, while an even greater reduction in relapse was noted when patients and high-EE relatives spent less than 35 hours in the same room each week. When both phenothiazine medication and reduced patient-relative contact were combined, the relapse rate was almost identical to that of low-EE families.

This suggests several potentially effective therapeutic strategies. The most obvious (and least expensive) would be the provision of adequate continuation medication with methods to ensure compliance, eg, minimally effective dosage to reduce unpleasant side effects, rapid follow-up of missed appointments and home visits if necessary, and the use of long-acting intramuscular preparations for persistent noncompliance. This could be combined with vocational counseling to enable the patient as well as family members to find work or other structured activities outside the home, so that contact between the patient and high-EE relatives may be reduced. The provision of day care centers or residential facilities may likewise facilitate such separation from detrimental family influences. Supportive care[9] constitutes a model of aftercare for the schizophrenic patient, combining these strategies with psychotherapy that focuses on assisting the patients with the here-and-now problems of living. Stein and Test[10] have demonstrated successful rehabilitation of schizophrenic patients with an active program of training patients in community living skills after aggressively separating the patients from all family contact. Another potential therapeutic strategy involves a more direct attempt to initiate changes in the family system. If it were possible to reduce the level of criticism and overinvolvement of family members sufficiently, this might result in a reduction of patient vulnerability towards relapse. It should be pointed out that the studies of the family factors that have implicated the family in schizophrenic relapse have also shown that the majority of families with schizophrenic members provide a supportive and beneficial living situation for the patients, and that relapse occurs infrequently. Thus, the negative connotation universally applied to schizophrenic family members, such as 'the schizophrenogenic mother'[11] is hardly justified in the light of these more recent findings, which suggest that negative family factors are present in only a relatively small proportion of schizophrenic families.

Family therapy has been widely applied to reducing family conflict in schizophrenia.[12-17] A recent controlled study suggests that as few as six sessions can effectively reduce relapse, at least in the short term, and where patients are maintained on adequate doses of neuroleptic medication.[18] It might be argued that the provision of adequate aftercare is an established procedure with established efficacy, and that alternative methods, such as family therapy, are technically complex and expensive. However, long-term continuing aftercare presents many problems: First, treatment may need to be lifelong.[19] Secondly, irreversible side effects (such as tardive dyskinesia) become more frequent with long-term neuroleptic medication. Third, the provision of adequate social and vocational rehabilitation is often limited by the patient's ability and motivation, as well as community resources and economic climate. Hogarty et al have pointed out some of the difficulties associated with intensive social aftercare programs.[20] In many cases, overenthusiastic rehabilitation may, in fact, lead to an increased vulnerability to relapse in the short term, with beneficial effects only accruing after at least a year's treatment. Residential care, whether in community-based boarding houses or long-term hospital wards, is seldom ideal; while institutional caregivers often show greater tolerance to aberrant behavior, lack of adequate personalized support often leads to a greater reduction in social functioning than when the patient is living at home.[21] Finally, despite apparently ideal aftercare conditions, compliance with all aspects of a rehabilitation program is often difficult to sustain over the periods necessary to ensure worthwhile gains. A family-based treatment program, on the other hand, offers an approach that avoids many of these difficulties. A stable reduction in expressed emotion and the development of a concerned, supportive household environment might be expected to lead to a stable reduction in relapse rate, a reduced need for long-term medication, and less pressure for the provision of vocational and social rehabilitation facilities. However, this assumes that family therapy can assist in providing a low-tension supportive family milieu and, in addition, that the detrimental family factors involved in high expressed emotion are themselves *directly* associated with relapse. At present, much of this must remain at a speculative level, although several studies currently under way should produce data to further clarify these issues.

A second series of studies of social factors has examined the impact of stressful life events on the course of schizophrenic illness. This research indicates that the risk of relapse is significantly increased during the three weeks following a stressful life change.[22] Once again, adequate neuroleptic medication offered some protection against such stress but was not sufficient in itself. To date, no study has examined extra- and intrafamilial factors concurrently. Zubin and Spring have outlined theory of vulnerability in which ongoing family stress and major life events may summate to exceed a threshold above which a relapse of schizophrenic symptoms is inevitable.[23] It is probable that relapse in families with low expressed emotion occurs as a consequence of such increased stress following a major life event, which, in spite of the family's support, exceeds the patient's vulnerabilty threshold. Efforts to enhance the patient's ability to cope with life crises have not yet been evaluated. Studies of schizophrenics' coping mechanisms indicate a lack of effective problem solving skills, as well as a delay in the mobilization of assistance from family and the social network until the relapse is well established.[24] Not only did the schizophrenic patient demonstrate ineffective coping behavior, but members of the patient's household appeared similarly deficient in the communication and problem solving skills needed to prevent a florid relapse of symptoms. This suggests that a further useful family intervention may involve teaching effective problem solving strategies to both the patient and the family, as well as improving mutual recognition of signs of excessive stress and imminent relapse.

Most schizophrenic patients and their families have extremely limited knowledge of their illness. It is apparent that many difficulties in community treatment programs are associated with insufficient understanding of the nature of the disorder, and the rationale for drug and psychosocial treatment by the patient and the family.[25] In order to further harness the care and support of the family network, and to reduce misunderstanding that may contribute to critical or overinvolved attitudes, basic education about schizophrenia may be valuable. Such education has been considered highly beneficial by patients and their families.[26]

It is concluded that an effective family therapy intervention program may incorporate the following variables: (1) education of the family about the nature and management of schizophrenia; (2) teaching more effective nonverbal and verbal communication to all family members, including the appropriate expression of dissatisfaction and concern, to reduce hostile criticism and overinvolvement; and (3) teaching more effective problem solving skills to help identify and cope with stressful life events.

A model of family therapy that combines education, communication, and problem solving methods has been developed by the author, in collaboration with Drs. Robert Liberman and Robert Aitchison at the UCLA/Camarillo Mental Health Clinical Research Center for the Study of Schizophrenia and the University of Southern California. These methods have been designed to directly counter the deleterious patterns of emotional expression found in the high expressed emotion families. The techniques have been applied equally well in families with nonschizophrenic members where similar communication and problem-solving deficits exist.

FAMILY THERAPY INTERVENTIONS

Family Education About Schizophrenia

At least two sessions at the beginning of the family program are devoted to educating the family and the identified patient about the nature, course, and treatment of the patient's schizophrenic illness. A didactic format is used, with handouts, diagrams, and other visual aids (Table 1). Family members are encouraged to discuss their experiences, misunderstandings, and anxieties. Schizophrenia is described as a stress-related biologic mental illness that leads to widespread problems of living in areas including problem solving, developing intimate relationships, work, study, personal care, and social and leisure activities. The major symptoms are clearly described, and the differentiation from other forms of mental illness are explained. The patient is encouraged to discuss personal symptoms with the family. This is often the first time such communication has occurred and usually results in a substantial clarification of family misunderstandings, and misperceptions of the patient when the patient has previously exhibited inappropriate or bizarre behavior. Biologic and environmental factors implicated in the etiology and subsequent course of the illness are described; the latest research findings are presented and critically discussed. Families frequently ask questions about new articles describing miracle breakthroughs in this illness. Megavitamin therapy and hemodialysis are two highly publicized treatments about which families frequently inquire in this discussion. Where clear-cut scientific evidence is not available, the therapists attempt to elucidate the pros and cons of any

Table 1
Summary of Curriculum of Family Education Sessions

- Schizophrenia: a stress-related biologic disorder
- Delusions, hallucinations, thought interference characteristic
- Affects all aspects of psychosocial function:

  Thinking and feeling
  Interpersonal relations
  Work
  Leisure
  Self-care

- Regular neuroleptics reduce relapse rate substantially
- Extra- and intrafamilial stress increases vulnerability to relapse

new treatments and avoid raising false expectations. The role of genetic factors is discussed in terms of a 10-fold increased risk of schizophrenia in first-degree family relatives. However, patients are not discouraged from procreation; the probability that multiple social and biologic factors are involved in the etiology of the illness is stressed. The biologic basis for drug therapy is outlined in terms of correcting an imbalance in the brain chemistry, the exact nature of which is not precisely understood. The importance of reducing environmental stress, both from within the family and from external stressors, is outlined together with a rationale for the family therapy approach as a way to minimize tension and maximize interpersonal support. Care is taken to avoid overtly or covertly implicating the family in the etiology or subsequent course of the illness. Family members are encouraged to discuss their guilt feelings concerning their perceived roles in the development of the patient's illness. They are told that despite a large amount of research and a number of widely publicized theories, there is no substantive evidence that child-rearing practices or family interaction patterns are specifically associated with the *onset* of schizophrenia. However, the important benefits that accrue from living in a supportive milieu and the deleterious effects of hostile, overinvolved family interaction on the *subsequent course* of an established schizophrenic disorder are emphasized. Therapists adopt an empathic role and encourage family members and patients to vent their frustrations, feelings of inadequacy, and, frequently, their dissatisfaction with previous community management of the illness. Patients and families are encouraged to adopt realistic yet hopeful expectations for the future. A large proportion of the criticism expressed about the identified patient tends to reflect unrealistic goals of parents for the patient. They tend to assume that with adequate therapy the patient will regain his or her former level of intellectual and social functioning, and when such progress does not seem to be occurring they become angry with the patient, or the therapists, or both. These initial family education sessions help members revise their notions of complete return to full premorbid functioning as a short-term expectation of drug and psychosocial therapy. They are encouraged to consider long-term goals for the rehabilitation process rather than the short–term goals of the medical 'cure' model for the management of schizophrenia.

The treatment of schizophrenia is outlined in terms of an integrated biologic and psychosocial rehabilitation program. The importance of long-term, regular, low-dose neuroleptic medication is stressed as a means of preventing the detrimental effects of stress. Once the patient and the family appear to understand the nature of schizophrenia and a rationale for long-term treatment, they are given more detailed information about drug therapy. After a brief overview of the drugs employed in psychiatry, the specific use of neuroleptic medication for schizophrenia is described. The effects of the major tranquilizers on florid schizophrenic symptoms are described, including the symptoms most and least likely to change and respond. The role of continued low-dose major tranquilizers in the prevention of relapse or exacerbation of florid symptoms is outlined. Evidence of the benefits of regular maintenance therapy is presented graphically to illustrate the high annual risk of relapse (70 percent) when not taking regular medication, as opposed to the much lower (30 percent) relapse rate on regular medication. In addition, the probable benefits of medication on reducing the social disruption of relapse are described, ie, rehospitalization, loss of job, etc, is less likely where ingestion of medication is maintained at the time of symptomatic exacerbation. The use of serial plasma level examination in gauging minimal effective dosage of medication is outlined. Unwanted physiological (side effects) and psychological effects (low self esteem, feelings of dependency) of long-term drug therapy are openly discussed. Possible irreversible effects, such as tardive dyskinesia, are described. Several methods of minimizing these unwanted effects are outlined. Finally, a warning is given against changing the drug regime without professional consultation, and against the use of nonprescription drugs such as amphetamines, LSD, PCP, or other hallucinogens. *Limited* alcohol and marijuana use is condoned where the patient's previous ingestion does not appear to have contributed to his or her symptomatology.

The patient and family are provided with written material outlining the issues discussed in the educational sessions. They are encouraged to read these handouts and to continue to discuss issues as they arise throughout the treatment program. An evaluation of the knowledge and understanding acquired during this phase of treatment has revealed a substantial improvement in almost all patients and family members. On a few occasions when the identified patient has still shown florid symptoms, these initial sessions may prove difficult to conduct. However, most families have reported changes in their attitude toward the patient and the patient's illness as a result of the educational sessions that have enabled them to structure a more consistent approach to the problem.

Communication Training

This treatment strategy aims to reduce the level of emotional tension experienced in the family on an everyday basis. The family members are taught effective communication of emotions in frequently occurring behaviors, such as conversations, making requests, and giving and receiving information, praise, affection, and criticism (Table 2). A detailed assessment that involves both individual interviews of family members and structured family interaction tasks is conducted prior to initiating family therapy sessions. An analysis of this standardized interaction is combined with close observation of the family interaction in unstructured conversation and in the educational sessions to help the therapist pinpoint specific assets and deficits in each family member's communication and problem-solving skills. Individual interviews enable an assessment of these skills outside the family group so that a distinction can be made between a general lack of communication skills and deficits specific to the family context. New skills may need to be taught to each deficient individual to remedy the former problem, while the latter problem may be resolved by facilitating appropriate communication within the family group as a whole. In one family, the schizophrenic patient spoke very rarely; when she did, in a barely audible whisper. however, it was noted that she communicated freely in individual interviews and with her friends. In this case the target problem involved enhancing her communication within the family system.

Once communcation difficulties with a high frequency of occurrence have been specified, the family members are invited to participate in repeated role rehearsal of situations that are not handled effectively at

Table 2
Summary of Communication Training Interventions

- Expressing specific positive feelings
- Making specific requests
- Expressing specific negative feelings
- Communicating information clearly
- Active listening
- Rehearsal of social skills

home. Dyads as well as larger family subunits demonstrate their usual patterns of communication in these situations. The therapist shapes more effective communication in subsequent rehearsals through the use of established behavioral strategies of instructions, modeling, coaching, social reinforcement, and performance feedback.[27,28]

Three major elements of communication are addressed: (1) *nonverbal behavior*, such as voice tone, volume, fluency; body posture and gesture; eye contact; and facial expression; (2) *verbal content* of the interaction; and (3) *reciprocity* of communication, including reflective, empathic listening; appropriate timing of interaction; the mutual exchange of affection; and agreement on shared goals and expectations.

Examples of situations often dealt with include the recognition, initiation, and expression of affection; giving praise and showing appreciation; asking for change in another family member's behavior in a specific, constructive way; initiating and supporting prosocial behavior; appropriately expressing anger, frustration, and disappointment; clarifying affective and informative messages. The use of generalized statements of emotional expression such as "You're such a wonderful person," or "Everything you do drives me crazy!" are discouraged in favor of praise or criticism for clearly specified behavior, eg, "I really enjoyed talking to you about your day at work," or "I am very annoyed with you for not having washed the dishes after you had promised me you would." Family members are encouraged to phrase requests for changes in another member's behavior in a positive, noncoercive manner. In most cases, the family members (including the patient) demonstrate the component communication skills, but tend not to use them effectively, communicating more frequently in a negative, demanding, and critical manner.

Family members are trained to keep communication highly specific, simplify the content, own up to their feelings, avoid attributing feelings to others without verification, and avoid excessive delays in the expression of both positive and negative emotions. These strategies minimize the risk of confused communication of the type characterized as the double bind.

During the sessions, the families continue to rehearse their communication strategies until they feel comfortable with the new approach, after which they are assigned specific homework assignments that involve the repeated performance of these alternative styles during their everyday lives. Reports of these homework efforts are recorded on diaries or worksheets kept by all family members. They are reviewed at the beginning of the next session. The therapy sessions are utilized as workshops during which family members may try out different communication skills in a supportive milieu. Often, the patients may demonstrate skill in an area of communication and may model this behavior to parents or siblings. Communication within the sessions may provide a focus for here-and-now inspection. Effective communication is praised, while impairment is noted and alternative expression prompted. In this respect, therapists are expected to communicate in a similarly effective manner during the session, so that they can demonstrate the model they expect the family to adopt.

As well as intrafamilial communication skills, patients and their families may rehearse with people outside the family using role-playing methods. Practice in conversation skills, interviews, and handling a variety of difficult encounters in the community may assist family members in coping more effectively with community living. In these instances, therapists and family members play a variety of roles such as shop assistants, welfare clerks, and personnel managers.

Problem-Solving Methods

This aspect of the family therapy seeks to reduce the stress encountered in the family after critical life events. These include extrafamilial stresses such as natural disasters (floods, fires, earthquakes), illness, injury, work and financial stress (eg, loss of job, delayed welfare checks), as well as intrafamilial crises—deaths, separations, major arguments. In addition, family members are taught to employ the same methods to cope with the less dramatic problems of day-to-day living. Where a family member continues to suffer from florid schizophrenic symptomatology (delusions, hallucinations, and interference with thought processes) his or her behavior may constitute a major ongoing source of family stress, to which end problem-solving methods may be employed to help both the patient and the family to cope more effectively. However, sources of tension within the family result from the behavior of each family member, and work on these problems constitutes a major focus of the problem-solving. Issues such as discord between the parents, rivalrous siblings, and scapegoating are frequent themes subjected to the problem-solving method. However, family members choose the problem themselves and thereby assume control of the content of the sessions. Although at times this will lead to families resisting confrontation of major issues, it provides some insurance that the family therapy sessions do not constitute additional sources of stress on an already burdened family system.

The problem-solving techniques detailed below are taught to the families and involve a structured procedure of identifying a problem, outlining, evaluating and implementing coping strategies, and reviewing the effectiveness of the chosen solution.

Identify a specific problem. This necessitates reflective listening to each member's description of the problem and seeking clarification when necessary, while avoiding interpretation and stereotyped solutions such as giving reassurance. The importance of reaching agreement on the nature of the problem is stressed, so that all of the potential solutions generated address the main issue and are functionally useful. Families very often accept the initial statement of the problem without further exploration and develop solutions that lack relevance to the core issue. For example, one family worked hard and persistently to find places where a very shy son could socialize with possible friends and girlfriends. But the problem their son sought help with was the acquisition of social skills he lacked in order to initiate conversation with potential friends without experiencing overwhelming anxiety and inadequacy.

Outline alternative strategies to cope with the problem without judging their possible merits. A list of at least five potential solutions is drawn up before making judgments of the effectiveness of each suggested strategy. Every suggestion is listed and acknowledged regardless of its obvious merits or demerits. This nonjudgmental brainstorming reduces the dominance of overpowering family members and permits even withdrawn patients to express their tentative solutions. Strategies which at first sight may not appear appropriate often prove, after being subjected to the greater reflection allowed by this method, the most effective. Thus, divergent or creative thinking is reinforced rather than suppressed, and all family members are accorded equal recognition for their attempts to produce solutions. Family members are encouraged to take turns to write out the list of alternatives so that none are overlooked in the subsequent discussion.

Evaluate the effectiveness of each of the listed strategies.   When a list of at least five potential solutions has been compiled, family members may then debate the pros and cons of each of the strategies in turn. The possible consequences, good and bad, of each strategy are discussed objectively.

Agree upon the most effective solution.   Given the available re-sources of the family system, the optimal strategy is then selected. This strategy may be a combination of several suggested solutions. Wherever possible, it should meet not only the immediate short-term crisis needs, but also be compatible with the long-term goals of personal and family growth: spending the family savings to buy a color television set may help reduce Father's boredom after being laid off work, but could lead to further crisis now that the family must survive on a lowered income. All family members are encouraged to reach a consensus at the completion of this step.

Carry out the best solution.   Successful execution of the selected strategy usually requires careful planning. A dry run may help the family prepare for potential difficulties. This may take the form of overt behavior rehearsal or merely talking through procedures step by step. Little details, such as bus schedules, using telephone services, adequacy of finances, understanding how to complete certain forms, etc, may lead to ineffective performance of the selected solutions if they are not accounted for in the planning.

Review problem status.   Once real-life performance of the selected coping strategies has been attempted, the family members involved are invited to recount systematically the detailed performance, and to note specific strategies that appeared to lead to problem resolution (Table 3). *Any* attempt to perform the agreed-upon strategies is praised, even when a successful outcome was not achieved. Failure of any attempt is examined in terms of partial success achieved. The family is encouraged to use the knowledge of their results to reconstruct a more effective strategy on future occasions. Care is taken to point out that many problems are very difficult to solve and that repeated problem solving is often needed.

The therapist may initially provide clear direction for the family. He/she may demonstrate and instruct the family in reflective listening

Table 3
Summary of Problem-Solving Interventions

- Pinpoint problem

- Generate potential solutions

- Evaluate potential consequences

- Agree on 'best' strategy

- Plan and implement strategy

- Review results; praise efforts

skills, suggest possible solutions, and help them evaluate and prepare effective strategies. As the family begins to master the problem-solving steps, the therapist's active guidance is gradually withdrawn.

The pretreatment assessments provide the therapist with an indication of possible critical situations. Stressors that have been identified as leading to previous family crises may be identified, as well as those that may be predicted in the future, eg, death of elderly parents, delay of a welfare payment. In addition to these potential major problems, lesser difficulties that arise between or during sessions serve as stimuli situations for training problem-solving techniques. Specific problem situations commonly encountered include:

1. *Family*: Physical illness or injury, prompting and supporting independent interests and behavior, visiting or entertaining friends, coping with identified patient's symptomatic behavioral disturbance, reducing expectations to realistic levels, seeking personal life space;
2. *Interpersonal*: Social rejection, refusing street drugs, living independently, marital and sexual problems, getting married, child-rearing, leisure planning;
3. *Community*: Job seeking, starting work, losing a job, gaining promotion, finding housing, financial problems, moving to another neighborhood.

Although many of these problems focus on the identified patient, they are usually valid, realistic issues that cannot be attributed to mere "scapegoating." The problem-solving method seeks to divide the burden of coping with the problem among all members of the family system, and to draw upon all family resources, including those available in the extended family and social network.

Homework assignments involving problem-solving behavior are usually not specified, but the family is instructed to report on stressors that impinge upon *any* family member between sessions. They are invited to describe their individual and joint efforts to cope with the problem. Support is given for attempts to use this problem-solving approach, either in its entirety, or, where appropriate, using components separately. A typical example of a problem solving attempt is provided in Table 4. Despite the apparent complexity of this method, remarkable success has been achieved in the training of severely disturbed and low socioeconomic families. Each new step is introduced only when the family has demonstrated proficiency at the previous level without prompting from the therapist. In several instances, families have managed to cope with major life stressors through employing the problem-solving approach. The structure provided has enabled them to stop and consider a wide range of alternatives when emotional tension is high. Such crises formerly led to feelings of frustration and helplessness with frequent hospital admission for identified patients.

Strategies for Coping with Symptom Behavior

Few families have an adequate repertoire of coping skills to deal effectively with the many problems associated with supporting a schizophrenic member in the community. While the problem-solving approach provides a structure that may facilitate family creativity in the development of novel solutions, the mental health professional may assist the family by sharing his/her behavioral management expertise with them. Within the problem-solving structure, issues such as the administration of medication, reducing side effects, dealing with delusions, or when to seek professional assistance may be discussed in a straightforward manner. Where a patient remains significantly handicapped by persistent symptoms, family members become the primary caregivers. Attention is given to teaching practical management strategies similar to those employed by skilled psychiatric nurses. In addition, many of these techniques may be integrated into the coping strategies of the family to be employed specifically to facilitate transactions within the family system. Some of these strategies include:

Contingency contracting. This strategy involves two family members agreeing upon discrete things that they would like to do for each other in a mutual exchange. Once each member has negotiated the pleasing behavior they would like the other to perform, a formally worded contract is drawn up and signed by each party. A woman who wanted her husband

Table 4

Example of Family Problem-Solving

Problem: Find structured activity for Jim to do on weekdays.

Alternatives	Positives	Negatives
Riding a bike	Good exercise; cheap	Bike needs repairs; boring
Going to the park	Can meet people	Nothing special there
Psychotherapy	Learn about self	Already in program
Gardening, mowing lawns	Good exercise; helps father; could develop into part-time job	Can't do it everyday
Going to gym	Healthful	Needs transportation; quite expensive
Getting a paid job	Rewarding; fills much of week	Might be too much stress at present
Going to day treatment center	Activities and psychotherapy available	Didn't like it before; too many people

Best solution: Getting a paid job.

Plan: Go to Department of Rehabilitation.
        Decide on type of job wanted.
        Phone local department stores.
        Look in newspaper for vacancies.
        Practice interviews with father.

Review: Jim phoned Department of Rehabilitation and attended for an assessment. They told him he was not ready for work but that they would be happy to help when he was better. Family felt discouraged and no further action was taken, pending further discussion with therapist. Therapist praised efforts and prompted further discussion of other alternative solutions.

to take her shopping negotiated a contract for him to "take me shopping and accompany me around the shops for one hour on one occasion weekly," while she would "accompany him on an activity of his choice on one occasion weekly." To avoid discord, each contracted behavior was agreed upon independently so that the husband's shopping assistance was not a prerequisite for his joint activity. Such contracts are particularly useful where neither person really wants to perform the behavior that pleases their partner.

Token economies.   A reinforcement program is occasionally employed to motivate one or more family members to perform more appropriate behavior by awarding points or tokens for performance of these behaviors, which can be readily exchanged for tangible reinforcers such as food, drink, entertainment, special attention, etc. All household members need to be involved in this process in order to provide consistent allocation of reinforcers. One patient who spent most of the day lying in his bed was motivated to assist in household chores, attend a local gym, and even to attend the family therapy sessions when his parents instituted a reinforcement program.

Shaping.   This involves the step-by-step prompting and reinforcement (usually with praise and warmth) for successive approximations to a specific desired response. One patient was praised for progressively larger segments of the front lawn he mowed, until he mowed the entire lawn without a break. This technique helps family members with unrealistic goals for the patient learn to be pleased with more modest short-term improvements.

Time out.   This procedure is taught to families so that members can excuse themselves from stressful situations politely when they feel under pressure. This enables patients and family members to escape from an overstimulating setting that might precipitate florid symptoms.

Setting limits.   A firm statement of the acceptable limits of a family member's behavior (preferably in the form of a positive request) is often a crucial part of providing a secure home environment. One patient's brother persisted in telling him that he was not mentally ill, and really needed to attend a faith healing religious cult the brother attended. The parents told the brother that they did not believe that faith healing could help the patient, and that taking him to such a meeting was quite unacceptable.

Identifying warning signals.   Specific prodromal signs indicating an impending relapse or exacerbation of florid schizophrenic symptoms are identified by the patient and family members. These warning symptoms frequently include sleep disturbance, social withdrawal, uncooperativeness, discussion of unusual ideas, mannerisms, irritability, headaches, and restlessness. But each patient may pinpoint two or three clear indicators that serve to warn the family to seek professional help as soon as possible in order to forestall a relapse. Patients and their families are provided with around-the-clock consultation from the therapy team.

Site of Treatment

Generalization of behavior learned in one setting (therapy) to another (home environment) is a problem all too often neglected in community psychiatry programs. This problem is particularly significant when treating schizophrenic patients, who show a low degree of transfer of learned skills across settings.[29] This problem can be reduced by several methods:

Overlearning. Family members repeatedly practice effective communication and problem-solving in the sessions until this behavior is initiated spontaneously during and between sessions by each participant.

Homework tasks. Specific assignments to perform skills practiced in the sessions are given to families at the end of each session. These tasks are reviewed at the beginning of the next session. Family members are given posters to remind them of skills trained in the sessions.

Family session attendance. All household members are included. Extended family members, friends, and neighbors are invited to join sessions when issues involving them are presented. Siblings are often supportive to the patient, particularly when issues of breaking over-involved parental ties are addressed. However, in the absence of adequate knowledge and understanding of schizophrenia, they may react in a critical way to their brother or sister. This negative attitude may be rapidly resolved after the family education sessions.

Transfer of behavior. In-home family sessions reduce the need for transfer of behavior from one physical setting to another. The sessions themselves become a more integrated part of the family system with the therapists invited to the home as supportive guests. Therapists are able to gain a clearer perspective of family life and can examine features such as seating arrangements at the dinner table, or the difficulties of living in substandard housing. Although the economy of in-home treatment is often questioned, fewer missed sessions occur and the time spent traveling to and from the home allows co-therapists time to discuss the family sessions and plan interventions.

Multifamily groups. These allow families to compare and contrast problems and coping mechanisms with one another. This sharing of fears, secrets, and resourcefulness serves to reduce the loneliness, help-lessness and frustration often evident but seldom expressed outside the nuclear family. This breakdown of barriers to the social network allows the family to restore their confidence so that they can begin to socialize again with friends and neighbors without guilt, shame, or fears of rejection. However, the disadvantages of the multifamily setting, which include a lack of specific focus on some problem areas (particularly sensitive family issues) limit the extent to which this mode is applicable as the main vehicle of therapy in families with a schizophrenic member. We have employed the multifamily groups in combination with single-family therapy, at times breaking an extended session into an initial multifamily phase followed by therapists meeting with each family separately.

Duration of Treatment

Schizophrenia usually runs a course of exacerbation and remission over several years. During the three months immediately following an acute episode, the patient is most vulnerable to further relapse. Relapse may occur any time in the subsequent two years. However, after two years without exacerbation, the risk of relapsing is low. The ideal family therapy program would, therefore, involve intensive treatment for three months after hospitalization for an acute episode, followed by gradual reduction to maintainence therapy in the second year after the onset of the illness. However, supportive family therapy aimed at continued reinforcement of effective communication and problem-solving skills may need to continue well beyond the second year. The Family Aftercare Program at the University of Southern California provides continuous family support and therapy over a minimum of two years. The initial three months involve intensive family therapy in the patient's home. This is followed by a less intense six-month phase where the patient is integrated with community rehabilitation services and the family interpersonal coping skills are consolidated. At nine months, family sessions are held once monthly till at least two years. During this phase, multiple family groups are conducted, aimed at developing a supportive community network and subsequent reducation of dependence on the family therapists. Whenever a relapse occurs, the Family Aftercare team provides more intensive support for the patient and the family, facilitates hospital admission when necessary, and assists in the inpatient management and discharge. Continuity of care is maintained throughout. Although medication is emphasized, particularly during the intensive treatment phase, monthly plasma levels assure that optimally effective dosage is maintained. The patient meets individually with a therapist prior to each conjoint family session when a metal status examination is conducted and individual problem issues are discussed. This enables the patient to feel supported by the therapist and allows the patient to express difficulties he or she is unable to express in the family session.

Assessment of Outcome

Although the outcome of schizophrenia is usually measured in terms of relapse of florid symptoms, a clear definition of a relapse is surprisingly difficult and often bears surprisingly little relationship with community functioning. The same can be said for hospital admission. Perhaps the most useful outcome measure is the level of social and interpersonal functioning, of not only the patient, but other family members as well. The role behavior of all family system members is assessed in this program. Good outcome is reflected in improved social function of *every* family member, more effective coping behavior when faced with stressful life situations, and a lessening of the burden of caring for a handicapped member. In addition, the very specific nature of the treatment interventions enables the assessment of observable changes before, during and after treatment. To date, observation of both structured and spontaneous interaction sequences indicate that most families are able to learn the specific communication and problem-solving techniques, and do in fact incorporate them into their everyday interaction. Furthermore, this results in a lowering of negative emotional expression. The current research program will seek to compare the family intervention program with the predominantly individual treatment approach, and to examine the long-term effectiveness of these therapies.

SUMMARY

Family interventions are indicated for families where excessive criticism and overinvolvement are expressed towards a member who has suffered a schizophrenic illness, where the family system lacks adequate means for reducing extrafamilial stress, or where insufficient skills for the effective management of a chronically psychotic person are evident.

A series of innovative family therapy techniques based on social learning principles are described:

1. *Education about schizophrenia.* A realistic, yet hopeful, account of the nature, causes, courses and management of schizophrenia is provided to patients and their families.
2. *Communication training.* This involves teaching nonverbal and verbal interpersonal communication skills through repeated role rehearsal, with instructions, modeling, and social reinforcement.
3. *Problem-solving training.* This involves teaching a structured sequential approach to generating effective solutions to specified family problems. After pinpointing the problem, a list of potential solutions is generated, evaluated, and the most effective is chosen. Finally, after implementation, the status of the problem is reviewed.
4. *Behavioral management strategies.* Families are trained to use a series of specific techniques to deal with problems commonly found in family systems, particularly where a member is handicapped by persistent or recurrent schizophrenic symptoms. These include *contingency contracting, token economy, shaping, time out, setting limits,* and *identifying warning signals.*

These techniques are employed within the framework of conjoint family sessions, conducted in the home. Combined with rehabilitation counseling, this constitutes the psychosocial component of a community-based program that aims to effectively support patients who have recently suffered a florid episode of schizophrenia and who are living with families where a highly emotional response to behavioral disturbance appears to carry a high risk of subsequent schizophrenic relapse. The family therapy component is directed towards strengthening environmental support and reducing stress by improving the social competence, including the coping skills, of *all* family members. The other major component of this program is carefully monitored neuroleptic medication. Results to date suggest that increased effectiveness of family communication and problem-solving can be achieved in many families; these are some indications that this may lower the risk of schizophrenic relapse. A controlled-outcome study is being conducted to fully evaluate the efficacy of this program.

REFERENCES

1. Bleuler M. Die Schizophrenen Geistesstorungen im Lichle Langjahriger Kranken-una Familiengeschichlen. Stuttgart, Thieme, 1972

2. Sullivan HS: The onset of schizophrenia. Am J Psychiatry 7:105–134, 1927
3. Jacob T: Family interaction in disturbed and normal families: A methodological and substantive review. Psychol Bull 82:33–65, 1975
4. Mishler EG, Waxler NE: Interaction in Families. New York, Wiley and Sons, 1968
5. Riskin J, Faunce EE: An evaluative review of family interaction research. Fam Proc 11:365–455, 1972
6. Hirsch SR, Leff JP: Abnormalities in the Parents of Schizophrenics. London, Oxford University Press, 1975
7. Brown GW, Birley JLT, Wing JK: Influence of family life on the course of schizophrenic disorderrs: A replication. Br J Psychiatry 121:241–258, 1972
8. Vaughn CE, Leff JP: The influence of family and social factors on the course of psychiatric illness: A comparison of schizophrenic and depressed neurotic patients. Br J Psychiatry 129:125–137, 1976
9. Mendel W: Supportive Care: Theory and Technique. Los Angeles, Mira Books, 1975
10. Stein LI, Test MA: Alternative to Mental Hospital Treatment. New York, Plenum Press, 1978
11. Fromm-Reichmann F: Notes of the development of treatment of schizophrenics by psychoanalytic psychotherapy. Psychiatry 11:264–273, 1948
12. Bowen M: A family concept of schizophrenia, in Jackson D (ed): The Etiology of Schizophrenia. New York, Basic Books, 1966
13. Jackson DD: Family interaction, family homeostasis and some implications for conjoint family psychotherapy, in Masserman J (ed): Individual and Family Dynamics. New York, Grune & Stratton, 1959, pp 122–141
14. Lidz T, Fleck S, Cornelison A, et al: Schizophrenia and the Family. New York, International Universities Press, 1965
15. Speck RV, Rueveni U: Network therapy: A developing concept. Fam Proc 8:182–191, 1969
16. Mosher LR: Schizophrenogenic communication and family therapy. Fam Proc 8:43–63, 1969
17. Rubenstein D: Techniques in family pschotherapy in schizophrenia, in Cancro R, Fox N, Shapiro LE (eds): Strategic Interventions in Schizophrenia. New York, Behavioral Publications, 1974
18. Goldstein MJ, Rodnick EH, Evans JR, et al: Drug and family therapy in the aftercare treatment of acute schizophrenia. Arch Gen Psychiatry 35:1169–1177, 1978
19. Mendel W: Schizophrenia: The Experience and Its Treatment. San Francisco, Jossey-Bass, 1976
20. Hogarty GE, Goldberg SC, Schooler NR, et al: The collaborative study group: Drug and sociotherapy in the aftercare of schizophrenic patients: Two year relapse rates. Arch Gen Psychiatry 31:603–608, 1974
21. Lamb, HR, Goertzel V: The long-term patient in the era of community treatment. Arch Gen Psychiatry 34:679–682, 1977

22. Brown GW, Birley JLT: Crises and life changes and the onset of schizo-phrenia. J. Health Soc Behav 9:203–214, 1968
23. Zubin J, Spring B: Vulnerability—A new view of schizophrenia. J Abnorm Psychol 86:103–126, 1977
24. Tolsdorf CC: Social networks, support, and coping: an exploratory study. Fam Proc 15:407–418, 1976
25. Creer C, Wing JK: Schizophrenia at Home. Surrey, England, National Schizophrenia Fellowship, 1974
26. Falloon IRH, Liberman RP, Lillie FJ, et al: Family therapy with relapsing schizophrenics and their families: A pilot study (unpublished manuscript, 1978)
27. Liberman RP, King LW, DeRisi WJ, et al: Personal Effectiveness: Guiding People to Assert Themselves and Improve Their Social Skills. Champaign, Ill, Research Press, 1975
28. Falloon IRH, Lindley P, McDonald R, et al: Social skills training of outpatient groups: A controlled study of rehearsal and homework. Br J Psychiatry 131:599–609, 1977
29. Liberman RP, Levine J, Wheeler E, et al: Marital therapy in groups: A comparative evaluation of behavioral and interactional formats. Acta Psychiatr Scand, suppl 266, 1976

H. Peter Laqueur

4

Multiple Family Therapy*

Dr. H. Peter Laqueur, one of the first to recognize the significance of multiple family group therapy, died at the age of 69 while his contribution to this volume was in preparation. Dr. Laqueur was born in Germany and received his medical education in Holland. He moved to the United States in 1947, did specialty training in psychiatry, and held a number of distinguished academic posts in New York City before moving to Vermont in 1968. He was Associate Professor at the University of Vermont, and Director of Family Therapy at Vermont State Hospital.

He is best known for his early recognition of the significance of multiple family therapy (MFT), and most of his publications deal with MFT. He was not only a pioneer of the use of MFT, but his work remains the foremost body of theoretical work on that subject. "Multiple Family Therapy" is reprinted from Family Therapy: Theory and Practice, edited by Philip J. Guerin, Jr., MD, and published by Gardner Press (New York), 1976 (pages 405–416), with the kind permission of Ria Laqueur, Dr. Philip J. Guerin, Jr., and Gardner Press. The many references to multiple family therapy in this volume are a testimonial to Dr. Laqueur's lasting contribution to the field of family therapy.

MRL

*Reprinted with permission from Laqueur HP: Multiple family therapy, in Guerin PJ Jr (ed): Family Therapy: Theory and Practice. New York, Gardner Press, 1976

HISTORY OF MULTIPLE FAMILY THERAPY

Multiple Family Therapy (MFT) was born in 1950 in a New York State Hospital where the author was in charge of a 100-bed ward of mostly young schizophrenic patients under insulin coma therapy. Noticing the well-known phenomenon of patients improving steadily until their first home visit and then returning to the hospital in worse shape, we decided to have a closer look at the families. Families were invited for informative question/answer meetings. This soon made the patients suspicious that the doctor 'conspired' with the families whom they generally saw as their adversaries. Joint meetings of patients together with their families were then instituted. After a few years, the sheer number of people present at these meetings made them ineffectual and we then decided to split these families up into groups of four or five families in a group.

Very soon we observed that this was not only expedient, saving time and personnel, but that the interaction of several families seemed to produce change in behavior faster than the treatment of individual families, which we also had used in some cases. It seems that certain mechanisms active in MFT, such as learning through analogy, indirect interpretation, and identification, make it easier for family members to improve communication and to try out new behavior in an atmosphere that is more permissive than when only one family is the center of attention at all times. MFT has been aptly called "a sheltered workshop in family communication."

We mentioned our work with families for the first time briefly in 1959, in a paper on our specific method of insulin coma therapy[1], but not until 1963 did we present a paper on Multiple Family Therapy[2]. Since then insulin coma therapy has practically been abandoned in this country and Multiple Family Therapy has progressed from a treatment for the most severely schizophrenic patients on an insulin ward to disturbed families with identified patients of the most diverse diagnostic descriptions in settings of all kinds—hospital, community mental health clinic, correctional facility, drug rehabilitation center and psychiatrist's office.[3-6]

DESCRIPTION OF MFT

A description of MFT is in order at this point. Four to five identified patients, hospitalized or ambulant, together with their families (parents, siblings, spouses, children) meet with a therapist, co-therapist, and observers (therapist trainees) in weekly sessions of 1½ hours. Meetings must be held in evening hours to make participation of working family members possible. Any large, acoustically acceptable, and decently ventilated room in which 25 to 30 chairs can be placed in an ellipse is suitable. Videotaping equipment is highly desirable to record the MFT session, both for immediate playback of important sections to the group as part of the therapy, as well as for the evaluation and training sessions of therapists, co-therapists, and therapists in training following the therapy session.

Groups are open-ended. A family leaving the group for whatever reason—for instance, improved identified patient and family relationships, so that the family does not feel the need for further participation; family moving away; change of season (particularly important in Vermont where families living at a distance grow weary of traveling at night over icy winter roads); or, occasionally, a family just dropping out—is replaced by a newly referred family.

After a trial-and-error period of selecting families for a common factor—for example, psychiatric diagnosis, educational level, or economic status—we found that it is best to make MFT groups as random as possible in their socioeconomic as well as their ethnic, religious, political, age, and other characteristics. Specific factor grouping carries with it the dangers of pseudointellectuality, and of superficial discussion around so-called common interests, instead of work on basic human behavior problems, such as marital relationships, or parent-child relationships.

The family's understandable request is that the treatment should produce improvement in the clinical condition of the member who has been classified as patient. Thus, the first task of the therapist is to explain that we don't believe in primary patient as opposed to healthy family members, but that we look for disturbed interaction patterns in the entire family in order to help them all. We explain that we see the specific symptoms in the identified patient as provoked, or at least contributed to, and therefore, alterable by the response of the family system. We aim to have other families in the group actively participate in the discovery of sickness-inducing mutual behavior, so that families become co-therapists and help each other find possibilities for change, and for coping with problems in new ways.

STRUCTURE OF DISTURBED AND HEALTHY FAMILIES

In our attempt to understand a family, we make use of perhaps somewhat oversimplified descriptions of the structure of disturbed as opposed to healthy families.

The most severely disturbed family is one in which everyone is turned off on everyone else. Each member lives in their own world and finds it difficult, if not impossible, to communicate with the others; they cannot talk about anything except perhaps the weather.

The second kind of family is split by the age-generation gap. The parents communicate with each other; the children are in touch with each other; but parents and children have little in common and cannot communicate.

The third family is split by sex. Father and sons form a subsystem, and mothers and daughters are another subsystem; there is little communication between the two.

In the fourth family, two members are intensely tied together emotionally, while other members are not connecting with the symbiotic pair or with each other.

The fifth family has one member, usually mother, in the control tower. Communications from everyone to everyone else go through her; direct communications from one family member to another are avoided. It must be understood that a control tower has also a 'loving' function—avoids collisions.

In the sixth kind of family, most members are in good communication with each other; but one is 'outside,' except for a weak connection with one other member, and is perhaps being scapegoated.

The seventh kind of family has a strictly hierarchical order; the person who is in the top position may not even appear with the family in the therapy session. He may be a grandparent or other significant personality who calls the shots for the whole family.

And finally, there is the 'ideal' family (which we still have to meet in real life), where everyone communicates freely with everyone else on every subject, on cognitive as well as emotional levels.

These models are, of course, only what we see as the most prevalent family types among hundreds of variants and combinations.

GENERAL SYSTEMS THEORY

We have found general systems theory[7] to be a most helpful tool in analyzing and understanding individual families, as well as the whole MFT group.

Living systems have a history of coming into being; of existing for a limited period during which they grow and expand in knowledge, skill, and capability for coping with the environment; and of ceasing to exist after having fulfilled their function. This history applies equally to families and the MFT group as a whole. The individual is seen as a subsystem of a higher system, the family, and this in turn as a subsystem of the next higher systems, the community, society, and environment (suprasystem.) Likewise, the MFT group consists of subsystems: the families and the therapeutic teams each consist of subsystems made up of the individual family members and the therapist, co-therapist, and therapist trainees.

All functioning systems, no matter how intricately composed of multiple parts (subsystems), have *input*; a *central processing unit* (CPU); *output*; and a *feeback loop* which informs the CPU of the quality of its performance and thereby allows control and correction of output.

The family system receives matter, information, and energy (input) from its members (subsystems), and the environment (suprasystem.) It processes this input into actions (output) that ensure productive and creative growth, or, at least, the survival of the system (family) and its subsystems (family members.) The joint decision-making apparatus of the family, whatever shape this may take—family council, informal consultation of family members, and so on—may be termed the CPU of the family system.

The MFT group—and for that matter, any form of psychotherapy—can be considered a system with input (human beings and relationships in need of help), a CPU (the therapeutic team, often in cooperation with family members who act as co-therapists), and output (better functioning of families and their individual members.)

Malfunction of an individual, a family, or the whole MFT group can be analyzed to find the primary focus of disturbance, and to devise methods for correction. Systems malfunction occurs when: the inputs are too powerful, or too scarce, or of irrelevant and useless nature; the CPU lacks data, information, organization, or perception/recognition/checking/planning apparatus to correlate incoming signals with output in a well-structured program and in satisfactory individual style; the output channels are obstructed, distorted, or poorly operating; feedback information is incomplete, wrong, or excessive, redundant, and misleading; and too much, too little, or the wrong kind of energy, matter, and information (cognitive and affective) passes through the interface from one subsystem to the other. Any of these occurrences may cause overloads, inadequate timing, improper reactions to internal and external sensors, friction between parts, faulty bypasses, or over- or underreactions.

In a system, no one part can move without influencing all other parts of the system. The therapist must be aware of this and at all times keep the MFT group and also the individual families in his mind *as* systems.[8] He then will be able to perform the function of a systems analyst, which consists of analyzing interface problems, feedback, perception, recognition, association, and planning for response; and proposing new and specific possibilities for the correction of malfunctions.[9-11]

DIFFERENCES BETWEEN MFT AND OTHER FORMS OF PSYCHOTHERAPY

We believe that MFT is unique insofar as it alone among the different forms of psychotherapy allows the suprasystem, the outside world, society, to enter into the therapeutic relationship.

In individual therapy, for theoretical reasons, the therapist and the patient close themselves off from the rest of the world. Information from 'out there' only enters through the patient's perception, and the therapist has no direct means of checking how correct this perception may be.

Peer group therapy brings the therapist together with several patients, but again information from the 'outside' only reaches the therapist through the patients' perception. He cannot see the patients' interactions with the significant others in their immediate environment, let alone with society.

Conjoint family therapy and social network therapy both focus primarily on the identified patient and bring in only persons directly concerned with the identified patient's problems and fate.

It seems to us that only in MFT is society, so to say, present in the form of several families other than the identified patient's, people who are not directly concerned with the identified patient's or his family's fate. The therapist not only directly observes the patient in the context of his family system, but also the family system in its relationship with a suprasystem, the MFT group. This makes the MFT group a truly open system for information input.

RECENT ADVANCES IN MFT

We have developed several techniques or adapted known techniques to our purposes in MFT by means of which we hope to expedite change and shorten the therapeutic process. Years ago we were not overly concerned with shortening therapy, because our identified patients were for the most part severely schizophrenic individuals, long term in-hospital patients. With the trend toward shorter hospitalization and faster reintegration of the identified patient into active life, we started looking for ways to also shorten MFT.

We devised an exercise for the very beginning of a new MFT group which seems to speed up the process of getting acquainted considerably.

The mothers of the group are asked to come to the center and tell the group what they think of themselves, and how they rate themselves as mothers and wives. Then the fathers in the group are asked to rate themselves as fathers and husbands.

The youngsters are asked to divide themselves into two subgroups, one the so-called 'good' children (usually the ones who consider themselves the 'healthy' children), and the other, the so-called 'bad' children (usually the identified patients). They are encouraged to state briefly their problems with the family; probably not surprisingly, the 'good' children also have many of these. This polarization—which of course works best with families who seek help because of behavior problems of one member—leads to a process of learning by analogy. After only two sessions, the group usually obtains a good awareness of the type of family problems in each family.

The therapist may also explain and diagram the previously described family structures for the group, and ask families to indicate which model they think comes closest to their own family.

In subsequent sessions we explore specific dyadic relationships with the help of some here-and-now exercises:

In the *yes-no exercise*: Two people with differences of opinion stand opposite each other with arms outstretched and hands on each other's shoulders. One states a wish or command and then shouts "Yes," while the other shouts "No." The shouting usually becomes louder and quickly is followed by a physical attempt to push the other away from the midline. Aggressive people try to win; passive people learn to muster more strength, and in the majority of cases both partners report that they find the emotional intensity of the exercise satisfying. Only a small number of people call this demonstration 'silly' or are 'ashamed to show feelings,' or are 'afraid of hurting or being hurt' or prefer to 'only talk' about their differences. There is diagnostic significance in how long it takes each person to express genuine emotion and activity; also in whether participants follow the rules or try to tickle or otherwise get the other off balance.

Three other exercises, the *yes-if*, the *yes-but*, and the *yes-and*, can be useful to explore how two people reach a tentative or qualified agreement, or if two people have to learn to agree to disagree in a friendly tolerant fashion, rather than to disagree in angry or resigned (shrugging shoulders) ways.

Another very challenging exercise is the so-called *back-to-back*. A couple is placed back to back, locking arms, and is asked to find a some way to extricate themselves from this position. Some turn around, seeking each other out, and some walk away from each other frustrated. From who does what when, we and the group as well as the participants in the exercise learn a great deal.

Hierarchy within the family can be made manifest by letting one person climb on a chair as 'boss,' and decide who should stand closest and who farther away.

We have somewhat modified the family sculpting technique of Peggy Papp and her colleagues. We not only ask a person to sculpt his family as he sees it now, but to model it over time, as it was when he was five years old, ten, 15/20 years of age, up to the present. This chronological family sculpture is also an excellent exercise for therapist trainees during the evaluation and training session that follows the MFT session. Similarly, we find the older psychodrama techniques of 'doubling,' 'monologue,' 'sociogram,' and 'act out a story' more useful in our training sessions for new workers than in the MFT session.

One of the most exciting innovations is the recording of MFT sessions on videotape, with its possibility for immediate playback to the group of important scenes, allowing us to study body language and contradictions between verbal and nonverbal signals. We record with two cameras, one at each end of the elliptically arranged MFT group. A special-effects generator allows the VTR director to show in a composite picture what goes on at one end of the group simultaneously with the reactions in the rest of the group.

PROCESS

For schematic purposes, we can divide the treatment process in MFT into three phases.

Phase I: Initial interest. Families experience an initial sense of relief and even some remission of symptoms as they see that something is being done about a painful situation. It is a kind of magical relief due to unreal expectations. But there is also the chance to observe at firsthand other families suffering (and improving), and thereby to have a spark of hope kindled.

Phase II: Resistance. The family begins to see that a change in attitude and behavior is required not only of one member (the identified patient), but in all members mutually and simultaneously. This is the time when their initial fears about exposing hurts and anxieties come to the fore, and resistance to treatment sets in. Doubt that 'anyone ever changes,' and fears about losing 'whatever little good relations we had' are voiced when they are asked to open up and to confront the sleeping dogs in their lives.

Before genuine changes in emotional response patterns based on something more than lip service can be obtained, individuals must first gain confidence that risk-taking and reaching out to the other person can be safe, and that the other person may respond positively and not with the accustomed withdrawal, irrelevancy, or rejection. Only when fear of failure gives way to mutual acceptance, can Phase II slide slowly into

Phase III: Working through. Significant changes begin to take place. With true openness and with increased confidence, families come to realize their deeper problems and also their ability to deal with them. They become more flexible in their recognition of the alternative options open to them. Families in this phase become helpful to other families in distress, and teach them by model and analogy.

MECHANISMS OF CHANGE

A description of some of the mechanisms operating in MFT may illustrate the nature of the transactions performed.[12]

Delineation of the field of interaction. Following Kurt Lewin's *Field Theory in Social Science,*[13] the therapist tries to see the total field of interaction between subsystems (patient, family) and suprasystem (the total social environment), and makes the participants in the group aware of the importance for sickness and health of this changing surrounding field. The range and variety of therapeutic approaches available to the therapist in this field of interacting forces is much wider than in a two-way communication with individual patients or single families.

Breaking the intrafamilial code. Families with a seriously disturbed member seem to develop secret codes for their internal verbal and nonverbal communications. These are often used to close off discussion of a dangerous area. Families have had a lifetime to learn each other's signals, and these are not readily understood by the therapist. Often other families, because of their own experience, are able to help in breaking these codes. At such moments, the therapist may be confused and unable to understand the direction things are taking, because he is unaware of the secret meaning of messages but *can* assist in circumventing this defensive process by insisting on discovering the real meaning of the transaction taking place, often with the help of explanations by other families.

Competition. Competition between systems (families) or subsystems (individuals) produces changes in the internal power distribution of the system faster than work with a single family could do. A threat to the status of a family or an individual stimulates competition, which leads, in turn, to productive interaction of the family members at an earlier stage in treatment. Later on, cooperation may take the place of competition.

Amplification and modulation of signals. A sensitive patient can pick up a signal from the therapist and amplify it to sensitize his family. Through his family, such a signal may be further amplified and modulated to other families who, without this amplification, might not yet have responded to the therapist's signal.

Learning through trial and error.. The MFT group provides its members with unique opportunities to try out new modes of behavior, reinforce them if they meet with the group's approval, or discard them if the group disapproves. The MFT group is characterized by the simultaneous presence of many authority figures—the therapist, mothers, fathers, and so forth. In this setting, the relationships between identified patient and various authority figures can be worked through rapidly by means of the comparatively nonthreatening process of understanding through analogy and identification. The therapist, in the role as parent-surrogate, may transiently diminish the parent's authoritarian status, thereby encouraging the identified patient to behave more independently, to be more 'daring.'

New insights may also be achieved through role-playing—for example, having the son of family A play the role of the father of family B. By acting as if he were that parent, son A may not only achieve for himself, but also transmit to the other children, a greater understanding of the role of the parent in this situation.

Learning by analogy. Members of the MFT group have many opportunities to observe analogous conflict situations and learn from these examples. The knowledge that others have been there is an important incentive to learn new ways of dealing with conflict; this situation occurs frequently in the MFT group, whose members present many different types of conflict.

Learning through identification. MFT offers many opportunities for identification. Fathers learn from other fathers; mothers from other mothers; youngsters identify with youngsters in other families. The fellowship of experience in the MFT group helps each to cope with existential and situational problems.

The use of models. The therapist in MFT uses the healthier aspects of one family as a model and a challenge as a way to motivate other families to change their behavior. The potential for this is enhanced by the fact that MFT groups are open-ended, so that in each group families at different stages of treatment are present.

Creating a focus of excitation. In our attempt to break through the resistance to change behavior that is manifested in most families, we asked ourselves: "How do people integrate new experiences in their outlook on the world and their preparation for future behavior?" Information theory postulates that those events that have the least probability of occurring, yet do occur, have the highest information value. A new pattern or a new sequence of signals that produces an excitation focus in the nervous system has high information value. Translated into MFT terms, a new more realistic type of behavior of one family, as distinguished from their usually observed behavior, can act as a focus of excitation for the whole group if it is used skillfully by the therapist. The use of humor, a drawing, or a video picture in this context can be very successful.

Use of families as co-therapists. The open-ended MFT group includes families in different stages of treatment and improvement. Often, the more advanced families, consciously or unconsciously, directly or indirectly, offer themselves as co-therapists; how the therapist uses these opportunities is indicative of his skill. In any of the above described mechanisms families can be used in therapeutic ways to help other families.

GOALS AND RESULTS

Therapy always aims to change a system of interaction between the primary patient and his environment, even if the stated goal is not crisis intervention, but only mediating and producing better insight. Insight, after all, in systems terms means becoming aware of more inputs to the regulatory system that maintains and steers the activities of the self. If one perceives and recognizes more external and internal forces and vectors, one subsequently can change one's behavior because of these insights. Every psychotherapist, from whatever school derived, strives to teach the primary patient and his environment to 'relate better'—that is, to be less easily offended, turned off, sulky, depressed, or unproductive; to learn self-confidence, even under stress; to stand up to formerly unconquerable obstacles and overcome them; to achieve a better understanding of inner conflicts and one's goals and purposes in life. This means that patients and families are encouraged and persuaded to gain a new perspective on life and environment, no matter how non-directive the therapeutic techniques applied are.

We consider a family improved if our therapeutic intervention has achieved the following: (1) Better function and creative operation of the family, even within environments that make family life more complex and difficult emotionally, economically, politically, or morally. (2) Better mutual liking and respect of family members for one another. (3) Better acceptance of shortcomings and capitalizing on each other's strengths. (4) Better ability to enjoy day-to-day living. (5) Greater capability for compassion, mutual love, understanding, support, and cooperation among family members. (6) Better insight and improved judgment. (7) Greater openness for new information. (8) Building of lasting and satisfying relationships with each other within the family, and with friends and environment.

It remains to be said that in the approximately 1500 families treated in our MFT groups over the last 25 years, we may have had no more than a handful of families where we thought MFT was contraindicated. These were cases where exposure of a vital secret might lead to explosive reactions. In general, however, we fully agree with Ackerman: "With great frequency I have found that these intimate matters, these so-called secrets, turn out not to be real secrets at all. Far more often they are common family knowledge, surrounded by a tacit conspiracy of silence. What is involved here is not so much a true secret but rather a barrier to emotional communication, a barrier to the free sharing of certain experiences."[14]

REFERENCES

1. Laqueur HP, LaBurt HA: Coma therapy with multiple insulin doses. J Neuropsychiatry 1:135–147, 1960
2. Laqueur HP, LaBurt HA, Morong E: Multiple family therapy, in Masserman JH (ed): Current Psychiatric Therapies (vol 4). New York, Grune & Stratton, 1964
3. Laqueur HP: Multiple family therapy: Questions and answers. Seminars in Psychiatry (vol 5), 1973

4. Laqueur HP, LaBurt HA, Morong E: Multiple family therapy: Further developments. Internat J Soc Psychiatry, pp 69–80, 1964
5. Laqueur HP, Safirstein SL: Comparison of treatment in the psychiatric division of a general hospital and in a state hospital. Excerpta Medica International Congress Series No. 150, Madrid, 1966
6. Laqueur HP, Wells CF, Agresti M: Multiple family therapy in a state hospital. Hosp Community Psychiatry 20:13–19, 1969
7. Von Bertalanffy L: General systems theory and psychiatry, in Arieti S (ed): American Handbook of Psychiatry. New York, Basic Books, 1966
8. Laqueur HP: Systems Therapy, in Masserman JH (ed): Current Psychiatric Therapies (vol 11). New York, Grune & Stratton, 1971
9. Laqueur HP: General systems theory and multiple family therapy, in Masserman JH (ed): Current Psychiatric Therapies (vol 8). New York, Grune & Stratton, 1968
10. Laqueur HP: General systems theory and multiple family therapy, in Gray W, Duhl FJ, Rizzo ND (eds): General Systems Theory and Psychiatry. Boston, Little Brown, 1969
11. Laqueur HP: Multiple family therapy and general systems theory, in Ackerman NW (ed): Family Therapy in Transition. Boston, Little Brown, 1969
12. Laqueur HP: Mechanisms of change in multiple family therapy, in Sager CJ, Kaplan, HS (eds): Progress in Group and Family Therapy. New York, Brunner Mazel, 1972
13. Lewin, K: Field Theory in Social Science. New York, Harper & Row, 1951
14. Ackerman NW: The Psychodynamics of Family Life. New York, Basic Books, 1958

Carol R. Bley

5

Multiple Family Therapy with Schizophrenics: Experiences with Single Males and their Families of Origin

Multiple Family Therapy (MFT) is a recent treatment modality, a three decades' blend of family systems and group theory. It is a treatment modality without a widely accepted theoretical foundation to render it readily applicable. Therefore, it is often used without full appreciation of its scope and is often erroneously though to be merely adjunctive to the real business of work with individual families. The possibility that MFT would be chosen over treatment of one family individualy is rarely considered seriously. In this chapter the strength and scope of this emerging modality, and its central importance in the treatment of an illness as serious and devastating as schozophrenia, will be addressed in a practical manner.

The case vignettes that follow will illustrate the difference between individual and family group therapy and will highlight the broad indications for use of MFT.

CASE 1: MANUEL M

Manuel's parents were embarrassed by his mental illness. They were a closely-knit Chicano family with no hint of the bizarreness often described in schizophrenic family transactions. They were a hurting family, and single family

---

The author wishes to thank Melvin Lansky, M.D. for collaborating on this chapter.

treatment did not ease their humiliation. A multiple family group allowed them to meet other families with the same problem. In this context they felt respected for being a caring family which was functional despite Manuel's psychosis. Manuel's emotional, sensitive father was adopted by two other sons in the group. Bonds formed. They asked about him when he was absent (an infrequent occurrence). This buttressed Mr. M's opinion of himself as a father more than any transaction with a therapist could hope to achieve. Mr. M regained the view of himself as a good father even though Manuel has been psychotic.

CASE 2: BRAD B

Brad was a chronically psychotic, Vietnam combat veteran, who attributed much of his torment to horrifying war experiences. However, he used his psychotic disorganization and rage in an intimidating way. Brad, 29 years old and separated, lived at home with his hardworking, middle-aged, divorced mother, and a younger sister who was enrolled in college. Unemployed since Vietnam, Brad spent long days at home drinking heavily and brooding about his empty life. Frequently he terrorized the household with unreasonable demands for special treatment. No one dared object out of fear that Brad would go into an uncontrollable rage, punching his fists through walls, breaking furniture, and threatening to harm family members.

The B's individual family meetings were tense. The sessions usually included only Brad and his mother. Mrs. B. feared any type of confrontation, so Brad got away with a lot of intimidation, but at the price of alienating himself from his family.

In multiple family therapy, Mrs. B found the support she needed to confront, even mildly, her potentially explosive son. The malignant course of Brad's illness changed little with therapy. Nonetheless, each member of the family, including Brad, was more accessible to support. Brad and his mother faithfully attended group. If they had had to choose, they would have chosen the group over individual family sessions, as would the therapists involved. Everyone felt that Brad's rage was too much to contain within the family or any small group. The multiple family group provided enough safety for all concerned to accomodate a potentially explosive family situation that was intermittently defused by hospital containment.

CASE 3: JEFF J

Jeff's parents were secretive in individual family sessions. They appeared polite, but engaged only superficially in treatment. Sessions were full of stubborn silences, not broken by the usual interpretations. Mr. and Mrs. J, flooded by self-recrimination, could not examine their motives and behavior. The family acted as though problems would go away if they were not addressed. This combination of denial and self-reproach resulted in stalemated communication between Mr. and Mrs. J and Jeff, who acted more like a boarder than a son. Jeff, 30, divorced from his pregnant wife, slept at home, at most of his meals there, but rarely spoke, not out of anger, but out of schizophrenic withdrawal and defeat. If he were not out driving alone in his car, he isolated himself in his bedroom and watched old war movies on television.

In multiple family therapy, the Js responded in the same defensive way: reserved and definitely uncommitted. Jeff was stiff and distant. Jeff and his parents saw other families struggle with similar conflicts. Eventually, Jeff and his father began to talk. Mr. J began, "Didn't we have good times fishing together last year? What has changed? I wat us to be close again, but you push me away." Both parents voiced worry about their troubled son, but they did not know how to break through the barriers, similarly reenacted in family treatment. The J family slowly became more communicative in and out of group, even occasional initiators of material for the group, but they still maintained some of their guardedness. They did attend group fairly regularly for eight months.

Jeff continued to live at home, but eventually took a full-time job and began providing financial support to his ex-wife and infant daughter. He has maintained himself out of the hospital and on the job during the two years since hospital discharge.

CASE 4: WALTER W

At the family intake, Walter, a 28-year-old, single, black man, arrived wearing a turban, jeans, a sports jacket with an American flag in the lapel, and small, hexagonal, mirrored sunglasses. His whole bearing communicated bizarreness and suspiciousness. Mr. and Mrs. W seemed at first to be well-intentioned parents, genuinely puzzled by their son's condition. Protesting that he was not like their successful, ambitious older sons, they asked, "Why did this happen to Walter? Weren't we good parents? What could we do help him?" Their attitude toward Walter seemed to vary from insisting that he straighten up and complete school to despairing totally and expecting nothing. The bizarreness of their communcations became clearer as time went on: the Ws bombarded the patient with irrelevant truisms and advice about diet, exercise, and discipline; produced note pads to get statements from therapists about what foods and exercise programs were best. Their combined impact left therapists and other group members with feelings of bewilderment and confusion.

The Ws were seen in single family and multiple family therapy. They participated regularly over two and a half years. Mr. and Mrs. W gradually modified their reactions to their son's illness, especially after Walter no longer invited their overprotective stance toward him. The parents began to consider what they wanted from each other after their retirement. Walter returned to a community college, initially taking one or two classes. The Ws terminated therapy when Walter was stable and family anxiety was down.

Walter has since gotten a college diploma. He maintains his own apartment, works part time, has a steady girlfriend, and has been out of the hospital for over five years.

LITERATURE REVIEW

Multiple family therapy has been practiced in various styles and forms since the early 1950s. Dr. H. Peter Laqueur is regarded as the original theoretician of multiple family treatment.[1,2,10] Laqueur's theory evolved from his experiences in treating young schizophrenic patients under formidable conditions: a crowded state mental hospital in the early 1950s. His curiosity about the pathologic influence of families upon his young schizophrenic patients developed into a treatment modality with stable groups of four or five families each. Laqueur observed the interaction of several families producing changes faster than the treatment of individual families. Laqueur labelled these mechanisms: competition and cooperation, learning by analogy, learning through identification constellations, learning through trial and error, use of the healthier aspects of certain families as models, and use of families as co-therapists.[2] He was the first to appreciate MFT as a unique modality that could mobilize simultaneously the supportive and confrontive features of the families and further the treatment of frightened, isolated, ashamed, and confused families.

Laqueur coined the term "identification constellation" for the opportunity for persons in multiple family groups to harness identifications with people in similar or complementary familial positions, and to use these identifications for problem solving, ego mastery, or reality testing in a supportive way. For example, a mother might be able to receive more support and constructive criticism from other mothers in the group than she could from group members who are not mothers or the therapist because, in crucial ways, the mothers are *like her*, and comments from them are simultaneously confrontive and supportive. A son might try asserting himself with the father of another family before trying some of the same negotiations with his own father.

Despite its 30-year history, the field of MFT is in the early stages of theoretical development. Few other than Laqueur have discussed MFT theoretically, and empirical studies on process and/or outcome are lacking.[1] MFT has been called the "overlooked treatment,"[3] a hybrid, a parallel method, rather than a subcategory of group therapy.[4] Despite its ever-expanding use in specific predicaments such as alcoholism, medical illness, and other psychiatric disorders, little attention has been paid to MFT per se. The confused conceptualizations, compounded by lack of convincing literature in the field, have perpetuated neglect of MFT as a major treatment modality.

This discussion is limited to the significance of multiple family therapy with a schizophrenic population, although the principles may be generalized to many other predicaments. I will be addressing practical issues: selection criteria, group composition, preparation of new group members, role of co-therapists, frequency of sessions, termination of therapy, and group process. Hopefully, an appreciation of the scope of MFT and a sense of its power and uniqueness will emerge.

SETTING

These observations will draw from seven years experience on a 20-bed male family-oriented inpatient unit at the Brentwood Veterans Administration Medical Center. This family treatment program provides a full range of psychiatric services covering everything from acute inpatient work to partial hospitalization to aftercare, and actively involves the family and/or significant others in every case.[5]

Two types of patients are most common in our program: young schizophrenics in their middle to late twenties, and men in their forties and fifties with character pathology accompanied by major affective components. Since this report is on schizophrenia, discussion will be limited to that population. Most of our schizophrenic patients are single and living with their families of origin. The predicament of the married schizophrenic will not be addressed at this time.

Diagnostically, our schizophrenic patients have front-rank Scheiderian symptoms and other clearcut diagnostic features. Schizophreniform psychoses are rare in our population. A significant number of our patients experienced their first psychotic break in or shortly after discharge from military service. It is not unusual for our young schizophrenic patients to be chronic at a very young age (early twenties) with continuous or multiple psychiatric hospitalizations since discharge from military service, and with marginal functioning in between hospitalizations. The population, therefore, is that of poor-prognosis schizophrenics.

The treatment philosophy of the program (from which these observations are drawn) views the family as central to the event of hospitalization.[5] Family involvement is required, and ongoing family meetings begin early in treatment. In that sense, the considerations discussed here may not be fully generalizable to other settings that use MFT principles without integrating it into an entire program tailored around family treatment.

RATIONALE

I view multiple family therapy as central to the treatment of schizophrenia. It is especially valuable as a vehicle of tertiary prevention by maximizing posthospital adjustment of schizophrenic outpatients. The indications are so vast that to consider contraindications is less useful than to consider the following general indications or selection criteria.

MFT for Socially Isolated Families

Many schizophrenic families have never seen another family's interactions. Phenomena referring to isolation in schizophrenic families have been described by Lidz et al as "prohibition of extrafamilial socialization,"[6] by Wynne as the "rubber fence,"[7] and by Bateson as the tertiary injunction of the "double-bind" transaction,[8] which prevents the victim from leaving the field.

CASE 5: KYO

Kyo, the young son of a traditional Japanese-American family, sat speechless as he watched a volatile, Italian-American family battle out their differences in one group session. He was used to his own family: quiet, overly polite, no overt disagreements, and definitely no shouting. What he witnessed amazed him and gave him a new perspective on how other families handle conflict. This view of other families added to his repertoire of the possible.

Almost without exception, the family members with a schizophrenic identified patient feel tremendous shame about the psychosis, and guilt over their shortcomings, real or imagined. Why did this happen to them? They want to hide. They do not feel this predicament is shared by other families. It is with relief, sometimes to the point of tears, that they meet other families with similar problems. Feeling that they are not alone is a crucial beginning to self-examination. To participate in MFT is an experiential exercise in family functioning, and often crosscultural exposure. Our groups work well with families of diverse ethnic origins and socioeconomic status.

CASE 6: PETER AND MANUEL

When Peter's stepfather, a materialistic man who prided himself on being self-made, talked about giving too much to Peter, Manuel's father replied,"I wish I had that to give to Manuel, but money ain't everything! Manuel knows I love him and would give my very life to help him." As Manuel's father wiped tears from his eyes, the group was silent. Peter's father was thoughtful. This questioning of family values could not have taken place as poignantly coming from the therapists or a member of his own family.

CASE 7: JIMMY J

Jimmy, a 23-year-old black man, was paranoid and excitable. He talked nonstop about being the son of God, fearful that "they" would get him and that hospital medicine was poisoned. He was certain police helicopters flying over his neighborhood were after him. His family lived in a high-crime area; the entire family tone was one of marked paranoia, reinforced by cultural mistrust, especially toward bureaucracies and white people. Jimmy was not willing to take medication on weekend passes. Mrs. J was uncooperative about supervising her son's medication or even returning him after weekend passes.

In MFT, Jimmy was told by the other young patients about the importance of taking medications; "Otherwise, man, you'll wind up back here [if discharged against medical advice] . . . or dead [in a provoked street confrontation]." Jimmy's mother got support from other mothers with her limit-setting difficulties: returning her son after passes, and not providing refuge when he left against advice. Since other families are not perceived as authority figures, Jimmy's mother is likely to listen to them.

MFT for Enmeshed Families

Much literature on schizophrenia describes a dysfunctional system with blurred generational boundaries and serious marital tensions that are projected onto vulnerable members of the next generation.[9] The family pattern of an overprotective mother, withdrawn father, and schizophrenic son with very few involvements outside of the family system may not be unique to schizophrenic families, but it is common.

CASE 8: FRANK F

Frank was the youngest son of working-class Italian-American parents. He was explosive and intimidating at times. Mrs. F, who was in an unhappy and sexually unfulfilled marriage, had overindulged and pampered Frank.

Within the family group, mother got both pressure and support to let Frank go, to allow him the space to make his own mistakes, and, in the process, not to feel responsible for him. Eventually Frank left home, moved into a halfway house, and, much to father's relief, started a job retraining program. Frank no longer used his illness to compete for mother's attention.

In our sample, the fathers often died or divorced the mothers when the patients were young, and there have been no adequate or substantial father substitutes to modify an intense mother-son dyad, which may be almost impossible to change.

CASE 9: DEAN D

In group, Dean's mother talked openly about her son's childhood and her husband's sudden death. Dean never knew his father; he was an only child. It was just the two of them; and Mrs. D suspected they might have been too close.

Thirty-three-year-old Dean, in partial remission from an acute schizophrenic break, was demanding in a gradiose way. He complained, "How dare the insurance company fire me? They are discriminatory. I'm too good, too competent for them!" Mrs. D encouraged Dean's externalizations, but at the same time resented his folly.

With group support, Mrs. D included her longstanding boyfriend in group sessions. The presence of this older gentleman seemed to diminish the intensity of the mother–son relationship. He thought Dean should be confronted with the unreality of his plans. The alternative seemed to be that Dean would never become independent and mother would never feel free to remarry. When other patients challenged Dean's plans, the Ds dropped out of group, but the group was of help in modifying the mother–son relationship and promoting better reality testing.

MFT for Families That Need
Predicament-Specific Information

Group members confront major issues concerning illness itself and the problem of attributing responsibility in the presence of recurrent psychosis. Parents wrestle with: "How much is the illness [and therefore should be overlooked or excused], and how much responsibility can by adult–child assume? Am I being too soft and indulgent? Do I ask too much of my child?" Patients encounter: "What is in my future? This illness you label psychosis, is there a cure? Will I need to take medicine forever? Can I ever expect to lead a normal life?" These questions are less anxiety-producing when addressed in a group of families.

CASE 10: FRANK F

Frank (see Case 8) announced one night in group that he wanted to be readmitted. There was so much conflict at home he felt he must return to the hospital to escape. Mr. and Mrs. F carried their feud over into group. His father thought rehospitalization unnecessary, but his mother was overanxious and looking for an answer. Other parents in the group challenged Frank with, "You really don't need to come back to the hospital. You just need another place to stay!" Frank moved into a halfway house, thereby averting an unnecessary and potentially demoralizing rehospitalization and, at the same time, removing himself from family tensions that he usually exploited.

MFT for Families That Need to
Check Out Their Perceptions

CASE 11: LEE L

Twenty-year-old Lee was an illegitimate child. His stepfather deserted the family when Mrs. L was pregnant with her last child. Lee's whole life revolved around his mother and four younger brothers. Mrs. L was only fifteen years older than Lee. Lee routinely babysat for her while she worked evenings as a cocktail waitress. He had no friends and no activities outside of the home, but he felt special to his mother. He only wished she was not so sad all the time. They shared confidences and dreams, more like siblings or lovers than parent and child. At times, he could not understand her logic. But Mrs. L was psychotic herself, which Lee never knew.

In their first multiple family therapy session, Lee witnessed mother's circumstantial conversations and other group members' confusion about the content. What emerged was a picture of a very disturbed woman. Lee could begin to see that and to separate out his autistic thinking from his mother's.

CASE 12: PETER AND JEFF

Peter sat back and watched his aggressive stepfather, Nate, confront every young man in group. Nate challenged Jeff, who was describing the frustration of job-seeking with, "You really don't want a job!" Peter could begin to recognize that Nate reacted to other young men in a similarly debunking, unempathic manner, and that this was Nate's style arising from his own deprived childhood. It was clear that no young man would get recognition from Nate. With the additional input from subsequent individual and group family sessions, Peter and Nate began to work out a more mutually satisfying relationship.

MFT for Resistive Families

CASE 14: RICHARD

Richard's father was a top salesman for a company based over 70 miles from the hospital. He was very worried about his oldest son, and questioned anxiously, "Is Richard's illness inherited?" Richard's mother had been mentally ill for over ten years. Father was unwilling or unable to get her committed. He wanted to participate in Richard's treatment, but could not come in during normal working hours.

Some families who are too resistive and/or unable for any reason to come in for individual sessions often will participate in multiple family groups, because groups can be experienced as supportive and quasi-social. Patients like group because they experience it as applying less pressure; usually they are not on the hot seat or scapegoated by the group. At times they will confide, "We come to group to help our parents!"

MFT Instills Hope

Nothing is more inspiring for the despairing family of an acutely disturbed inpatient than interacting with a stable outpatient who has been through the same predicament. This experience is worth more than months of encouraging words from a therapist.

Basically there are no contraindications for multiple family group therapy. However, if the family will not come, or comes so irregularly as to jeopardize the intactness of the group for other families, then it is necessary to enforce the boundaries and officially drop that family from group. Likewise, if there are significant family secrets that cannot be revealed and that are in the center of the family's difficulties, the therapist may be in an untenable situation with dual loyalties to family and to group dictating opposite responses. Acute psychosis in one or more members is not a contraindication for MFT.

IS MULTIPLE FAMILY THERAPY ENOUGH?

In our setting, multiple family therapy rarely starts out as the only treatment modality. The typical treatment package for acute inpatients includes a multiple family group, individual and group psychotherapy, individual family sessions, and medication. During the acute phase, when major issues of family roles, projections, scapegoating, and unresolved symbiosis must be addressed, MFT is central to the treatment plan and actually facilitates and enhances the maximal therapeutic gain from the other modalities. Once the acute phase of family treatment is complete, MFT is an excellent modality to facilitate the family work. However, for unresolving, deep-rooted family system problems, MFT must be supplemented by intense individual family work.

CASE 16: ALAN A

Alan is a severely regressed schizophrenic inpatient who eludes treatment by running away from the hospital, impeding process within individual treatment sessions, and escaping into his own autistic world. Alan sits, mute, as his parents openly debate in group about what they call "Alan's condition." Alan's mother thinks that Alan is sick and that all of his abnormal behavior should be excused. Recently, while out of the hospital on a pass, Alan set fire to the living room drapes while his parents were on vacation, but he did manage to put out the fire before it caused any serious damage. Mrs. A writes off all of this behavior as due to Alan's illness and never looks beyond the surface behavior to what her son might be communicating. She sees his actions as unintelligible, but Mr. A adamantly insists that Alan knows what he is doing. His parents debate Alan's capacity for responsibility: this also goes on at home. Reflecting on the process and gaining strength through identification constellations enabled this family to resume individual treatment where actual negotiations could be completed in a more direct way than in MFT.

THE GROUPS THEMSELVES

My conduct of MFT is based upon experiences with several long-term multiple family groups of single schizophrenic men and their families of origin. Thirty-five families were treated with 60 percent remaining in group nine months or longer. One recent group has met regularly for four years. Membership is maintained at about five or six families. The group is open-ended and there is no time limit. The core membership changes as some families terminate. At any one time, group membership will include acute inpatients and stabilized outpatients.

Composition

Originally our groups were heterogeneous as to diagnosis but homogeneous as to family constellation, ie, groups of young, single patients with parents or marital couples groups. It soon became apparent that this method of selection posed serious impediments. For instance, the wife of a withdrawn schizophrenic man could not talk to the wife of a neurotically depressed man, as the withdrawal behavior was not comparable. This was not what Laqueur would call an "analogue conflict situation."[10] Also, the wives of depressed men could not understand the predicament of the schizophrenics' wives, nor could they offer relevant suggestions and/or support. This was soon evident even to the couples themselves. The wife of one schizophrenic group member became increasingly frustrated and despairing. We had decided to pull that particular couple out of group when the couple themselves asked to be reassigned. A comparison of psychotic withdrawal and manipulative neurotic withdrawal stimulated much discussion, to the relief of all involved.

Multiple family groups for single schizophrenic patients should contain acutely ill inpatients and stabilized former inpatients, all with their families of origin. This combination maximizes the potential of MFT. If the group contains all stable outpatients, the impetus for group work is less than when more advanced patients can see themselves as helpers and more acute patients can gain reassurance. On the other hand, if the group is composed of all acute inpatients, then the group is overwhelmed by the chaos and the despair and cannot work profitably. An inpatient who is too disturbed to sit through group is asked to leave the session, usually to the relief of the patient as well as the other group members. Such disruption is material for the group—material that resonates with the experiences of every member in the group, so these comparatively rare occurrences are useful. If a patient's family cannot attend a particular session, the patient still participates. Occasionally, the group will encourage a patient to continue alone in group after his parents have precipitously dropped out, as long as this arrangement does not compromise the availability of identification constellations for other families.

The group is functional as long as most families are represented by two generations. If families cannot or will not make the commitment to attend group regularly, the group boundaries are critically jeopardized and cohesiveness is destroyed. Adolescent and young adult siblings are usually integrated easily, but active young children may be too disruptive. Sex, socioeconomic status, and cultural/racial differences rarely become obstacles for these groups.

Preparation

Families should have some preparation for a multiple family therapy group. Family members are curious. They wonder, "What is group like? What can we expect?" Prior to the family's first MFT session, they meet with the group's therapists to answer these basic questions and to begin to establish rapport. In our experience, it is best to describe the group as supportive and to explain that they will meet other families with similar problems that have been through the same crises and survived. This emphasis on empathy rather than confrontation is more likely to reduce anxiety by anticipating the families' heightened sensitivity to being blamed and to having demands made on them.

Families come to group with similar agendas. Without exception, families feel guilty and responsible for their ill member's condition, and they fear the mental health professional will openly blame them. They come prepared for the worst. We tell families, "We are not here to judge. We do not fully understand what causes this illness." By these explanations and by consistently demonstrating our commitment to the *entire* family, the family's fear of being blamed gradually diminishes. We don't presume that the family caused the illness, but we do point out what the family might be doing unintentionally to perpetuate their child's problems.

Without exception, families fear they will be coerced into providing more materially than they are willing or able to provide. The widowed mother with an unemployed and manipulative adult son does not want to be told to provide room and board, nor should she. Once families realize our goal is to help patients to achieve as much independence as they are capable of handling, and that the family will not be asked to do anything more than come to group, family anxiety underlying the resistance goes down.

In the Family Treatment Program from which these observations are drawn, the MFT groups hold an elitist position. Patients volunteer to join the group and are disappointed if they are not included. They want to be a part of the family group, symbolically and literally.

Co-therapy

The co-therapists for our schizophrenic groups have been male/ female or both female. The advantages of using a co-therapist usually outweigh the pitfalls when working with many families. It is impossible for one person to be in touch with a complex process when so many variables are operative. If and when one therapist gets overinvolved in nonproductive transactions with a family or families, the observing co-therapist can provide the necessary objectivity. After group we hold a wrap-up to discuss process and ongoing assessment of group members. At these staff sessions, one's own observations can be validated or challenged. When the therapist is working with schizophrenic families who can induce him or her into their pathologic framework, it is vital to have supports and opportunities to test reality.

Critical questions to ask when considering working with a particular co-therapist are, "Do you have a basic respect for each other's abilities? Are you able to work well together, or are you pursuing one focus and you co-therapist another? Are you able to communicate directly and air differences openly?" If therapists can disagree openly, this openness provides modeling that may be more effective than interpretation in dealing with group members' anxiety about the expression of one's own anger. Working out these differences within group is inherently reassuring for schizophrenic families.

My own group experiences have been with both male/female and two female therapy dyads. Although the literature emphasizes the advisability of using male/female co-therapists, we have not been impressed that having two female co-therapists necessarily changes group process. Issues of nurturance, authority, envy, competition, sexual attraction, and conflicts over sexual roles are still played out, and if the co-therapist can deal with these issues, they are available for work.

Rules

There are few rules other than regular attendance and no violence. This is deliberate, since it is best to resolve issues interpretively by making them group issues and working with them in that way. There are no rules about socializing on the part of group members, and it is made clear that the therapist cannot be expected to keep secrets. Fees are not charged in our setting.

Frequency of Meetings

The group of schizophrenic young men and their families of origin meets for an hour an evening every other week. Our original groups met every week, but we were more impressed with the importance of overall length of treatment (one or two years) and modified the frequency to make it suitable for increasing family commitments outside the hospital. If a family is very resistant, the biweekly schedule may justify their forgetting which week the session was held, but this issue can be handled interpretatively by the group. If a family is motivated, biweekly scheduling is not a problem.

Termination

An important practical issue is termination. When? How? From our observations, the family usually decides, and appropriately so.[11] Since the time span of our multiple family group is indefinite, termination is a separate matter for each family. Individual family members and/or the family unit itself may use MFT as a support for as long as necessary. Typically, the family drops out because of diminished anxiety and increased ability to cope, more or less as the reasons for coming to the group subside in the course of treatment. They enjoy the social function of group, but at some point the inconvenience of attendance takes over and the family talks about terminating. Usually the family situation has been stable for many months, often for over a year. Termination is talked about in group, family members say their good-byes, and leave. At termination they are told that re-entry is possible and negotiable. A newly terminated family might keep in touch with one or more MFT families outside of group. It is not unusual for a family member to come to the ward for another purpose but to ask about various group members while there.

If the family terminates precipitously, while there are still unresolved turbulent issues with the hospitalized patient or within the family, this has been a poor prognostic sign. Often, the group will try to confront the family and keep them in group. Of the few families who have left precipitously (usually a decompensating patient or paranoid, distrustful parents), the patients have often been rehospitalized.

CASE 17: PETER

Following a very intense group session in which Peter's mother angrily confronted him with making endless demands and seeing himself as a special customer, she announced she would not return to group. At that point Peter had stopped taking his medication and was rapidly decompensating. He received much support from group that session (as had mother) and decided to continue group on his own. Since Peter had been a member of the MFT group for over a year, the other group members responded favorably to that idea.

After missing two or three transition sessions, Peter did return and began stabilizing. Now he is seen by the other group members as a successful outpatient, who has attained a goal still to be achieved by the less stable inpatients. Although this creates some pressure for Peter (he now has an image to uphold), it has served as a reorganizing experience within the family.

Conduct of Group

The room in which group is held has comfortable sofas, large padded vinyl chairs, cocktail tables, and pictures—as close to a living room as a hospital budget allows.

The tone of the group is set from the beginning, when arriving members are welcomed as they would be in the therapist's own home. This sets an atmosphere of basic friendliness rather than an anticipated trial. Issues of blame and demands have been addressed prior to group but always re-emerge as part of the group's ongoing work. Arriving families have engaged in socializing before group. Typically, this cuts off as the therapists enter the room. This is group time; time to get down to business.

Therapists comment on who is missing and inquire about the absentees. If there are sufficient two-generation families present and if the group includes acute inpatients and some outpatients, the group usually takes off. It is only on rare occasions that a total standstill of the group's work requires attention from the therapist.

Resistance does show itself. It requires attention when scapegoating maneuvers appear in the form of unhelpful and unempathic advice or outright blame attributing personal defectiveness and conveying the message that nothing except the scapegoat is a problem within that family. Frequently, the scapegoat will do something to provoke or invite the criticism. Attention to the timing of this provocation suggests that the provocation or even the psychotic episode itself served to take attention away from the group as a whole, or from another part of the family in particular. Covert antagonism or marital tension are common stimuli that provoke scapegoating behavior and thereby relocate the problem within the system. The therapists' most difficult task is making the group aware of such maneuvers.

The helping process with MFT occurs primarily as described by Laqueur[10] and expanded by Lansky and his coworkers.[12] Part of the group process is problem solving, some experiential (role playing with other group members in parallel positions), and some didactic.

Therapists maintain a family orientation; the group is there for the *entire* family. We strive not to overidentify with the patients or the parents or any other subgroup. We consciously avoid scapegoating of patients and family. It is amusing to hear MFT members talk about group: patients like group because it helps their parents; parents like group because it manages patients. When a parent has a personal crisis, we encourage him or her to talk about it. We restate our treatment philosophy: it's a family group. Support is available for whoever needs it.

Some of the most interesting phenomena occur after group. Families stay behind and talk. They shake hands and reestablish contact. It is not unusual for members to spend time trying to lift the spirits of a discouraged group member. Many times an informal session continues long after the formal group has ended—in the parking lot. Some families socialize with one another outside group. Practically all families will inquire about former group members. Bonds have formed. In contrast to some therapists, I do not discourage extratherapeutic contact among members. In my opinion, the real relationships have far more to offer our unusually isolated and shame-ridden population than the alternative of a group where acting out is forbidden. With less disturbed families, matters might be different.

MECHANISMS OF ACTION

The central feature that makes MFT unique is the therapeutic use of identification constellations.[10] In a group of schizophrenics and their families of origin, people have an opportunity to share ego strength if the therapist can assist them in making and using identifications with members in parallel familial positions who face similar predicaments.[13] Mothers, for example, may be able to do more reality testing in a supportive way with other mothers. Issues like self-recrimination, guilt, shame and anger, parental roles and family rules, can be explored in group as nowhere else. Schizophrenic patients profit by identification with others at varying stages of illness. Not uncommonly, problems such as residual psychosis and resistance to drug therapy, can be introduced intrepidly by one patient and added to by others until problems that might never have been discussed are faced openly. It is mutually advantageous for schizophrenics in varying phases of illness to respond to each other. Sons may also try out newly acquired skills and behaviors with other families before beginning negotiations in their own families.

In this supportive setting, confidence, camaraderie, trust, and hope replace isolation, panic, shame, and despair. New opportunities become available for families to learn about the illness, and to learn from encountering group members as members of a task force dealing with residual pathology that follows acute treatment.[14] Groups progress to a general feeling of mastery and success even with some difficult episodes of illness. Even in a case of completed suicide, the family had gotten much from a long course of treatment.

CASE 18: ANTHONY A

Anthony was the only son of working-class Italian-American parents, who were genuinely bewildered by their son's illness. Anthony's younger sister, Marie, was married with a baby of her own, while at 28, Anthony still lived at home. He seemed locked into hostile–dependent relationships with his overprotective, infantilizing mother and withdrawn, competitive, critical father. Anthony had physically attacked his father and destroyed some household furnishings in an explosive episode which led to his most recent hospital admission. He was alienated from all of his immediate and extended family (other than his mother), as they were frightened of him. Anthony listed his problems as depression, auditory hallucinations, and loneliness. This was his fourth hospitalization since discharge from military service; he was considered chronic. We accepted him into our family treatment program as a last resort.

The family system symptoms which prompted referral to the multiple family group were. (1) an isolated, humiliated, defeated family; (2) a lack of communication between Anthony and his parents, compounding their conflicts and contributing to an atmosphere of near-explosive tension between them; and (3) an overprotective, overinvested, infantilizing mother and disengaged father.

Anthony's family attended group regularly for 10 months. Initially, Mr. and Mrs. A used the group as a place to unload their anxieties about their difficult son, and to gain support from other parents. Much later Mrs. A acknowledged her role in keeping Anthony spoiled and, later still, confessed her own fears and anxieties without projecting all of her own out-of-control feelings onto Anthony. During this process, she dramatically loosened up her mothering and allowed her son more breathing room and independence. Mr. A changed less dramatically. Initially, he came across as a solid, infallible patriarch, hostile and skeptical about psychotherapy. Later, he acknowledged his anxieties and mistakes regarding the family business and other family decisions. Eventually, through identification with the therapists, he became an active group participant.

During this time, Anthony maintained a satisfactory posthospital adjustment despite major reality stresses: quitting several jobs, losing unemployment benefits, abandoning his apartment, facing fears of rehospitalization, emergency placement in an halfway house, and finally returning to live harmoniously with his parents.

At the point where Anthony had begun a 12-month vocational rehabilitation training program and was feeling, for the first time, really good about himself and at peace with his parents, the A family decided to terminate from the group. They knew that returning to the group could be negotiated. Anthony did complete his training curriculum; it was the first thing he had ever completed in his life.

The A's treatment did not consist of only MFT, but the supportive environment of this modality and confrontation from other families enabled the As to look nondefensively at how they perpetuated their son's illness, and make the necessary changes.

REFERENCES

1. Strelnick AH: Multiple family group therapy: a review of the literature. Family Process 16:307–325, 1977
2. Laqueur HP: Multiple family therapy, in Guerin, Philip J (ed): Family Therapy, Theory, and Practice. New York, Gardner Press, 1976
3. Nevin D: Multiple family therapy, the 'overlooked' treatment approach: It's alive and ready for use. Am J Orthopsychiatry 44:223, 1974
4. Handlon JH, Parloff MB: The treatment of patient and family as a group: Is it group psychotherapy? Int J Group Psychother 12:132–141, 1962
5. Lansky MR: Establishing a family-oriented inpatient unit. J Operational Psychiatr 8:66–74, 1977
6. Lidz T et al: Schizophrenia and the Family. New York, International Universities Press, 1965
7. Wynne LC, Ryckoff IM, Day J, Hirsch, SI: Pseudo-mutuality in the family relations of schizophrenics. Psychiatry 21:205–220, 1958
8. Bateson G, Jackson DD, Haley J, Weakland J: Toward a theory of schizophrenia. Behav Sci 1:251–264, 1956
9. Bowen M: Family Therapy in Clinical Practice. New York, Jason Aronson, 1978
10. Laqueur HP: General systems theory and multiple family therapy, in Gray W et al (eds): General Systems Theory and Psychiatry. Boston, Little, Brown & Co, 1969
11. Lansky MR: On the idea of a termination phase for family therapy in the hospital. Group and Family Therapy, 1980. New York, Brunner Mazel
12. Lansky MR, Bley CR, McVey GG, Brotman B: Multiple family groups as aftercare. Int J Group Psychother 28:211–224, 1978
13. Lansky, MR: Personal communication
14. Detre T, Kessler DR, Sayers J: A Socio-Adaptive Approach to Treatment of Acutely Disturbed Psychiatric Inpatients. Third World Congress of Psychiatry Proceedings I. Canada, University of Toronto Press, 1961, pp 502–506

PART III

The Affective Disorders and Suicide

Judith S. Musick, Frances M. Stott,
Bertram J. Cohler, and Jerry Dincin

6

Posthospital Treatment for Psychotic Depressed Mothers and Their Young Children*

The child learns to become a competent member of the social community and to develop the skills for communicating with others within the context of the family. Social, personality, and even intellectual characteristics emerge slowly as an interaction between the relationships the child forms with others and his or her own biologic organization and propensities. The human is *presocial*;[1] that is, requires development within a social world to become fully socialized. For the young child, the social world is the family. Just as the biologically endowed infant shapes and modifies his or her social world so that child is, in turn, structured by it and his or her biology is modified and given direction. Positive guidance in a caring and responsive interpersonal environment is of critical importance for the later development of competence.[2]

THE MOTHER–CHILD RELATIONSHIP

Within that special subsystem of the family, the mother–child relationship, the child develops language and thought as well as basic social and personality attributes. Although the mother–child relationship is only one aspect of the larger family system, for the infant and young child

---

*The authors wish to thank Roseanne Clark for her most valuable theoretic and clinical contributions, and for helping develop and implement the program upon which this chapter is based.

91

it is the matrix from which the child extracts the first understanding of the self and the world, teaching the earliest and most critical lessons in becoming a thinking and social being. While we are cognizant of the mother-child relationship as an integral part of the larger family system, we have chosen for both theoretical and practical reasons to focus primary treatment efforts on the dyad.

Psychoanalytically oriented theorists have long been interested in the mother–child relationship[3–8] as it relates to all aspects of early ego development. Developmental psychologists, on the other hand, have looked at particular ego functions such as thought and language as though they existed in isolation from the child's human environment. Mother–child interactions were understood to be important for social and personality development, but were generally ignored when more cognitive functions were being investigated. Recently this perspective has changed radically, as we have come to see the roots of the child's knowledge and intellectual competence in early social interactions.[9–16] It is therefore largely as a result of relationships with family members, particularly the mother, that young children come to view the world and themselves in a particular kind of way, to select, take in, and process information.

The capacity for learning itself is nurtured in the back-and-forth interactions of responsive, involved mothers with their young children. Efficacy, competence, curiosity, and the thirst for knowledge are powerfully influenced in the early years by the quality of the mother–child relationship. The sense of having control over one's environment is critical for the development of the desire to learn, for persistence in problem solving, and for the basic idea that the world is a safe and interesting place to explore and learn about. The child who has found that 'what I do and what I want, does make a difference' will run towards the world as if it were a giant playground—trusting, caring, learning, growing, and sticking with difficult challenges until they are mastered. This child has developed a sense of himself or herself as a someone who counts. Without a suitable environment, the growth of these basic human attributes can be most severely affected. The whole critical package of competencies necessary to cope and survive in our society cannot develop in the absence of secure and meaningful interpersonal relationships.

The abilities of the human being to establish social relations are acquired early in the mother–child relationship, and behavior disorders or emotional disturbances may be the outcome of an early distorted relationship with the mother.[17,18] When this relationship is disturbed, the child will frequently lack the adaptive abilities necessary to effectively interact with the environment. This should not be surprising, since these abilities are an outgrowth of ongoing experience with an empathetic, consistent, and contingently responsive mother who helps the child to understand and to structure his or her world, as the child internalizes the mother's caring. This kind of mother is able to see her child as a separate individual and respond to the child's particular behavior and developmental needs.

Beyond competence, the basic sense of security so critical for ego development or a sense of self is developed within the primary object relationship. If the mother's ego support is absent, weak, or patchy, the child seems to lack this sense of self. Winnicott noted that without "good enough mothering" the child is merely a collection of reactions to impingement.[19] There is little energy left to devote to appropriate developmental tasks when the child must direct all efforts towards engaging a distant, unresponsive caregiver, or towards soothing and comforting him- or herself.

Finally, across cultures one sees a certain 'joie de vivre'; an enjoyment, involvement, and playful enthusiasm in interaction between mothers and their young children, which overrides the various methods of socialization found among different cultures, subcultures, and families. These 'universals' must have a very special role in the child's development, teaching vital interpersonal lessons on a multitude of levels. The absence of these universal behaviors, conversely, could be regarded as depriving and potentially harmful to a young child. What happens when the mother is incapable of providing these kinds of experiences for her child? Why might she be unable to create a healthy, nurturant child-rearing environment?

MOTHERHOOD

Motherhood is a stage in the life cycle that arrives with shocking suddenness. Lopata has said that only widowhood or other significant losses by death pose a greater crisis for women in our society.[20] During pregnancy, the woman, her husband, and their extended families can prepare for this new role, but no preparation can anticipate the full reality of the event itself. With the birth of her infant, the mother must have the welfare of another uppermost in her own thoughts. For the first time in her life, concern for self is explicitly secondary to concern for another. Her time, energy, and emotional resources must be shared, and even sleep is sacrificed for her child's welfare. Motherhood is a socially defined role, but it is also a developmental issue that must be negotiated by the mother in order for her to feel a sense of adequacy. Failure to negotiate this issue leaves the woman vulnerable to feelings of frustration, despair, isolation, and increased self-absorbtion.

Caring for a young, dependent child with little support or help, while having to meet familial as well as other obligations, is replete with stress and potential conflict. Since, in our society, the care of children still primarily falls to the mother, the emotional well-being of mother and child are interdependent. The capacity to nurture young children requires considerable physical and emotional resources, which mental illness is likely to impair or deplete. For the mother with a serious emotional disturbance, the tasks of motherhood are often difficult or impossible.

MOTHERHOOD AND MENTAL ILLNESS

Research reported by Grunebaum, Cohler, and their colleagues presents a composite picture of the woman who becomes psychiatrically ill during the first year after childbirth.[21] This woman has, from her own childhood, been unable to achieve closeness with others. Largely unable to trust others or to achieve reciprocal and interdependent relationships, this woman is unable to assume the multiple differentiated relationships required of an adult in our society. Her primitive emotional needs impair her ability to achieve mutuality with her husband and to obtain satisfaction from her roles as wife, homemaker, and mother. For the woman with longstanding conflict regarding nuturant care, the responsibilities of childcare evoke feelings of intense resentment and conflict. Naturally these feelings will have implications for the development of her children. Her psychopathology may be communicated to them, leading to impairment in such adaptive skills as the capacity to appraise and act in accord with reality, and the capacity to develop close relationships with others.

Impairment in the child's cognitive and social/emotional development may combine with increased genetic risk to predispose the child of a mentally ill mother to far greater vulnerability to subsequent psychiatric and psychological disorder than the child of a well mother. Recent studies have indicated that the children of women with psychiatric disorders (schizophrenia, schizo-affective disorder, manic-depressive illness, psychotic depression) are at 'high risk' for the subsequent development of social/emotional and intellectual impairment.[22-24] It is important to remember that vulnerability to psychiatric and psychological risk is a function of the ongoing interaction between the developing biologic organism and the animate and inanimate environment. Thus, when the child of a mentally ill mother develops poorly, it is partially as a result of genetic and biological/temperamental factors within that child, partially as a result of parental and other environmental factors, and partially as a result of the dynamic interaction between these variables.

Maternal Depression

Although the children of schizophrenic mothers have been more thoroughly studied, it may be that the child of a severely depressed mother is at as great a risk as the child of a schizophrenic mother for subsequent impairment. The impact of a uni- or bi-polar psychotic affective disorder is just as likely to have a deleterious effect upon the child's development as a schizophrenic disorder. Genetic risk for both disorders is roughly equivalent, and both are characterized by repeated hospitalizations.[25,26] The children of schizophrenic mothers may be even somewhat at an advantage, because they are more frequently cared for by others on a long-term basis.[27] In addition, the child of the schizophrenic mother is more clearly able to discern differences in the mother's present adjustment and to disregard episodes of clearly bizarre behavior. The apathy and withdrawal characteristic of the depressed patient, together with the lack of involvement and degree of irritability and resentment expressed about child-rearing,[28] may be more harmful than the distorted or bizarre behavior of the schizophrenic mother. It appears additionally, that depression is not merely a disorder of *mood*, but that like schizophrenia, it has a *cognitive* component as well. Beck[29] and Cohler et al[30] hypothesize that such a combined cognitive and affective disturbance may have a more profound impact upon the child's development than a cognitive disturbance alone.

The risk of the mother losing control and abusing her child may increase as a consequence of maternal depression.[31] In a review of 131 cases of parental child murderers, Resnich found that 71 percent of the mothers were depressed.[32] The danger of abuse is increased with evidence of hostility towards the favorite child of a hated spouse, or when the content of the depressive thought is directed towards the child, eg, hostile feelings, fear of harming the child, or anxiety about the child's health.[33] Musick, Clark, and Householder comment that the flattened or negative affect of the depressed mother, combined with her general lack of empathy, connectedness, and enjoyment of the child constitutes a syndrome of psychological neglect that may be more lethal to the child's developing sense of self-competence than actual abuse.[34]

Effects of Maternal Depression in Children

Although the consequences of depression may be subtle and do not always appear as gross disturbances,[35] maternal depression at any point during the first two years of a child's life may be associated with increased

tendency to depression in the child.[36,37] Chronic depression leaves little
room for a child's natural, spontaneous curiosity and urge to explore and
create. A pessimistic mother may induce a sense of failure in her child,
along with a feeling of responsibility for her unhappiness. A preoccupied,
depressed mother somehow limits the freedom of her child to meet and
engage the environment.[35] The outcome can be quite serious in terms of
cognitive and/or social/emotional impairment. In striving to adapt to a
less-than-optimal environment, children learn to think and feel about
themselves and the world in ways that do not bode well for healthy
development.

As earlier noted, the children of depressed mothers represent a
neglected group in the research on children at risk, although there have
been some provocative findings on the basis of previous studies. Cohler
found that young children of depressed mothers showed both greater
intellectual impairment and greater disturbance in the ability to deploy
attention than the children of either schizophrenic or well mothers.[30]
Welner et al[38] and McKnew[39] have both found a high incidence of
depressive symptoms in the children of adults who suffer from a
depressive illness. The depressive symptoms take different forms according to the child's develomental level, but the underlying themes relate to
the child's efforts to compensate and express bereavement at the mother's
depression and subsequent emotional unavailability.[40] Infants may
respond to maternal depression by withdrawal and "failure to thrive",[41]
whereas preschool and school-age children of depressed mothers display a
wide range of behavior and learning problems.[42,43]

Because depression is so common among mothers of young children,[42,31] these findings give a sense of the wide-ranging consequences of
maternal depressive illness and present an urgent challenge to the mental
health field. Recognizing that depression interferes with a mother's ability
to respond to and meet the needs of her child, and recognizing the hardship
of trying to provide for the child when she herself feels so depleted, makes
the design of an intervention program to meet the needs of both mother
and child and to go beyond a mere surface or temporary 'crisis intervention,'
particularly problematic. Fostering an attachment including connectedness and a sense of mutual joy in a mother–child pair that is characterized
by sadness, anger, or lonely detachment is a challenge to existing
programs. This was the major factor influencing the design of the present
intensive treatment program for severely (psychotically) depressed mothers and their children.

As a result of what is known about the development of vulnerable
children of mentally ill mothers, in tandem with the role of the mother–
child relationship in affecting both the child's development and the

mother's self-conception as a woman and a mother, it is difficult to conceive of an effective program of intervention not including three specific goals: (1) the mother's own psychiatric rehabilitation; (2) a special therapeutic nursery program for the child; and (3) ongoing evaluation and clinical efforts with the mother–child *relationship* itself. The Thresholds Mothers' Project was developed to realize these three goals.

THE CLINICAL PROGRAM

The program, developed for the treatment of depressed mothers and their children, is a funded as part of our larger National Institute of Mental Health clinical research and intervention program[43] for psychotic (schizophrenic, schizo-affective, manic-depressive, and psychotic depressed) women and their children under 5 years of age. Mothers and children attend an intensive clinical intervention program on a daily basis for a period of approximately 12 to 15 months. This program includes group and individual therapy sessions, a didactic child development course, social and vocational programs for the mother, as well as a therapeutic nursery for her child. The program was structured both to provide therapeutic intervention for these high-risk families and to afford the clinical and developmental research teams the opportunity to conduct ongoing assessments of mother, child, and mother–child relationship. This group will later be compared to a second group receiving treatment in the home, as well as with a third group of mothers who have never experienced a psychiatric illness and their young children. The 'well' mothers, recruited from the community, were equated with mothers in the two intervention groups on six variables: age and sex of youngest child, mother's age, marital status, race, and socio-economic status (mother's education and father's occupation).

The Mothers' Project is an integral part of the Thresholds agency. It offers additional services, designed specially for the needs of mothers and children, which are not part of the program for Thresholds' other clients. The rehabilitation program at Thresholds is the foundation upon which the Mothers' Project rests. Mothers participate in most aspects of the Thresholds program, which is characterized by an emphasis on behavior, a utilization of the experiential approach, and the prevention of rehospitalization. The work-readiness program, and the many facets of the social rehabilitation program—problem-solving groups; evening, weekend, and summer programs; therapeutic family camping; skill rehearsal; and social placement—form a core of activities around which a large portion of the mother's time is spent. In addition, a number of mothers have taken advantage of the academic program at Thresholds to improve basic skills and complete high school education.

In addition to the social and vocational rehabilitation programs of the agency, intensive, specialized clinical intervention program components have been designed to provide for the unique needs of this group of mentally ill mothers. The staff of the Mothers' Project includes Thresholds case workers, vocational rehabilitation counselors, psychiatrists, and a psychiatric nurse. In addition, a specialized team of clinical and research personnel (including clinical and developmental psychologists, a psychiatric social worker, a teacher–therapist, an assistant teacher, a student teacher, a driver/videotape consultant, a pediatric nurse-practitioner consultant, graduate students, and several volunteers) make up this large and diverse staff.

The specialized program is twofold, encompassing therapeutic and educational interventions. The women in the group require much in the way of empathetic and nurturant experience to be able to take advantage of the educational and skill-building aspects of the program. This is necessary before a mother is able to relate to her child in more positive and growth-fostering ways, which she acquires through her participation in the project.

The most effective intervention program for depressed mothers appears to be one in which support is provided in helping them deal with ambivalent feelings regarding childcare, while at the same time providing support and assistance as they learn the skills of child-rearing. In addition, because her own needs and those of the child are so closely intertwined, the mother is encouraged to develop a sense of separateness (including a separate life for herself), independent of her role as mother. Finally, psychotherapeutic intervention is utilized, accompanied by more directed efforts in the development of mothering skills and increased capacity to respond to the child as an independent person. This is complemented by couple and family therapy involving husband and, if necessary, other members of both wife's and husband's extended families. In sum, traditional psychiatric treatment following hospitalization is supplemented by rehabilitation directed at the mother's roles as mother, homemaker, and wife, encouraging development of a wide sphere of competence and greater and more varied sources of life satisfaction, including some independent activities outside the home, such as work or school. It is also critically important to provide direct assistance to the mother in her ongoing relationship with her child in order to help them interact in healthier and more satisfying ways.[44]

Soon after a mother and child enter the program, they receive an intensive battery of personality and intellectual assessments. The information derived is utilized along with expressed maternal perceptions of current problems, nursery observations, family history material, mothers' current level of functioning in the social and vocational program, and videotapes of mother–child interaction, to develop a treatment plan for the mother, the child, and the dyad. This results in the conceptualization of current relationship issues for the dyad, and development of treatment goals utilizing the specialized interventions described below.

The Mothers

MOTHERS' GROUP

This is a weekly therapy and peer support group that meets for 1½ hours per week. A psychiatric social worker and a clinical research psychologist are the group therapists. The group is extremely diverse in terms of psychological functioning, symptomatology, level of cognitive functioning, age, social class, racial/ethnic group, and marital status. In spite of this heterogeneity, the group provides a forum for sharing common life stresses, problems of readjusting to the roles of wife and mother, medication compliance, and core issues such as one's own maternal relationship and fears of the effect of their illness upon the child.

CHILD DEVELOPMENT COURSE

As the program was developing, we became aware of the mother's lack of general, basic childcare knowledge. The need for another group with a more structured and didactic approach became apparent. The child development course meets weekly and is jointly supervised by the project director and the nursery teacher–therapist. The format is varied, as can be seen by the list of topics covered in the last year (see Table 1).

In addition to the Mothers' Group and the Child Development Course, there is a Friday Mothers' Group, which takes field trips to museums, art galleries, flower shows, and, locally, the Evanston Childrens' Clothing Association Annual Clothing Sale. This group takes on special projects such as making Christmas gifts, baked goods, or crafts. Mothers also enjoy going 'out to tea' with staff on Friday afternoons at one of the neighborhood restaurants.

The milieu approach of the agency, in conjunction with the clinical staff of the project, provides an atmosphere ready for coping with the multiple crises in the lives of these women and children. All staff members, including the driver (who at times has had to dress and feed

Table 1. Topics and Guest Speakers for Child Development Course

Topics
- Theories in Developmental Psychology
- Prenatal Development through the Birth Process
- Infancy
- Learning and Development
- Language Development—how children learn to talk
- Social and Emotional Development
- Play and Learning—the importance of play
- Physical and Motor Development
- Behavior Problems—eating, sleeping, toilet training
- Childhood Fears and Anxieties
- Sexuality
- Aggression and Jealousy
- Discipline or Child Abuse?
- The Parenting Experience—a mutually rewarding relationship
- Fathering—should childrearing be shared? What do fathers contribute to a child's development?
- Attachment and Separation
- Crying—can one spoil a child?
- How to Pick a Good Preschool for Your Child
- Toys and Games to Make Together at Home
- Getting Your Child Ready for Kindergarten

Guest Speakers
- Pediatric nurse practitioner (one class a month): issues include nutrition, childhood illness, accidents and how to avoid them.
- Family Service Bureau social worker (one class every two months): issues include stresses on the working mother, childhood sexuality, finding and using community resources for mother and child.
- Parental Stress Volunteer: Child abuse and neglect.
- Parents as Resource Volunteers (one class every three to four months): Making hand puppets, making toys from material found in your home.

Special Sessions
- What to expect from your: infant (less than 1 year old), toddler (1–3 years old), preschooler (3–6 years old), school-age child (6–11 years old), adolescent (11–18 years old).
- Films and filmstrips: one session monthly.
- Field trips: toy lending library, Educational Resource Center, area preschools and daycare centers, public library (local branches and main library).

children, or coax a mother out of bed), serve a therapeutic function; mothers are also seen individually by their caseworker on a once- or twice-weekly basis.

Whenever possible, the project staff also develops a relationship with the husband, since his support is viewed as crucial to the successful involvement of the family. However, it should be noted that most of our mothers do not presently have viable marriages. Indeed many a mother's struggles in order to function in a healthier manner are met at first by resistance and hostility from a spouse who has an investment in being the sole 'healthy' member of the family. If there is no husband in the home, it is often possible to involve the maternal grandmother when she is the significant other living in the home. We have, however, met with more than one grandmother's reluctance to support her daughter's efforts to be more competent.

In spite of these difficulties we firmly believe that the significant others in the mother's and child's life must be seen and involved. First, they can be helpful in dispelling the mother's distrustful feelings; and second, if they take part in the program *they* feel less threatened, displaced, or out of control. Significant others will, ultimately, be relating to the mother, and it is they who seek guidance about developing new and better ways of relating to the mentally ill family member. Finally, if support and recognition can be provided for other family members, they are often able to give something back to the mother in a more meaningful way, and to better understand the mother's problems as *family* issues.

The Children

The children vary in age from birth to 5 years of age and come from a broad range of socioeconomic groups and ethnic backgrounds. They also differ in the kind of family network and parenting experiences they have had. What is shared among these children is that each is the child of a mother with some form of depressive illness which inevitably has affected her ability to adequately parent her young and vulnerable child.

Certain areas of development are of special concern for those who work with the children of depressed mothers: language is usually delayed, as well as used inappropriately for communication; attentional skills are marked by lack of ability to focus and sustain attention to relevant animate and inanimate stimuli in the environment; and attachment and separation issues are poorly negotiated, since there is usually a striking lack of healthy mutual bonding between mother and child. There is instead either a sense of great distance and mutual mistrust, or a symbiotic mother–child fusion where boundaries are blurred and the child does not act as an autonomous, separate individual. These children also lack spontaneity (or joie de vivre). They seem rigid and depressed, display little affect and seem without the natural childhood attributes of curiosity and the urge to explore.[44]

The Therapeutic Nursery

The nursery of the Mothers' Project is designed to provide an educational and therapeutic environment for the young children (5 years of age or younger) of mentally ill mothers. Over the past 3 years, the project has served a total of 40 mothers and 42 children in the nursery, with 10 mother–child pairs involved in the program at any given time (although in two instances, mothers have had two children in the nursery at one time). The nursery serves as both a remedial and preventive program for these children, who are at high risk for developing emotional and intellectual problems because of repeated separation, genetic factors, and the effects of living with a severely depressed mother. Staffed by a head teacher–therapist and an assistant teacher, and aided by volunteers and student teachers, the nursery is in session five mornings a week from 9:00 to 11:30 AM, and three afternoons a week (M, W, F) from 1:00 to 4:00 PM, year-round. For the children, the nursery provides a safe, responsive, consistent environment offering educational stimulation and emotional support. It also offers support and modeling for the depressed mother who spends 1½ hours per week in the nursery room with her child.

These are the primary issues considered in programming for the nursery. However, the program is adapted to meet individual needs. For a 3-year-old child who is attached symbiotically to his mother, skills in mastery and independence are especially important in promoting more adequate individuation. For a 2-year-old who communicates by hitting, grabbing, or grunting incoherently, language skills are essential in developing better relationships to peers and less frustrating relationships with adults. For a 'tuned out,' poorly relating, environmentally delayed 7-month-old, intensive work is provided to establish bonds of love and mutuality with mother and with one member of the nursery staff. We simultaneously work on providing the child with experiences of sensitive responsive interactions as the adults in the nursery introduce the child to the stimulating world of objects, events, and people.

The nursery curriculum is varied and based upon a philosophy of individualized planning for each child, encompassing reality testing, responsiveness, and the development of a trusting relationship within a safe, structured, predictable, and accepting environment that permits expression of feeling. This environment serves as the matrix from which more adaptive learning and coping skills can be developed by these children. Indeed, the nursery is such a powerful therapeutic milieu that often a child's developmental level must be reevaluated after a month in the program because change is so drastic during that time. For example, one toddler was assessed at entrance and found to be borderline-retarded with precursors of autistic behavior. Several weeks later we realized this little girl needed a reevaluation, and found that her score on the Bayley Scales of Infant Development had increased strikingly as her abberant behavior had disappeared. In another case, the 2½-year-old child of one of our most seriously disturbed mothers entered the nursery as primitive as a feral child—licking mirrors, grunting, eating with his fists, and unable to remain still long enough to attend to any task, object, or person. Within several weeks, the nursery and clinical staff became aware that a competent, extremely winning, and clever child was emerging. Within the nursery's safe, structured environment, a child's potential strengths are allowed to develop. Although almost all of the children are, to some degree, delayed and/or deviant in certain areas of development, we do have strong evidence that they are functioning at a much higher level than when they entered the program and are making significant gains in learning and adaptive skills.

The foundation upon which all nursery planning rests is the weekly all-staff meeting, providing the basis for day-to-day nursery planning. The nursery staff bring their own clinical observations, progress notes, and descriptions of the child's (and the mother's) behavior to the nursery. They also bring a completed nursery assessment form on the child who is being staffed that week. This form has been developed and refined over the past three years, and gives, we believe, an accurate picture of a child's strengths and weaknesses. These forms are filled out on each child four times a year, and are used for research as well as nursery planning purposes. The information from the nursery assessment form is used in conjunction with that derived from the development and personality assessments completed at entrance to the program. This information is also used as an early screening mechanism helping in the diagnosis and treatment of problems existing which may target the child for abuse (hyperactivity, nonresponsiveness, etc.) or severe learning disorders (motor, speech, language, and intellectual dysfunctions).

The Mother–Child Dyad

MOTHERS IN THE NURSERY

A special time is set aside each week for the mother to visit with her child in the nursery, and to be observed by project staff as she interacts with her child. Special assistance is provided for the mother in teaching her how to determine and meet her child's needs and to realize a more mutual relationship. As a result of observing the nursery teachers and other project staff with the children, mothers come to maintain a more tolerant approach to child care, and also are provided with specific ideas about caring for their children. The nursery provides a partial (trial) separation of mother and child. Mothers may also work with children not their own in the nursery if, at first, it is too stressful to be with their own child. A mother's time in the nursery is tailored to her capacity to relate to her child, as well as to her personal skills and abilities. For example, one mother plays the guitar and sings beautifully. She is often asked to assist at music time. We try to find activities that can be mutually enjoyed by mother and child—reading a story together, having a pillow fight, playing infant-like games, tickling, assembling a puzzle, puppets, make-believe, etc. We have found that mothers grow in their capacity to understand and care for their children as they experience success in the nursery.

LUNCHTIME INTERVENTION

Mothers and children lunch together daily, mothers having full responsibility for their children during the lunch period. Lunchtime is supervised by two Mothers' Project staff members. It is their responsibility to monitor the atmosphere and to provide nurturance as well as to act as models for mothers by interacting with the children in positive and constructive ways.

The mothers find this time with their children to be very stressful, as the feeding (of infants) and eating (of older children) is an area of much symptomatic behavior. Struggles for autonomy, testing the mother's ability to set limits and to *give* to her child are issues that must be negotiated on a daily basis. Indeed, for the mothers themselves, food and the issues surrounding eating appear to be related to their own desperate neediness. We often see a mother shoveling a large amount of food into her own mouth while her child, quietly hungry, sits next to her. One mother who experienced guilt over her separation from her child and what she considered to be her "inability to relate" to her child, would stuff her child's mouth with food, having little or no awareness of the child's inability to swallow as fast as she was feeding. Almost all of the mothers manifest inappropriate ideas about what is a suitable amount of food to expect a young child to eat; the mothers fill the toddler's plate with portions of meat, vegetables, and rice, suitable for a very hungry adult. This behavior is seen among middle-class and poor mothers, and is understood as symptomatic of deeper issues, beyond feeding per se.

There are occasions when, after several observations (and careful consideration of issues involved at our weekly staffing meeting), a decision is made, and plans are developed for specific staff intervention at lunchtime. An attempt is made to begin with the mother's current understanding of her relationship with her child, and to recognize and appreciate cultural differences in approaches to childcare and discipline. There are two basic rules with which all mothers are asked to comply: (1) they are not to hit the children, and (2) mothers assume responsibility for their children during the lunch period and must stay with them, although additional staff support is available during this often stressful time.

VIDEOTAPE INTERVENTION

The work with the mothers in the nursery and at lunchtime is supplemented by regular videotaping of the mother and child together. These videotapes, made when the mother and child enter the program and at regular three- to four-month intervals thereafter, are used as the subject of discussion with the mother regarding her relationship with her child. The advantage of the videotape over the classroom sessions is that the tape can be stopped so that the mother and her staff worker can discuss the mother–child interaction and current issues in their relationship. When the mother–child interaction becomes the focus of discussion between a mother and her worker, the mother's feelings about childcare and the maternal role acquire a sense of immediacy missing in the ordinary contact between a mother and her therapist in the consulting room.

The video consultant (Jill Metcoff, M.S.W., who has an extensive background in the uses of videotape in mental health settings) and the mother's staff worker meet to plan the session after the worker and the mother have jointly decided upon an issue or problem to address. Case material from the weekly staffing is used when preparing for the video intervention in conjunction with the ideas and observations of the worker and the video consultant.

The goals for the videotape intervention are:

1. To sensitize the mother to her child's cues and to help her to respond based on her child's needs, not her own
2. To help her to recognize her child as a separate individual
3. To support her in her role as an adult decision-maker who helps to structure her child's environment, set limits, and introduce the world of objects and people to her child
4. To increase her opportunities for positive interaction with her child.

The video intervention fosters and focuses on interaction within an environment that is consistent, safe, protective, and individualized for each mother. Mothers can experience increased mastery within this situational and time-limited exercise in which they work on important developmental tasks such as separation/individuation, specific parental

Table 2

Goals Central to Therapeutic Efforts with Mothers and Children in the
Thresholds Mother's Project

Engage the mother in the project:
1. Helping her to identify what is there for her: a support group; relief from all-day childcare; vocational training; furthering her education; getting to know her child better; or simply getting out of the house
2. Involving the family, and, where possible, enlisting them as our allies in helping the mother and child
3. Providing transportation

Help mother and child to achieve some order and stabilize their lives:
1. Medication maintenance, which helps to prevent rehospitalization
2. The daily structure of both the mother's and child's program at Thresholds
3. Concrete support in obtaining adequate housing, or the temporary services of a homemaker to help with household and childcare chores if needed
4. Acting as the mother's advocate to obtain funds as needed or appropriate

Help the mother establish a mutually satisfying relationship with her child:
1. Working with her to establish a reasonable routine and pattern of care commensurate with the child's basic needs (feeding, sleeping, appropriate dress, etc.)
2. Helping her to clarify her own needs before concentrating on the more subtle problems of mother–child interaction. Mothers must have some personal needs met before they are able to give to their children emotionally.
3. Beginning to focus on interpersonal issues by helping the mother to derive some enjoyment from her child. We help both to discover mutually enjoyable activities, and then help the mother to elaborate and extend them.
4. Helping the mother to sensitively observe the child's cues and to respond appropriately to the child's needs.
5. Helping the mother, in individual treatment sessions and mothers' group, to acknowledge and accept ambivalent feelings towards her child. We help her deal with the intrapsychic issues which interfere with her ability to adequately parent her child in conflict-laden areas such as autonomy, separation, or dependency needs.
6. Encouraging her to supply developmentally appropriate experiences to her child.

We conceive of these steps in the order given above, but often must skip a step or work on two steps simultaneously.

Help the mother establish mutually workable relationships with husband and/or family:
1. Family and/or couples treatment.
2. Encouraging husband and/or family members to view us as allies; participate in our program as much as they are able; and feel comfortable turning to us for support when they feel overwhelmed by the mother's difficulties.

Help mother and child to become a part of the larger community:

1. Assisting the family in finding and making use of programs in the community such as family drop-in centers, parent–child gym/swim programs, and courses given at community centers, the YMCA, and Settlement Houses.
2. Working with our nursery teacher to help the child make the transition into kindergarten, to a new preschool in the community, or to a therapeutic program, if necessary.
3. Make certain that the mother has ties with another source of support by the time of termination in the Mothers' Project. The treatment of choice is most often individual psychotherapy for her, as well as supportive treatment for the family when feasible.

---

behavior such as limit setting, and general competencies, such as learning to observe and communicate better. During this time, no matter what the task, a warm, affective exchange is encouraged between mother and child. The outcome is extremely rich, both for the staff and for the dyad itself.

The Mothers' Project staff utilizes the material from the video intervention in conjunction with other material from the mother–child staffing, and with the research videotapes (three 5-minute segments of feeding, structured and unstructured play) to plan the future direction and focus of their therapeutic efforts. The mother and child have shared an enjoyable experience and have a sense of mastering a task, or learning something new together. Finally, the mothers are helped to reflect on their role and their feelings about it.

About a week after the video session, the mother is asked to choose her favorite segment from the taping and to share it with all the other mothers at the followup group session. The mother explains to the group why she likes the particular segment. This generally initiates a group interchange of ideas and feelings about mothering. The video consultant acts as a group facilitator, but encourages the mother to lead. These sessions have been found to be very special occasions for all concerned, and especially for that mother, who becomes the 'star of the day.'

MOTHERS' PROJECT GOALS

We have learned a great deal from these women, their children, and the larger families of which they are a part since we opened our doors in the fall of 1976. We are always learning as we continuously evaluate and refine our intervention and treatment methods, and reflect upon what has happened between a mother and child, how and why it has happened, and what its meaning may be for other mothers and children with similar issues to be negotiated. Although we are always cognizant of the need to see and treat each dyad as unique, we know also that certain goals (Table 2) are central to remedial efforts with *all* our mothers and children. In a sense they are more than goals; they are steps that must be taken and the basics around which each individual treatment plan is designed.

CASE STUDY: A SEVERELY DEPRESSED MOTHER AND HER CHILD

Mother's History

Betty T is a 35-year-old married woman who came to the Mothers' Project following her seventh hospitalization. Betty's complaints at each admission included overwhelming feelings of depression with suicidal ideation. Her suicide attempts, in the form of overdoses, have primarily been in response to rejections, her first attempt occuring after her first husband divorced her. The precipitants for her more recent hospitalizations included a post partum depression, a difficult and disappointing marital situation, and feelings about being an inadequate mother to her 20-month-old daughter, Penny.

Past history included what Betty described as an unhappy childhood. Her mother died of cancer when Betty was 11 years old. She was not allowed to see her mother leave for the hospital or to attend the funeral. Betty did not even know the cause of her mother's death until several years later. She described her relationships with her two stepmothers as unhappy, characterizing these women as ungiving and overcontrolling. Betty viewed the period following her divorce, when she lived alone and worked as a medical technician, as the high point in her life. She has a history of working successfully and strongly wishes to do so again.

Betty's present marital family situation was the core of her distress. Her husband, Andrew, was the battered child of mentally ill parents, and had experienced the most deprived of childhoods himself. He was presented as a rather domineering individual who had high expectations of Betty. He wanted to be able to depend and rely on Betty, and was furious that during her depression she had been unable to support him emotionally. Betty sees Andrew as insensitive and aloof, and fears that he will leave her because of her illness. At the same time, she wishes to symbiotically merge with him, hoping that he will provide the personal strength and structure which she is unable to maintain herself.

Child's History

Penny was a healthy, full-term infant of average size. Betty breast-fed her daughter during the first month, but Penny cried continuously. Betty feels that this crying was due to insufficient milk supply, since Penny stopped crying as soon as she was put on formula. When Penny was 1 month old, Betty was hospitalized for a severe postpartum depression.

From this time until she entered the program at 23 months, Penny was cared for by a series of temporary housekeepers who gave her routine but uninvolved care.

Initial developmental testing at 23 months revealed average fine and gross motor skills, but Penny's cognitive functioning was considerably lower, indicating an uneven pattern of abilities—always a cause for concern. The most notable deficit in Penny's profile was her lack of attention; she did not attend to or focus on many tasks. She demonstrated better attention in manipulative tasks such as placing keys in a pegboard than she did in verbal tasks, such as responding to pictures by pointing or naming, or tasks requiring her to imitate the examiner. These latter tasks are of particular significance because they are highly dependent on a significant social relationship.

When Penny entered the nursery program she appeared to have severe problems. Of particular concern was her language use. While Penny seemed to understand spoken language, and had an impressive vocabulary, especially a memory for names, she rarely used language meaningfully or to communicate well with others. For a long time, she demonstrated an inappropriate use of pronouns often associated with childhood psychopathology, particularly in substituting "you" for "I." Thus, while Penny's rote language skills were high, her communicative competence was very low. She also seemed to tune people out—to not listen.

As was true on the formal testing, Penny's attentional problems interfered with her ability to concentrate in the nursery. Her attention span was extremely short, she was distractible, couldn't focus on an activity, and was stimulus-bound, responding to the slightest noise or change in the environment. She demonstrated poor ego development by her inability to explore the environment and examine it in order to learn. Penny showed no pride in her creative products (eg, drawings), and had difficulty with mastery, wanting to do things she was clearly unable to do. She did not know how to elicit appropriate help; rather than use an adult as a resource, she would scream when needing assistance. Her frustration tolerance and impulse control were also minimal. Essentially, Penny appeared to be a child with quite imprecise personal boundaries who had never established a bond with a caretaking person. This was illustrated by the almost frantic way she flitted from person to person, as well as by her inability to attend to and learn from her environment.

Dyadic/Relationship Issues

When mother and daughter first entered the Mothers' Project there was a distinct lack of connectedness between them. This was epitomized by Betty's constantly telling people that she had "inherited a 2-year-old child." Betty was uncomfortable with and overwhelmed by Penny; she seemed even to be frightened of her. Her inability to respond to her child was exacerbated by Penny's lack of ability to initiate social behaviors. Her inconsistent experiences with multiple caregivers and subsequent lack of attachment, in combination with her own biological/tempermental qualities, made Penny a child who had little to offer her mother. She seldom looked or smiled at her mother, much less approached or spoke to her. These behaviors are the child's contribution to the mother–child relationship, and have been found to be very important in increasing maternal responsiveness.[11] Penny appeared to have no trouble in separating from her mother—letting go of her all to easily, and seeming to prefer strangers! She knew the names of most of the people in the agency and would repeat them in a parrot-like fashion. Whenever Betty appeared in the nursery to pick her up, Penny would say, "Go back to work, Mommy," seeming to resent the intrusion in her play.

Betty's overanxiousness and particular insensitivity made it very difficult for her to respond to an already troubled child. She was unable to engage Penny, or to understand what she really wanted. Betty was harsh, stilted, and unable to establish an interdependence of rhythm or dialogue between herself and her child. She could not respond to Penny in a warm, contingently responsive manner, nor with affectionate playfulness. Rather than setting appropriate limits, Betty would be overcontrolling and engage in angry power struggles. When she did communicate with Penny in nonstressful times, it was often in an offhanded manner, as if Penny were a much older child or an adult.

Course of Treatment

MOTHER

The initial goal of involving Betty in the Mothers' Project was not particularly difficult to realize. Clearly, Betty was in need of a nurturing environment. Initially, referred by the psychiatrist who had treated her during her hospitalization, Betty came alone to the agency for her first interview. When Penny's sitter suddenly quit, Betty began to bring Penny, and the mother and child then became part of the Mothers' Project.

When Betty entered the program she cried continuously and did not want to leave at night to return to her husband. After 6 to 8 weeks she began to function somewhat better, but then began to feel increasingly depressed. At this time she was assigned to a male therapist, with whom she quickly established a relationship (a familiar pattern for Betty with men). Her medication (an MAO inhibitor) was also stabilized at this time. At this point she was involved in and committed to the program.

The second major goal of the project, that of helping mothers to achieve some order and stability in their lives, was also not a particular problem in Betty's case. Because of her husband's job and her own middle-class background, Betty had adequate housing and was reasonably able to cope with homemaking routines. If anything, she was compulsive, and her home was extremely orderly.

The third major goal of the project, helping mothers establish a mutually satisfying relationship with their children, soon became a major focal point in Betty's and Penny's treatment. The first phase of this goal was to ensure a reasonable pattern of care for Penny. Due to her many hospitalizations and the series of surrogate caretakers provided for Penny, Betty was virtually a new mother of a 23-month-old child.

Betty was apprehensive about suddenly being alone with Penny. Since she now had responsibility for her daughter at home, we focused on caring for the baby's needs and on working with Betty to deal with Penny at lunch. A staff member was always present for a model and to talk to Betty about appropriate portions, limit setting, etc. The Child Development Group became a perfect format for giving Betty an understanding of the ways in which children develop in general, as well as the specific needs of toddlers.

Having ensured Betty's capability of basic caretaking, it was possible to move directly to the second phase of the larger relationship goal, helping Betty clarify her own wants and needs before concentrating on the mother–child interaction. When she initially entered the program, Betty had a great deal of trouble spending time with Penny in the nursery. She was frazzled, unable to follow Penny's lead in play activities. She was constantly leaving the room to make phone calls, go to the washroom, or smoke a cigarette. It was decided to wait until Betty could consolidate her own strengths and until Penny was more settled before bringing Betty into the nursery.

It was during the resolution of this phase that the rehabilitative aspects of the larger agency became particularly important for Betty. Initially, she worked in the 'crew,' where she was able to regain some of her previous work skills and increase her confidence. After several months, Betty was promoted to assist with some of the actual agency clerical work. This made use of her excellent job skills and further increased her sense of competence.

Betty's needs were also being addressed in the clinical aspects of the project. Her case worker began to focus on helping her understand the nature of her depression. She evinced particular guilt about the early separation and possible damage she might have done to her daughter during the times she was hospitalized and depressed. She was also having problems maintaining a viable relationship with her husband and was frequently in conflict with her roles of mother and wife.

For several months, Betty used the Mother's Group primarily as an arena for ventilating her anger. Initially she was angry and bitter about her husband. She was sick and tired of his watching television, and his fussiness, and often spoke of divorce. She next turned her anger on the nursery teacher, Wendy, who took them out into the cold too much, allowed Penny to mess in paints, and generally "spoiled" her. At this point Betty threatened to remove Penny from the nursery. She was concerned only with the concrete, literal aspects of Penny's care rather than with her emotional needs. Betty was clearly uncertain of herself as a mother but covered this with a false bravado. Indeed, her defensiveness was all-pervasive during this phase. She used her position as a clerical assistant to dominate the other mothers, acting much like a staff member. On one occasion she told a visitor that she was a volunteer. It became difficult for the staff to relate to Betty's underlying disappointments and issues rather than respond to her manifest anger and caustic defensiveness.

The third phase of the relationship goal was initiated while the staff was still trying to help Betty clarify her own needs. As soon as she became somewhat comfortable in the agency, plans were made to work on the interpersonal issues between herself and Penny. On the most basic level, we directed our efforts towards helping Betty enjoy Penny. Betty was phased back into the nursery one morning a week. Each week the staff would set up situations in which Betty would feel comfortable and competent, eg, reading a book to Penny. This aspect of the total treatment program did not always progress smoothly with Betty. There were times when, for example, she would spend her time in the nursery balancing her checkbook.

The video intervention focused on helping Betty set limits for Penny in appropriate, reasonable and nonpunitive ways. Gradually, Betty became somewhat more comfortable with her daughter, showing particular pride and satisfaction in Penny's appearance and vocabulary. Betty was also delighted by the attention Penny got for remembering everyone's name in the agency.

Toward the end of this phase in Betty's rehabilitation, it was felt that Betty and Penny had formed a real attachment, which they hadn't been able to do earlier because of Betty's illness and series of hospitalizations. One day at lunch, about 6 months into the program, Betty reported to one of the staff that she had found Penny awake and sitting up when she returned home after an evening out. Penny's greeting was, "Mommy, take your coat off." Betty was obviously pleased at the implications of this and reported that Penny had also begun to pucker her lip when leaving. The first time Penny cried when Betty started to leave the nursery, Betty's eyes filled with tears. The reunions of mother and child in the nursery were also becoming warmer, and Penny began to ask for Mommy in times of stress.

CHILD

Penny had also made her own significant strides in the nursery. Probably the most notable change was her increasing ability to relate more meaningfully to her teacher. She began to differentiate between people and showed a more trusting response to her teacher (as well as to her mother). Initially she vacillated from clinging and whimpering to being irritating and demanding. She had had no internalized controls to comfort or support herself. She slowly began to internalize the consistency, predictability, and warmth of her teachers. She began, for example, to imitate her teacher during times of stress, repeating, "It's okay, it's okay."

This progress in forming relationships had an impact in all areas of Penny's functioning. She began to use language to communicate in a much more feeling and reciprocal manner, rather than merely repeating things by rote. She was also gradually beginning to be able to focus her attention for somewhat longer periods of time. In an eight-month period, her IQ, went from 84 (on the Bayley Scales of Infant Development) to 106 (on the Stanford-Binet), a remarkable increase!

MOTHER AND CHILD TOGETHER

Now that mother and daughter had become attached to a reasonable extent—Penny having become a more lovable, responsive child, and Betty experiencing enjoyment in their relationship, it was possible to consider the next phase. We began to attempt to help Betty sensitively observe and identify Penny's cues, and therefore respond to her needs. While Betty enjoyed interacting with Penny, she did so largely on her own terms. Using both the video intervention and time in the nursery, Betty was encouraged to notice what Penny liked to do best, and to help her to key into and elaborate those activities. Betty was shown how to entice Penny with games, rather than trying to force her to do something.

It was also possible to simultaneously work on the next phase of helping Betty to supply developmentally appropriate experiences. Betty was an apt student in Child Development Group, quickly learning what toddlers needed to do. She was more responsive to the more intellectual kinds of stimulation, however, and resisted less structured activities such as taking Penny for walks and playing outside. She was unwilling to come to the agency-wide therapeutic camp with Penny, despite our attempts to get her to do so. We felt that the intensity of being with Penny for four days running, in full view of everyone, in a primitive and unstructured setting such as camp, was just too much for Betty.

Betty has made considerable gains in her ability to respond to Penny's needs and cues. However, these gains have largely been in conflict-free areas. Betty is still experiencing a great deal of difficulty in negotiating her depressive symptoms, which may be partially due to the stage of Penny's development. This has highlighted the phase of the treatment plan for Betty as of this writing—that of helping Betty acknowledge and accept her ambivalent feelings toward Penny. What is particularly pertinent is the need to help Betty deal with her intrapsychic issues, which interface with Penny's normal developmental needs.

Penny is at a stage when the issue becomes the extent to which the child can establish self-assertion—and at what cost—in the interaction with the mother.[45] Betty seems to be perpetually engaged in power struggles with Penny. This is particularly evident in her toilet training efforts. Despite the many hours of discussion with staff in response to her questions, Betty continues to insist that Penny sit on the potty chair every hour. Although she is able to intellectually understand that Penny needs to exercise some control, Betty is unable to relinquish it. Autonomy/control issues appear in other areas as well—what Penny eats for lunch and in what order, whether she is able to play in her bath, etc.

Betty's Interpersonal Aperception Test, an extension of the Thematic Aperceptic Test, also indicated that control is a salient and unresolved issue for Betty. Her response to a card showing a mother on a park bench watching her small child playing nearby epitomizes her struggle in this area. After describing how nice it is for both mother and child to be outside, she offers the following resolution:

"Well, there may be some argument because mother may have to get in the house and the little boy is going to want to sit outside and play. But, mother is *still bigger* [italics author's] than the little boy, and she'll probably say, "Well, now we have to go make dinner, we'll come back tomorrow.""

It seems that Betty is having difficulty with Penny, who is struggling with striving toward some sense of autonomy while still needing very much to have her dependent needs met. Caring for her daughter has evoked anew Betty's own unresolved conflicts around provision and acceptance of maternal care. While she sometimes wishes Penny were still a helpless baby who she could simply care for, Penny's dependency is very anxiety-provoking. For example, Betty bought Penny a tricycle so "she could be more independent." Penny rides off in a spurt of independence, becomes frightened and wants Mommy to come and get her (reminiscent of Mahler's rapproachment phase,[8] in which the child needs to touch home base). Betty experiences this as manipulative on Penny's part and becomes furious.

What is clear is that for Betty to continue to progress in the program, her own limitations in interpersonal relatedness need to be modified. While Penny has made considerable progress in cognitive development, further gains in the affective domain are highly related to Betty's predisposing and enduring character traits. Betty's dependency and hostility interfere with her ability to be a warm, consistent, and responsive mother. Betty continues to need help, guidance, and direction in order that she may meet similar demands placed on her by Penny.

As of this writing, Betty is beginning to use her individual case worker and Mothers' Group to deal with some of her own feelings. While much of her concern is still at an intellectual level, it is hoped that she will be able to come to terms with her angry feelings. Video interventions are planned with the hope of helping her see that Penny's strivings for autonomy are not aimed to "get her."

FATHER

While the goal of helping Betty establish a mutually satisfying relationship with Penny has not been fully realized, there has been sufficient progress to encourage work towards the next goal, that of helping Betty establish a mutually workable relationship with her husband.

In trying to understand the family system, one is struck with how very similar the core issues are for both husband and wife. Like Betty, Andrew experiences severe conflict around dependency and control. As implied earlier, Andrew married a woman who he viewed as competent and controlled. On one hand, he needs to see her as adequate; on the other hand, he may be repeating his own history as the child of a mentally ill mother. This marriage is therefore an opportunity for him to repeat, conquer, and express ambivilence towards his mother. He does this by controlling Betty.

Penny has become the focal point of Betty and Andrew's shared issues. For example, Andrew constantly derides Betty for not doing a better job of toilet training their child. Here Andrew's extreme concern with cleanliness, his past history as an eneuretic, and his fear of loss of control, combine to inflate this issue far out of proportion to its' concrete seriousness. This interacts with Betty's unresolved core conflicts about control, and about pleasing people so they will not abandon her. Again we can see the ways in which a child's developmental issue—in this case, toilet training, and its' attendant issues of autonomy and control—can stir up and exacerbate the parent's own core issues.

Mothers' Project staff felt that Andrew needed to be involved in the treatment plan not just for Penny, but to help him face some of his own terror about becoming mentally ill, like his mother. This task was made practically impossible by Andrew's strong resistance to coming to a place that was, as he often said, "full of crazy people." In addition, massive repression and lack of insight made him extremely resistant to treatment. For Andrew, therapy would represent the dismantling of his carefully constructed 'overadequate' persona.

In spite of these obstacles, it was felt that Andrew had to become involved in Betty's treatment or he would sabotage her efforts to change. Husband and wife needed to progress together developmentally for mother's and daughter's gains to be maintained. The goals established in attempting to engage Andrew were (1) to demystify the setting and help him face his own fears, (2) to work towards his becoming willing to enter individual and/or marital therapy, (3) to educate him about child development issues, and (4) to help him to see the connections between his concerns about his daughter and his concerns about himself. Just as Betty has been helped to understand that Penny is not "out to get her" when she resists toilet training or is negatively assertive, Andrew needs to be helped to see that his wife's illness and daughter's strivings for autonomy are not directed against him.

This form of intervention is not only helpful for the family system but is preventive as well. Although Penny is not yet the identified patient, she could easily become so because of her role as the focal point of her parents shared psychological issues. It is not difficult to imagine the conflicts that might surface as Penny negotiates the tasks of the latency years, which involve moving into the world of school and peers. The separation and symbolic abandonment of Penny's entrance in this wider world could be very stressful for both parents. Add to this the increasing demands of a school-age child for attention, assistance with homework or other activities, and the noisy and playful boisterousness of her friends in the house, and the situation is ripe for anger and tension to be focused on Penny.

While Penny's role as the focal point of her parents' shared issues is the clinical predicament, it is also the beginning of the solution. By inviting Andrew to a Parent Conference in the relatively conflict-free sphere of an educational setting—our nursery—we were able to induce him to come to the agency. Since the approach of the project is one of milieu treatment, the nursery teacher was a logical first therapist. Once they establish a relationship in which Andrew feels comfortable, he may be able to move from dealing with Penny's issues to an understanding of how they relate to his own concerns. If Andrew can clarify these concerns he might be willing to work with a Mothers' Project case worker, and to participate in some beginning marital treatment with Betty.

Long-Term Project Goals

The long-term goal of helping this family to become a part of the larger community will be approached on several levels. First, when Penny is 4 years old she will be placed in a carefully chosen, sensitively run, preschool in the community. This will be done because the Mother's Project is time-bounded (children must leave before they reach 5 years of age), and because Penny will need the experience of being in a regular preschool setting in order to successfully make the later transition to kindergarten. Mothers' Project staff begin working on school placement about 6 to 10 months before a child 'graduates' from the nursery, and are in close contact with the new school both before and after the child begins. While nursery staff are helping Penny to make the transition to the larger community, clinical and vocational staff will be assisting Betty in her quest for a job outside of the agency. Betty both needs and wants to work, but will require a job with somewhat shorter or more flexible hours until Penny is older.

Finally, although Betty could remain at Thresholds as a regular (non-Mothers' Project) client, the agency is basically an aftercare milieu treatment facility. This family will require the kind of lifelong supportive services that are best offered by settings which specialize in individual and family therapy. Also, while Betty has made considerable gains with her Thresholds case worker, it seems clear that she will ultimately need to deal with her early and core issues. This would probably best be accomplished by long-term individual treatment.

CONCLUSIONS

Preliminary findings on the relationships between severely depressed mothers and their children indicate that it is not that these women lack mothering skills or knowledge, but rather that the underlying affective relationship is characterized by a striking lack of connectedness. Information on parenting and assistance in parenting skills will be less meaningful than a mother's ability to become genuinely engaged with her child. Initially the mothers are either detached from their child; unempathetic, unresponsive to the child's needs, and unable to respond contingently and appropriately; or they are fused with the child and unable to acknowledge or empathize with the child's needs as separate from their own. Mothers are unable to nurture their children; to be playful, joyful, or engaged with them, because they themselves are so desperately needy and lacking internal structure or resources. Depressive systems put the mother in the untenable position of having to give when she needs to receive. Both acute and chronic depression significantly impair a woman's capacity to adequately mother her child. It is particularly difficult for these mothers to deal with their feelings, especially their ambivalence towards affection and hostility. They also experience severe conflict around their child's developmental issues, as these often trigger core, unresolved conflicts of their own.

The most effective treatment plan is one in which there is prompt treatment of the mother's depressive illness in conjunction with an intensive therapeutic experience for the child. Thus we may be able to break the cycle of mother–child disharmony, as relief of symptoms helps the mother to care more about her child, who is simultaneously becoming more competent and easier to care for. We know that one cannot teach a mother to love her child, and further that those aspects of the mothering process most likely to give rise to developmental problems are the least ameable to this form of intervention. We must go beyond a didactic 'how to' method in order to enhance interpersonal relatedness. Therefore primary treatment methods should be directed towards fostering the mother–child bond, and towards helping a mother to become attached to a child who is almost a stranger to her. Only after a mother has had some of her own deep needs met, will she be able to genuinely know and love her child.

Finally, it is unrealistic to think that even an intensive 1- 2-year experience will be enough for these multiproblem families. Rather, we must recognize that the depressed woman and her family will continue to need supportive services for many years to come.

REFERENCES

1. Richards MPM: First steps in becoming social, in Richards, MPM (ed): The Integration of a Child into a Social World. London, Cambridge University Press. 1974, pp 83–97
2. Lidz T: The Person: His or Her Development Throughout The Life Cycle, (revised ed). New York, Basic Books, 1976
3. Spitz R: A Genetic Field Theory of Ego Formation. New York, International Universities Press, 1959

4. Escalona SK: The Roots of Individuality: Normal Patterns of Development in Infancy. Chicago, Aldine, 1968
5. Erikson E: Childhood and Society, (ed 2). New York, W W Norton, 1963
6. Freud A: Normality and Pathology in Childhood. New York, International Universities Press, 1965
7. Winnecott OW: Playing and Reality. New York, Basic Books, 1971
8. Mahler M, Pine F, Bergman A: The Psychological Birth of the Human Infant. New York, Basic Books, 1975
9. Caldwell BM: The effects of infant care, in Hoffman ML, and Hoffman LW (eds): Review of Child Development Research (vol 1). New York, Russell Sage Foundation, 1964
10. Vigotsky LS: Development of Higher Mental Functions, in Psychological Research in the U.S.S.R. Moscow, Progress Publ, 1966
11. Clarke-Stewart KA: Interactions Between Mothers and Their Young Children: Characteristics and Consequences. Monographs of the Society for Research in Child Development, 1973, vol 38, (Serial No. 153)
12. Newson E, Newson J: On the Origins of Symbolic Functioning, in Varma V, Williams P (eds): Piaget, Psychology and Education. Itasca, Illinois, Peacock Publications, 1976, pp 84–96
13. Yarrow LJ, Pedersen FA: The Interplay between Cognition and Motivation in Infancy, in Lewis M (ed): Origins of Intelligence: Infancy and Early Childhood. New York, Plenum Press, 1976, pp 379–399
14. Bruner J: The organization of early skilled action, in Richards MPM (ed): The Integration of a Child into a Social World London, Cambridge University Press, 1974, pp 167–187
15. Bruner J, Sherwood V: Peekaboo and the Learning of Rule Structures, in Bruner J, Jolly A, Sylva K (eds): Play: Its Role in Development and Evolution. New York, Basic Books, 1976
16. Bruner J: On Prelinguistic Aspects of Speech. Oxford University (to be published)
17. Spitz R: The First Year of Life. New York, International Universities Press, 1965
18. Rutter M: Maternal Deprivation Reassessed. Middlesex, England, Penguin, 1972
19. Winnicott DW: The Maturational Processes and the Facilitating Environment. New York, International Universities Press, 1965
20. Lopata H: Occupation: Housewife. New York, Oxford University Press, 1971
21. Cohler B, Grunebaum H, Weiss J, Hartman C, Gallant D: Life Stress and psychopathology among mothers of young children. Am J Orthopsychiatry 45:58–73, 1975
22. Anthony EJ, Koupernik C, (eds): The Child in His Family: Children at Psychiatric Risk. New York, Wiley, 1974
23. Cohler B: Character, mental illness, and mothering, in Grunebaum H, Weiss J, Cohler B, et al: Mentally Ill Mothers and Their Children. Chicago: University of Chicago Press, 1974, pp 234–132

24. Garmezy N: The Study of competence in children at risk for severe psychopathology, in Anthony EJ, Koupernik C (eds): The Child in His Family: Children at Psychiatric Risk, New York: Wiley, 1974, pp 77–98
25. Mendlewicz J, Rainer J: Adoption Study Supporting Genetic Transmission in Manic-Depressive Illness. Nature 268:327–29, 1977
26. Cadoret R: Evidence for genetic inheritance of primary affective disorder, Am J Psychiatry, 135:4,463–466, 1978
27. Rutter M: Children of Sick Parents: An Environmental and Psychiatric Study. Institute of Psychiatry, Maudsley Monographs no 16, London, Oxford University Press, 1966
28. Weissman M, Paykel E: The Depressed Woman: A Study of Social Relationships. Chicago, University of Chicago Press, 1974
29. Beck A: The Development of Depression, in Friedman R, Katz M (eds): The Psychology of Depression: Contemporary Theory and Research. Washington, VV Winston, 1974, pp 3–20
30. Cohler B, Grunebaum H, Weiss J, Gamer E, Gallant D: Disturbance of attention among schizophrenic depressed and well mothers and their young children. J Child Psychol Psychiatry 18:115–135, 1977
31. Richman N: Depression in mothers of preschool children. J Child Psychol Psychiatry 17:75–78, 1976
32. Resnich PJ: Child murder by parents: A psychiatric review of filicide. Am J Psychiatry, 126:1414–1420, 1969
33. McDermaid G, Winkler EG: Psychopathology of Infanticide. J Clin Exp Psychopathol 16:22–41, 1955
34. Musick J, Clark R, Householder J: Issues surrounding abuse and neglect among the children of mentally ill mothers. Paper presented before the Governors' Conference on Child Abuse, National Committee for the Prevention of Child Abuse, Springfield, Illinois, May 1979
35. Bemesderfer S, Cohler S: Depressive reactions during the period of separation: Individuation and self among children of psychotic depressed mothers, in Morrison H (ed): Children of Depressed Mothers. New York, Grune and Stratton (in press)
36. Freud, A: The ego and the mechanisms of defense (1936), in The writings of Anna Freud (vol 2). New York, International Universities Press, 1966
37. Anthony EJ, Benedek T (eds): Depression and Human Existence. Boston, Little, Brown & Co, 1975
38. Welner A, Welner Z, McCrary M et al: Psychopathology in children of inpatients with depression: A controlled study. J Nerv Ment Dis 164: 408–413, 1977
39. McKnew D, Cytryn L, Efron A, et al: Offspring of patients with affective disorders. Br J Psychiatry 134:148–152, 1979
40. Phillips I: Childhood depression: Interpersonal interactions and depressive phenomena. Am J Psychiatry 136:511–515, 1979
41. Fraiberg S, Adelson E, Shapiro V: Ghosts in the nursery: A psychoanalytic approach to the problems of impaired infant-mother relationships. J Am Acad Child Psychiatry 14:387–421, 1975

42. Malinquist C: Depressions in childhood and adolescence. N Engl J Med 284:887–1893, 955–1961, 1971
43. Dincin J, Cohler B: The Rehabilitation of Psychotic Mothers and Their Children. Public Health Service Grant MH 28143-04, 1975.
44. Blutstein W: Characteristics of the Children of Mentally Ill Mothers. Read before the Annual Conference of the National Association for the Education of Young Children, Atlanta, Nov 1979
45. Sander L: Issues in early mother–child interaction in Rexford E, Sander L, Shapiro T (eds): Infant Psychiatry: A New Synthesis. New Haven, Yale University Press, 1976, pp 127–147

Yolande B. Davenport

7

Treatment of the Married Bipolar Patient in Conjoint Couples Psychotherapy Groups

This chapter explores the efficacy of group psychotherapy for homogeneous married couples as a treatment modality in the long-term management of bipolar patients on lithium carbonate. Less troubled with disruptive mood swings when maintained on prophylactive drugs, bipolar patients are able to engage with their spouses in psychotherapeutic efforts to examine and change symptoms of marital and family dysfunction. Patients with a bipolar history are difficult to treat in traditional dyadic psychotherapy, even during symptom-free intervals between episodes. Many hospital readmissions occur because of patient failure to comply with medication; at least 20 percent of diagnosed patients do not respond to available drugs; and the lives of many are disrupted by marital failure. The effects of this illness, generally assumed to have a genetic basis, have profound impact upon family members.

INTRODUCTION

No matter how satisfying the marriage may have appeared prior to the onset of illness, distressing changes in the relationship result when bipolar manic-depressive illness befalls a marital partner. The despair, withdrawal, and dependency of severe depression and the provocative, alienating behavior of mania may leave lasting scars long after symptoms remit.

Clinical awareness of continuing and disturbing interpersonal and

123

intrapsychic problems of the bipolar patient is often obscured by drugs that control the wide mood swings and distressful behavior associated with the disorder. The malignant quality of this recurrent familial disease is often overlooked. The functional impairment found among many bipolar patients in follow-up studies, and the disruptions due to the illness reported in family, occupational, and social life, suggest the persistence of problems despite adequate pharmacotherapy.[1,2]

DEFINITION

To understand how psychopathology in a bipolar spouse can so disturb a marital or family system, it is necessary first to define and describe the illness and its most prevalent symptoms. A person diagnosed as having the bipolar form of manic-depressive illness has experienced episodes of both mania and depression, in contrast to the person with a unipolar illness, who has a history of depressions only. Bipolar illness tends to run in families and is considered to have a strong genetic component. It is a serious, chronic, recurrent disorder requiring professional treatment, often including hospitalization.

Most adults have experienced depression in the form of mild transient sadness (the 'blues') generally related to a specific life event, a mood that dissolves without psychiatric intervention. Grief and mourning related to loss and death are 'normal' depressive feelings. The clinically depressed person, however, is afflicted with an acute, persistent mood disorder characterized by feelings of despair, helplessness, and low self-esteem. Motor retardation, inability to concentrate or make decisions, disturbances of sleep and appetite, withdrawal, extreme dependency, delusions, loss of energy, feelings of self-reproach, agitation, and recurrent suicidal ideation or gestures are among the symptoms associated with a clinical depression. When prolonged, the illness and its symptoms impair everyday functioning, and the affected individual requires professional help and possibly hospitalization. The onset of a depressive episode may occur suddenly or may develop over a period of weeks. When first episodes occur, patient and family sometimes delay seeking help. When this happens, spouse and/or family are often profoundly affected by this period of the patient's pathological or aberrant behavior.

The beginning of a manic episode may also go unrecognized and untreated. The high spirits, creativity, energy, and euphoria typical of the early stages of some manic episodes (ie, hypomania) are often infectious and may not be viewed as abnormal. A manic episode may be characterized by euphoria, hyperactivity, overtalkativeness, flight of ideas, grandosity, irritability, distractability, decreased need for sleep, and increased libido. When the manic patient writes checks without funds, makes unwise purchases and investments, uses obscene and abusive language, is sexually provocative, or becomes violent, the illness is of psychotic proportion and requires hospitalization. The patient may feel extremely well, and many families will engage in incredible struggles, using all of their pursuasiveness and wiles before they are able to convince the patient of the necessity for hospitalization. Bankruptcy, loss of employment, and alienation of friends may result from the turmoil, and in turn result in social isolation and deeply felt shame and humiliation.

Most patients have periods between episodes in which they are relatively symptom-free and may be perceived as stable. In spite of adequate drug prophylaxis, some bipolar patients continue to experience less severe 'mini-episodes' of depression and mania, which seldom require hospitalization and permit routine occupational and social functioning. We see many such patients in our groups whose moods are clearly attentuated by lithium. They continue to have manageable episodes outside of the hospital, requiring considerable understanding and forebearance by the spouse.

Spouse and family are apt to be more aware of these subtle shifts in mood than are friends and acquaintances at work. On the job, the patient is often able to maintain a relatively normal appearance. In the early stages of a manic episode, for example, irrational anger, sleeplessless, and increased activity alert the family that the patient may be hypomanic or becoming so. Families often inform us that they can detect slight changes, which they perceive as clues to the mood shift, that occur in tone of voice, dress, mannerisms, or in affect. For example: "He gets 'that look' in his eyes every time he starts to get high" "Suddenly, we realize that she is neglecting the housework, too busy doing things in the neighborhood." For some patients, with the onset of each episode, there is indeed a recurrence of the same prodromal patterns of behavior, which serves as a warning: "It always starts with his getting angry with the children over nothing" "I know it has begun again when I hear him screaming at them when he comes up the walk from work." "She begins to stay up later each night, and then decides to clean the kitchen and takes everything off of the shelves... it always starts with the kitchen." "He always decides to go on a strict diet." "She begins to smoke again."

Undetected hypomanic behavior is potentially and ultimately destructive to the marital relationship. One spouse, who has experienced several episodes of hypomania with an outpatient spouse, has been unable to detect the onset of the mood change. Several times, she has become aware belatedly when the monthly bank statement (possibly left by the patient to be discovered) revealed the expenditure of near-ruinous sums of money. Members of a couples group are very quick to note slight changes in each other. As this is tolerated, it often permits medication adjustment and modification. Although some of our patients have learned to monitor their sense of becoming hypomanic or depressed, and will report this voluntarily, many seem unable to detect their own shifts.

As for depressive episodes managed outside of the hospital, one patient in a couples group described his depressions: "When I am depressed, I cannot be a solicitous husband or father. I cannot be the caretaker of my house, garden, and car. I can only eat, and sleep, and think about how badly I feel. It takes all of my energy to get dressed every morning to go to my office to sit all day and do nothing." In the meantime, his wife struggles alone with the responsibilities of home and children, and discusses in the group her feelings of being demeaned by the demands of the illness, and of anger with her husband. She feels his depression controls her life.

These painful circumstances are typical of the predicament of bipolar patients we see in our groups. Although they are treated actively with medication and are able to remain at home, they lead lives that by most standards are chaotic and disorganized. The stable appearance of the patient between episodes and the shared inability of patient and spouse to disclose the reality of their relationship causes many problems to remain untreated. Far too often, a major crisis is required to expose the ongoing difficulties.

BACKGROUND AND REVIEW OF THE LITERATURE

Affective illness has been a concern of the mental health practitioner since biblical times, presenting serious treatment difficulties for centuries. In the late nineteenth century, Kraepelin systematically described manic-depressive illness, distinguishing it from schizophrenia.[3] Later, psycho-analysts such as Freud and Abraham, in their investigations into the nature of the illness and the refractoriness of these patients to individual psychotherapy, developed concepts that they hoped would aid study of etiology and of treatment. The loss of narcissistic input, rage at the lost object, and failure to mourn loss stem from a faulty mother–infant relationship, a "primal parathymia," that they claimed predisposed to the illness and presented continuing problems for the person with an affective disorder.[4,5] Abraham described the manic-depressive patient as unable to maintain firm object relations and object constancy, feeling continually threatened by a sense of impending loss and doomed to perceive the lost object as a disappointment and target for rage, given the patient's insatiable narcissistic demands. He noted that the predominant character structure of the manic-depressive patient is 'abnormal' and observable even during symptom-free periods.[6]

Other analysts began to consider the significance of childhood events in the manifestation of the illness in the early family life as well as in the marriage of the patient. Cohen et al,[7] Fromm-Reichman,[8] and Gibson[9] referred to the unusual and inconsistent conformity to rigid rules noted in the nurturing family of the manic-depressive patient. Fromm-Reichman, in 1949, alluding to the dilemma of the clinician, said "manic-depressives can only be treated successfully if the therapist is able to help them break through their clinging dependence on the family and its substitutes, and to reevaluate the conventional group values of the family."[10] Smith described the emotional withdrawal of the mother during the infancy of the prospective manic-depressive as an effort to deny and avoid anxiety about separation.[11] Finley and Wilson referred to the "walled-in existence" of the future patient in the manic-depressive family setting, which causes "guilt and hostility" leading to " . . . depression, or an explosion outward which appears as mania."[12] Jacobson, in a classical study of the interaction of psychotic partners, found that in the manic-depressive marriage, the "seemingly close, over-warm marital relationship, is actually of a symbiotic type," with the " . . . partners actually feeding on each other; . . . a position which becomes inevitably unstable, facilitating easy, rapid, and drastic cathectic changes on the slighest provocation."[13] She suggested that many patients are "very masochistic" in their choice of a marital partner, selecting one who becomes a "super-ego figure," and an "over-valued love-object" important to the self-esteem of the patient. Realistically, the "healthy partner is actually the more passive, more selfish, more frankly demanding character type." Jacobson also remarked on the problems of individuation in the bipolar marriage, which she regarded as characteristic.

Beginning in the 1950s, the influence of rich, descriptive material from the early psychoanalytic literature began to lessen, having failed to achieve lasting therapeutic change. At about the same time, notable breakthroughs in drug treatment began. This was accompanied by an increased understanding of the genetic and biologic nature of manic-depressive illness. New and effective drugs, the tricyclic antidepressants and lithium carbonate, were introduced in the 1950s and 1960s, drastically changing treatment approaches. In addition, continuing Kraepelin's earlier efforts, diagnostic scales and instruments were developed leading to more reliable diagnostic classification and selectivity in pharmacotherapy.[14,15]

In the pre-drug era, treatment depended almost exclusively on the psychotherapeutic patient–therapist relationship. There is very little in the analytic literature which clearly substantiates that diagnoses were accurate or that remissions were attributable to the treatment. This changed with the advent of the new drugs; chemotherapy successfully controlled the troublesome, recurrent manic and depressive episodes for most patients.

The new emphasis on biochemical and genetic features of the illness tended to de-emphasize the search for etiology (and blame) in the individual intrapsychic processes, and in the family interactional patterns. Characteristics attributed earlier to the person with manic-depressive illness, including problems with intimacy and social adaptation, were ignored or minimized. Early pharmacologic-based treatment was reported as though the patient lived in isolation. The true extent of disturbance in the patient's marital relationship and support system could be concealed from the clinician by the defensive character structure of many bipolar patients if the clinician emphasized only the 'magic pill' now available to control the more obvious symptoms of illness. This occurred, ironically, at a time when the significance of external human events (including the marital relationships of patients) was also gaining recognition as a variable with powerful effects on the course of illness.

In the post-drug era, psychiatric literature focusing primarily on the psychotherapeutic treatment of the bipolar patient is meager and unconvincing. Bipolar patients (characterized by provocativeness, opacity, fitful compliance with medication, and antipathy to traditional psychotherapy) continue to be the despair of many clinicians. The same alienating, manipulative, demanding style that mitigated against a successful dyadic psychotherapeutic alliance was perceived as interfering with the patient's ability to function optimally in a therapy group modality heterogenous for diagnosis. Yalom described the presence of a bipolar patient as one of the "worst calamities" to befall a group, and suggested that it was "unwise" for a group to invest time in treatment when there was "such little likelihood of success."[16] The usefulness of lithium carbonate in the maintenance treatment of the bipolar patient is well established. The paucity of studies available which considered the significance of psychotherapy in conjunction with drug therapy in the treatment of bipolar illness may be a reflection of the prevailing general psychotherapeutic pessimism.

More studies are now available of the psychotherapeutic treatment of the unipolar patient. These range from examination of supportive interventions when the patient is severely depressed to descriptions of various theoretical approaches, including psychoanalytic, behavioral, and cognitive psychotherapy.[17–19]

Research efforts have also assessed the benefits of drug therapy and psychotherapy in the treatment and outcome of unipolar depressed patients.[20] The marriages of unipolar depressed patients have also been examined to explain how the marital interaction of couples contributes to depression.[21]

There have been few studies that attempt to assess the usefulness of psychotherapy in the management of the lithium-controlled patient. One recent study reported on the effectiveness of group psychotherapy conducted for bipolar patients exclusively. These investigators found that hospital readmissions decreased, and that patients seemed to have made a more satisfactory employment, interpersonal, and social adjustment during the 2-year period of group participation.[22] Brodie and Leff found extensive marital conflict among bipolar patients they studied.[23] In a series of male and female patients with a history of mania, 57 percent at follow-up were reported to be divorced or separated, compared to 8 percent of the patients in the study who had unipolar depressions only.

Fitzgerald examined the effectiveness of psychotherapy with bipolar patient and spouse, and stressed the importance of working with the interpersonal relationships of these patients and their families for improving compliance in taking lithium.[24] Demers and Davis studied the influence of prophylactic lithium treatment on the marital adjustment of the bipolar patient.[25] They reported that chemotherapy did not increase spouse ratings of the patient's "desirable attributes." Greene described the marital adjustment of a group of patients with primary affective disorder.[26] Given adequate counseling by the clinician, it was reported that the spouse could be successfully engaged as an "assistant therapist." Heterogenous group therapy was ruled out for the bipolar patient in this study; it was felt that fragility of ego boundaries and the underlying illness might not be recognized by other group members. Homogenous groups are not discussed.

Ruestow et al found that the overall marital adjustment of bipolar males was good, based on a validated self-rating scale.[27] The authors had a "clinical impression" that married, bipolar, female patients had greater problems with dependency issues than male patients. This suggested that women might benefit from couples therapy focusing on their dependency problems. Based on these results, the authors were dubious about the necessity for long-term psychotherapy for married male patients.

In an earlier study of the psychodynamics and interpersonal relationships of manic patients and their spouses, a research team including the present investigator alluded to differences in the marriages of bipolar male and female patients. It was our impression that men may be equally dependent, but defended against it through denial and selection of a dominant spouse. The marital choice is felt to have replicated an earlier relationship with a dominant mother who met their needs by being continually present.[28]

THE BIPOLAR MARRIAGE

As observed earlier, many marriages break up when one spouse has bipolar illness. Many bipolar patients are divorced because of the unwillingness of a well spouse to tolerate the agression of mania or the dependency of depression. If a marriage is to survive the destructive assault and damaging effects of manic or depressed behavior, certain psychological factors must be present. What is the cement, then, that holds some well partners in such pathologic relationships? It is assumed that the spouse who remains in the marriage is someone who empathizes and can be supportive. However, the anhedonia of the depressed patient is contagious, and many well spouses become chronically depressed.[29] If pleasure in the marriage is no longer derived by the patient from sexual activity, seeing friends, taking trips, etc, the well spouse who needs and encourages these once-pleasurable activities eventually relinquishes them when confronted with the patient's negativism and apathy. It is not surprising that the spouse, whose omnipotent feelings are continually challenged by the patient's covert message that "you really can't help me, no matter how hard you try," feeling unappreciated and unsupported, sinks also into a state of anhedonia and depression. It may be that it is the spouse, unable to tolerate these latter feelings, who flees the marriage. When the patient is hypomanic, concealing basic insecurity and neediness with hurtful verbal abuse, the spouse feels assaulted and equally unsupported. It often appears as if there is no carry-over of goodwill upon which the spouse can depend. The scarcity of emotional supplies in the relationship effects both both patient and spouse.

Not surprisingly, studies of assortative mating in the affective disorders suggest that the bipolar patient has a special talent for selecting a spouse with complementary characteristics. Well spouses frequently have affectively ill parents or siblings in their families of origin, and it has been proposed that their choice of mate may be an attempt to replicate the earlier familial relationships and adaptations.[30,31] No matter the basis of selection, the extent of discomfort and dismay experienced by the well partner in such marriages is great. The well partner who remains married must endure humiliations, verbal insults, and abuse during hypomania, and unreasonable expectations, demands, and complaints during depression, meanwhile fulfilling the role of responsible spouse and parent. The security of being needed to hold the marriage together is seldom sufficient to compensate for depressive tendencies in the so-called well spouse.

The bipolar patient's problems with identification and individuation shared by the spouse increases the difficulties many couples experience in modifying a repetition of earlier parenting models. Failure to differentiate, difficulty in establishing autonomy, and generally unclear ego boundaries are patterns transmitted from the earlier family to the relationship with spouse, and, eventually, children. The spouse as caretaker becomes the recipient of all primary love, and is thus invested with the omnipotent expectations of the patient, so the marriage appears as a life-sustaining relationship. This type of symbiosis makes the exploration or testing of a less restrictive relationship very difficult; the symbiosis is reinforced powerfully by the illness.

In marriages of bipolar patients, a typical conflictual constellation becomes evident when the patient is depressed, passive, and dependent. The patient is unable to make decisions and is teetering on the brink of a situation where decision is mandatory. The power to decide is of necessity given to the spouse, but the patient often says later, "You took advantage of me because I was depressed," and becomes angry. The criticism stems from an omnipotent expectation of perfection that can never be met. The spouse, too, becomes angry at being put in such a position and at being made to feel responsible though unappreciated.

Manic-depressive patients are thought to marry mothering persons who will take care of them and assure happiness. But often the spouse has also suffered early deprivations, is needy, and unable to provide constant nurturing to meet the patient's insatiable needs. Again, disappointment in omnipotent expectations angers the patient. The bipolar patient's self-perception in the marriage is of a helpless individual who needs a strong person to control urges and impulses, and who blames the spouse for not being omnipotent and onmiresponsible.

In a recent study at the National Institute of Mental Health (NIMH), 19 currently married bipolar couples were interviewed separately from their spouses using the NIMH Family Attitudes Questionnaire (FAQ). The FAQ was designed to quantify individual perceptions of patients and spouses about the etiology, familial risk, and chronic burden of bipolar illness, to assess attitudes toward marriage and child bearing, and to provide a data base for genetic counseling. Marriages ranged in length from 1–45 years (22.2 ± 3.2 SEM). Spouses perceived the illness as a profound burden, seriously disrupting their lives with damaging psychological and economic consequences. For example, 53 percent of spouses, in contrast to 5 percent of the patients ($p < 0.1$), indicated they would not have married, and 47 percent of spouses compared to 5 percent of patients

($p < 0.1$) would not have had children had they understood the nature of bipolar illness prior to making these decisions. Only 11 percent of patients thought that more knowledge about the illness would have prevented their spouse from marrying them. This suggests an unawareness or denial on the part of the patient of the burden and regret the spouse has experienced. On the other hand, 47 percent of the spouses knew of the existence of the illness prior to marriage, and 67 percent of the couples had children after the onset of the illness. Although these study couples remained married, the overall data reflects the plight of the marriages, the existence of spouse pathology, and the demands imposed on both patient and marital partner by a severe, recurrent, psychiatric illness; the tyranny of memories and patterns from earlier family experiences, and the patient's tendency to deny the significance of the illness for spouse and other family members.[32]

This study also revealed that some spouses perceived the illness as transient, and felt the patient's basic spontaneous and outgoing personality traits during well phases would help maintain the marriage. Other spouses in the study indicated that moral or religious scruples, guilt, children, age, financial circumstances, and lack of employablity were reasons for remaining together. There are those couples who recognize the tragedy and disruption caused in their lives by the illness. Yet when asked why, they refer to memories of the good years together prior to the onset of the illness, and their sense of commitment to the idea of marriage. Also, there are those who believe in the curative power of medication as a reason not to abandon the marriage. Denial and self-deception may be active mechanisms for some who remain in a bipolar marriage 'for better or for worse.'

In a recent study[33] of 32 symptom-free, manic-depressive patients and their spouses examined separately, we found that both patient and spouse appear to hold a similar, faulty perceptive world view when tested on the Weissman Dysfunctional Attitude Scale.[34] This is a 40-item scale in which 30 items labeled maladaptive are considered characteristic of depressed persons. A major finding of our study was the lack of significant differences in scores of patients and spouses on both functional and dysfunctional items. The data suggests and confirms our clinical impressions that in their depressive view of the world, patient and spouse share the same pathogenic views, thus accentuating the resemblance of the partners and having important treatment implications as well. If the distorted cognitions, the perfectionistic standards and demands, and the sense of low self-esteem are present in both partners, then treatment planning must take into account the unavailability of the spouse to provide reality-based interpretations.

Earlier research on the interpersonal relationships and psychodynamics of married bipolar patients reported on themes and features specific to this patient population and significant to their marital relationship. They included (1) the pervasive fears of patient and spouse of the recurrence of an episode of mania or depression, in spite of medication; (2) a sense of helpnessness and dependency in an intense marital relationship; (3) the need to avoid expression of all affect and to defend against closeness; (4) the use of massive denial to manage feelings of hostility, anxiety, loss, and grief; and (5) themes related to earlier parental loss and failure to grieve.[28]

We noted further that the prominent pathology in both spouses reflected dynamics identified by the earlier psychoanalytic writers. The notion that conflict and feeling expressions are to be avoided (since they might lead to abandonment) and the mutual dependency of the marital pairs are major pathologic issues and were addressed in the treatment for all of the couples in the therapy groups.

In a recent study, we also examined and reported on characteristics and psychodynamic features of families in which manic-depressive illness has occurred in at least two generations. Repetitive patterns and maladaptive responses consistent among the families were identified cross-generationally, which may further explain why many of the couples stay together. These additional characteristics included (1) unrealistic standards of conformity and self-expectation among all family members; (2) displacement of parental feelings of low self-esteem onto their own children; and (3) the tendency for members of these families to remain bound together and isolated in a closed, rigid system with little socialization outside the family network, thus limiting the opportunity for the introduction of new and different responses.[31] Singularly, these characteristics are not unique and are to be found in many family constellations, but their combined existence in the bipolar family beset with episodic illness is damaging. Parental inability to attend to their own wants and needs results in an incapacity to mourn for themselves and for the tragedies and suffering in their lives attendant to the illness. This repression of grief and awareness of feelings filters down and is transmitted to their children. It may be that this is the manner by which the family culture helps to sustain the depressive system.

The relationship between the couples supports denial of feelings, and this continual repression of rage, grief, and affection during well stages reinforces the feelings of the pair that such expression is not safe. Provocative behavior in bipolar marriages can often be understood by its proximity to situations signifying loss. There are continual circumstances within the marital dyad that perpetuate turbulent and destructive features of the system; the intent to do so is probably beyond the conscious awarenes of the participants. The turmoil provides a form of stability and permanency in the marriage. Previous comments illustrate that, in spite of medication, many couples continue to lead their lives as if there is nothing but the despair of depression or the euphoria of mania. In the safety of the couples psychotherapy groups, however, we find we are able to confront the defensive maneuvers and intervene in the ubiquitous and repetitive patterns that compound and deepen depressions.

THE COUPLES GROUP PARADIGM

More than ten years ago, we began to study and treat bipolar patients and their spouses in psychotherapy groups homogeneous for diagnosis in an outpatient clinic at the Clinical Center of the National Institutes of Health. Each group consisted of three to five couples with one spouse of each couple having been hospitalized at least once for an acute manic episode and meeting diagnostic criteria for bipolar manic-depressive illness. Index patients, generally symptom-free at time of entrance into the group, are admitted with their spouses either following discharge from the hospital or from an outpatient medication supervision group in the clinic attached to our ward. Selection for a group is basically random within our population sample, and is based on space available and geographic accessibility to NIMH. The groups have been in existence for some time. They have a reasonably good record of helping people stay out of the hospital, and most couples are well-motivated to attend. The group members have the advantages of continuity of care, because the therapists have known most of the couples on the ward or in the clinics. Both patient and spouse have been exposed to a setting where the illness is defined as basically biochemical; this attitude itself may be supportive. Thus, the setting provides a benign institutional transference that allows couples to recognize the existence of problems of adaptation and of adjustment requiring more than pharmacotherapeutic efforts alone.

Our groups meet 1½ hours weekly; attendance at meetings is good, and the drop-out rate is low. Serum blood levels are drawn monthly. Although this takes place outside the group time, discussion of the biochemical elements of the illness and of lithium treatment and side effects are inevitable and, perhaps, desirable. The biologic aspects of illness are no longer the main focus of meetings, which they were when lithium was first introduced and when spouse involvement in medication management was the primary rationale for the group's existence. When a prolonged discussion of medication occurs, especially in some of our advanced groups, it is perceived as digressive. Access to the physician co-therapist is provided for in a 15-minute period prior to each session for individual discussion of medication or physical problems. Prior to admission to a group, extensive interviews were held with the couple to obtain history, and so the therapists could learn the current state of the marital relationship.

We have strongly advocated the female–male co-therapist model. This design reflects the earlier parental relationship, and provides the group members with a new set of 'parents' whose ego boundaries are distinct and who will help them to temper their perfectionistic, omnipotent strivings by providing a corrective model and facilitating cooperative endeavor. The co-therapist model displays the differences, splits, and communication problems that are part of the fabric of any active, viable relationship. When one therapist has been absent by necessity, we have noticed that the drain on the other therapist can be exhausting. Manic-depressive patients tend to 'cannabilize' the lone therapist, and counter-transference issues are very difficult with these patients. In a group setting, crisis may be frequent, and occasions when all group members are simultaneously symptom-free are not the rule. We have also incorporated weekly consultations wth a senior psychoanalyst consultant into our model. These sessions provide the therapists with continuity and support, and they also serve as a forum for discussion of pathology, etiology, dynamics, treatment, and research.

Although patients with major psychopathology are not considered good risks for many psychotherapy groups, our experience suggests that the demandingness and potentially explosive behavior of the bipolar patient can be contained and treated in groups consisting of other diagnostically similar patients, their spouses, and two therapists. Patient and spouse come into the groups and are viewed as two people who 'have a past history and a future together' and meet with other couples who share their predicament.[35] The primary focus in therapy is on interaction between each married couple rather than on the group process. Similarities between couples are recognized by the pairs as they disclose themselves in the group. This is particularly true for the spouse, who often has felt isolated and alone when illness is treated in oblivion to its effects on the family. In one newly formed group, when everyone disclosed previous behavior during manic episodes, and spouse feelings of helplessness and anger, the members quickly concluded they were surely 'computer-matched' because of the similarity of experiences.

Much support is required when a member of a group is depressed or manic. The groups readily discuss many problems that directly effect the couple and their families. In one group, following a serious manic episode which led to hospitalization of one member, the group spent several sessions discussing methods to relieve the plight of spouses when a manic patient must be committed to a hospital. There was active discussion of the need for community support of the spouse, and of the necessity of having informed relatives and friends whose help could be sought. Measures which would facilitate rapid action by the spouse were discussed, including the desirability of keeping savings in a bank in the spouse's name only so that it would be possible to manage temporarily. Practical suggestions such as these were accepted and have been implemented by some of the couples. The idea of a voluntary waiver of the patient's rights in order to facilitate the spouse's obtaining hospitalization has been discussed, as well as bestowing responsibility for patient's medication on the spouse. These ideas seemed more threatening to the patients at first, but did confront the fact that the hypomanic or manic patient often lacks self recognition of the state and has difficulty seeking or accepting help. Ultimately, such plans are a source of great relief, for the spouse who must cope with antagonistic behavior, and for the patient who needs immediate protection and care.

One group also discussed what they termed a 'spouse-syndrome,' which occurs in the immediate postmanic or postdepressive period. This was defined as the time when the patient, feeling quite stable again, and often successfully repressing memory of the offensive behavior during the episode, demanded the return of normal affection and sexual attention. Patients were invariably bewildered by the anger and sense of being demeaned and exploited expressed by all of the spouses. The spouses proposed a 'waiting period.' A crucial aspect of the negotiation was their willingness to confront feelings themselves and to tell the patient spouses about them.

How is it that change occurs or therapeutic progress is maintained? In view of the basic omnipotence and grandiosity of the bipolar patient's reasoning, can there be real cognitive improvement? Psychoanalytic observers noted a basic flaw in the personality of the manic-depressive patient. We, too, have observed that the bipolar patient has difficulty in relinquishing the grandiosity and omnipotence, in becoming responsible and working at the emotional realities of relationships. In addition, we have observed these couples through the years noting the rigidity, constant denial, and forgetfulness from one session to the next; it often appears that the cognitive functioning of the bipolar patient is impaired. The spouse's irritation when the patient claims not to remember is also frustrating for the therapists.

Some investigators ascribe cognitive changes to medication-induced side effects. Their preliminary work in this area supports a theory of deficiency in the cognitive functioning of bipolar patients treated with lithium.[36,37] What may appear to be cognitive dysfunction has profound effect upon the lives of these patients, their families, and those who try to treat them. It incites feelings of helplessness, despair, and fury in many clinicians, resulting in rejection of the bipolar patient for any more than medication supervision. In time, repeated rejections reinforce the patient's crucial vulnerabilities, and leads to further symptomology, often of massive proportions. Memory loss and cognitive deficiency may be a response to the distress these patients feel as well as the stress under which many of them live, rather than an organic impairment which limits their interactional possibilities.

One example of an apparent deficit with clear dynamic origins occurs regularly in our groups, which are designed so that after a period of approximately two years, the male co-therapist leaves for another assignment. After many years of witnessing this phenomenon, we can depend on our patients to either forget entirely or mispronounce the name of the new therapist for at least the next nine months, and sometimes even to the end of the physician's tour. Although it remains frustrating, we have learned to accept this denial as symptomatic of an earlier failure to resolve separations and losses and a manifestation of anger at being left, rather than the result of an actual cognitive deficit. The loss of significant parenting persons experienced by many of our patients,[28] combined with exaggerated dominance of the remaining parent, reinforce character traits, including dependability, emphasis on performance, and perfectionism. Infantile omnipotence, grandiosity, and narcissism are thus reinforced. These become significant adaptive traits and also serve a major defensive purpose in dealing with loss and separations. Treating the manic-depressive patient requires an awareness of the enormous sensitivity to the slightest clue or anticipation of loss. The therapist must be continually aware that the bipolar patient is unable to deal with, integrate, or resolve this constant predicament.

Some have postulated that cognitive deficiency is based on the bipolar patients' inability to directly express feelings, difficulties in integrating positive feelings, and seeming unwillingness to consider alternative forms of conflict resolution. For most patients, everything is polarized, with nothing inbetween. There are no gray areas; everything is either black or white. Calling such failures of integration cognitive deficits is questionable. Nonetheless, the integrative failures must be understood in order for therapy to be effective. For example, during a hypomanic episode, a patient threatened to leave his wife; such threats were frequent and state-dependent. As his mood modulated and with the encouragement of the group, he enumerated his wife's many admirable qualities, admitted fears that she no longer loved him, and decided he could "forgive" her self-protective behavior during the episode. However, when his wife informed him in the same session that she intended, nonetheless, to become self-supporting, he became enraged and reverted again to threats proclaiming that she obviously no longer cared for him and that the marriage was no longer viable. It was as if her positive qualities, and the reasons for maintaining the marriage no longer existed. Compromise was impossible. Sustained group support in the next several sessions was required to focus on the distortions, and examine the patient's pathologic thinking and its potentially destructive consequences.

We have often noted the uncanny ability of our group members to identify the weakness in the relationship of other couples; to observe, correct, and emulate. The members learn new adaptive modes from the modeling of other group members and their therapists. Modeling may appear relatively benign, but actually is a powerful force for change among group members who seek social approval. Patient and spouse identify with similar couples, and realize that their own behavior may not be constructive or adaptive. It is important for a bipolar couple to deal with fantasies that the patient is basically bestial, and to learn that the patient is, in fact, suffering from a diagnosable illness. This realization lessens the terror surrounding the illness. The spouse, as well as the patient who is dysphoric or hypomanic, can find comfort and unique understanding in a therapeutic group relationship with others who identify with their experiences and who are not rejecting. When the couple also identifies with the others' conflict and does not reject them, this is empathetic support which allows for growth. The couples contribute in ways that go beyond problem-solving. When members empathize and endure with a couple through a crisis, the struggling pair learns that others find them of value. This is the exact situation so tentative and precarious in the psychodynamic constellation of bipolar patients, and this sense of validation of self-esteem in the group may be decisive.

In this way, homogenous groups provide a setting for the disclosure of maladaptive responses and interactions which maintain faulty personality functioning. When defensive organization among group members is similar, there is less opportunity for dissembling by the couple being discussed. This facilitates reconstruction, and allows exploration to take place. Intervention occurs through interruption of the transactions of the bipolar couple. For example, in one session, a hypomanic patient angrily discussed a long-standing pattern of resentment toward his supervisor in a company where the patient had been employed many years prior and subsequent to the onset of his illness. In the past, impulsive and volatile action on the patient's part had led to demotion and cancelled the likelihood of further promotion. The patient was willing to examine this in the group and listen to suggestions to put his present complaints in writing, as well the experiences of others regarding the "unfairness" and "stupid-ity" of supervisors. A long-standing resentment of authority figures was confirmed by the spouse, who also revealed her unwillingness to even discuss the current crisis at home, because she knew the patient's rage would descend upon her. It is worth noting that the group was able to acknowledge the resemblance of the behavior in both work and family systems.

In our therapeutic work, we attempt to treat and alter the symbiotic relationship of the couple. For the patient to accomplish this alone without psychotherapeutic intervention would be difficult. The bipolar patient's narcissism with its omnipotent expectations of the spouse must first be identified and examined before the patient can appreciate its significance, and begin to relinquish it. For example, in one group, a hypomanic, irritable patient brought to the session an irrational rage which she felt toward her spouse and children. The family was notified that a special-delivery package was being held at the post office during the hours the patient was at work. She became enraged when her husband and children decided that they could not call for the package during the appointed hours, and that it could wait until the weekend when someone would be free. The patient was unable to accept that her husband and sons had examined their priorities and made a responsible decision. The patient thought the consequences were catastrophic and that she would be held responsible. It was as if she sensed that the symbiosis was broken, someone would have to accept blame, and in her omnipotence, the patient was the chosen one. This particular couple are at a stage in their group treatment where the patient wants to continue the symbiotic relationship, and the spouse wants to individuate. The material they bring to group is used to focus on the patient's unrealistic expectations and on the manner in which she sets herself up for disappointment.

We have emphasized, almost exclusively, the pathology in the marital relationship of bipolar couples. Although the couples we have described may have sought each other out to supplement self-deficiencies antedating their marriages, there are, nevertheless, elements of human warmth, affection, and responsibility in their relationship, which are essential ingredients in any lasting marriage. On many occasions in the group, unusual stamina has been displayed by couples faced with a severe episode recurrence. The appearance of an acute episode of bipolar illness in a child requires even greater fortitude. Many marital conflicts which are discussed in the group are similar to those seen in most marital therapy groups. The identification of one spouse as a patient on medication, and the pathologic affect so often visible in the group setting are unique qualities. Minimizing the impact of these factors on the marriage is the purpose of the group.

SUMMARY AND CONCLUSIONS

There are several specific therapeutic advantages that the couples psychotherapy group modality provides for bipolar patients: (1) spouse involvement counteracts patient efforts to distort, deny, and flee treatment; (2) diffusion of transference reduces anxiety about intimacy and close-ness; (3) a supportive group copes with fears about the genetic component of the illness; (4) mutual sensitivity results in early warnings, permitting earlier drug or psychotherapeutic intervention; and (5) group cohesiveness with the common denominator of affective illness supports the thrust toward socially desirable behavior. Sharing the predicament offers unique sources both of support and of limit-setting.

These conclusions derive from a study in which the outcomes of 65 married, bipolar patients, previously hospitalized at the NIMH for an acute manic episode and discharged with a recommendation for continued lithium therapy, were compared. The followup study occured 2 to 10 years (mean, 3.9 years) after hospital discharge, and included 12 patients from our clinic who were receiving couples group psychotherapy, in conjunction with lithium maintenance. We found that the overall outcome was poor for the 53 patients not in a couples group. Eighteen patients had experienced rehospitalization for recurrence of a manic or depressive episode; 14 patients were divorced and two separated; 3 had committed suicide; and, overall, 39 patients had suffered unfavorable changes in job status or reported impaired occupational functioning. However, the 12 patients who were in couples group therapy at follow-up had no rehospital-izations or marital disruptions, and appeared on a more benign post-hospital course as measured by current work status, social functioning, family adjustment, and mental status.[38]

A finding of no major life disruptions among the patients receiving both lithium maintenance and couples group psychotherapy did not definitively establish the effectiveness of the couples' modality for bipolar patients. Methodologically, the sample was small; it was not possible to control for pretreatment differences, or for the self-selecting factors of staying in a group. In addition, we were unable to find control groups in the community for comparison. On the other hand, we felt the lessening and avoidance of major life disruptions were, in part, attributable to the uniquely sustaining quality of the couples' alliance with the group.

The therapeutic task has been primarily one of intervention, interpre-tation, and re-education. The therapeutic work at times seems repetitious, but the social isolation experienced by many bipolar patients and their families suggests a continuing need for group interaction, which sustains reeducation and provides new learning tools. Ongoing interpretation of the interaction of a couple is essential if the quality of their lives together is to change.

We hoped that the group modality would permit intervention early enough to prevent rehospitalization, and this has happened for most of our patients. We had also hoped that marital treatment might have some impact on the children of these marriages. However, two rehospitalizations have occurred among the adult members of our current groups. In addition, there have been several psychiatric hospitalizations of young adult offspring from these families. Our sample is too small for true measurement of the effectiveness of the groups, and cannot separate out which positive changes are due to medication effectiveness or due to psychotherapeutic effectiveness. Nor can we say with certainty that learning new coping skills will lessen the impact of a genetic vulnerability, in site of overall good results found in couples treated in our groups and their families. Nonetheless, our impression is that combined therapy including homogeneous groups is significantly more powerful—often decisively so—than drug treatment alone.

It is to be expected that the effectiveness of lithium carbonate treatment with its good prognosis for approximately 80 percent of bipolar patients will mean that more will marry and have children. A recent survey indicated that primarily because of misdiagnosis, between one third and one half of persons with bipolar disorder in the United States are currently not receiving treatment.[39] The economic impact of failure to treat, or inadequate treatment, of persons with manic-depressive illness is astronomical, quite apart from the unnecessary human suffering and misery caused by this illness. We know that medication is essential in any consideration of the treatment of the bipolar patient. Methodologic problems remain as to the relative efficacy of medication and psychotherapy, especially when used in combination. New systematic studies are needed, but in the meantime, our clinical observations suggest that the homogeneous married couples group does provide an effective therapeutic approach for altering malignant defenses and providing opportunities for change and growth.

REFERENCES

1. Carlson GA, Kotin J, Davenport YB, Adland ML: Follow-up of 53 bipolar manic-depressive patients. Br J Psychiatry 124:134–139, 1974
2. Winokur G, Morrison J, Clancy J, Crowe RR: The Iowa 500. Arch Gen Psychiatry 27:462–464, 1972
3. Kraepelin E: Manic-Depressive Insanity and Paranoia, Barclay M (trans). Edinburgh, ES Lovington, 1921

4. Freud S: Mourning and melancholia, in Collected Papers, vol 4. London, Hogarth Press, 1956

5. Abraham K: A short study of the development of the libido, viewed in the light of mental disorders, in Seclected Papers on Psychoanalysis. London, Hogarth Press, 1949

6. Abraham K: Notes on the psychoanalytical investigation and treatment of manic-depressive insanity and allied conditions, in Selected Papers on Psychoanalysis. London, Hogarth Press, 1949

7. Cohen MB, Baker G, Cohen RA, Fromm-Reichman F et al: An intensive study of 12 cases of manic-depressive psychosis. Psychiatry 17:103–137, 1954

8. Fromm-Reichman F: Intensive psychotherapy of manic-depressive: Part II. Confin Neurol 9:158–165, 1949

9. Gibson R: The family background and early life experience of the manic-depressive patient. Psychiatry 21:71–90, 1958

10. Fromm-Reichman F: Discussion of English, O Spurgeon: Observations of trends in manic-depressive psychosis. Psychiatry 12:125–134, 1949

11. Smith J: The metaphor of the manic-depressive. Psychiatry 23:375–383, 1960

12. Finley C, Wilson D: The relation of the family to manic-depressive psychoses. Dis Nerv Syst 12:39–43, 1951

13. Jacobson E: Interaction between psychotic partners: I. manic-depressive partners, in Eisenstadt (ed) Neurotic Interaction in Marriage. New York, John Wiley, 1956

14. Feighner JP, Robins E, Guze SB: Diagnostic criteria for use in psychiatric research. Arch Gen Psychiatry 26:57–63, 1972

15. Spitzer RL, Endicott J, Robbins E: Research diagnostic criteria, rationale, and reliability. Arch Gen Psychiatry 35:773–782, 1978

16. Yalom I: The Theory and Practice of Group Psychotherapy. New York, Basic Books, 1970

17. Ostow M: Drugs in Psychoanalysis and Psychotherapy. New York, Basic Books, 1962

18. Lewisohn PM: A behavioral approach to depression, in Friedman RJ, Katz MM (eds): The Psychology of Depression. Washington, Winston & Sons, 1974

19. Beck AT, Shaw BF: Cognitive approaches to depression. in Ellis A, Gruger R (eds): Handbook of Rational Emotion Theory and Practice. New York, Springer, 1977

20. Klerman G, et al: Treatment of depression by drugs and psychotherapy. Am J Psychiatry 131:186–203, 1974

21. Friedman AS: Interaction of drug therapy with marital therapy in depressive patients. Arch Gen Psychiatry 32:619–637, 1975

22. Shakir SA, Volkmar FR, Bacon S, Pfefferbaum A: Group Psychotherapy as an adjunct to lithium maintenance. Am J Psychiatry 136:455–456, 1979

23. Brodie HKH, Leff MJ: Bipolar depression—a comparative study of patient characteristics. Am J Psychiatry 127:1086–1090, 1971

24. Fitzgerald R: Mania as a message: treatment with family therapy and lithium carbonate. Am J Psychiatry 26:547–555, 1972

25. Demers R, Davis L: The influence of prophylactic lithium treatment on the marital adjustment of manic-depressives and their spouses. Compr Psychiatry 12:348–353, 1971

26. Greene BL, Lustig N, Lee, RRL: Marital therapy when one spouse has a primary affective disorder. Compr Psychiatry 19:565–570, 1978

27. Ruestow P, Dunner DL, Bleecher B, Fieve RR: Marital adjustment in primary affective disorder. Compr Psychiatry vol 19, no. 6, 1978

28. Ablon SL, Davenport YB, Gershon ES, Adland ML: The married manic. Am J Orthopsychiatry 45,5:854–866, 1975

29. Davenport YB, Adland ML, Gold PW, Goodwin FK: Manic-depressive illness: psychodynamic features of multigenerational families. Am J Orthopsychiatry 49:24–35, 1979

30. Gershon ES, Dunner DL, Sturt L, Goodwin FK: Assortative mating in the affective disorders: A preliminary report. Biol Psychiat 7:63–74, 1973

31. Dunner DL, Fleiss JL, Addanizio G, Fieve RR: Assortative mating in primary affective disorder. Biol Psychiatr 11:43–51, 1976

32. Targum SD, Dibble ED, Davenport YB, Gershon ES: The family attitudes questionnaire: patients and spouses view bipolar illness. Arch Gen Psychiatry (in press)

33. Dibble ED, Davenport YB, Guroff, JJ: Maladaptive Attitudes of Manic-Depressive Patients and Their Spouses: Measurements and Therapeutic Implications. Presented at annual meeting of the American Orthopsychiatric Association, Washington, DC, 1979

34. Weissman AN, Beck AT: Development and validation of the dysfunctional attitude scale. Paper presented at the Annual Meeting of the Association for Advancement of Behavior Therapy, Chicago, 1978

35. Framo JL: Marriage therapy in a couples group, in Block DA (ed): Techniques of Family Psychotherapy, New York, Grune & Stratton, 1973, pp 87–97

36. Reus VI, Weingartner H, Post RM: Clinical implications of state-dependent learning. Am J Psychiatry 136:7, 1979

37. Reus VI, Targum SD, Weingartner H, Post R: Effect of lithium carbonate on memory processes of bipolar affectively ill patients. Psychopharmacology 63:39–42, 1979

38. Davenport YB, Ebert MH, Adland ML, Goodwin FK: Couples group therapy as an adjunct to lithium maintenance of the manic patient. Am J Orthopsychiatry 47:3, 495–502, 1977

39. Bipolar Disorder: A State of the Science Report. Medical Practice Information Demonstration Project, Baltimore, Policy Research Incorporated, 1979

Joseph Richman

8

Suicide and the Family: Affective Disturbances and Their Implications for Understanding, Diagnosis, and Treatment

This chapter will explore the interaction between the suicidal patient and the family, with emphasis upon affective features as they are evidenced in diagnostic and therapeutic family interviews. Additionally, it will examine some of the roots of suicidal behavior in family dynamics and structure, and discuss their implications for psychotherapy. The presentation will inevitably touch upon earlier statements on the subject, but the affective emphasis and much of the data are new.

Suicide has been called a basically individual[1], irreducibly social[2], or fundamentally biologic act. All of them are, in some sense, correct. Suicide is best understood as the end result of a process or pattern of biologic, psychological, familial, and social (as well as accidental), circumstances. Any single suicidal act may be attributed to any one of these factors, such as a biologically based psychotic depression. However, 'cause' is a misleading concept here. A depression does not cause suicide, any more than psychodynamic pressures, marital tensions or family conflicts do; rather, all contribute to the total situation. In therapy, for example, both the depression and the family problems would be treated, not the depression alone.

Indeed, suicide *is* intimately related to family factors; likewise is the overcoming or healing of a suicidal despair intimately related to the family. Individual motives and precipitants almost always appear in a context of other individuals whose motives and strivings are relevant; and all are part of a familial and social network. The biologic predisposition of one member of the network may be relevant to the suicide of another member; similarly, the presence of facilitating social circumstances occur within the social network. Suicide is best studied, therefore, as the act of an individual in the social context.[3] The most fitting setting in which to examine this phenomenon is the family, where we can simultaneously look at those interactions between the individual and the significant others which may lead to a self-destructive resolution.

The deceptiveness of the individual component, when viewed outside of the social context, was brought home early in personal experiences with suicidal patients. In 1965, the author interviewed a 57-year-old man with intractable, unremitting pain as the progressive result of a variety of physical ailments: diabetes, an ulcer, severe arthritis, and an inoperable tumor of the spine that, while benign, kept him imprisoned in a wheelchair in a third-floor walk-up apartment. Finally, in disgust, he slashed his wrists and ankles, and was brought to our emergency room.

I naturally sympathized with the man's plight on the basis of his account and believed that I would do the same under those circumstances. However, the context changed when I called in his son to notify him that his father would be hospitalized. The son was eager to talk, and described his father as a tyrant who controlled his wife and children through his ailments, making everyone suffer. On the day in question, there had been a tremendous quarrel, culminating in the family members walking out, leaving the man alone. It was on this occasion that he made his suicide attempt.

The son's story, so different from his father's, was a revelation at the time. It was that experience which formed the basis of my diagnostic assessment of suicidal potential, consisting since then of a series of individual interviews and evaluations, followed by a family interview. The family interview also discloses family patterns and difficulties that are usually concealed, often unknown to the other family members but nonetheless relevant to the suicidal act.

In the assessment and family treatment of suicidal patients over a 15-year period, seven characteristics of these families have consistently emerged:

1. An inability to accept necessary change, including:
   - An intolerance for separation
   - A symbiosis without empathy
   - A fixation upon infantile patterns and the primary or earliest family relationships

2. Role conflicts, failures, and fixations

3. A disturbed family structure, including:
   - A closed family system

- A prohibition against intimacy outside the family
- An isolation of the potentially suicidal person within the family
- A quality of family fragility

4. Affective difficulties, including:
   - A unipolar pattern of aggression
   - A family depression, hopelessness, etc.
   - Pervasive separation and death anxiety
   - Sexual disturbances
   - An intolerance of all affects

5. Unbalanced or unipolar intrafamilial relationships, including:
   - A specific kind of scapegoating
   - Double-binding sadomasochistic relationships
   - A turning of the potentially suicidal person into the bad object for the entire family

6. Transactional difficulties, including:
   - Communication disturbances
   - Excessive secretiveness

7. An intolerance for crises

AFFECTIVE DISTURBANCES

This section concentrates upon the fourth family characteristic noted above: the area of affective disturbances and their treatment implications. In order to round out the picture, attention will be given to the other aspects, especially problems around separation, social role functioning, and the closed family system; all of these will be examined in their relationship to affect and therapy.

Affective disturbances refer to the family system components involved in the arousal, type, and discharge of tensions. It concerns the social context rather than psychiatric or biologic classifications. Within this social framework two main features stand out: the rules governing drive expression and discharge, and the prevailing affect or mood in the home conducive to depression and morbidity. Thus, the material in this section is derived largely from clinical observation and some strikingly confirmatory instances in the literature on the expression of feelings, emotions, and drives within the family context.

Since Freud's *Mourning and Melancholia*,[4] suicide has been considered the outcome of the vicissitudes of aggression. Thus, suicide has been described facetiously as "murder in the 180th degree," aggression against someone else turned against the self and a response to the death wishes of significant others.[4,5]

While the value and validity of all these formulations must be recognized, they nonetheless can be criticized for their exclusive emphasis upon the aggressive drive. Suicidal persons have anxiety reactions, depressive reactions, and sexual as well as other impulses which are often prominent components of the tensions leading to a suicidal act. As such, a broad range of areas will be considered under the rubric *affect*, including affective expression (or its tolerance) in general, anxiety, sex, aggression, depression, and hopelessness, in particular.

There is a noteworthy similarity between the phenomena to be described here and the borderline syndromes described by Kernberg and others.[6,7] In the author's experience, the majority of suicidal individuals have been diagnosed as borderline. A family-oriented approach is particularly valuable with such patients, for its contribution to the understanding of splitting, fragmentation, primitive affective reactions, panic anxiety, and so forth; in dual regard to the origins in the past and their maintenance in the present. Such disturbances can be resolved or alleviated through the renewal of the healing and growth forces in the family.

Intolerance of All Affects

In the families we have seen, withdrawal and impulsivity are polarized responses to emotional situations which may be overtly frowned upon yet covertly reinforced. Genuine spontaneity, on the other hand, is perceived as a threat, and the free expression of feeling is reacted to with discomfort and various indications of disapproval. Feelings, however, may be discharged impulsively after a buildup of tensions, but rarely as an expression of the individual. Feelings induced within the family framework are another matter: The induction of humiliation and shame, for example, are frequent methods of control in order to maintain homeostasis. One major implication is that impulsivity is a learned phenomenon which, at least in part, follows social and family rules.

This paucity of spontaneity has been discussed elsewhere as an aspect of the disturbance of empathy in the suicidogenic family.[8] Briefly, to have an emotion is a uniquely individual act; a feeling is indubitably one's own, and an announcement that one is a separate entity. Of course, an intolerance of affects does not mean an absence of affects. Because these affects cannot be discharged appropriately within an interpersonal context, they cannot become directed into sublimated or socially acceptable channels, or be manifested in a situation of emotional rapport.

Instead, they remain primitive, raw, fused, and undifferentiated. Due to the autonomy implied by an individual's freedom of feeling, this results in an overwhelming resistance to the recognition of the presence of such feelings. This pattern precludes an ability to cry with others, for example, or to laugh together.

A 17-year-old, suicidal, epileptic girl was hospitalized because of an overdose. She began crying shortly after the family interview began. Her mother's response upon entering the room was to become furious and angrily exclaim, "You don't care for me; you only think of yourself."

Such reactions may encompass warm as well as angry feelings. One daughter said to her mother, "I want to have a positive relationship with you." Again the mother became furiously angry, and replied, "You say that now. Why did you wait all these years?"

Anxiety

Anxiety is the emotional spur behind the basic experiences of separation, symbiosis, and early fixations, which, in effect, direct all that follows: Its prevailing expression is in the form of anxiety about death and separation. A more accurate term might be *separation/symbiosis/fixation anxiety*, but for brevity and convenience, the term *separation anxiety* will be used throughout. Such anxiety is seen, for example, in the turmoil and fights in the family surrounding a teenager's choosing companions, and choosing self-destructive activities like drug addiction;[9,10] it is also central to suicide attempts surrounding the dissolution of a marriage or love affair. In each of these cases, the threat of loss by autonomy, death, or separation proves overwhelming. In more or less subtle forms, the separation anxiety and family contexts of these situations may be less evident, but they are the forces behind suicides associated with financial failure, social disgrace, illness, or the death of loved ones.

A 28-year-old man was the last child still living at home. His mother became intolerably anxious whenever he left the house. All the other children had moved out, and he was chosen (as it were) by siblings to be the companion for their depressed and lonely mother. The young man was a polio victim who believed that his physical disability was the cause of his mother's depression. It was also a major reason given for his serious suicide attempt, which he made while having difficulties fitting his leg braces. On fuller consideration, the suicide attempt seemed based upon his assigned role as the 'security blanket' for his mother.

A 40-year-old suicidal man illustrates the same point. He had miraculously survived a six-story fall from his apartment, which occurred while his mother was having her second heart attack. As in the previous case, his brother was able to leave home, marry, and work productively. The older son was never able to separate, and is at present a very disturbed, chronically schizophrenic alcoholic. He was, nonetheless, well-motivated for psychotherapy, and his family (including the married brother) all agreed to enter family therapy. Therapy began with a very promising agreement about financial and living arrangements. The patient was to attend a day hospital program; he also joined Alcoholics Anonymous. In a few weeks, however, mother and son became embroiled in severe conflicts. The mother began making what seemed like insatiable demands for money and care from her suicidal son, expressing the belief that she would soon die. His needs, which had so recently received recognition, were submerged. As a result, the patient became depressed, regressed, and murderously angry, demanding hospitalization. The therapy is still continuing on an outpatient basis. The basic problem is the mother's panic anxiety whenever her son leaves (to go to the day hospital, or, for that matter anywhere else). She is afraid that she will die alone while he is away. This is not a new reaction. When her son was 17 and left the house to go out on a date, she was subject to the same panic attacks. She would imagine that something had happened to him and would scream, "He's dead; I know he's dead!" making her husband telephone the police. In essence, her separation and death panic only subsided when her son was physically with her.

Sexual Disturbances

The issue of aggression has tended to dominate the psychodynamic investigation of suicidality. However important aggression may be, it is valuable to return to the speculations of the early psychoanalysts. In an historic psychoanalytic symposium on suicide in 1910,[11] pioneering analysts reported that masturbation guilt was often a prominent feature in the suicidal behavior of young people. Sullivan[12] also saw adolescent suicide as rooted in masturbation guilt and sexual conflicts.

Times have changed, and so, allegedly, have sexual mores. Nevertheless, a recent confirmation of the significance of sexual conflicts may be drawn from the paper by Resnik,[13] in his study of death by strangulation in teenagers. He found that many of these youths had actually killed themselves by accident in the course of a masturbatory ritual, which consisted of fastening a noose around their necks while masturbating. Incidentally, such procedures occur with much greater frequency than is ordinarily recognized.

In addition to the factors of masturbation and sexual impotence, we found that the amount of incestuous sexual contact within the families of our suicidal patients was quite remarkable. (Most of these subjects were girls, but boys were involved too.) In this context, it is of interest to note that Virginia Woolf, who committed suicide at age 59 after a long history of suicidal behavior and several unsuccessful attempts, had been sexually molested from the age of 6 until well into her teens by a half-brother who was 14 years her senior.[14] The phenomenon of incest in the background of suicidal persons is not limited to any one class, but extends into all social and economic levels. With young suicidal males, these incestuous acts are more concealed than in females, and they become the nucleus of a widening sense of guilt and depravity.

Another feature noted in these families was the pervasively sado-masochistic nature of the sexual relationships outside the home. As a result, successful, mature relationships were not possible, and there was little happiness or satisfaction in the relationship. It is evident that the function of these unworkable, unstable, unhappy, and unsatisfactory sexual arrangements may well be the avoidance of intimacy and commitment by both partners, in order to maintain the earlier infantile fixations or primary relationships that would otherwise be threatened. Primary relationships refer to ties to the first objects in the child's life, usually those of mother, father, and siblings. A major step in ego and social development is the move from primary to secondary relationships, ie, with a person outside the original family.

While incest, masturbation, and their equivalents may be a problem for the youthful suicidal individual, sexual impotence is a serious and frequently fatal precipitant of depression and surrender in the elderly. An example is that of a widowed 70-year-old man, who, when involved with a younger woman, found himself impotent.[15] He told a cousin, "If I can't be all man with her, then I don't want to live." He took an overdose of medication, and while in the hospital, jumped from a window to his death. There was much more to this man's suicide, of course, than his relationship with the younger woman; a great deal of study is needed regarding the relationship between sex and suicide.

In summary, sexual disturbances and conflicts appear to be as common findings in histories of suicidal situations as are overt problems with aggression. There are many good reasons for this association: Sexuality is associated with role definition and personal differentiation. Sexuality also impels people outside of their family of origin and primary object relationships into new relationships and the beginning of families of one's own. The high cost of individuating is why sexuality is such a problem for suicidal persons and their families of origin, and why incest is so frequently found. Sexuality and aggression are not separated, but rather fused and confused. Aggression, however, has wider manifestations than sexuality alone, as shall be seen.

Nonreciprocal Aggressive Impulses

This is a most important area, addressing tremendously angry feelings and the communication of death wishes and instructions for the suicidal person to commit suicide. There is much clinical evidence in the literature of the presence of these phenomena,[16] although not all investigators have accepted the value or even the truth of these findings. Kobler and Stotland,[17] for example, in their investigation of an epidemic of suicides in a hospital, reported an account of a social worker who interviewed the mother of a patient shortly before the patient's suicide. The social worker wrote: "One interview was so full of death and morbidity in one form of another, including her statement that it would be easier to adjust to her son's death than to his mental illness, that I felt quite concerned about her ability to hold together." The authors admonished the social worker, and presented her account as an example of the prejudice that exists against relatives. However, that anonymous social worker's description was a faithful rendering of what we have heard repeatedly from relatives of suicidal patients, and we regard such statements as a basis for family treatment, not for condemnation.

DEPRESSED FAMILY ATMOSPHERE

Every home has an atmosphere, and a prevailing mood that lends the home familiarity and therefore comfort. In most homes there is also a variety of moods, depending upon changing times and conditions. In suicidogenic homes, however, there is less variety. Rather, gloom and doom are pervasive (at least when the family is together and there are no outsiders present). It is difficult for those dwelling in such a setting to escape depression, if only by osmosis. The fragile individual, who dominates the family, is most often at the center of this depression.[18] There is also one who must remain with the depressed (but dominant) fragile other, who is not permitted to leave. Just as there is a pattern whereby one person cannot leave, there is also a pattern whereby most family members can escape the noxious atmosphere. All others may, for example, go to their rooms while at home, remain out of the house a great deal, or marry early. But the potentially suicidal person cannot do this. Too-centrally a part of the suicidal family pattern; the potentially suicidal person has been designated for the role from a very early age. The individual may possess some physical or mental disability or weakness, be the youngest or oldest child, be the only girl or only boy, or symbolize some significant person in the family's past.

In the case of the 40-year-old suicidal man described in the discussion of anxiety, his mother expressed her belief that the problem stemmed from the family situation at the time of his birth. Her husband, the patient's father, had broken his back in an accident on the job just before the patient was born. The mother said she had therefore spent the first four years of her son's life in a state of constant fear and insecurity. This particular problem had presumably been resolved by the time her second son was born.

It is noted, then, that the affective atmosphere and the rules governing affective expression are essential aspects of the suicidal situation. It is suggested that these are designed to maintain infantile and pathologic patterns, prevent separation, and maintain homeostasis.

HOPELESSNESS, DESPAIR, AND GIVING UP

Hopelessness is another major aspect of the affective family situation, and its increase at the time of a suicidal crisis is a major danger signal. Like depression, despair may be a very contagious commodity. The oft-heard statement from the relatives of chronically suicidal patients, "Maybe he would be better off dead," is not necessarily a death wish or only a death wish. It is also an expression of that relative's hopelessness and having given up. These feelings in the significant relatives, verbalized or not, often precede an actual suicide or the more lethal attempts.

Bishop Pike, for example, reported feeling hopeless the day before his son committed suicide.[19] Another example is found in *In A Darkness*, written by the James Wechsler family, about the death of their son Michael.[20] Both the son and the family had been worn out by years of psychiatric problems and suicide attempts, and by a succession of therapists who had been largely ineffectual. Towards the end, Michael and his father had a quarrel, in which the son told him, "My doctor tells me I can't get better unless I can express my aggression." Wechsler recalls. "I remember an emotion of despair, a sense of futile reenactment at this reversion to the Freudian jargon... I also believe Michael must have seen an expression signifying hopelessness and that it must have in some way compounded his own deepening fears about himself." It was shortly afterwards that Michael ended his life.

Despair, hopelessness, and giving up, then, can be regarded as social systems phenomena, not purely individual feelings. Perhaps this family reaction (the presence of which is a secret and unbearable burden) is the primary reason why the family must be worked with and helped, not only the suicidal individual. The major lesson for those therapists who wish to help the seriously suicidal individual is, therefore, not to give up, to despair, or above all, to feel hopeless about feelings of hopelessness on the part of the family as well as the patient.

TREATMENT IMPLICATIONS

Three of my most recent referrals were an 11-year-old boy whose father had committed suicide and who was threatening to do the same; a 70-year-old man with a senile, demented wife and brain-damaged son, who was thinking of killing himself and taking his helpless family with him, and a 67-year-old paraplegic, a stroke victim in a nursing home, who slashed his wrists when his family did not visit him on Father's Day. In all cases, family-oriented therapy was decided upon as the treatment of choice, although the details of treatment differed. A treatment plan in which family therapy is included is necessary for each individual but is not necessarily the only ingredient.

Each plan is also age-dependent. The age-dependent differences in procedures range from play therapy with children to the establishment of supportive and social therapy with the elderly. (There *is* an overlap, and conceivably, for example, appropriately designed play therapy could be a potent therapeutic medium with the aged; but in general, there are age-related differences in treatment.) However, there are also commonalities in the family-oriented approach to assessment, management, and treatment. What follows applies to all age groups.

Assessment

In the context of this paper, assessment refers primarily to the evaluation of suicidal intent and the risk of a serious suicidal act. Within this frame of reference, the psychiatric diagnosis is relevant. Depression is rampant in most suicidal patients. Large numbers of suicidal patients have indulged heavily in alcohol or drugs. Impulse control tends to be poor and sporadic; the splitting of objects into good and bad is typical; and psychotic reactions (ranging from a few moments to several months) are frequent. These manifestations are best regarded as evidence of stress, strain, and decompensating controls. They are, therefore, indicators of severe suicidal potential. Past history, especially a history of early loss of a parent, family disorganization in childhood, and other historic and personality factors are vital to understanding why a person is suicidal; but they do not explain why a person is suicidal at this particular time. For the latter, it is necessary to know the nature of the person's current situation, the crises that are present, and social and familial features. The step-by-step procedures for evaluating suicidal potential[21] include a thorough evaluation of the suicidal person, an individual evaluation of each relative, a diagnostic family interview, and an exploration of the current situation, especially the changes and crises that are occurring.

The assessment method is based upon the belief that suicide is the outcome of three conditions: (1) the exhaustion of resources of the suicidal individual, so that the individual can no longer cope with the demands of life; (2) the exhaustion of family resources together with the unavailability, inability, or exhaustion of the resources of other social support systems; and (3) the presence of a crisis, which is perceived as insoluble and hopeless by everyone.

The assessment procedure is best conducted by the future therapist, because the evaluation method described here is a fruitful beginning for treatment. The conjoint family interview is the most important and vital part of the procedure. The interviewer has the opportunity to know each member of the family directly, not only to hear about them.

Nevertheless, this family-oriented approach is recommended only for those therapists who already have training and experience, and who have the ability to appropriately intervene to make contact with the family as a family, and to simultaneously be in touch with the suicidal patient. For such tasks, the skills of both the family therapist and suicidologist are required. Otherwise, there is a major danger that the interviewer may become part of the problem and lose therapeutic leverage. It has been an all-too-frequent experience that the family refuses to come for a interview on the grounds of unfortunate past experiences with family meetings, invariably with an inexperienced therapist.

Treatment

Considering the range, pervasiveness, and intensity of the affective disturbances in the suicidal patient and family, it comes as no surprise that the initial family therapy sessions are characterized by an outpouring of affectively-based reactions and complaints, including expressions of massive rage, death wishes, and the extremes of blaming and scapegoating. This is a desirable beginning, since the initial goal of treatment with the suicidal patient and family is to reduce anxiety and stress, although it is not always recognized as such. Too many therapists become alarmed and pessimistic in the face of these outbursts, and may even terminate therapy. Nevertheless, this release of tension is usually necessary. It is the beginning of a catalytic process which presages ultimate success. Since the anxiety behind these outbursts is basically a separation anxiety, the family is reassured at the outset that they do not need to separate until they are ready.

Social Role and Therapy

Role is an area at the interface between separation problems within the family, and relations with the outside world. It is, therefore, a powerful area for therapeutic intervention. It is advised not to deal directly with separation and related issues, but instead to aim to strengthen social role competence.

Suicidal people are characterized by failure in meeting their social role obligation in virtually every area of functioning at the time of the suicide attempt.[22] This holds true even in the case of someone as seemingly exceptional as Ernest Hemingway, who had been awarded the Pulitzer and Nobel Prizes for literature shortly before he killed himself. At the time of his death, however, he was brain-damaged, unable to write, and his family and social network were either unavailable or unable to support him.[23] Psychologically, then, Hemingway was in the same position as the suicidal patients described above.

In the study of social roles and suicide,[21] role failures associated with attempted suicide were found to be considerably more far-reaching and pervasive, and somewhat less tied to traditional role definitions than would be anticipated by earlier sociological studies.[24] Those early studies had concluded that suicide in men was associated with problems in their occupational roles, while suicide in women was associated with their sexual and familial roles. However, in our population, men were failures in their family, parental, and sexual roles, as well as in their work; while women were failures at work, as well as in their sexual and familial roles.

How is one to account for these role failures in the suicidal population? The answer lies, I believe, in the previously discussed difficulties in dealing with separation, with a resulting intolerance of outside contacts not controlled by the family system. The major role problem, therefore, is that of development and change from earlier roles to more mature roles. These changes seem to threaten the early relationships and the survival of the family system. The family thus takes steps to restore the family member to a previous role, thereby, maintaining the homeostasis.

Another factor to be considered in treatment is the presence of marked ambivalence over success or failure in social role competence. Because of the perceived threat, success is often considered as great a danger as failure. Nevertheless, the family is unduly sensitive to external demands and pushes the potentially suicidal person to succeed, while also communicating the message to fail. The patient may receive one message to succeed in work and school, for example, because that is expected by 'them' or 'others'; and yet another message to fail, because to do otherwise would raise the spectre of separation and loss. A painful bind may thus be created, which can only be resolved by psychosis or a suicidal act.

The role concept offered here outlines very helpful guides for therapy. First, some consideration of what not to do: because of the strength and tenacity of the early bonds, it is unwise to prematurely attempt to separate the suicidal person from the family or social system. Instead, it is through strengthening role competence that the therapist can best achieve what Tabachnick called the goal of "lessening the pathological relationship".[25] This occurs as the family members interact with each other in the family sessions. As tensions relax and the anxiety over separation subsides, the potentially suicidal person does begin to work, go to school, acquire less destructive companions, or even marry.

Nevertheless, concern has been expressed in some quarters about the potentially destructive effects of interfering in the family's role pattern. Experience has illustrated that the family therapist must, indeed, adhere to the Biblical injunctions: "Thou shalt not uncover thy father's nakedness," and "Honor they father and thy mother," no matter how unworthy the parents may appear. With suicidal patients, this attitude is a positive step toward improving the role relationship within the family.

Communication and Therapy

Most studies of suicide and communication deal with communications of suicidal intent by the self-destructive person,[26] but few if any suicide researchers have asked how these communications were received. From a family perspective, however, communication is best understood as part of a social pattern or system, with rules that include all the members of the communication network.[27]

For example, in the author's study of communications relevant to the development and appearance of suicidal tendencies, as well as verbalizations of depressive and suicidal ideation by the patient himself,[28] it was found that direct or indirect verbalizations of death wishes by significant others were prominent. Moreover, nonverbal communications were even more striking and central to the development of suicidal acts than those which were verbalized. Such nonverbal communications may include:

1. Ignoring or being impervious to expressions of suicidal intent
2. Physically leaving after hearing despairing of suicidal thoughts voiced
3. Physically turning away or turning one's back to the significant other

4. Being secretive, keeping suicidogenic communications of the family within the recesses of the home and concealed from the outside world
5. Presenting medical symptoms or illness by one or another family member with the implicit accusatory message, "You are killing me" (and thus must kill yourself)

A case in point was a 66-year-old woman whose suicide was attributed to psychotic depression. Initially, she was helped by electro-convulsive therapy but relapsed almost immediately into an intractably depressed state. Her husband developed chest pains, which were described as prodromal to a heart attack, and her son developed stomach pains, the presumed precursor of an ulcer. The woman said repeatedly, "I am killing my family. Everyone would be better off if I were dead." The family silently but eloquently agreed with her statement. Finally, she took a fatal dose of sleeping pills and antidepressents. In this particular case, the physical illnesses of her husband and son were communications that she was, in fact, killing her family, and would, therefore, have to kill herself if they were to survive.

The opportunity to directly intervene in these communication patterns is a major reason why family therapy can be of unique value. For example, in family therapy, anger and destructive wishes are expressed explicitly, rather than in the form of physical symptoms or other covert messages. That this occurs in the presence of a professional outsider, in and of itself changes its meaning. The therapist sympathetically labels such verbalizations as emotional expressions of an exasperated person, rather than as concrete instructions for someone to commit suicide.

In conclusion, although there are many other meaningful features relating to affective disturbances in the family therapy of suicidal persons, the areas of separation, the strengthening of social role competence, and the handling of suicidogenic communications are among those features that are most important, and ultimately, life-preserving.

SUMMARY

Arguments, anger, and intense destructive interchanges take place in most, or perhaps all, families, not only in those where suicide occurs. The family is both a battleground and a comfortable, safe basis. This chapter has focused upon the disturbances and disruptions that take place within the family which are conducive to a suicidal outcome in one of its members. However, an emphasis solely upon what is divisive and wrong can be too one-sided. There are positive features in those families we have seen, forces of integration and love.

There are no easy solutions to the problem of suicide; but, as noted, the key to successful relationships is a mutual committment of people to each other and the presence of a sense of humor.[29] It is through faith in these troubled families and their healthy potential that treatment and healing becomes possible.

REFERENCES

1. Dublin LI: Suicide: A Sociological and Statistical Study. New York, Ronald, 1963
2. DeVos G: Suicide in cross-cultural perspectives, in Resnik HLP (ed): Suicidal Behaviors: Diagnosis and Management. Boston, Little Brown, 1968, pp 105–134
3. Richman J: The social contexts of a suicide, in Litman RE (ed): Proceedings of the Sixth International Conference for Suicide Prevention. Ann Arbor, Edwards Brothers, 1972, pp 260–265
4. Freud S: Mourning and melancholia. Standard Edition (vol 14). London, Hogarth Press, 1957, pp 237–258
5. Rosenbaum M, Richman J: Suicide: The role of hostility and death wishes from the family and significant others. Am J Psychiatry 126:128–131, 1970
6. Kernberg OF: Borderline Conditions and Pathological Narcissism. New York, Jason Aronson, 1975
7. Kohut H: The Analysis of the Self. New York, International Universities Press, 1971
8. Richman J: Symbiosis, empathy, suicidal behavior, and the family. Suicide and Life-Threatening Behavior 8:139–150, 1978
9. Stanton MD: The addict as savior: Heroin, death, and the family. Family Process 16:191–197, 1977
10. Reilly DM: Death propensity, dying, and bereavement: A family systems perspective. Family Therapy 5:35–55, 1978
11. Friedman P (ed): On Suicide. New York, International Universities Press, 1967
12. Sullivan HS: Schizophrenia as a Human Process. New York, Norton, 1962, pp 338–339
13. Resnik HLP: Erotized repetitive hangings: A form of self-destructive behavior. Am J Psychother 26:4–21, 1972
14. Bell Q: Virginia Woolf. New York, Harcourt Brace Jovanovich, 1972
15. The individual, the institution and suicide: A case conference of the Department of Social Medicine, Montefiore. The New Physician 20: 646–649, 1971
16. Richman J, Rosenbaum M: A clinical study of the role of hostility and death wishes by the family and society in suicidal attempts. Israel Annals of Psychiatry and Related Disciplines 8:213–231, 1971
17. Kobler AL, Stotland E: The End of Hope. New York, Free Press, 1964

18. Richman J: Suicide and the closed family system. Proceedings of the Tenth International Congress for Suicide Prevention and Crisis Intervention. Ottawa, Canada, June 17–20, 1979, pp 329–332

19. Pike JA, Kennedy D: The Other Side. New York, Dell, 1969

20. Wechsler JA, Wechsler NE, Karpf HW: In a Darkness. New York, Ace, 1972

21. Richman J: Family therapy of attempted suicide. Family Process 18: 131–142, 1979

22. Richman J, Rosenbaum M: Role relationships in suicidal and nonsuicidal psychiatric patients, in Fox R (ed): Proceedings of the Fifth International Conference for Suicide Prevention. London, 1969

23. Baker C: Ernest Hemingway: A Life Story. New York, Bantam, 1970

24. Breed W: The suicide process, in Farberow NL (ed): Proceedings of the Fourth International Conference for Suicide Prevention. Los Angeles, Delmar, 1968, pp 286–291

25. Tabachnick ND: Interpersonal relations in suicide attempts: A psycho-dynamic formulation and some indications for treatment. Arch Gen Psychiatry 4:16–21, 1961

26. Murphy GD, Robbins, E: The communication of suicidal ideas, in Resnik HLP (ed): Suicidal Behaviors: Diagnosis and Management. Boston, Little Brown, 1968, pp 163–170

27. Watzlawick P, Beavin JH, Jackson DD: Pragmatics of Human Communication. New York, WW Norton, 1967

28. Richman J: The communication of suicidal intent within the family. Presented at the Sixth Annual Meeting of the American Association of Suicidology, Atlantic Beach, Florida, Ap 2, 1974

29. Reedy M: Review of "Walter and Sally," a 35mm filmstrip. Gerontologist 20:13–14, 1980

PART IV

Character, System, and Symptom in the Personality Disorders

Melvin R. Lansky

9

Treatment of the Narcissistically Vulnerable Marriage

Distinguishing a marriage that is characterized by narcissistic vulnerability from one that is not is crucial, not only in overtly conflictual marriages, but also in clinical situations affected by marital tensions that may find expression in other types of symptomatology. The latter situations include such varied phenomena as alcoholism or depression in a spouse; underfunctioning, aggressiveness, or promiscuity in children or adolescents; sexual dysfunctions; behavior disorders; addictive disorders; and a host of apparently straightforward psychotherapeutic situations that end in stalemate. For a couple without narcissistic vulnerability of clinical significance, many types of therapeutic experiences and even nonprofessional growth experiences may be helpful. For those marriages where narcissistic vulnerability is in evidence, understanding of the features of this vulnerability is essential in planning the strategies of technique to avoid inflicting narcissistic injury in the treatment process and to provide an experience in which truly generalizable emotional learning takes place. Most enduring marriages of narcissistically vulnerable patients occur between two such partners.[1] Experienced clinicians are often astounded at the underlying similarity between seemingly different type in such marriages. The major bond in the marriage is the opportunity for unconscious collusion in defensive operations that keep everyone in the family from being flooded with the awareness of inadequacy. This is the primary psychological gain.[2] There may be secondary gains superimposed. Considering the prevalence of such marriages, the difficulties posed in treatment, the refractoriness of symptomatology if the marital difficulty persists, and the variety of clinical situations in which narcissistically vulnerable marriages prove to be the central and primary focus of therapeutic intervention, the distinction between a narcissistically vulnerable marriage and one that is not cannot be emphasized too strongly.

BLAME AND COLLUSION: FOUR HISTORIES

Case 1

A woman in her early forties entered conjoint therapy with full knowledge that she resorted to blame a great deal. "I'm a yeller. I yell and get it all out of my system and then it's all over." She berated her husband constantly for dominating her, influencing her decisions, and making all the decisions in the marriage with no input from her. There was little sex in the marriage. There was constant quarreling. Sessions organized around negotiating decisions came off to her apparent satisfaction, but she remained skeptical even when she admitted that the agreements were kept; she maintained that her husband would change his mind anyway and do what he pleased. He was a businessman, and she worked in his office. Efforts to examine the consequences for the marriage of working so closely together resulted in protestations that she was not really trained but did professional-level management. They came home together but rarely spoke. She spent time by herself and he read. They quarreled about in-laws, vacations, expenditures, decorating, their children, and the office.

She complained of marked depression, weight loss, and broken sleep, and was begun on amitryptiline, 75mg daily. There was marked improvement. Blaming stopped. They began having fun together. Mood and appetite improved, and friction around the house diminished. She stopped the medication, saying that it only left her in more of a position to be taken advantage of. She was less guarded and aggressive and could the more be dominated. The equilibrium quickly reverted to the previous state in a matter of days, but she refused to resume medication. "He says 'take your pill' as though I'm the crazy one." Her husband agreed that he was quite picky about how he wanted the house decorated; the office run; restaurants, friends, and vacations chosen; and many features connected with raising the children. He, too, was dissatisfied and contemplated divorce, but the idea of her working in a separate place was unthinkable, and he could not manage to spend so much as an afternoon engaged in his own pursuits. The couple's only friends were business contacts with whom they socialized as couples, presumably for business reasons.

In conjoint sessions and in the few individual sessions that were scheduled, each spoke of difficulties as if they emanated solely from the shortcomings of the other spouse. When this was pointed out to them after lengthy conjoint therapy, they both agreed but continued to talk, without any notion that, for there to be changes in the marriage, both must see change as coming from themselves. Her parents' marriage was characterized by surface domination by her father and perpetual threats of separation by both parents; she was drawn in as peacemaker at an early age. His parents lived an unhappy life together without overt talk of separation.

Case 2

A couple in their fifties appeared for therapy shortly before the last of their children left home, leaving them together for the first time in several decades. They wanted to rework their marriage. She, in particular, was unhappy with it. She was furious about the number of extramarital affairs that her husband had had. The couple had agreed to let bygones be bygones, and to try to negotiate a better relationship. The issue of trust came rapidly to the fore, and every effort to make the relationship deepen was met with constant reminders on her part about the past, and anger because she could not count on him. He protested that the affairs had occurred some years before, and were not ongoing currently. She felt that he habitually slighted her socially—when the two of them were together with his associates—and that she still couldn't trust him. He admitted that he had done so, and one focus of therapy became his public insults and broadcasted infidelities that assured her mistrust and invited her suspiciousness and blaming. Getting caught for transgressions was a dominant issue in his childhood and adolescent struggle for recognition from his parents; after these issues were discussed, he assured her that his misconduct was entirely in the past that he wished to negotiate a better marriage. She said she would have to be certain.

The therapist asked if she could really imagine circumstances that would put her at ease, and she couldn't. Her thoughts went to the professional career that she had given up, and all that she had passed up to hold the family together. The implications of her feeling cheated early in life were explored, but the feelings remained unchanged, as did her conviction that she had been cheated in the marriage. As her own reluctance to negotiate a better marriage became more and more evident, she withdrew from the therapy and complained of lifelong depression and emptiness. The suggestion was made that this issue be explored conjointly and, perhaps, in individual sessions with another therapist. She gave the idea some thought but progressively withdrew more and more from the sessions, finally breaking off the therapy.

Case 3

A man in his late thirties berated his wife for being a few minutes late to a conjoint therapy session. He screamed and yelled, hurling vile epithets at her for being unreliable, undependable, and causing him to worry about her protection. She was like a little girl, he said, and couldn't take responsibility, couldn't be reliabile, couldn't even apologize for letting him down. The therapist pointed to the vehemence of his response (without success), in getting him to consider if the vehemence were fed by other issues. The issue seemed trivial, but her constant placating seemed to invite more blame and abusiveness from him and to keep him in an almost frenzied state as they argued session after session. Both spouses had been left by one parent early in life, and the other parent before adolescence. The wife had secured some attention from her sisters by inviting and enduring their constant criticism and harassment. The husband had been raised by a grandmother and two aunts who belittled men and made fun of his masculine traits throughout his upbringing. Similar incidents peppered a very chaotic therapy almost constantly, until the husband was jailed for a lengthy period of time following his apprehension during the clumsy execution of a burglary.

Case 4

In a session between a depressed man with a cardiac condition and his wife, blaming was the typical transaction. His wife berated him constantly for his shortcomings, and he attacked her for her personality traits. At the end of one session, he remained afterward to tell the therapist (begging her to keep it confidential) that he would kill himself if his wife left. Later that day she phoned the therapist to say, in confidence, she presumed, that she was leaving. The next session began with the couple quarreling about some trivial matter external to the marriage. The therapist was experienced enough not to agree to secrecy and tactfully brought up both communications, the secrecy and the apparent indifferenc to the weighty matters being discussed. The particular crisis subsided after their attention was drawn to their communications, but the blaming transactions continued. Some months later the husband had a myocardial infarction and was admitted to the medical ward. At that time his mood improved markedly and the relationship improved dramatically while he was on the medical ward. They did not return to marital therapy.

FEATURES OF THE NARCISSISTICALLY VULNERABLE MARRIAGE

The more overt type of chronically conflictual narcissistically vulnerable marriage may be easily seen in an initial interview with a couple presenting with marital difficulties. Such marriages are easier to spot than when difficulties are covered over by overt symptoms in one spouse identified as a patient or in a child. In marriages free of narcissistic vulnerability, anger generally resides in a specific situation and recedes with the resolution of the issue being contended. Fights are capable, in principle at least, of resolution. In vulnerable marriages, disagreements serve as opportunities to express infantile rage and vengefulness in the form of blame. The manifest issues serve as justifications for low-level defensive operations, usually projective in nature, that bring to the forefront fear of being let down, left alone, not being taken care of, and disappointed. In more normal marriages, spouses can get to the point of asking for what they want. Demandingness and entitlement pervade vulnerable marriages so that nothing seems capable of fulfilling omnipotent expectations. In normal marriages, disputes based on differing preconceptions of the marriage can often be seen as derivatives of marriages of the spouses' parents. The differences can often be negotiated. In vulnerable marriages, there is usually an obvious trauma in upbringing with the derivative themes replayed in the marriage and unresolvable in principle. Such trauma consist of gross defects or sudden changes in parental nurturance; parentification or blame by parents; triangulation of the child in chronically quarrelsome or vulnerable marriages; or physical or sexual abuse by a parent or with parental knowledge.[3] In normal marriages, ignorance of intimate situations is often resolvable with better communication and goodwill once major conflicts are resolved. With vulnerable marriages, emptiness and preoccupation with disappointments early in life leave, in both partners, a feeling of incompleteness and inadequacy that make intimacy a terror to be warded off. The awareness of the terror becomes yet another humiliation requiring vigorous defense. In vulnerable marriages, low-level projective mechanisms accompanied by vengefulness and self-righteousness leave the blamer lost so much in the issue at hand that an observing ego is not available during the conflict, and a completely different ego state is present when the couple are not in comflict. In more normal marriages, it is clear what areas of richness hold the marriage together; vulnerable marriages have spouses with either few subliminatory channels or so much that is disowned about the couples' need for each other that it is difficult to see what holds the marriage together. The discourse of narcissistically vulnerable patients is replete with frustrations and shortcomings in life described as though they emanated from shortcomings in the spouse. This, in other contexts, is referred to as the use of projective-introjective mechanisms; it is the extreme of unempathic relatedness.

Narcissistically vulnerable marriages that are less typified by overt conflict may be more difficut to recognize in the consulting room or in the history of patients who do not appear to have been offspring of traumatic marriages. Outright symptomatic dysfunction in a spouse, in the form of substance abuse, a behavior disorder, or an affective disorder, may alert one to the presence of such vulnerability.[1] More subtle are situations that present as plausible loyalty conflicts—between family and job, between family of origin and family of procreation, or between marriage and children. Such preoccupations may not superficially differ from normal complex loyalties, but often cover up preoccupied states of mind and an inability to participate in the marriage at all. The use of some special status of overriding loyalty serves to disguise the difficulty in bonding in the marriage. Other clues are the character traits of contempt, self-righteousness, self-pity, blaming, debunking, or undue suspiciousness in any context.

In a family with an identified dysfunctional member, narcissistic vulnerability in the nuclear marriage may evince none of these features. This concealing of inadequacy by projection onto a spouse or a child who acts dysfunctionally in a field of seemingly normal family members has been pointed out by many family therapy theorists as the seemingly individual disturbance that is found to serve the needs of the entire family system. Experienced family therapists of any persuasion are familiar with the ability of families to give the appearance of symptoms residing only in one member. It is the rule for manifest narcissistic vulnerability to appear, often explosively, if such an identified patient improves and begins to find freedom from the demands of the system in which the patient serves as a focus for projections of inadequacy. The scapegoat serves this function vicariously for the family; as long as this function is performed by the identified defective, there is some feeling of well-being in the rest of the system.

Other systems aspects of the narcissistically vulnerable marriage are the clinginess and fear of abandonment that may be inferred from behaviors that reassert the stably unstable dyad. Moves of independence are met with behavior that reestablishes even an unsatisfactory dyad as the primary focus of its members' attention. The behavior is usually felt to be symptomatic, antisocial, or frankly psychotic: infidelities broadcast to the spouse, drinking, suicide attempts, and so forth, that give one party a chance to demand, uncover, and blame—preoccupied states offering much relief in themselves when the split-off state is allowed to express itself—and the other, a chance to inflict punishment by the behavior. Both resume an unpleasant union, attachment to which is disowned, but attention to which is undivided and unremitting.

CLINICAL DIFFICULTIES

Marriages not characterized by narcissistic vulnerability and treated for difficulties stemming from conflict alone, or from simple inexperience in the absence of vulnerable features of the personality, may respond to a wide variety of techniques.

Understanding of the narcissistically vulnerable marriage leads to appreciation of features of such relationships; that task requires specific techniques. The vulnerable marriage, perhaps best characterized by the full-blown chronically conflictual or blaming couple, is not organized around satisfaction, enjoyment, or desire. Such marriages are organized around the containment and expression of massive rage, by the collusive exchange of projective defenses warding off the experience of inadequacy and the humiliating realization that abandonment (or even the threat) results in debilitating anxiety and fragmentation experiences.[2,4] The security operations in the marriage may come entirely at the expense of satisfaction. Accordingly, shedding light on the operations within the marriage risks exposing the partners as clingy, empty, angry, envious, and intensely dependent on a spouse who is also held in contempt. The humiliation of such awareness must be warded off by these patients, who have usually been sensitized by actual experiences of humiliation in their early nurturing relationships. This humiliation-proneness may make even the simplest descriptive statement by the therapist appear as blame itself, and, hence, mortifying. Interpretation of process that is, with healthier couples, best done by pointing out patterns of communication, may result in a transient subsidence of a crisis, but without generalized learning or enduring change. In the narcissistically vulnerable marriage, the therapeutic activity of pointing out what the spouses actually do, ie, describing patterns of communication or action, is often humiliating to the point of endangering treatment. The model of metacommunication as the essence of therapeutic intervention, like the model of interpretation alone for psychoanalysis, is insufficient for the treatment of narcissistically vulnerable marriages.

The collusive defenses, often obvious if the couple is observed over even a short time, are difficut to point out: they are lost in projections and actions—invitations to blame, provocations to act up, and (what comes to be predictable) responses that reestablish the blaming equilibrium. Blaming behavior or provocative blame-inviting action is difficult to get into therapeutic focus, because the ego state that blames or provokes blame by drinking, bungling, gambling, and so forth, is split off from the more usual state of consciousness, which is the one that presents to the therapist. At such times when a normal state of consciousness is present, the patient is bewildered by the behavior, oblivious to it, ashamed of it but, above all, not in control of it. This combination—split-off ego states accompanied by low-level projective defenses and actions—make appeal to an observing ego nearly impossible. The same difficulties oppose the chance for therapy to become a situation where an effective observing ego can generalize learning in the sessions to other situations. Hence, there is difficulty in establishing even *that* a patient or a couple *defends*, much less *how* or against *what*. It further complicates matters that such patients have actually been traumatized. Sustained trauma before the age of 10 is almost ubiquitous. As has been mentioned, this trauma consists of outright abandonment or deficit in nurturance—due to evident character pathology in parents rather than to chance—involvement in a narcissistically vulnerable parental marriage by being parentified, scapegoated, or blamed; or outright aggressive or sexual abuse with the knowledge of a parent who fails to institute appropriate protection. The result is a constant preoccupation with security operations, abandonment, injustice, and holding oneself together that carries over into adulthood, especially in intimate situations. Accordingly, such vulnerable marriages are characterized not just by conflict, but by deficits originating from shortcomings in real, protective, empathetic nurturance early in life.

The techniques of treating the couple with narcissistic vulnerability should, optimally, be aimed at these features: collusive defenses; humiliation proneness; terror of abandonment; infantile rage with the specific flavor of injustice; vengefulness; excessive gratification from aggressive discharge;[5] splitting of the ego and low-level defenses interfering with an observing ego that can learn from the therapeutic experience; and a history of unsatisfactory nurturance inferred from repetitive themes in the patient's life that repeat in derivative forms the traumata of childhood.

PRINCIPLES OF TREATMENT

Treatment strategies for narcissistically vulnerable couples are rarely formed with specifics of the pathological difficulties in mind. Adherents of particular treatment modalities (eg, individual, family, or drug therapy), may claim success with some patients using only the type of treatment that they advocate. Undoubtedly some successes are attained with one treatment modality alone, but in literature devoted to psychotherapy, pharmacotherapy, or family therapy, emphasis is very rarely on treatment failures, and even more rarely on methods (outside of the type of treatment being advocated) that might overcome those difficulties.[6] When the emphasis is on avoidance of the treatment failure, rather than the preservation or advancement of any one method, different sets of choices confront the therapist. In the present state of our knowledge of therapeutics, it cannot be reasonably maintained that any one treatment suffices.

The limitations of any one treatment modality brings forth the need for an eclecticism based on specific treatment strategies that are mindful of specific obstacles posed by the psychopathology in question. Psychoanalysis, individual psychotherapy, family therapy, pharmacotherapy, and hospitalization all have a place in the treatment of narcissistically vulnerable couples. However, an eclectic approach does carry the risk of haphazard or hypomanic decisions on the part of the therapist. The patients being treated have an extraordinary degree of emptiness, futility, depression, and rage. These, together with the well-established ability of such patients to impart those feelings to others, raise the risk that the therapist may become involved in such feelings, intolerant of them, and do something with an eclectic rationalization that actually constitutes a devastating piece of acting out that may doom the treatment to failure. If multimodal treatment is not well thought out, the risk of countertransference-motivated acting out increases. What is needed is a sufficient understanding of the treatment modalities and what difficulties are addressed by each. In this way, a blend of treatment possibilities can be developed that addresses the specifics of the pathology: collusive defenses, discharge by blaming or discharge in action, humiliation proneness, terror of abandonment, splitting, emptiness, and deficits in the personality and capacity for intimacy referrable to an incohesive sense of self.

Aspects of family psychotherapy, individual psychotherapy, multiple family group therapy, pharmacotherapy, and hospitalization that apply specifically to the problem of narcissistic vulnerability will be discussed in this paper. These components of an overall treatment strategy have specific justifications for use in the treatment of narcissistic vulnerability. The blend of modalities is a separate matter and, at this stage of our knowledge, must be discussed more conjecturally.

MARITAL PSYCHOTHERAPY

Conjoint psychotherapy of spouses and, perhaps, others in the family may be necessary if treatment is stalemated by overreactivity, collusive defensive operations, sabotage by family members, or if individual therapy becomes stalemated by *complaining*. The latter may denote a therapeutic split: the therapist is idealized and the spouse is denigrated at the cost of all progress in either the treatment or the marriage.

One may see conjoint therapy as the main vehicle of change, with individual therapy, pharmacotherapy, and hospitalization being stabilizers or facilitants for work that is basically done in the conjoint sessions. Family therapy should not always be regarded as primary; it may enable more definitive work in individual therapy or psychoanalysis, a parameter of technique[7] that allows the more individual work to proceed. The latter use of family therapy, as a stabilizer and enabler of individual therapy, is common practice in the treatment of adolescents, but fairly little has been written about its use with couples.

Family therapy is not the same for narcissistically vulnerable couples as it is with less-disturbed patients with neurotic levels of inhibition or even ignorance or inexperience in intimate relationships as the basis for marital difficulties. For the latter, a great many techniques are effective in uncovering feelings in a permissive, supportive setting. Vulnerable couples, whose transactions are typified by overreactivity and failure of repression, become submerged in feeling and require techniques that structure therapy so that transactions go through or are conducted by the therapist. For humiliation proneness, it is crucial to make empathic contact with each spouse repeatedly, and to take more than usual care that the treatment be experienced as just by all concerned. Another technique for addressing humiliation-proneness is the use of intergenerational reconstructions that do not arise directly from the transference. In the treatment of couples, assigning tasks and giving advice may be the therapist's response to feelings of futility, rage, emptiness, or depression transmitted by the patient. These maneuvers serve to avoid these affects in patients and the therapist, and work against ultimate success in the treatment.

Collusive defensive operations and the magnitude of infantile rage in blaming marriages preclude profitable use of models that simply facilitate interaction between spouses. Their difficulties are largely in becoming lost in feelings, not in being unaware of them, and the gratification in discharging rageful feelings does not lead to constructive change or learning from experience. Failure of repression, rather than inhibition, is the hallmark of the blaming couple. Murray Bowen[1] has developed the technique of having all transactions go through the therapist to break up collusion and overreactivity. This technique also makes the therapist available as a role model for empathetic contact that cannot possibly occur when blaming, disowning, and collusion is going on.

Case 5

In an initial interview with a couple, the husband was explaining what led to him beating his wife and requesting hospitalization. His wife interrupted, saying that he had the story all wrong and was up to his old tricks. They began arguing. The therapist, after ascertaining from both that such stormy stalemated arguments were typical, explained that therapy would proceed best if he talked to one spouse for a while, with the other trying to listen empathically while the therapist talked to the first. The wife was asked to try this. She was told that this would be difficult because of her fears, her opinions, and her past and present dissatisfactions; but that it was crucial, since change was unlikely to occur unless an atmosphere was created where both partners felt understood. She was asked to try to put aside her pain, her fears, and her view of the situation, and to listen and to attempt to spot her own tendencies to contradict, argue or blame. The therapist continued talking to the husband in a search for an empathic understanding of the shame, fear, and hurt that triggered his violence. Roles of talker- and listener-spouse alternated several times during the session.

For humiliation proneness, it is necessary to emphasize the potentially destructive effect of interpretations pointing out character traits including communication style.

Case 6

A man in his mid-fifties appeared complaining of inability to hold off ejaculation long enough to satisfy his wife. He wanted individual treatment. When he was told that treatment was optimally conjoint, he balked, but finally agreed to have his wife appear for a subsequent session. She appeared and talked contemptuously of her hsuband, of his coarseness, his inadequacies, his weakness as a provider, and his failure to appreciate her relationship to her mother who lived with them. When asked by the therapist if she thought she made a contribution to the marital unrest, she became enraged that the therapist felt it was all her fault, and bolted out of the room, never to return.

To avoid such mortifying interpretations, including metacommunicative interpretations or systems interpretations, therapy must start from an empathic grasp of the person's experience and progress only later to the effects of what was done. The too-abrupt labeling of character traits, by foisting more humiliation on patients than thay can bear, is more on the side of reinforcing undesirable behavior than of extinguishing it. Interpretation of patterns of behavior has the same effect as blame for the vulnerable patient.

A crucial technique for dealing with humiliation is the use of intergenerational constructions.[1,8] These may be done formally early in the therapy, with the construction of a genogram, or throughout therapy by the constant relation of the pertinent themes originating with the family of origin over several generations to the situation being dealt with currently. The history of the traumata mentioned above, extracted and recapitulated empathically, will go a long way in helping the patient to understand why he or she is sensitized to issues such as abandonment, terror, rage, possessiveness, envy, futility, and repetition of life themes that have been untelligible prior to an understanding of them over generations. Any psychotherapy deals with the here and now, but the selective use of past history will allow patient to understand *himself* or *herself* empathically as one who has unwittingly been dealing with traumata of the past and, hence, is the result of an understandable and intelligible process rather than a defective, incomprehensible, and contemptible product. My emphasis on intergenerational reconstructions, as aimed specifically at humiliation and shame, differs from that of others, emphasizing the intergenerational approach. The use of themes derived from past history is in dealing with overwhelming effect in the here and now. Intergenerational reconstructions, then, are essentially aimed at resistances and the powerful affects, (especially shame and humiliation) behind them, that oppose the work of treatment.

Case 7

The violent husband (case 5) reacted to his wife's interruptions with rage, blaming, and despair. He claimed that she stifled all initiative and capsized every effort at self-reliance. Somewhat later, he cried as he related that his father, a punitive disciplinarian humiliated him constantly and in public. When the therapist linked this to his sensitivity to his wife's criticism, the patient added that he at the same time wanted advice and was humiliated by intrusiveness. Both spouses felt understood at this point, and the husband went on to describe his relationship with his father and how it had colored his relationships not only with women (in two previous marriages), but also with men in authority in numerous jobs which he quit explosively. He desperately wanted structure and guidance, but felt humiliated when anybody told him what to do. Exploration of the same issue in his wife's life showed her response to be colored by her relationships with her hardworking father who was seldom home, and her depressed resentful mother, whose blaming attacks drove him away. She had had three previous marriages, all with similarities to her present one and to that of her parents.

Viewed intergenerationally, issues in the here and now may be approached with the goal of eliciting the patient's empathic *self-understanding* and giving the patient the experience of empathic understanding from another. These are the preconditions of change and of learning from experience in those for whom a curt description of their self-protective operations is humiliating. It is from the intergenerational point of view that themes of abandonment and efforts to ward off separations, feelings of emptiness, and of repetition of traumatic situations can best be brought to the patient's attention without being experienced as blame by the therapist.

In the treatment of situations involving deficits in the personality, in contrast to those dealing only with conflicts that do not stem from ego deficits, it is crucial to insure that the threat of abandonment is not underestimated. Risk of losing the relationship if the patient differentiates too much are often factors in the marriage and the therapy as they were in childhood; likewise with fears of intimacy.

Case 8

In the course of brief conjoint treatment for premature ejaculation, a couple persisted in arguing over interferences to their doing prescribed pleasuring exercises. The manifest issues were with children, circumstances of privacy, scheduling of time together, and other worries until the therapists suggested that the frequency of such arguments (nightly) might have something to do with anxiety about the exercises themselves or the intimacy involved. The circumstances provided less occasion for argument in the subsequent sessions but arguments continued, now about the unreliability of the other, and the many past issues that remained sources of bitterness. The couple decided—probably quite wisely—to terminate therapy after quarreling had reached the stage of outright mutual character assassination.

Separateness is what cannot be risked by spouses in a blaming marriage; the fear of independence is too great. For such couples, it is usually best to recommend conjoint therapy, using empathetic understanding as the point of departure for change, but supplying also a second treatment situation that provides an experience of secure symbiosis that is not at such risk. This kind of security is what such patients did not have in childhood or in the marriage. This is a necessary condition for improvement, but it is often neglected by therapists emphasizing change at all costs, or by those valuing interpretation or metacommunication without full consideration of the role of other factors in emotional growth.

It is doubtful that conjoint therapy of a single marriage or family with severe narcissistic vulnerability can concurrently provide an atmosphere for change and the experience of symbiotic acceptance; both are necessary for the definitive resolution of the difficulties. Conjoint sessions must be supplemented either by long-term individual psychotherapy, or psychoanalysis, or with multiple family group therapy with couples in similar predicaments being treated together.

INDIVIDUAL PSYCHOTHERAPY

Individual psychotherapy may be seen as an adjunct to marital therapy; or, conversely, family therapy may be seen as a precondition or enabler of individual therapy, a parameter of technique. It is arguable that unmodified psychoanalysis or psychoanalytic psychotherapy offers the advantage of dealing not only with the needs for support and change, but with the problem of responsibility that is so hard to address in persons with predominantly projective defenses. Indeed, for those seeking psychotherapy or psychoanalysis for the purpose of making changes in themselves, such treatment is probably the treatment of choice. But such patients are a small minority of those in this type of marriage. Not uncommonly, when such patients come to psychotherapy, the disowning of symbiotic needs in the marriage that are seen in conjoint sessions as blaming behavior becomes, in the therapeutic dyad, complaining. It is often impossible for persons in collusively-disowning conflictual marriages to engage in meaningful psychotherapy; indeed, the presence of such a marriage is felt by some to be a caution (if not a relative contraindication) to unmodified psychoanalysis for most patients. These difficulties within the therapeutic dyad are compounded, not only by difficulties of time and expense, but also with the technical difficulty of getting such patients to agree to appear without those family members who carry their projections. Intensive psychotherapy alone does not have the potential to reach the vast majority of such marriages.

The situation is different when a judicious combination of family therapy and individual therapy (including psychoanalysis) is used. The emotional constancy and support of individual psychotherapy, together with the empathic addressing of collusive maneuvers in family therapy, may have a synergistic effect and allow for change in the presence of emotional constancy.

It is quite likely that the technique of treating narcissistic vulnerability will advance considerably under the influence of the psychology of the self that has come into prominence in the last decade, especially following the work of Heinz Kohut.[4] Kohut has drawn attention to transference phenomena that he calls mirror and idealizing transference, and to the special handling of these specifically narcissistic transferences; to the lack of cohesiveness in self-structure in narcissistically vulnerable persons who are prone to fragmentation experiences; to narcissistic wounding by the process of treatment itself; and on the centrality of shame rather than guilt in the defensive activities of such patients. The psychology of the self and its influence on all psychotherapeutic techniques can be expected to enhance treatment possibilities for many patients hitherto felt to be untreatable.

MULTIPLE FAMILY THERAPY
OR COUPLES GROUPS

Multiple family therapy (MFT), composed of couples in similar predicaments, tends to be less wounding than is therapy where comments outside the family system come only from a therapist, as they would in the treatment of a single family or couple.[9] Further, the group can draw on what Laqueur[10] has called identification constellations, the ability of the group to draw ego strength from members in similar family constellations, or to try out new behaviors with those in complementary relationships.

Case 9

In a multiple family group, an alcoholic man was constantly berated by his wife for drinking. Her daughter from a previous marriage was disrespectful and downright insulting to him, and this was an issue that sparked contention between husband and wife. He was hospitalized and demanded Antabuse for his drinking. He stopped drinking entirely. The group, the wives most emphatically, pointed to enormous pressure on him to resume drinking when he was blamed and noted that he resisted quite well. He seemed in control of resisting drinking when he impulsively went off the wagon, became abusive, and lost his job. These drunken episodes served to invite his wife's blaming even more. He found sex distasteful and was reluctant to have intercourse despite his wife's eargerness for sex. She reminded him constantly that she was never satisfied. After he had gone several months without alcohol, the wife's accusations still continued; her father and first husband had been alcoholics. Intergenerational explorations by the therapist converged with here-and-now behavioral integration from the group. She made herself and her family of origin a project for study and, over subsequent months, gained much control over her blaming behavior.

MFT widens the opportunity to learn from experience while minimizing the risk felt so strongly in the marriage itself—that a sustaining relationship can tolerate no basic change. Such groups can allow a beneficient symbiosis to develop, often over several months to a year. Multiple family therapy remains a neglected modality which more often than not should be included in treatment combinations of first choice.

MEDICATION

The decision to use medication in combination with psychotherapeutic modalities is problematic. Much destructive and malignant affect can be managed without detriment to the psychotherapy by the judicious use of antidepressant medication in moderate dosages. This must be done in such a way to insure that the bulk of the treatment remains psychotherapeutic. To the humiliation-prone patient, just the act of being medicated may be experienced as blame and sadistic control by spouse and therapist in collusion.

Case 10

A 26-year-old mother of a 1-year-old baby came for marital counseling. She felt her husband to be unreasonable with his professional time spent away. She quarreled with him constantly. She had been horrified that her feelings about the baby were not what she thought they should be. She hated the baby at times, and wondered what kind of a mother she should be. Her relationship with her mother had been extraordinarily close, but highly conflictual. She felt strongly about traditional sex roles and the baby's arrival had precipitated all sorts of unwelcome feelings about men, women, caretakers, and those taken care of. She felt that she wanted a divorce, then considered her part in the marital squabbling, and felt that she was unreasonably demanding and expected the world to be perfect, resented the caretaker role, and envied her husband as the one taken care of. She wanted to feel better, not to spend endless time in psychotherapy. Her libido was diminished, intercourse was nonexistent, she awoke unrefreshed early in the morning, and her appetite and concentration were impaired. She was begun on amitryptiline, 75 mg at bedtime, with dramatic results over the next two weeks, at which time she said that she was entirely herself and never felt better. She felt that she would rethink psychotherapy. Her husband's schedule eased, perhaps in response to her being more pleasant. On a weekend away together, she discontinued the medication and called to say she didn't want any more therapy and that the marriage was intolerable.

There may in fact be blaming and controlling, as well as a host of other reactions to the patient, acted out in the countertransference. The therapist's inability to cope with the futility emanating from a grasp of the difficulties of such marriages may prompt action that feels definitive as a response, ie, medicating the patient. If medication becomes a continual focus in therapy, countertransference difficulties should be suspected. Medication is an adjunct rather than a central feature in the treatment. Little is to be gained in the use of tranquilizers. Medication, for practical purposes, is confined to moderate amounts of antidepressants. The wisest strategy is usually to agree on a reasonable, set pattern of medication for a period of time, and to keep that dose relatively constant. If things are done otherwise, the problem of responsibility for change becomes inextricably complicated and effective psychotherapy is usually sacrificed for very little in return.

HOSPITALIZATION

Hospitalization may be required, especially initially, particularly to ensure the safety of one or both spouses, but also to lessen the destructive effects of impulsive action, and to preserve the therapeutic situation that might otherwise never blossom into definitive treatment. It is a comon error to neglect the decisive importance of family psychotherapy in the hospital and to ignore the extent to which central difficulties found in the family recapitulate in the hospital setting.[3,11,12] Foremost among these is the appearance of the same superficial disowning of deep symbiotic ties to marriage or to hospital. If these are not presumed and dealt with, discharge can be a precipitous undoing of all the stability gained from hospitalization. It is only a small exaggeration to say that the treatment of such patients and their spouses in the hospital should always consider the significance of the containment provided by the hospital. Family psychotherapy in the hospital should concentrate from the start on termination of hospitalization and progress to a well-defined termination phase. This termination phase in the central and primary feature of family therapy of the narcissistically vulnerable patient in the hospital.

TREATMENT COMBINATIONS

Discussion of treatment combinations for the narcissistically vulnerable couple must be mindful of the fact that the justification for such combaintions may be influenced by therapist competence, zeal for one or another of the modalities deployed, and striking failures or successes that may unduly influence anecdotal reports. Treatment combinations vary depending on whether the central and primary focus of the treatment is to be the symptom, the system, or the personality.

If symptoms such as substance abuse, suicidality, or antisocial action are harmful to the point that they must be stopped to prevent the occurrence of a dangerous situation, the task of symptom control takes precedence over detailed exploration of the system or the personality. One cannot treat, for example, the family or the personality of an alcoholic while uncontrollable and destructive drinking is going on. The same applies to the suicidal patient, the drug user, and the violent patient. While such symptoms are out of control, emphasis is necessarily on the use of medication and hospitalization to stabilize the situation and to make the patient or couple available for definitive treatment.

If the symptomatology is dysfunction in a child or spouse that is not uncontrollable to the point of overwhelming the clinical picture—the above-mentioned symptoms in less fulminant form or dysphoria, underfunctioning, sexual dysfunctions, or depression—treatment strategies should be focused on the family system with particular emphasis on the marriage. This is so even if the symptom seems unconnected to the marriage. Symptoms often wax and wane with the state of the marriage or fill the void of an empty marriage. Hospitalization and medication are either adjunctive or not used. Family therapy, marital therapy, or multiple family group therapy become central and primary. Individual psychotherapy becomes more a supportive venture with the aim of furthering the work of family therapy. In many cases, where a dysfunctional spouse or child reflects a disorder in the system (and not simply the reaction of the system to a disturbed member), individual therapy introduces more confusion than it reduces and should not be used. Treatment strategies are aimed at the system requiring an 'identified patient' with the goal of making the system one in which a specific defective is not required.

If overt conflict dominates the clinical scene, say, in a marriage chronically characterized by blame but uncomplicated by suicidality, substance abuse, or antisocial action that necessitate external controls, emphasis should be placed on strategies paving the way for personality change. This is especially true if external circumstances are fortunate and if the spouses are able to take some responsibility for their roles in the marriage. In such marriages, marital therapy or multiple family groups with techniques specifically adapted to problems posed by narcissistic vulnerability are necessary, especially early in the treatment and serve primarily as parameters of technique or enablers or the intensive individual work (in some cases, even unmodified psychoanalysis) in which personality change and dimunition of narcissistic vulnerability can occur. Decisive working through of narcissistic difficulties is in the therapeutic dyad, not the marital dyad. Nonetheless, competent marital therapy may be synergistic with individual therapy if the two are simultaneous. In fortunate cases, both spouses improve and the marriage re-equilibrates at a higher level of personal functioning. After family work addresses collusive factors perpetrating a conflict-ridden marriage, substantial progress can often be made in long-term individual therapy for each spouse, with antidepressant medication used judiciously.

Control of major destructive symptomatology must be accomplished before work can be completed on freeing the symptomatic individual from the system that requires the dysfunction. Freedom from the system—no matter how this is accomplished—is usually prerequisite to personality change. Once destructive symptoms are under control, new strategies may become central that address the system; and once the dysfunctional person becomes less entangled by the system, strategies are better directed toward the personality system. Whether treatment strategies change, as the patients and families do, is quite another matter and depends on the flexibility of the treatment source, the availability of resources, and the motivation of the clientele. Programs aimed at symptoms, eg, alcoholism or suicide, may progress from symptom control through just enough examination of the family system to modify symptomatic behavior. Much family therapy stops short of definitive personality change if the family therapist only does family therapy and will not adapt the treatment to the newer needs of the improving persons. From the point of view of treatment failures, the situation may be seen in reverse order. Much work aimed at personality organization fails because of collusive activity in the family system that systematically undercuts the work of the therapy. The family system should have been dealt with first. Failures result from refusal, on the part of the psychotherapist or psychoanalyst, to recognize this. Much work on family systems is rendered impossible if major symptomatology is not controlled first; the work cannot result in generalizable learning from experience.

VISTAS FOR RESEARCH

The foregoing attempt to delineate the rationale for various treatment strategies for narcissistically vulnerable couples raises far more questions than it puts to rest. Does the conceptualization of narcissistically vulnerable couples distinguish a type of marriage that is really discernible from a marriage without significant narcissistic vulnerability? Can families with dysfunctional or symptomatic spouse or child be shown to be narcissistically vulnerable? What is the real prevalence of such marriages? Do they discriminate those in whom treatment difficulties are found, eg, in the treatment of alcoholism of sexual dysfunction, or of intractable behavior disorders in children? Is the past familial background of such patients predictable; have they suffered sustained childhood trauma that differes form that sustained by more normal couples with marital difficulties?

Other questions concern the treatment strategies: Do they help more patients to be engaged in treatment? Does the technique under scrutiny really address the difficulty for which it is used? Do the techniques open the way for overall treatment success or improvement, where one might expect to find treatment failure? What about other modalities? Are monoamineoxidase inhibitors more specific to narcissistically vulnerable dysphorias than are tricyclic antidepressants? Is videotape of use in enhancing a weakened observing ego? Should many generations appear in the therapy instead of just the couple? Should the couple be seen by opposite sex therapists who themselves meet with a consultant?

The issue of treatment in a multimodal approach presents problems for evaluation that go beyond the usual difficulties in psychotherapy research. The emphasis placed here on the priority of addressing collusion in the system before personality change can be accomplished would require a massive and sophisticated research effort before the conclusion could be reached that this point of view is more fruitful than others.

There is a convincing, albeit unsystematic, collection of results from the psychoanalytic treatment of narcissistically vulnerable persons that indicates that such pathology is much less refractory to definitive change that was once believed.[4] The clinician who is aware of the complexities of the clinical possibilities and the requirements of definitive research can seldom wait for the results of conclusive research. It is necessary to evaluate treatment outcomes in any way available for scrutiny, including (perhaps, especially) those paitents who refuse treatment or those who do not improve. This is the most meaningful source of clinical hypotheses.

REFERENCES

1. Bowen M: The use of family theory in clincal practice. Compr Psychiatry 7:345–374, 1966
2. Lansky MR: On blame. Int J Psychoanal Psychother 8:429–456, 1980
3. Lansky MR: On the idea of a termination phase for family therapy in the hospital. Group and Family Therapy 1980—An Overview. 323–334
4. Kohut H: The Analysis of the Self. New York, International Universities Press, 1971
5. Kernberg A: Borderline Conditions and Pathological Narcissism. New York, Jason Aronson, 1975
6. Lansky MR: Research in Family Therapy, in Serafetinides EA (ed): Methods of Biobehavioral Research. New York, Grune & Stratton, 1979
7. Eissler KR: The effect of the structure of the ego on psychoanalytic technique. J Am Psychoanal Assoc 1:104, 1953
8. Stierlin H: Psychoanalysis and Family Therapy. New York, Jason Aronson, 1977
9. Lansky MR, Bley CR, McVey GG, et al: Multiple family gorups as aftercare. Int J Group Psychother 28:211–224, 1978
10. Laqueur HP: Mechanisms of change in multiple family therapy, in Sager and Kaplan (eds): Progress in Group and Family Therapy. New York, Brunner Mazel, 1972
11. Lansky MR: The initial phase of family therapy in the hospital. Int J Family Psychiatry (in press)
12. Lansky MR: Establishing a family oriented inpatient unit. J Operational Psychiatry 8:66–74, 1977

David A. Berkowitz

10

The Borderline Adolescent and The Family

While originally used to indicate a diagnostic entity on the border of psychosis, today we use the term "borderline personality organization" to denote a relatively stable type of personality structure characterized by primitive defenses, poor impulse control, and low frustration tolerance. Although psychotic regressions may occur, they tend to be transient and to occur specifically under stress evoked in close interpersonal relationships.

Descriptively, Gunderson and Singer, as have Grinker and Werble, suggested six operational criteria for diagnosing the borderline patient,[1,2] namely: (1) the presence of intense affect, usually of a strongly hostile or depressed nature; (2) a history of impulsive behavior, which often may include self-destructive acts such as drug dependency and promiscuity; (3) a certain social adaptiveness; (4) brief psychotic experiences, which are likely to have a paranoid quality; (5) a tendency toward loose thinking in unstructured situations; and (6) interpersonal relationships that vacillate between transient superficiality and intense dependency with devaluation, manipulation, and demandingness.

Modern understandings of the structural characteristics of the borderline personality has been aided by, among others, Klein, Bion,

This chapter represents, in part, work initiated at the National Institute of Mental Health, in collaboration with Drs. Roger Shapiro, John Zinner, and Ed Shapiro. My thanks for a helpful reading of an earlier draft of this manuscript to them, and to Drs. Gerald Adler, Louis Berkowitz, and Paul G. Myerson.

Knight, Frosch, Guntrip, and especially Kernberg.[3-9] Klein described the primitive defenses of the infant mind as splitting, idealization, and projective identification. Bion described a type of mental functioning involving an intolerance of frustration, a prevalence of aggressive impulses that become manifest as a hatred of internal and external reality, and a fear of imminent annihilation. Because of heightened aggressive impulses, according to Bion, the 'psychotic personality' makes use of splitting and pathologic projective identification to attack aspects of the self, internal, and external objects. This results in the principal mental activities and the links with objects to appear torn to pieces. In his seminal work, Kernberg (following Klein), has described the borderline patient's persistent reliance on 'lower level' defensive operations, including splitting, primitive idealization, projective identification, denial, and devaluation. In Kernberg's view, borderline personality organization presents a pathologic condensation of genital and pregenital instinctual strivings with a predominance of pregenital aggression, accounting for the condensation of sexual, dependent, and aggressive impulses.

From the viewpoint of inner experience and past history, the borderline patient suffers from a pervasive fear of abandonment and sense of aloneness, ranging from empty despair to overwhelming panic.[10-12] The borderline is unconsciously and sometimes consciously convinced of eventual abandonment and is unable to trust. Rage over deprivation and abandonment results in lowered self-esteem, primitive guilt, and fears of retaliation, all of which reinforce the fearful expectation of abandonment. Furthermore, as Adler has pointed out, escalating demands and poor object choices compound these feelings of deprivation. These difficulties of the borderline patient significantly influence all of the patient's interpersonal relationships, including the relationship with a therapist, where they lead to major problems in establishing a therapeutic alliance.

Developmentally, the borderline issues described above are felt to be related to maturational failures in the earliest years of life. Adler has related the central problems of the borderline patient to a complex interplay between the child's emotions and early experiences of frustration, deprivation, and marked literal or emotional abandonment.[10] Kernberg has suggested that the borderline personality sustained a developmental failure during the period after self-object differentiation but before the development of object constancy.[8,9] Mahler and her co-workers have described their careful observations of the separation–individuation period (five months to three years) and subdivided this period into four subphases.[13] Many authors now believe that borderline psychopathology is related to difficulties in the parent–child relationship in the particular subphase of separation–individuation that they have called "rapprochement," and that occurs from 16 to 25 months.[14-18] Here the toddler's obliviousness to the mother's presence, which is characteristic of the preceding "practicing" period, is replaced by active approach behavior, increased separation anxiety, a constant concern with the mother's presence, and a need for her to share in the child's developing autonomy.[13] However, as Mahler and Kaplan point out, to present a coordinated system of subphase-related failures in one subphase of the separation–individuation process with a corresponding specific form of narcissistic or borderline personality organization may well be too oversimplified.[19]

SEPARATION ANXIETY

Buie and Adler explain the borderline's inability to allay separation anxiety as a result of achieving self-object differentiation but not yet having developed adequate *holding introjects* (ones that provide a sense of soothing, comforting security) for the degree of internal soothing which would allow a person to be physically separated and yet not vulnerable to separation anxiety.[20] They suggest that the borderline patient has a specific vulnerability to *evocative memory*, the capacity Fraiberg described that develops at about 18 months of age to retain and evoke the image of the mother in her absence.[21] As distinguished from recognition memory,[22] evocative memory is based on the child's developing the capacity for object permanence during rapprochement.[23] According to Adler and Buie, the capacity for evocative memory is prone to regress under the impact of the borderline patient's rage, when the patient is liable to lose what holding introjects he or she does possess, and must rely to a large extent on others to provide this function of soothing.[11]

Kohut and Wolf view the borderline as suffering from a central defect in the nuclear self covered by complex defenses.[24] They postulate that the borderline child's need to establish an autonomous self was thwarted by the repeated intrusions of the parent exactly when the early self of the child required the accepting mirroring of its independence. In this connection, some self-endangering and other-endangering acting-out behavior has been understood from the vantage point of narcissistic vulnerability.[25]

One important issue emerging from the literature, then, is the relative emphasis given to the role in the genesis of the borderline disorder of stage specific trauma on the one hand, or to the more chronic, cumulatively-traumatic family relationships, on the other. Attempts to correlate failures in specific develomental subphases probably run the risk of representing, as Mahler and Kaplan[19] suggest, a vast oversimplification. Such correlations fail to follow a truly epigenetic viewpoint that would hold that strengths and weaknesses in each prior developmental subphase influence succeeding ones. Mahler and Kaplan argue that in assessments of the personality organization of narcissistic and borderline child and adult patients, the overriding dominance of one subphase distortion or fixation must not obscure the necessary consideration that there are always corrective or pathogenic influences from the other subphases.[19] One problem inherent in sorting this out retrospectively is that where there has been empathic failure by the parents in anyone subphase or developmental issue, there is likely also to have been difficulty, although not necessarily to the same degree, in others. Thus an emphasis on a sustained traumatic situation would appear to make greater conceptual, clinical, and therapeutic sense than an overly narrow focus on stage-specific trauma alone.

DOVETAILING OF ADOLESCENT AND BORDERLINE ISSUES

For the borderline adolescent, the issues described dovetail with and further complicate an already stormy and vulnerable period of development, a phase which has been designated the *second individuation process* .[26] Blos states that what occurs in infancy, in Mahler's phrase, a "hatching from the symbiotic membrane to become an individuated toddler,"[27] becomes in adolescence the shedding of family dependencies and the loosening of infantile object ties in order to become a member of the adult world. Successful disengagement from infantile objects leads to the finding of new extrafamilial love objects in the outside world, while object choice remains restricted to simple replication and substitution without that successful disengagement.[26]

Anna Freud has documented the internal difficulties inherent in the adolescent developmental task and the concomitant interferences to treatment.[28] Many of the latter arise from the adolescent's desperate attempts at self-defense against the regressive dependent strivings with which the adolescent struggles. The adolescent needs to defend against the instinctual upsurge and against the infantile object ties, with defense against the latter sometimes resulting in flight. Treatment problems, in Anna Freud's view, result from the unavailability of libido for investment in the past or in the therapist because it is tied up both in mourning old objects and in seeking new ones. Anna Freud invokes this economic viewpoint to explain such common problems as the adolescents' reluctance to cooperate, their lack of involvement in the therapy or in the relationship with the therapist, their battles for the reduction of weekly sessions, their lack of punctuality, their missing of treatment sessions for the sake of outside activities, and their propensity to suddenly break off treatment altogether. To this lack of stability in the usual adolescent treatment situation, we must add for the borderline adolescent the problems of heightened impulsivity and lack of control, low frustration tolerance, deep distrust, and severe separation anxiety.

THE FAMILY OF THE BORDERLINE ADOLESCENT

Let us briefly review the developmental task of the adolescent phase from the side of the parents. For the adolescent's development to be successful, the family must promote (or at least allow) the individuation process during this period. In order to do this, the family must provide a facilitating or *holding environment* during the child's adolescence.[29-31] In Winnicott's original description of the holding environment, the mother 'survives' her child's instinctual assaults without retaliation or withdrawal, thus demonstrating to the infant her own autonomy and independent existence. Elsewhere the requisite holding environment during adolescence has been described as one that provides a consistent context within which the child can develop an integrated self concept and an integrated conception of others in the development of what Erikson has termed an *ego identity*.[32-34]

In a similar vein, Brodey ascribed to the parent the task of relating to the child with an awareness of the child's "objective existence," allowing the child separateness while remaining within "responsive communicative distance."[35] The family, then, must provide an empathic setting in which the child is aided gradually to separate and differentiate without being devalued or threatened by a withdrawal of support.

The task of this phase is a developmental one for parents as well, and offers them an opportunity to arrive at what Benedek has called a "new level of integration."[36] Whereas this stage in the life of the parents holds potential for further growth or, to use Erikson's term,[34] *generativity*, it is inevitably stressful and, in the family of the borderline adolescent, often one of despair. In working with these families, we often find, in cases of the borderline adolescent improving through treatment, a parallel improvement in relationships in the family as a whole, and in the parents' marriage. For example, one mother of a borderline adolescent had constantly tried to vicariously raise her self-esteem through the accomplishments of her husband and children. She continually berated her hospitalized adolescent daughter for poor grades in school, feeling that all the problems resided with the daughter. However, through family treatment the mother came to realize that she was herself feeling impoverished. Once acknowledging this, she was able to discover within herself dormant interests and talents. She struggled to overcome her anxiety in entering a complicated and creative profession which provided her much satisfaction in the long run. Gradually, she became able to support her self-esteem from within, mitigating to an extent the previous reliance on her husband and daughter for narcissistic sustenance.

Generalities about the family of the borderline adolescent risk inaccuracy and must be understood as oversimplifications. Psychopathologic outcome is a complex matter, including the dynamics of each of the individuals involved, the specific circumstances of the particular family at a particular time, small group processes, shared fantasies, and the meaning of the designated child to the family, to mention only a few of the relevant factors. Nevertheless, a common assumption is that borderline patients have suffered early and repeated actual frustrations in the form of literal or emotional abandonments and real failures of empathy in inconsistent, controlling, and/or rejecting parental responses to their developing and individuating selves.

Thus, the family of the borderline patient seems to fail in the essential task of providing a holding environment. Despite various claims, it should be emphasized that at this point no specific type of family can be said to alone be pathognomonic for the borderline. Various types of empathic failures in these families have been observed, including the implicit rejection of the child's essential self resulting from parental wishes for merger and control on one hand, overt rejection and abandonment on the other, and combinations of the two. In any case, the borderline child has experienced these failures in parental empathy as implicit or explicit rejection and abandonment, and has felt emotionally unresponded to with profound effects on the developing personality structure, defensive organization, and sense of self.

Shapiro has carefully documented the development in the literature from earlier, dyadic, and more static formulations, such as that of unconscious conflict in the parent being acted out by the child, to a broader view which included all family members as well as shared defenses and family group dynamics.[37-40]

In a retrospective study comparing case records of matched samples of hospitalized borderline, schizophrenic, and neurotic patients, Gunderson, Kerr, and Englund found families of the borderline patient to be characterized by the rigid tightness of the marital bond and a consistent pattern of neglect of the borderline offspring.[41] Masterson[14,15] and Masterson and Rinsley[16] have suggested that the mother of the borderline patient is herself borderline, and that she rewards the borderline patient for regressive behavior (such as clinging dependency) and she threatens abandonment by withdrawing libidinal supplies in response to the border-line child's attempts to separate and individuate.

From their observations of the interaction of borderline patients with their families, Zinner and Shapiro[42], and Shapiro et al[32] have suggested that the parents, while not necessarily borderline, do have a relatively deficient resolution of symbiosis and formation of an ego identity, a deficiency that sets the stage for them to regress, as will be described later. Zinner and Shapiro have described how, in its regression, the family presents the patient with a carrot and a stick: The carrot is the implicit promise of an all-gratifying relationship with certain family members who are purged of all "bad" qualities. The stick, on the other hand, represents the threat of emotional abandonment via expulsion or threatened death or illness in response to the child's autonomous pursuits. The borderline adolescent is then faced with an all-or-nothing dilemma in the family: to progress, grow, and develop is to risk abandonment; to preserve the good relationship is to sacrifice autonomy. Much of the rage of the borderline patient can be understood in this familial setting.

It is important to try to make sense of some of the apparent discrepancies in the various views of the borderline family in the literature. One possibility is that if each of these authors is looking at the same phenomenon, then each is doing so from a somewhat different perspective. Thus, each may be seeing the phenomenon from a different vantage point. These issues will be further clarified in this and subsequent sections of the chapter.

Both the individual psychopathology of the parents' personalities and the resultant regressive group processes in the family as a unit play a role in the family's failure to sufficiently support the developmental task of the borderline adolescent. In order for the parents to function successfully as facilitators of the adolescent individuation process, they must have had relatively good developmental experiences in their own families of origin. They need to have emerged from their own struggles over individuation with psychological integrity, relative maturity, and sufficiently adequate capacity for regulating narcissistic equilibrium. These tools enable them to survive the adolescent's devaluation and assault integral to the stormy attempt to disengage from infantile object ties.

From the standpoint of individual psychopathology it appears that the parents of the borderline patient have failed to adequately resolve conflicts around dependency and autonomy and issues of separation–individuation and that they "parentify" their children.[32,43,44] In a similar vein, Stierlin has described parental binding of separating adolescents.[45] Many of the parents appear to fit Kohut's description of the "merger-hungry person-ality".[24] One type of disorder of the self, the merger-hungry personality perceives the child or adolescent as a "selfobject" in Kohut's term,[46] ie, an object which is psychologically "experienced as part of the self," rather than as a separate and independent individual. Since the "other" is needed to function as part of the self, used to stabilize and complete the self through merger, that other cannot be perceived as separate and independent. Due to a fluidity of boundaries between themselves and others, merger-hungry personalities are unable to discriminate their own thoughts, wishes, and intentions from those of the selfobject. Intolerant of the other's independence, extremely sensitive to separations, they expect and demand the selfobject's continuous presence.[24] These parents are themselves highly vulnerable to anxiety over abandonment, and from this springs their enormous need to control.

In contrast to providing a facilitating environment, and despite heartfelt avowals to the contrary, many of these families often resort to a variety of counter-separation attitudes and behaviors under the impact of the adolescent period. To varying degrees, these parents attempt to hold their borderline adolescent close, to possess their child, and to prevent individuation. Strictness regarding the adolescent often is rationalized by the parents as based on the existence of dangers outside the home—rapists, murderers, sex, drugs, etc.,*—and real events are cited as justification for a paranoid and phobic view of the world. Inevitably, these parents find fault with their children's object choices outside the family. Occasionally in therapy they may admit their wish to have been able to stop the passage of time when the children were small. Under tactful questioning, such families reveal that no one has much of a life outside the family. These parents have few friends, and the children often feel responsible for their parents' well-being.

In their desperate attempts to fend off perceived separation and loss, these families may resort to increasingly regressive behaviors, including ostracism of the separating adolescent, whose move toward autonomy is experienced as a personalized rejection.[32,33,42,47] Such an angry repudiation of the departing adolescent may appear superficially to be simply a manifestation of rejecting parents. Other regressive family behaviors evoked in response to the borderline adolescent's separation may involve incest, bribes, exacerbations of physical illness, and threats of abandonment through death and suicide.[48] Thus, during this second opportunity for resolving issues of individuation, many families of borderline adolescents manifest a variety of counter-separation attitudes and behaviors inimical

---

*Clinically speaking, expressions of concern by the parents about these specific items usually reflect a reaction to the underlying issue of separation.

to the adolescent developmental task, and contribute to reinforcing the failure of maturation characteristic of the borderline.[26]

Many other parents of borderline adolescents who appear at first glance to be simply rejecting parents are, in fact, responding out of their enormous vulnerability to separation anxiety and dread of abandonment by defensively rejecting and abandoning their adolescent child before the child can abandon them. This same dynamic can operate in possessive parents when the loss of the separating adolescent appears irretrievable and inevitable.

FAMILY REGRESSION '

Such narcissistic vulnerability in the parents, in addition to making absolute control over the child or adolescent imperative, also sets the stage for a regression in family functioning and defensive reactions in response to shared unconscious fantasies about separation of the adolescent off-spring. As described previously,[33] these parents experience their adolescent's phase-appropriate separation–individuation as a personalized narcissistic loss and injury, since behaviors of the adolescent which herald separation and autonomy threaten the parents' precarious self-esteem. In this regression, boundaries between individuals are weakened, and primitive defensive functioning is increased, including projection of disavowed parental aspects into the adolescent, and the adolescent's collusive participation in this process.[40,49] In this family regression, in response to revived, unresolved issues of adolescence, family members may take unrealistic, stereotyped positions with prominent use of denial and distortion.[37] The borderline adolescent is scapegoated, inviting, as well as becoming the recipient of, projections from family members.

Often we find that dependent needs which had been frustrated early in each of the parents tend to be humiliating and must be managed by denial and projection onto the borderline child or adolescent. These needs may be felt to come from the adolescent in a hostile, draining way.[32] Then the disowned needs of the parents seen in the child may be thwarted by the parents who had felt those same needs thwarted in their own development. At other times, needs for autonomy that were conflictual in the parents may be disowned and projected onto the borderline adolescent.[12,32] In either case, during such a family regression, solid boundaries and differentiation between self and other are weakened. As part of this regressive group process and in response to parental anxiety and threat of loss of parental love, the borderline adolescent often colludes with parental projections and assumes the role parental defensive requirements demand. In addition to maintaining family homeostasis by meeting parental needs in this way, the borderline adolescent is afforded opportunities for drive discharge as well through acting-out behavior.[50] Impulsivity serves to avoid separateness; it is also overdetermined by poor impulse control.

CASE STUDIES

Four brief case vignettes will illustrate typical examples of borderline adolescents in interaction with their families.

Case 1

An adolescent girl was admitted for an inpatient evaluation after severely beating her mother and then slashing her own wrists. The mother and daughter had been physically fighting for several years prior to the admission to the hospital. The adolescent had abused both drugs and alcohol, and demonstrated uncontrolled outbursts of rage at the mother, lack of impulse control, and inability to tolerate frustration or limits of any kind. A work-up for temporal lobe epilepsy was negative. The patient's biologic father had abandoned the family early. The mother had remarried and separated from an alcoholic stepfather who sexually abused the patient during latency and early adolescence. Currently, the mother relied on the daughter to keep her constant company, and to run interference for her in her own stormy relationships with men. Mother and daughter refused to consider a temporary separation from one another. The mother bribed the daughter to return home, saying that she would support her truancy if she came home, but would force her to attend school if she moved in with her grandmother, which the mother perceived as an intolerable abandonment.

Case 2

Another mother complained that her adolescent daughter, an only child, had been lighting fires, provoking authority, and physically assaulting her. It emerged that the mother had often beaten the girl severely and felt very threatened by any of the girl's age-appropriate demands for mothering, because the mother felt so insecure and in need of mothering herself. For example, since she considered herself an inadequate cook, she felt threatened when her daughter wanted to help her in the kitchen. Further inquiry revealed that the girl was very phobic, particularly fearful of the dark—she imagined chopped-off heads on the bureau, monsters in the shadows, and big teeth in the patterns on the blanket. The girl was terribly ashamed of her fears and embarrassed over the fact that, because of these fears, she had been sleeping with her mother for the past six years. At first the mother stated that she and her husband mutually agreed to this arrangement because they each needed their sleep, and it was the least complicated way to deal with a demanding, frightened child.

Six years ago, the parents took separate bedrooms. The father had moved into the daughter's bedroom, and the daughter had moved into the mother's bedroom to share the double bed with her. The mother and daughter were, by the time of the interview, so symbiotically linked that neither could go to bed alone or at different hours, lest either one become anxious. The mother then explained that she has always been fearful of intimacy, particularly of a sexual kind, and while she likes to be cuddled by her husband, inevitably he gets aroused and wants to have intercourse, which frightens her. This always resulted in her pushing him away. Invoking economic necessity, the father has worked long hours six days a week. When the mother wants cuddling, he usually pushes her away. The arrangement with the daughter is thus convenient and helps protect the mother from her loneliness. "After all," she asks, "what can you do with a child who is so afraid of sleeping by herself?"

Case 3

A borderline young woman was hospitalized for repeated impulsive, self-destructive, and suicidal behavior. She felt that she was the black sheep of the family. The patient was the youngest of four children, the rest of whom had left home. Her father, a depressed and controlling man, threatened that he would not pay for her college tuition if she were to leave home. He had himself suffered maternal loss at two years of age and had been cared for reluctantly by several different relatives during his earliest years. The mother referred to the patient as "my baby" and claimed that she felt closer to her than to any of the other children. During a family interview, the mother tearfully described how in her own early childhood a baby sibling had died, and her mother had suffered a "nervous breakdown" at the time.

Case 4

In another case, a borderline adolescent young woman suffering from empty depression and marked self-hatred was admitted to an inpatient service for repeated running away and promiscuous behavior. In an interview, her mother accused her in an enraged tone of voice, "Oh, now are *we* sleeping with every Tom, Dick, and Harry?" The young woman's father, who later called her a slut, surreptitiously handed her the keys to his boat so that she and her date might have some "privacy."

TREATMENT

In the treatment of the borderline adolescent and the family, one starts with a reluctant set of patients. All members of the family are invested in seeing the problems as residing within the borderline adolescent; the family maintains that they are only there to be helpful to the index patient. Painful as the situation is, all members of the family including the index patient are covertly invested in maintaining the status quo. No therapeutic alliance yet exists, and adolescent and family are largely guarded, suspicious, and unlikely to really trust the therapists. Therapists are perceived as a potential threat to the family's shared unconscious fantasies and collusive transpersonal defensive functioning felt to be so vital to family equilibrium. At the outset, members of the family will be far more invested in having the therapists take sides than be helpful to the family as a whole.

To the extent that the internal intrapsychic difficulties of the identified patient are inexorably intertwined with or represent efforts to resolve interpersonal difficulties in the family, we have found involvement of the family in evaluation and treatment to be important for the resolution of problems of the individual borderline adolescent or young adult. Chronologic age is less a determining factor in this matter than the extent to which the individual's problems remain entangled with and energized by the dynamics of the family. For example, if the individual's phase-appropriate thrust toward individuation meets a developmental inter-ference in regressive, counter-separation attitudes of the family that mobilize guilt in the youngster, then these attitudes and their underlying motivations must be addressed if an alliance is to be developed and therapeutic progress is to be made. This has been discussed elsewhere in terms of managing the "external resistances" to the treatment, as these reinforce the internal resistances of the borderline adolescent.[47,51] It follows that treatment of the family, concurrent with individual therapy for the adolescent, is an important and at times necessary adjunct for addressing the special difficulties of forging a therapeutic alliance in the individual psychotherapy of the borderline adolescent. At times this will be able to be accomplished on an outpatient basis. However, often provision of a more intensive holding environment through hospitalization is necessary, especially to de-escalate explosive fighting or seriously self-destructive behavior.

Under ideal circumstances, the goals of treatment for the borderline adolescent and his family are accomplished by providing two therapists. The individual therapist sees the adolescent twice or three times a week in intensive, long-term, exploratory, psychoanalytic psychotherapy aimed at characterologic change. The individual therapist also functions as a co-therapist in a weekly family therapy session. This necessitates the therapist's ability to shift roles, so that he or she does not fall prey to the trap of siding with the adolescent against the parents, but maintains a therapeutic stance that is guided by the intention to be helpful to all members of the family. The other therapist sees the parents in a weekly marital therapy session and also functions as a co-therapist in the conjoint family sessions. Again, this therapist too must shift roles, both co-therapists attempting to help the entire family to mobilize its own resources and facilitate the phase-appropriate growth and development of each of its members. Family treatment emphasizes a psychodynamic understanding of the current familial interactions in light of the parents' own experiences in their families or origin, with intergenerational reconstruction a salient goal. Siblings who are involved with the family are included in the family sessions, preventive work being accomplished as the social context of their own development is altered. Some siblings seek individual therapy at a later point as they become aware of their own difficulties. The treatment format described above is of at least one- to two-years' duration, and usually continues in some form for several years in order to accomplish character change. Depending on the severity of psychopathology, treatment often involves hospitalization of the adolescent at the outset, frequently for several months. Such hospitalization provides a sufficient holding environment for treatment in spite of the patient's long-standing anxiety about abandonment and intrusion, and the primitive defenses the patient employs to manage that anxiety. While a single therapist may attempt treatment of both adolescent and parents, this is usually a much more difficult and complicated matter. Forming an alliance with the adolescent, already a formidable task—in the adolescent because of his or her great distrust, fears, and guilt over betraying family loyalties,[44] and in the parents because of their dread of abandonment and object loss—may prove impossible with a single therapist. Whatever the actual details of the treatment program, one guiding principle cannot be overemphasized: individual psychotherapy of the adolescent index patient alone, without providing some form of treatment for the parents, is almost always doomed to failure.

The adolescent must gain an opportunity to see that efforts to become an independent individual do not destroy the vulnerable parents. On the contrary, he or she may observe in treatment their parallel efforts to reach new and more adaptive levels of integration and more mutuality in the parents' marriage. All members of the family may be able to arrive at a more mature and realistically gratifying set of interrelationships over time. At this higher level of family functioning, it is clear that collusive transpersonal defenses will be less necessary to maintaining family homeostasis, and therefore greatly reduced. There can be new and more realistic perceptions of the adolescent by the parents, of the parents by the adolescent, and of the marital couple by one another.

In the concurrent treatment of the family of the borderline adolescent, where problems of individuation are paramount, it is essential to develop a working alliance with the entire family.[52] That alliance is founded upon attempts to empathically understand all the family members, with sensitivity to each of their life stresses, unresolved griefs, and feelings of abandonment. Despite the family's frequent wish to scapegoat the border-line adolescent, the therapist tries to expand the family's perspective of the presenting problem to include their roles in generating, perpetuating, and resolving the current crisis and the more deeply ingrained developmental problem.[53] In the context of the developing alliance, projections may be taken back, denied affects may be reclaimed,[54] and intrapsychic conflicts previously managed by externalizing them into the interpersonal family setting may be reinternalized. At times it may be necessary to gently confront both denied affects and distorted perceptions. For example, on the one hand, it was necessary to suggest to the mother in case 4 that she seemed invested in maintaining the distorted view that her daughter was promiscuous. On the other hand, it was equally necessary to point out to the daughter how she seemed to provocatively invite her mother's sus-picions. Such work is slow and repetitive, with regressions as frequent as salutary developments.

Vulnerable parental narcissism, with its possessiveness and its claims for absolute, omnipotent control, or its identification-with-the-aggressor rejecting behavior, is usually rooted in the parents' unresolved grief over past losses. Those losses may be acute and discrete but more often are chronic and cumulative, resulting from frustrating and depriving relation-ships in which the parents felt emotionally abandoned in their families of origin. The specter of loneliness, abandonment, rage, and emptiness raised by the separation of the adolescent offspring in such families stirs up unfinished preoccupations with former traumatic losses or a cumulative sense of loss. If parents can prevent separation of the offspring and awareness of their own separateness, it is as if they can mitigate the old hurts and deprivations or recapture, replace, and restore aspects of the old objects.

As Fraiberg, Adelson and Shapiro have underlined (following Freud), where there has been repression and isolation of painful affects related to childhood disappointments and deprivations in the parents, the stage is set for the parents to unwittingly inflict pain on their own children.[55,56] Old traumatic situations are painfully repeated and re-enacted. Interruption of this cycle may be accomplished by providing the parents of the borderline adolescent the opportunity for completing belated grief work.[54,57]

The therapists' technique should be designed to encourage the parents to elaborate in detail and associate to the shut-out, frozen-out feelings lying behind their angry outbursts, their projective distortions of the adolescent, and their subtle cues that support the adolescent's remaining in a troubled but nonseparated position. Such an exploration should lead to the unresolved grief in the parents' own early lives as this is triggered by sadness over current separations and losses. For instance, the mother of the borderline adolescent in case 4 was helped to trace the origins of her rage at her daughter to a profound yearning for her own mother's approval and an intense rivalry with a physically ill and, in her perception, favored younger sister. In a family session, the mother sobbed as she began to remember the painful feeling she had as a child that nothing she did ever seemed to please her own mother.

In such a treatment setting, the borderline adolescent's tendency to deepy distrust the therapist often yields to a progressively solid therapeutic alliance in the context of which the adolescent may begin to work toward a resolution of his or her developmental impasse and character restructuring.

IMPLICATIONS FOR FUTURE RESEARCH

It appears that a comprehensive treatment program involving a combined individual and family therapy, established during an initial period of hospitalization, has repeatedly been found highly beneficial by clinicians engaged in the therapy of borderline adolescents. However, follow-up studies and controlled-outcome studies are needed in order to validate this common clinical observation. In addition, specific treatment techniques also await further elaboration. There is no doubt that, whatever the psychopathologic process underlying the development of the borderline adolescent, such a treatment situation can largely resolve it over time. While the paucity or availability of affect, the severity of the ego deficit, and the extent of reliance on primitive defenses seem to determine which patients' pathology can be resolved and to what extent, such prediction represents a complex area requiring future research.

While our theory of treatment in large part derives from the conceptual understanding and formulation of the problem, both conceptual understanding and treatment represent a more advanced state of knowledge by far than the complicated matter of etiology. Etiology of the pathology in the borderline child, adolescent, and adult patient, remains poorly understood despite many excellent contributions. Certain authors attribute the pathology to elements in the innate endowment of the borderline, while other authors highlight the effects of emotional trauma from the environment during critical developmental periods. The issue of *nature versus nurture* in the development of the borderline personality is far from settled, and any definitive conceptualization will have to take into account the interaction of both of these elements. At this point in our knowledge, there seems to be a range of personalities and dynamics found in the family of the borderline patient, as noted in observations of family interaction, and as ascertained through case histories and in information gleaned from psychotherapy, especially through re-creations in the transference. The common denominator of these varied family influences seems to be feelings in the borderline adolescent of abandonment, rejection, and certain felt and actual parental failures in support for individuation. It appears that the quality of interaction with the caretaking figures is far more influential than quantifiable measurements of actual loss. Adolescence recapitulates some of the earlier issues of separation–individuation and the family members' capacity to provide a holding environment in the face of these issues, or their propensity for a shared regression. These data have made it tempting to hypothesize about earlier phases of development and about developmental origins of the borderline personality. However, it is here, in the matter of etiology, that, in conjunction with continued child observation and continued observation of the dynamics of family group interaction, careful longitudinal studies of personality development as well as careful in-depth studies of the parents' individual personalities are vitally needed.

REFERENCES

1. Gunderson JG, Singer MT: Defining borderline patients: An overview. Am J Psychiatry 132:1–10, 1975
2. Grinker R, Werble B: The Borderline Patient. New York, Jason Aronson, 1977
3. Klein M: Notes on some schizoid mechanisms. Int J Psychoanal 27:99–110, 1946
4. Bion WR: Differentiation of the psychotic from the nonpsychotic personalities. Int J Psychoanal 38:266–275, 1957
5. Knight R: Borderline states. Bulletin of the Menninger Clin 17:1–11, 1953
6. Frosch J: Psychoanalytic considerations of the psychotic character. J Am Psychoanal Assoc 18:24–50, 1970
7. Guntrip H: Psychoanalytic Theory, Therapy, and the Self. New York, Basic Books, 1971
8. Kernberg OF: Borderline Conditions and Pathological Narcissism. New York, Jason Aronson, 1975
9. Kernberg OF: Object-Relations Theory and Clinical Psychoanalysis. New York, Jason Aronson, 1976
10. Adler G: The usefulness of the "borderline" concept in psychotherapy, in

Mack JE (ed): Borderline States in Psychiatry. New York, Grune & Stratton, 1975

11. Adler G, Buie D: Aloneness and borderline psychopathology: The possible relevance of child development issues. Int J Psychoanal 60:83–96, 1979

12. Shapiro ER: The psychodynamics and developmental pathology of the borderline patient: A review of the literature. Am J Psychiatry 135: 1305–1315, 1978

13. Mahler MS, Pine F, Bergman, A: The Psychological Birth of the Human Infant. New York, Basic Books, 1975

14. Masterson, JF: Treatment of the Borderline Adolescent: A Developmental Approach. New York, John Wiley & Sons, 1972

15. Masterson JF: Psychotherapy of the Borderline Adult. New York, Brunner Mazel, 1976

16. Masterson JF, Rinsley DB: The borderline syndrome: The role of the mother in the genesis and psychic structure of the borderline personality. Int J Psychoanal 56:163–177, 1975

17. Settlage CF: The psychoanalytic understanding of narcissistic and border-line personality disorders: Advances in developmental theory. J Am Psychoanal Assoc 25:805–834, 1977

18. Blanck G, Blanck R: Ego Psychology: Theory and Practice. New York, Columbia University Press, 1974

19. Mahler MS, Kaplan L: Developmental aspects in the assessment of narcissistic and so-called borderline personalities, in Hartocollis P (ed): Borderline Personality Disorders. New York, International Universities Press, 1977

20. Buie D, Adler G: Definitive treatment of the borderline patient: I. Theoretical considerations of the primary sector of borderline psychopathology (submitted for publication)

21. Fraiberg S: Libidinal object constancy and mental representation. Psychoanal Study Child 24:9–47, 1969

22. Spitz R: The First Year of Life. New York, International Universities Press, 1965

23. Piaget J: The Construction of Reality in the Child. New York, Basic Books, 1937

24. Kohut H, Wolf E: The disorders of the self and their treatment: An outline. Int J Psychoanal 59:413–425, 1978

25. Berkowitz D: The vulnerability of the grandiose self and the psychotherapy of acting out patients. Int Rev Psychoanal 4:13–21, 1977

26. Blos P: The second individuation process of adolescence. Psychoanal Study Child 22:162–186, 1967

27. Mahler M: Thoughts about development and individuation. Psychoanal Study Child 18:307–324, 1963

28. Freud A: Adolescence. Psychoanal Study Child 13:255–278, 1958

29. Winnicott DW: The depressive position in normal emotional development, in Collected Papers: Through Pediatrics to Psychoanalysis. New York, Basic Books, 1958

30. Winnicott DW: The theory of the parent–infant relationship. Int J Psycho-anal 41:585–595, 1960

31. Winnicott DW: The use of an object. Int J Psychoanal 50:585–594, 1969

32. Shapiro ER, Zinner J, Shapiro RL, et al: The influence of family experience on borderline personality development. Int Rev Psychoanal 2:399–411, 1975

33. Berkowitz D, Shapiro RL, Zinner J, et al: Family contributions to narcissistic disturbances in adolescents. Int Rev Psychoanal 1:353–362, 1974

34. Erikson E: The problem of ego identity. J Am Psychoanal Assoc 4:56–121, 1956

35. Brodey WM: On the dynamics of narcissism: I. Externalization and early ego development. Psychoanal Study Child 20:165–193, 1965

36. Benedek T: Parenthood as a developmental phase. J Am Psychoanal Assoc 7:389–417, 1959

37. Shapiro ER: Research on family dynamics: Clinical implications for the family of the borderline adolescent, in Feinstein S and Giovacchini P (eds): Adolescent Psychiatry, VI. New York, Jason Aronson, 1978

38. Szurek S: Genesis of psychopathic personality trends. Psychiatry 5:1–16, 1942

39. Johnson AM: Sanctions for superego lacunae of adolescents, in Eissler K (ed): Searchlights on Delinquency. New York, International Universities Press, 1949

40. Johnson A, Szurek S: The genesis of antisocial acting out in children and adults. Ps An Quart 21:323–343, 1952

41. Gunderson J, Kerr J, Englund D: The families of borderlines. Arch Gen Psychiatry 37:27–33, 1980

42. Zinner J, Shapiro ER: Splitting in families of borderline adolescents, in Mack JE (ed): Borderline States in Psychiatry. New York, Grune & Stratton, 1975

43. Schmideberg M: Parents as children. Psychiatr Q (Suppl)22:207–218, 1948

44. Boszormenyi-Nagy I: Loyalty implications of the transference model in psychotherapy. Arch Gen Psychiatry 27:374–380, 1972

45. Stierlin H: Psychoanalysis and Family Therapy. New York, Jason Aronson, 1977

46. Kohut H: The Analysis of the Self. New York, International Universities Press, 1971

47. Berkowitz D: The disturbed adolescent and his family: Problems of individuation. J Adolescence 2:27–39, 1979

48. Gutheil T, Avery N: Multiple overt incest as family defense against loss. Fam Proc 16:105–116, 1977

49. Zinner J, Shapiro R: Projective identification as a mode of perception and behavior in families of adolescents. Int J Psychoanal 53:525–530, 1972

50. Zinner J, Shapiro R: The family as a single psychic entity: Implications for acting out in adolescence. Int Rev Psychoanal 1:179–186, 1974

51. Shapiro R: The patient, the therapist, and the family: The management of

external resistances to psychoanalytic therapy of adolescents. J Adolescence 1:3–10, 1978

52. Shapiro ER, Shapiro RL, Zinner J, et al: the borderline ego and the working alliance: Indications for family and individual treatment in adolescence. Int J Psychoanal 58:77–87, 1977

53. Zinner J: Combined individual and family therapy of borderline adolescents: Rationale and management of the early phase, in Feinstein S and Giovacchini P (eds): Adolescent Psychiatry, VI.New York, Jason Aronson, 1978

54. Berkowitz D: On the reclaiming of denied affects in family therapy. Fam Proc 16:495–501, 1977

55. Fraiberg S, Adelson E, Shapiro V: Ghosts in the nursery. J Am Acad Child Psychiatr 14:387–421, 1975

56. Freud S: Beyond the pleasure principle, in The Standard Edition of the Complete Works of Sigmund Freud (vol 18). London, Hogarth Press, 1955, pp 7–64

57. Paul NL: The role of mourning and empathy in conjoint marital therapy. in Zuk, G, Boszormenyi-Nagy I (eds): Family Therapy and Disturbed Families. Palo Alto, California, Science and Behavior Books, 1967

E. Mansell Pattison and Edward Kaufman

11

Family Therapy in the Treatment of Alcoholism

The intimate relationship between alcoholism and the family has been recognized since 1940 in the alcoholism literature. Yet, the utilization of family therapy and other family intervention strategies in the treatment of alcoholism has only slowly emerged since 1970. The literature in the alcoholism field has focused mainly on alcohol use as the primary problem and has ignored family dynamics.[1] At the same time, it is striking that the family therapy literature is almost totally devoid of consideration of alcoholism. Thus, the fields of alcoholism and family therapy have gone their separate ways, even though, from a clinical standpoint, family treatment should be a major component of alcoholism rehabilitation. There are several reasons for this situation. First, most mental health professionals still hold stereotyped negative attitudes toward alcoholics, despite many significant improvements in treatment.[2] Second, despite clinical recognition of alcoholism problems in family treatment settings, clinicians often will work only with family problems per se and ignore the alcoholism.[3] Third, the successful treatment of alcoholism requires a variety of family intervention strategies and modification of family therapy techniques to deal with the specific problems associated with alcoholism.[4]

Therefore, in this chapter we shall stress the interactive dynamics of the family and the use of alcohol. Particular emphasis is placed on the importance of identification of different family patterns in alcoholism, and the necessity for family interventions appropriate to specific family patterns. We term this a *differential* treatment approach.[5-10]

FOUR FAMILY SYSTEMS WITH ALCOHOLISM

From a descriptive standpoint we shall present four different family systems in which alcoholism is a major problem, to illustrate that there are indeed different family constellations, with different interventions required in different families.

The Functional Family System

The Broadway family consisted of Bob and Mary, married for 15 years, and two latency-age sons. The marriage was stable and happy, and the sons were well-adjusted. Both parents occasionally drank, but Bob, a college professor, became increasingly depressed and alcoholic. Mary, a physician, tried everything possible to help Bob with his problem, only to become increasingly depressed, frustrated, angry, and helpless when everything she did failed. The sons began to exhibit school problems and misbehavior at home when Bob drank heavily at home. Marital co-therapy that focused on the dynamics of the couple proved ineffectual, as agreed by both therapist and the couple.

Family therapy involving the parents and both children was intiated in the home, with a focus on the family response to Bob's drinking behavior. Contracts were negotiated with Mary and with the sons as to the limits of their responsibilities and the responses they should make to Bob, both when sober and when intoxicated. This clarification of family roles and responses quickly amerliorated the emotional symptoms of Mary and the sons. The family was then able to function effectively. However, Bob continued to engage in sporadic drinking bouts. He was placed on an Antabuse regime and seen in intensive individual psychotherapy. Concomitantly, the family was seen in monthly family sessions to reinforce and maintain appropriate family function.

The Neurotic Enmeshed Family System

Sue and Brian Smith had been married for 20 years, and had five children. As a sales manager, Brian was away from home frequently, drank heavily in social business meetings, and was considered a problem drinker at times by his employer, although he maintained his job. There had been incessant marital quarreling over the years because of Brian's absences, job preoccupation, job conflict and the rearing of the children. She felt the whole responsibility of the home and children was hers. She felt Brian ignored and disdained her. Their good times were always at parties where both drank heavily. Gradually, Sue drank more and more until, she drank constantly at home. In turn, Brian turned against Sue because she had become a lush. Each of the children became delinquent. Brian and Sue each blamed the other for poor parenting. They took turns threatening divorce, but one of the children would usually get into trouble at such times, serving to bring Sue and Brian back together.

The threat of job loss forced Brian to ameliorate his drinking, which he did. Sue joined Alcoholics Anonymous (AA) and became sober. Yet, marital conflict endured, and further delinquency among the children continued. Brief couples therapy did not ameliorate the marital and familial conflicts. Finally, family therapy was sought, in which the behavioral rules of family function were the focus of treatment. This resulted in marked improvement in the behavior of the children and a diminution of scapegoating between the parents. Brian's continued drinking remained an issue, but not a major problem. The couple continued a neurotic relationship with minimal personal satisfaction, but relatively effective family function.

The Disintegrated Family System

Harry Jones dropped out of high school to marry Jane, and they quickly had four children. Although he was a skilled mechanic, Harry was relatively poor, because the children had come before the family had become economically established. Soon he began to stop off for a few beers with the boys before coming home. Beleaguered Jane was angry over the modest expenditures for beer because they could not afford it. Harry resented her jealousy of this small pleasure. He began to drink constantly on weekends while repairing junk cars for more pocket money. They began to fight and argue, which escalated to physical violence when Harry drank heavily. Jane and the children became frightened of Harry's violence, because he would attack the children if they irritated him. Harry started leaving home to drink and not showing up for work. He was fired, and Jane took the children and left him. Both Harry's and Jane's families blamed Harry for all these events and ostracized him, refusing him money, clothes, or shelter. Harry hung around bars, and panhandled from his drinking buddies until they, too, refused him any help.

After two years of marginal existence, Harry finally applied to a half-way house. He was dirty, depressed, shabby, and dispirited. He could not get work as a mechanic, for his reputation was well-known. In the halfway house, Harry was fed, clothed, and reoriented about alcoholism according to AA principles. He learned to take responsibility for himself and stop blaming his wife, family, and former buddies for letting him down. After three months of sobriety, he was placed in vocational retraining, while regularly attending AA meetings. The social worker at the halfway house contacted Jane and helped her join Al-Anon. There Jane learned to reinterpret her marital and family problems which had resulted from Harry's alcoholism. After six months of sobriety, Harry obtained a new job as an apprentice electrician. Concomitantly, the social worker began to hold family sessions with Harry, Jane, and the children, although there was no reconciliation. Eventually, these family sessions included Harry's and Jane's respective families; both were resentful and suspicious of reconciliation. Over six months, these extended family sessions resulted in a renegotiation of the marriage, after Harry had a stable job. A symbolic remarriage was celebrated with the families on both sides in attendance.

The Absent Family System

Anna Brown was born into a poor family in the Los Angeles slums. Her father was alcoholic, and her mother supported the six children with hand work. Anna ran away from home at 16, after a beating by her father. She married a 35-year-old salesman, who was a philanderer and an alcoholic. He beat her, too, even when she was pregnant. After giving birth to three children in three years, she divorced her husband, and went to work as a waitress. She ran around with pick-up dates and drank heavily. She drifted to work in sleazy restaurants, finally ending up on welfare. She drank up her welfare checks. Her children were neglected and finally placed in foster care. She was admitted to state hospital alcoholism wards five times in two years. The staff could not locate any family or relatives. She had no friends or social relationships. She was jailed for public intoxication, and lived in junkyard boxes.

Anna was finally admitted to a Salvation Army shelter home for women. She was not interested in any type of psychotherapy; she did not like to think about herself, her feelings, or her miserable life. She achieved sobriety through a religious conversion, and remained on the staff of the Salvation Army center for three years. She became a member of the mission church and formed friendships there. She enrolled in secretarial training and obtained a secretarial job. After five years, she married a non-drinking member of AA. They have now established a stable and satisfying marriage and family.

ALCOHOLISM AND THE FAMILY—A SYNOPSIS

There is substantial literature on alcoholism and the family regarding a variety of major issues. We will not review this but will rather summarize basic themes and conclusions. Several major reviews have been published that detail the existing literature.[11-19]

The Effect of Alcoholism on the Family

Regardless of the family system, alcoholism is a major stress on individual family members and the family system. Alcoholism is an economic drain on family resources and can threaten job security. Drinking behavior may interrupt normal family tasks, cause conflict, and demand adjustive and adaptive responses from family members who do not know how to appropriately respond. In brief, alcoholism creates a series of escalating crises in family structure and function, which may bring the family system to a system crisis.[20-25] In addition to these psychological consequences, alcoholism creates physical problems, most notably sexual impotence or dysfunction, which in turn produce further marital conflict.[26,27]

The Effect of the Family on Alcoholism

A converse dynamic occurs, in that marital and family conflict may evoke, support, and maintain alcoholism as a *symptom* of family system dysfunction, as a *coping mechanism* to deal with family dysfunction, and as a *consequence* of dysfunctional family styles, rules, and patterns of alcohol abuse. In this case, alcoholism is not the cause, but rather the effect of family dysfunction.[28]

Early studies focused on the personality structure of the husbands and wives, with the assumption that personality conflict was a basic dynamic.[29,30,31] Most focused on the male alcoholic and his non-alcoholic wife. It was often implied that the wife was neurotic and chose an alcoholic husband, or that the wife later became neurotic because of her husband's alcoholism. Or perhaps even more misogynistic was the view that the wife drove her husband to drink. In retrospect, these studies were marred by selective biased samples, lack of comparative controls, and reductionistic interpretations of psychodynamics as psychopathology.[32-44] In sum, the fable of the noxious wife is just that—fable.[45] There is no validity to several earlier typologies of typical wives of alcoholics, nor can one conclude that wives of alcoholics are somehow specifically different from other wives.[46-48] The same problem obtains in the study of men who marry women alcoholics. Although little studied, these reports often indicate significant psychopathology among these men—but better samples and comparative data may likewise demonstrate no specific type of male spouse of an alcoholic woman, although there are often typical marital patterns.[49,50]

A more fruitful approach has been the study of marital interactional dynamics, role perceptions, and marital patterns of expectations and sanctions about the use of alcohol. Couples with alcoholism appear to engage in neurotic interactional behavior similar to other neurotic marriages, which are both dissimilar from healthy marital interaction. Thus, alcoholic marriages are not unique, but rather neurotic marriages in which alcoholism is part of the neurotic interaction.[51-63]

The Family and Alcoholism as a System Problem

Recent family research has moved away from a focus on the marital partners toward a consideration of the family system, the families of origin, the consequent lifestyle of children of alcoholic families, and the kin structures of the extended family system. This provides a much broader view of alcoholism as a family problem.

The first conclusion from experimental observations of family systems is that alcohol use in a family is not just an individual matter. The use of alcohol and the consequential behavior of drinking are dynamically related to events in the family system. Thus, the use of alcohol is *purposeful*, *adaptive*, *homeostatic*, and *meaningful*. The problems of alcoholism are not just the consequences of drinking per se, but more importantly, the *system functions* that drinking serves in the operation of the family.[64-71] Thus, we may properly consider alcoholism as a family systems problem.[72-74]

We can extend the systems approach to a larger consideration of the nuclear family embedded in generational and kinship systems. The problem of alcoholism runs in families, across generations, and into the kinship system. Alcoholism can be idiosyncratic to an individual. Cotton reports that different samples report 47–82 percent of cases where there is no familial alcoholism. On the other hand, he reports that 33 percent of alcoholics have a parent who is alcoholic, and in 82 percent of cases there is another member of the extended family system with alcoholism.[75] It has been considered by some that alcoholism is a genetic syndrome.[76] While genetics may determine differences in metabolic and physiologic responses, and thus contribute to the vulnerability to alcohol abuse, genetic differences seem implausible as the major determinant of the *behavior* of alcoholism. Numerous studies have carefully delineated the psychological transmission of alcohol abuse patterns from parents to children across generations;[77-81] similar patterns of alcohol abuse among kinship systems[82] and the choice of marital partners vulnerable to alcoholism based on alcoholism experience with parents.[83-85] Thus, the problem of alcoholism is not simply an individual problem, or a problem of marital partners, or a problem in the nuclear family system, but reflects larger alcoholism-generating family systems.

Alcoholism and Children in the Family System

Much of the alcoholism family literature has focused on the marital partners, neglecting the roles and functions of children in the family, and the consequences of alcoholism for the children. Margaret Cork named them "the forgotten children."[86] In the immediate situation of the alcoholic family, children are often the most severely victimized. They have growth and development problems, school and learning problems; develop emotional problems, and frequently exhibit significant behavior dysfunctions.[87-95] Further, these children are often subject to gross neglect and child abuse.[96] Teenage children are not immune to these adverse consequences, even though they are often considered less vulnerable.[97-99] Just as significant are the long-term adverse consequences on personality patterning, identity formation, and dysfunctional attitudes toward alcohol.[100-103] Thus, family intervention must truly consider the needs of all the children in the family, both in terms of short–range problems and longer-term preventive concerns.

The Family as a Determinant of Rehabilitation

In keeping with the observations of alcoholism as a system problem, the attitudes, structure, and function of the family system is the one most important variable in the successful outcome of alcoholism treatment. The alcoholic enters treatment from a family system and returns to that family system. If the system is dysfunctional it may vitiate any individual treatment gains. If the family changes or adapts more appropriate functions, however, it may sustain improvement and change in the alcoholic member.[104-110]

FAMILY TREATMENT METHODS

The development of family treatment interventions for alcoholism parallels the development of the conceptual framework of alcoholism as a family systems problem. The first family treatment approaches were developed in the 1950s in social work agencies and appear primarily as individual case work methods.[111-114] This was followed by marital therapy of alcoholic couples.[115-118] A variant on this theme is the joint hospitalization of marital couples, although only one is alcoholic.[119-121] Group therapy for just the wives of alcoholics was developed;[122-127] then, group therapy of alcoholic couples.[128-133] These trends resulted in clinical reports on specific family therapy of whole families with alcoholism as a problem focus.[134-140]

From a general systems perspective, clinical reports have focused on more extended family systems. This perspective includes Al-Anon as an adjunct social system for spouses;[141,142] support groups for children and adolescents;[143,144] multiple family alcoholims groups;[145,146] the inclusion of relatives and friends in the familization of hospital treatment programs;[147] and the development of social networks to assist re-entry into the community.[148-151] The social network approach deals with generational family systems, kinship systems, and community systems, detailed by Pattison.[152-157]

In sum, there is no one family therapy approach, but rather a variety of family intervention methods available, which can be utilized appropriate to the needs of a specific alcohol problem and family constellation.

TYPICAL FAMILY DYNAMICS

Like most symptoms of family dysfunction, alcoholism is a systems-maintaining and a systems-maintained device. Drinking may serve as a symptom or expression of stress created by conflicts within the family system. Excessive drinking often occurs when family anxiety is high. Drinking stirs up higher anxiety in those dependent on the one who drinks. The anxiety causes everyone to do more of what they are already doing. Drinking to relieve anxiety and increased family anxiety in response to drinking can spiral into a crisis, lead to collapse, or establish a chronic pattern.[74] Drinking frequently triggers anger in the drinker and provocation in others, which then ignites further anger and provocation despite attempts by the alcoholic to absorb the anger with alcohol. Drinking contributes significantly to provocation, verbal abuse, and physical violence.

Triangulating family systems are prone to alcoholism. In such systems, conflict or distance between two parties is automatically displaced onto a third party (eg, an in-law, lover, therapist, or child), issue, or substance (alcohol or drugs).[74] This is in contrast to a threesome in which each member can move freely with the other two.

Female alcoholics tend to marry male alcoholics, but male alcoholics usually do not marry female alcoholics. Despite different male/female alcoholism rates, marital patterns are more likely to reflect psychosocial role dynamics.[84,85] Individuals tend to choose spouses with equal levels of ego strength and self-awareness, but with opposite ways of dealiing with stress. We frequently see that opposites attract in male–female relationships, particularly obsessives and hysterics. In such relationships each person describes giving in to the other. The one who gives in the most becomes *deselfed* and is vulnerable to a drinking problem.[74]

Even after a pattern of alcoholism is established, these couples continue in a highly competitive relationship. The alcoholic repeatedly tries to control the situation, yet avoid responsibility through subtle, passive-dependent techniques. The spouse tries to control by being forceful, active, blunt, and dominating. Neither wins dominance, but the fight continues indefinitely. The adherence to a competitive style blocks the possibility of mutually satisfactory ways of interaction, and prevents the kind of risk-taking that leads to growth.

Spouses frequently blame each other for the family's problems. This dual projection blinds the couple from seeing their respective roles in creating problems. They frequently fight endlessly about "who started it," and readily duplicate this position in therapy with the hope that the therapist will judge right from wrong. Drunkenness is an important stage in the communication problems of such couples. Attempting communication with a drunk is frustrating and exasperating. The usual response is to let the drunk person set the rules, follow his or her lead, cease trying to communicate, and withdraw. Withdrawal involves long periods of silence and leads to escalation of negative feelings and distrust, and, ultimately, to explosive expressions of anger.

Some individuals marry alcoholics or potential alcoholics to meet certain needs and pre-existing traits of their own. These and others who are "normal" develop many personality changes in response to living with an alcoholic.

The alcoholic leaves the spouse starved for attention and affection. Early in the marriage, love is expressed through sex and material possessions. Spouses then withhold affection because it leads to sex, an act the alcoholic believes forgives all past transgressions, particularly drinking. As alcoholism progresses, the alcoholic becomes progressively unable to perform sexually, and the marriage becomes asexual.

The alcoholic loses the parental role in areas other than sexual functioning. The male alcoholic readily gives up his role as a father. Other roles (such as household chores and maintenance) are also rapidly abandoned and given over to others. The role of breadwinner is the last to go, and job loss may be necessary before treatment is sought. These families develop a chronic atmosphere of silence and tension, and their children complain of a lack of fun and laughter.[65,120]

Alcoholism breeds alcoholism and drug abuse. A nonalcoholic wife may encourage the older son to take over responsibilities abdicated by the father, placing the son in overt competition with the father in both behavior and drinking. Daughters in such families feel that the alcoholic father prefers them to the mother and feel that, if the mother were more loving, the father would not drink. They believe the ills of weak men can be cured by love, and they tend to marry alcoholics, repeating this pattern in multiple marriages.[77,80,81]

As nonalcoholic members take over full management of the family, the alcoholic is relegated to child status, which perpetuates drinking. Coalitions occur between the nonalcoholic spouse, children, and in-laws, which tend to further distance the alcoholic.[28] Children are terrified of the violence common to alcoholic families.[89] School phobia may result from the child's desire to stay home to protect the parent(s) from harm.

Alcoholic fathers are prone to child abuse through violence, sexual seduction, or assault.[96] Alcoholic mothers are more prone to child abuse through neglect. The nonalcoholic spouse may neglect children through directing the child's attention to the alcoholic.[91] Although not all alcoholics seriously abuse or neglect their children, the majority have difficulties in child rearing.[86-88] The emotional disturbance that characterizes alcoholic families leaves the children feeling rejected and unable to identify with either parent.[101,103]

The patterns that develop in family members of the alcoholic have been labeled as the disease of *co-alcoholism*. In the early phases of coalcoholism, there is denial and rationalization with the hope that the alcohol-related behavior will improve; there is responsibility and guilt for the alcoholic's behavior and some withdrawal. In the middle phases, there is hostility, disgust, pity, preoccupation with protectiveness, and shielding of the alcoholism. The co-alcoholic will drink with the alcoholic as a way of tolerating alcoholic behavior. In the advanced stages, the hostility, withdrawal, and suspiciousness become generalized to the total environment. In the final stages, responsibility for and quarrelling with the alcoholic are all-encompassing. Outside interests decline, and needs to maintain the self are disregarded. Psychosomatic symptoms or drug and alcohol dependence may occur, and separation is threatened or demanded. Frequently, the alcoholic will become sufficiently motivated for treatment when the co-alcoholic reaches the detachment aspects of these final phases.

Thus, the spouse and family build up defenses, which create problems if and when the alcoholic gets sober. If the alcoholic stops drinking, the spouse no longer fights about drinking, but about whether the alcoholic will resume drinking, which paradoxically triggers resumption of drinking. The alcoholic who is sober and doesn't want to be is still psychologically drunk and punishes everyone in the family system because he or she expects and doesn't receive exceptional rewards for giving up alcohol.

The romance of sobriety wears off after a while, and the slightest stress may tip the alcoholic off again. The grief of giving up alcohol may last for months or years.[68,70] During this period of prolonged grief and high, unfulfilled expectations, the recovering alcoholic is referred to as a *dry drunk*. If the family system is not worked with during this phase of the cycle to form new patterns of relating to each other to replace those developed during alcoholism, then the old system will draw the alcoholic and the family back to symptomatic consumption of alcohol.

Certainly, these observations emphasize the importance of family therapy for the ultimate benefit of the total system. What has frequently been neglected is the importance of involving the total family system including children, parents, and in-laws, in order to ameliorate or stop the drinking of the alcoholic. A 6-year-old may encourage a parent to drink to quiet the violence or to loosen controls to a point where affection is shown. An alcoholic mother drank herself into a stupor "because" her son would not cease daily pot smoking. A 15-year-old helped provoke a cycle of drinking and fighting in his parents so that they would be unable to set limits and enforce punishments. After 15 years of marriage, one wife finally found a sufficient sense of her own resources to be able to leave her charming alcoholic husband. He fled 3000 miles away to another woman, who soon tired of him. His mother then flew to him, to drive his car and him back home. On the seven-day trip back, she kept him constantly supplied with huge quantities of alcohol "to placate him."

What is seen most commonly is a family system where the non-alcoholic parent has made a crossgenerational coalition with a child, generally of the opposite sex; this excludes, alienates, and infantilizes the alcoholic. Such coalitions are also common between the co-alcoholic and his or her parents or a lover, or between the alcoholic and a lover (generally one who is the child of alcoholics). Thus, attention to familial relationships outside the alcoholic–spouse dyad are essential to understanding and changing the alcoholic as well as maintaining sobriety after it occurs.

FAMILY THERAPY METHODS

In working with alcoholics and their families, the therapist is faced with an unique problem, that of *wet* and *dry* family systems. A wet system is one in which the alcoholic continues to drink problematically; a dry system is one where active drinking is not a problem but the family's problems continue. Some therapists, particularly those who work in AA-oriented programs, will only work with dry systems. In our opinion, this should *not* be a precondition of treatment with family systems. A dry system is always preferrable, but it may be an unreasonable expectation for many families at the onset of treatment. In all families, the therapist should suggest measures to effect a dry state, at least temporarily, and in some instances the therapist should insist on these measures.

Achieving a Dry System

If the alcoholic is drinking so severely that he or she is unable to attend sessions without being under the influence and/or if functioning is severely impaired, then the first priority is to interrupt the pattern of drinking. Thus, the first goal is to persuade the family to pull together to initiate detoxification. This may be done on an outpatient basis, but if the drinking is severe, this may require immediate short-term hospitalization.[155] If the drinking is only moderately severe or intermittent, then the family should be offered alternatives to initiate a temporary alcohol-free state. These should include social detoxification centers, Alcoholics Anonymous, Antabuse, and very rarely, minor tranquilizers. Antabuse should not be given to a family member for daily distribution as this tends to reinforce the family's being locked into the alcoholic's drinking or not drinking. Minor tranquilizers are discouraged because they tend to become a part of the problem rather than a solution. Appropriate medication for treatment of that minority of alcoholics who drink because of underlying affective or other psychotic disorders may also help produce a dry system. If the alcoholic refuses to initiate abstinence, then we are left working with the wet system.

Working with Wet Systems

Since the wet system is a reality, the therapist should have techniques available to work with such families. When a member arrives at a session intoxicated, the therapist should not deal directly with this problem. Rather, the therapist should ask the sober spouse and family members to deal with the intoxicated person. This offers an excellent opportunity to observe the family interactions during one of the most critical phases of family system function. In subsequent sessions this behavior can be reexamined. In general, it is easier to ask the hyperfunctioning partner (sober) to change than the underfunctioning (alcoholic) one.

In working with wet systems, it is critical that the therapist not maintain the illusion that problems are being resolved because the family is "in therapy" when, in fact, the problems are still being reinforced. Provision of support systems for the other family members may help reduce the emotional intensity fixated on the alcoholic (or therapist). Al-Anon is a valuable support system as are significant others and social network systems of relatives and friends. Other supports, such as vocational training, jobs, social agencies, pastors, and attorneys, may be essential.

The therapist can offer the spouse only threes alternatives:[73] (1) keep doing exactly what you are doing, (2) detaching or emotionally distancing from the alcoholic, or (3) separating or physically distancing from the alcoholic.

When the family members choose not to change, the choice is overt; thus one can label what they are doing. If they do not choose option (2) or (3), then the therapist can tell them they are choosing option (1). In choosing (2) they are not criticizing drinking, but are asked to accept it, live with the alcoholic, and be responsible for their own reactivity regarding drinking. Al-Anon reinforces option (2) by teaching powerlessness over the spouse's alcohol intake to the sober spouse with the goal of getting the spouse to stop asking the alcoholic to control his or her drinking. If they choose (3), the alcoholic may frustrate eviction attempts, so the family may have to move out, which is initially considered impossible.

Thus, the famly is presented with three apparently impossible choices. The problem is resolved by choosing one of three courses of action and following through, or by experiencing the helplessness and powerlessness of these situations being repeated and clarified. The therapist insists that these are the only options, and should not expect one to be adopted right away. The family members then share despair and hit bottom sufficiently to become responsible for themselves rather than continue to try to change the alcoholic. The alcoholic may then get worse, in order to get the family back into the entanglement. The therapist must predict this situation and prepare the family. If the family can say, "We prefer you not to kill yourself (or us), but we are powerless to help you," it is unlikely that the alcoholic will commit suicide or murder. These options then open the door to consider new family adaptations apart from whether the alcoholic is wet or dry.

Interventions with Different Family Systems

Different schools of family therapy tend to utilize different vocabularies, techniques, or strategies. There are little data to compare the efficacy of different family methods, much less as applied to alcoholism. The integration of structural, systems, psychodynamic, and behavioral methods suitable to individual therapist styles, work settings, and types of family alcoholic problems encountered is stressed here. A summary follows, outlining some general principles for working with the four descriptive types of family systems.

In the *functional family system*, families have learned to function with a minimum of overt conflict. Such families often avoid psychologically oriented interventions. Here, *family-educative* approaches are often helpful. Explanation of the medical effects and complications of alcoholism may be the most useful initial entry into family participation. Such families will often then participate in educative–cognitive exploration of family roles and explicit and observable behavioral interaction. Exploration of implicit family rules and behavioral expectations can be followed by the development of family contracts and behavioral role practicing. Intensive family exploration of personal and interpersonal dynamics may not be necessary or may be resisted. However, some such families may progress into more intensive psychodynamic work. Many will respond to the more cognitive and behavioral approaches outlined.

In the neurotically enmeshed family system, many of the same initial approaches to family involvement and commitment as outlined above may be necessary. In most cases, much more active psychodynamic work will have to be done by the therapist. In these families, educative and behavioral methods may provide some initial relief, but will not be likely to impact the enmeshed neurotic relationships. Explicit family psychotherapy is usually required here. Often, multiple generations and kinship systems are interlocked with the nuclear family dynamics, and the involvement of the larger social systems, where possible, will probably be salutary. In the functional family system, work with the nuclear family is usually sufficient; in the neurotically enmeshed family system, work with just the nuclear family may often be insufficient. Further, mechanisms for disengagement of the enmeshed nuclear family members are required. Concomitant involvement with AA or Al-Anon may be very helpful, together with involvement of family members in more significant kinships, friendships, and community relationships.

In the disintegrated family system, the use of family interventions might seem irrelevant. However, many of these marriages and families have fallen apart only after severe alcoholic behavior. Further, there is often only *pseudo-individuation* of the alcoholic from marital, family, and kinship ties. These families usually can not and will not reconsitute during the early phases of alcoholism rehabilitation. Thus, the initial and early stages of treatment should focus primarily on the alcoholic individual. However, potential ties to spouse, family, kin, and friends should be explored early in treatment, and some contact should be initiated. There should be neither explicit or implicit assumptions that such familial ties will be fully reconstituted. When sobriety and personal stability have been achieved over several months, more substantive family explorations can be initiated to re-establish parental roles and family and kinship relationships—still without reconstitution. These family definitional sessions can then serve as the springboard for either appropriate redefinition of separated roles, or for reconciliated family structure. In either case, it is important for both the alcoholic and his or her family system to renegotiate new roles and relationships on the basis of a rehabilitated alcoholic. Some families may not wish reunion, but can achieve healthy separation. Families desiring reunion must establish a new base for family relationships.

The absent family system presents rather different problems. Here the issue is *not* reconstitution, but rather the development of new social networks, new social systems, and new lifestyles. Often alcoholics in such circumstances have little ability to form effective social relationships and do best in partially insitutionalized social support systems. However, as illustrated in the opening case study, some of these alcoholics do learn to participate in effective social systems over time, in graduated fashion, and even build functional families.

MODIFICATIONS OF FAMILY THERAPY
FOR ALCOHOLISM

In adapting the techniques of family therapy to alchoholism we have found that a synthesis of structural, systems, behavioral, and psychodynamic approaches is most helpful.

In using a psychodynamic approach, we avoid the role of the passive listener, which is ineffective with alcoholics as well as their families. Rather, the therapist is involved with the family as a genuine human being who deals with the immediate, shared moment of experience. Nevertheless, we feel that a family history of each family member is helpful in understanding the repetition of triangulating patterns from one generation to the next.

Past history can be extremely helpful if it is utilized without blaming, guilt induction, or dwelling on the hoplessness of long-standing, fixed patterns. The repetitive patterns and their derivatives are pointed out to the patient and family. Their maladaptive aspects to themselves and their family are pointed out, and they are given tasks to help them change these patterns in the here-and-now.

In utilizing the structural method, we use the structural map diagnostically. The genogram is helpful as an information-gathering and synthesizing device. "Joining" the entire family is much easier with the dry system, as it is almost impossible to join with the drinking alcoholic in a therapeutic way. The restructuring techniques which we have adapted to the family treatment of alcoholics include the therapeutic contract, assigning tasks, utilizing the symptoms of the index patient, enactment, marking boundaries, education, teaching, and the use of the total family network.

The Therapeutic Contract

This deals with establishing the terms, duration, and cost of therapy. With the alcoholic family, the issue of drinking and how it will be dealt with should be made a part of the contract. The way a family deals with the drinking should vary according to the type of family and extent of drinking. The family's involvement in AA and Al-Anon may also be a part of the contract, though such a commitment may be a later goal in therapy. The contract should be an agreement to work on resolving disagreements.

Assigning Tasks

Tasks may be assigned either within the session or as homework. The best task is one which uses the presenting problem to make a structural change in the family. It is preferable for a task to be accomplished in the session before tasks are given to be performed at home. A couple might be asked to speak to each other in the session while facing each other directly and without a child sitting between them. If this is successful, then the couple can be assigned to eat dinner in a restaurant without their children, or to take a vacation by themselves. The tasks should be compatible with the therapist's goals for restructuring the fmaily at each given point in the therapy. Therapeutic homework assignments permit the therapists and the therapeutic work to live with the family until the next session. Another way to give tasks is to assign the direction of a task; have the family choose the specifics and then reinforce their choice. A father who had neglected his medical and dental care because he was worried about his wife's drinking was asked to make an appointment with a dentist. A wife who was overinvolved with the amounts of alcohol her husband was consuming daily was given the task of estimating how many drinks he had every day and writing it down without telling him. He was asked to write down the actual amounts, and they were compared in the next session. The discrepancies demonstrated the futility of her efforts and diminished her overinvolvement in his drinking. This task was also a paradoxical one, the nature of which will be described below.

Utilizing the Symptom of the Identified Patient

The symptom of the identified patient (IP) is in a very special position, and the first goal should be to influence the rest of the family to help the identified patient with the symptom. If the symptom of some other family member is focused on before the IP's symptom is alleviated, the family may be unduly stressed and leave treatment. The symptom may be exaggerated in order to emphasize the family's need to extrude it. An example of this is encouraging a family to continue the "glories" of overindulging and infantilizing the alcoholic. A symptom that is an externalized acting-out of family conflicts can be prescribed to be performed within the family so that the family can deal with it, eg, adolescent stealing, secret drinking.

The Paradoxical Nature of Symptoms

The recognition and the use of paradoxical directives can achieve change. Such tasks may appear absurd; they require families to do what they have been doing rather than change, because the latter is what "everyone else" has been demanding. If the family then follows the therapist and continues what they have been doing, then the therapist assumes power over the symptom. If the family continues to oppose the therapist, then they will reverse the symptom. If they comply with the therapist, then they can acknowledge their power over the symptom and have the power to change it. The paradox "short-circuited" the ability to disown the conflict, kept at a distance through symptoms. Previously the symptomatic behavior seemed impersonal and uncontrollable, but the paradox makes it volitional. The command to "own" the symptoms bring them into volitional responsibility, and also brings the basic conflict into the person. When properly delivered, the paradox leaves the family chafing at the bit to make desired changes.

Relabeling or reframing the symptom may be very helpful, as when adolescent acting-out is an attempt to bring disengaged or divorced parents together, or to relieve parent–child responsibilities.

Re-Enactment (Actualization)

Patients usually direct their communications to the therapist. They should be required to talk to each other. They should be asked to enact transactional patterns rather than describe them. Role playing and family sculpture (a visual model of family roles) are helpful ways to facilitate actualization of patterns (as well as change them). Manipulating space (by changing seating or placing one member behind a one-way mirror) is a powerful tool for generating actualization. Working with the family when the alcoholic is inebriated creates a powerful re-enactment of family interactions. The family should resolve current conflicts in the sessions rather than talk about post disagreements. When a therapist becomes bored with a session, it is frequently because actualization or change has not occurred.

Marking Boundaries

This is done by delineating individual and subsystem boundaries. Individuals should not answer or feel for others, should be talked to and not about, and should listen to and acknowledge the communication of others. Nonverbal checking and blocking of communications should also be observed and, when appropriate, pointed out and halted.

The parental subsystem should be protected from intrusion by children as well as other adults in and outside of the family. Frequently, in order to strengthen the executive, parental system, sessions which exclude everyone else should be held. When individuals are deprived of a key role by a new boundary that did not previously exist in the family, they should be provided with a substitute role. If a member is placed behind a one-way mirror, that person can be given the role of expert observer and permitted to comment later.

Education and Teaching

Giving the family knowledge about alcohol and alcoholism is almost always helpful. The support and nurturance that a family can appropriately offer its members should be taught, understood, and encouraged. The therapist may have to assume executive functions as a model, and then step back so the family can assume them. Families may be taught how to handle schools or social agencies, parents taught how to confirm each other or react differently to their children. Children may be taught how to deal with their peers, including using peers as co-therapists. Helpless family members can be taught to tap their potential in social and vocational areas.

Use of the Total Family Network

Other significant family and social network members, including employers, housekeepers, siblings, aunts, uncles, neighbors, and friends may be involved. Families who present as only two persons are very difficult to change. Couples' groups or multiple family groups can provide some leverage by supplying other parental figures to such systems. Invariably there is another person, such as a boyfriend, sibling, aunt, or grandparent who can be extremely helpful in changing family systems; eg, the triangle which led to the problem is reversed, in order to achieve otherwise impossible structural changes. In the same manner, significant others can indeed become significant change agents in family systems.

Countertransference

Alcoholics and their families provoke specific types of emotional reactions in therapists. The alcoholic's dependency, relationship, suction and repulsion, manipulativeness, denial, impulsivity, and role abandonment will provoke countertransference reactions in the therapist depending on the therapist's emotional makeup. However, as family therapists, we view our emotional reactions to families in a systems framework rather than a countertransference context. Thus, we must consider how these families will replay their problems with the therapist, attempting to detour or triangulate their problems with the therapist. In these families, the therapist must be particularly sensitive about becoming a co-alcoholic who tries to over-protect, or becoming provoked to reject the alcoholic.

The relationship between the therapist and the family with alcoholism replicates what happens within the family at home. One example of this is the therapist who alternates between saving and persecution, to first allow the alcoholic to do almost anything, even coming to sessions drunk, and then switching to a punitive position such as demanding sobriety before the patient will be seen. In addition, the problem of countertransference must be distinguished from a more generalized negativism or hostility toward alcoholics. Both are antitherapeutic.

SUMMARY

This chapter has outlined the intimate relationship of the problem of alcoholism to family systems. This relationship may be rather singular, as in the case of highly localized individual alcoholism in a stable and healthy family system, or it may be quite generalized, as in the case of multi-generational and multi-kin involved multiple cases of alcoholism. We have presented four descriptive types of family systems of alcoholism based on related research.[156,157] These are not definitive types, however, but illustrate a broad spectrum of family involvements in alcoholism. In turn, we emphasize the need for the differential utilization of different types of family treatment interventions. Alcoholism is, in our opinion, best viewed as a family system problem, which poses a challenge for innovative system interventions.

REFERENCES

1. Orford J: Alcoholism and marriage: The argument against specialism. J Stud Alcohol 36:1537–1563, 1975
2. Pattison EM: Ten years of change in alcoholism treatment and delivery systems. Am J Psychiatry 134:261–266, 1977
3. Cohen PC, Krause MS: Casework with Wives of Alcoholics. New York, Family Service Association of America, 1971
4. Pattison EM: A conceptual approach to alcoholism treatment goals. Addict Behav 1:177–192, 1976
5. Pattison EM: Rehabilitation of the chronic alcoholic, in Kissin B, Begleiter H (eds): The Biology of Alcoholism, Clinical Pathology (vol 3). New York, Plenum Press, 1974
6. Pattison EM: Management of alcoholism in medical practice. Med Clin North Am 61:791–809, 1977
7. Pattison EM: The Jack Donovan Memorial Lecture 1978: Differential approaches to multiple problems associated with alcoholism. Contemp Drug Probl 9:265–309, 1978

8. Pattison EM: The selection of treatment modalities for the alcoholic patient, in Mendelson JH, Mello NK (eds): The Diagnosis and Treatment of Alcoholism. New York, McGraw-Hill, 1979
9. Pattison EM, Kaufman E: Alcohol and drug dependence, in Usdin G, Lewis JM (eds): Psychiatry in General Practice. New York, McGraw-Hill, 1979
10. Pattison EM, Sobell MB, Sobell LC: Emerging Concepts of Alcohol Dependence. New York, Springer, 1977
11. Ablon J: Family structure and behavior in alcoholism: a review of the literature, in Kissin B, Begleiter H (eds): The Biology of Alcoholism. Social Pathology (vol 4). New York, Plenum Press, 1976
12. Bailey M: Alcoholism in marriage: A review of research and professional literature. Q J Stud Alcohol 22:81–97, 1961
13. Hanson KJ, Estes NJ: Dynamics of alcoholic families, in Estes NK, Heinemann ME (eds): Alcoholism: Development, Consequences, and Intervention. St. Louis, CV Mosby, 1977
14. Janzen C: Families in the treatment of alcoholism. J Stud Alcohol 38:114–130, 1976
15. Krimmel HE: The alcoholic and his family, in Bourne PG, Fox R (eds): Alcoholism: Progress in Research and Treatment. New York, Academic Press, 1973
16. Paolino TJ Jr, McCrady, BS: The Alcoholic Marriage: Alternative Perspectives. New York, Grune & Stratton, 1979
17. Scott EM: Struggles in an Alcoholic Family. Springfield, Ill, Charles C Thomas, 1970
18. Steinglass P: Experimenting with family treatment approaches to alcoholism, 1950–1975: A review. Fam Proc 15:97–123, 1976
19. Steinglass P: Family therapy in alcoholism, in Kissin B, Begletier H (eds): The Biology of Alcoholism. Social Pathology (vol 4). New York, Plenum Press, 1977
20. Bailey MB, Haberman PW, Alksne H: Outcomes of alcoholic marriages: Endurance, termination, or recovery. Q J Stud Alcohol 23:610–623, 1962
21. Burton G, Kaplan HM: Marriage couseling with alcoholics and their spouses: II. The correlation of excessive drinking with family pathology and social deterioration. Br J Addict 63:161–170, 1968
22. Jackson J: The adjustment of the family to the crisis of alcoholism. Q J Stud Alcohol 15:562–586, 1954
23. Kephart WM: Drinking and marital disruption: A research note. Q J Stud Alcohol 15:63–73, 1954
24. Lemert EM: The occurence and sequence of events in adjustment of families to alcoholism. Q J Stud Alcohol 21:679–697, 1960
25. Orford J, Oppenheimer E, Egert S, Hensman C: The role of excessive drinking in alcoholism complicated marriages: A study of stability and change over a one-year period. Int J Addic 12:471–445, 1977
26. Lemere F, Smith JW: Alcohol-induced sexual impotence. Am J Psychiatry 130:212–213, 1973

27. Schuckit MA: Sexual disturbance in the alcoholic woman. Med Aspects Hum Sex 6:44–65, 1971

28. Jacob T, Favorini A, Meisel SS, Anderson CM: The alcoholic's spouse, children, and family interaction: Substantive findings and methodological issues. J Stud Alcohol 39:1231–1251, 1978

29. Ballard RG: The interaction between marital conflict and alcoholism as seen through MMPI's of marriage partners. Am J Orthopsychiatry 29: 528–546, 1959

30. Chassell J: Family constellation in the etiology of essential alcoholism. Psychiatry 1:473–482, 1938

31. Karlen H: Alcoholism in conflicted marriages. Am J Orthopsychiatry 35:326–326, 1965

32. Clifford BJ: A study of wives of rehabilitated and unrehabilitated alcoholics. Social Casework 41:457–460, 1960

33. Denicker P, Saugy D, Ropert M: The alcoholic and his wife. Compr Psychiatry 5:374–383, 1964

34. Dinaburg D, Glick ID, Feigenbaum E: Marital therapy of women alcoholics. J Stud Alcohol 38:1247–1258, 1977

35. Fox R: The alcoholic spouse, in Eisenstein V (ed): Neurotic Interaction in Marriage. New York, Basic Books, 1956

36. Futterman S: Personality trends in wives of alcoholics. J Psychiatr Soc Work 23:37–41, 1953

37. Kogan KL, Jackson JK: Role perceptions in wives of alcoholics and of non-alcoholics. Q J Stud Alcohol 24:627–632, 1963

38. Kogan KL, Jackson JK: Stress, personality, and emotional disturbance in wives of alcoholics and nonalcoholics. Q J Stud Alcohol 26:595–604, 1965

39. Kogan KL, Jackson JK: Some concomitants of personal difficulties in wives of alcoholics and nonalcoholics. Q J Stud Alcohol 26:595–604, 1965

40. MacDonald D: Mental disorders in wives of alcoholics. Q J Stud Alcohol 5:620–627, 1945

42. Rae JB, Forbes AR: Clinical and psychometric characteristics of wives of alcoholics. Br J Psychiatry 112:197–200, 1966

43. Wall J: A study of alcoholism in women. Am J Psychiatry 93:943–955, 1937

44. Whalen T: Wives of alcoholics: Four types observed in a family service agency. Q J Stud Alcohol 14:632–638, 1953

45. Kogan KL, Jackson JK: Alcoholism: The fable of the noxious wife. Met Hyg 49:428–453, 1965

46. Edwards P, Harvey C, Whitehead PC: Wives of alcoholics: A critical review and analysis. Q J Stud Alcohol 34:112–132, 1973

47. Paolino TJ Jr, McCrady B, Diamond S, Longaburgh R: Psychological disturbances in spouses of alcoholics. J Stud Alcohol 37:1600–1608, 1976

48. Tarter R: Personality of wives of alcoholics. J Clin Psychol 32:741–743, 1976

49. Busch H, Kormendy E, Feverlein W: Partners of female alcoholics. Br J Addict 68:179–184, 1973

50. Rimmer J: Psychiatric illness in husbands of alcoholics. Q J Stud Alcohol 35:281–283, 1974
51. Becker JV, Miller PM: Verbal, and nonverbal marital interaction patterns of alcoholics and nonalcoholics. J Stud Alcohol 37:1616–1624, 1976
52. Billings AG, Kessler M, Gomberg CA, Weiner S: Marital conflict resolution of alcoholic and nonalcoholic couples during drinking and nondrinking sessions. J Stud Alcohol 40:183–195, 1979
53. Bullock SC, Mudd EH: The interaction of alcoholic husbands and their nonalcoholic wives during counseling. Am J Orthopsychiatry 29:519–527, 1959
54. Drewery J, Rae JR: A group comparison of alcoholic and nonalcoholic marriages using the interpersonal perception technique. Br J Psychiatry 115:287–300, 1969
55. Gorad SL: Communicational styles and interaction of alcoholics and their wives. Fam Proc 10:475–489, 1971
56. Gorad SL, McCourt WF, Cobb JC: A communications approach to alcoholics. Q J Stud Alcohol 32:651–668, 1971
57. Haberman PW: Psycholgoical test score changes for wives of alcoholics during periods of drinking and sobriety. J Clin Psychol 20:230–232, 1969
58. Hanson PG, Sands PM, Sheldon RB: Patterns of communication in alcoholic marital couples. Psychiatr Q 42:538–547, 1968
59. Hersen M, Miller P, Eisler R: Interaction between alcoholics and their wives: A descriptive analysis of verbal and nonverbal behavior. Q J Stud Alcohol 34:516–520, 1973
60. Kennedy D: Behavior of alcoholics and spouses in a simulation game situation. J Nerv Met Dis 162–23–34, 1976
61. Mitchell HE: Interpersonal perception theory applied to conflicted marriages inwhich alcoholism is and is not a problem. Am J Orthopsychiatry 29:547–553, 1959
62. Mitchell HE: The interrelatedness of alcoholism and family conflict. Am J Orthopsychaitry 24:547–559, 1968
63. Rae JB, Drewery J: Interpersonal patterns in alcoholic marriages. Br J Psychiatry 120:615–621, 1972
64. Davis D, Berenson D, Steinglass P, Davis S: The adaptive consequences of drinking. Psychiatry 37:209–215, 1974
65. Davis P, Stern DR, Van Deusen JM: Enmeshment-disengagement in the alcoholic family, in Seixas FA (ed): Currents in Alcoholism (vol 4). New York, Grune & Stratton, 1978
66. Fisch M: Homeostasis: A key concept in working with alcoholic families of active and inactive alcoholics. Fam Ther 3:133–140, 1976
67. Jackson JK, Kogan KL: The search for solutions: Help-seeking patterns of families of active and inactive alcoholics. Q J Stud Alcohol 24:449–457, 1963
68. Steinglass P, Weiner S, Mendelson JH: Interactional issues as determinants of alcoholism. Am J Psychiatry 128:275–280, 1971
69. Steinglass P, Weiner S, Mendelson JH: A systems approach to

alcoholism: a model and its clinical application. Arch Gen Psychiatry 24:401–408, 1971

70. Weiner S, Tamarin JS, Steinglass P, Mendelson JH: Familial patterns in chronic alcoholism: A study of father and son during experimental intoxication. Am J Psychiatry 127:1646–1651, 1972

71. Wolin S, Steinglass P, Sendroff P, Davis DI, Berenson D: Marital interaction during experimental intoxication and the relationship to family history, in Gross M (ed): Alcohol Intoxication and Withdrawal. New York, Plenum Press, 1975

72. Berenson D: A family approach to alcoholism. Psychiatr Opin 13:33–38, 1976

73. Berenson D: Alcohol and the family system, in Guerin PJ (ed): Family Therapy: Theory and Practice. New York, Gardner Press, 1976

74. Bowen M: Alcoholism as viewed through family systems theory and family psychotherapy. Ann NY Acad Sci 233:115–122, 1974

75. Cotton NS: The familial incidence of alcoholism: A review. J Stud Alcohol 40:89–116, 1979

76. Goodwin DW: Is Alcoholism Hereditary? New York, Oxford University Press, 1976

77. Hoffman N, Noem AA: Alcoholism among parents of male and female alcoholics. Psychol Rep 36:322–323, 1975

78. Penick ED, Read MR, Crowley PA: Differentiation of alcoholics by family history. J Stud Alcohol 39:1945–1948, 1978

79. Swiecicki A: Adult adjustment of children from alcoholic and nonalcoholic families: A 10-year follow-up study. Probl Alkzmu 17:1–7, 1969

80. Wolin SJ, Bennett A, Noonan DL: Family rituals and the recurrence of alcoholism over generations. Am J Psychiatry 136:589–593, 1979

81. Zucker RA: Parental influences upon drinking patterns of their children, in Greenblatt M, Schuckit (eds): Alcoholism Problems in Women and Children. New York, Grune & Stratton, 1976

82. Jones RW: Alcoholism among relatives of alcoholic patients. Q J Stud Alcohol 33:810–823, 1972

83. Lemert EM: Dependency in married alcoholics. Q J Stud Alcohol 23:590–602, 1962

84. Paolino TJ Jr, McCrady BS, Diamond S: Statistics on alcoholic marriages: An overview. Int J Addic 13:1285–1294, 1978

85. Rimmer J, Winokur G: The spouses of alcoholics: An example of assortive mating. Dis Nerv Syst 33:509–511, 1972

86. Cork MR: The Forgotten Children. Toronto, Addict Res Found, 1969

87. Chafetz ME, Blane HT, Hill MJ: Children of alcoholics: Observations in a child guidance clinic. Q J Stud Alcohol 32:687–698, 1971

88. El-Guebly N, Offord DR: The offspring of alcoholics: A critical review. Am J Psychiatry 134:357–365, 1977

89. Fox R: Children in the alcoholic family, in Bier WC (ed): Problems in Addiction: Alcohol and Drug Addiction. New York, Fordham Univ Press, 1962

90. Haberman PW: Childhood symptoms in children of alcoholics and comparison group parents. J Marriage Fam 28:152–154, 1966
91. Hecht M: Children of alcoholics are children at risk. Am J Nurs 73:1764–1767, 1973
92. Mayer J, Black R, MacDonald J: Child care in families with an alcohol addicted parent, in Seixas FA (ed): Currents in Alcoholism (vol 4), New York, Grune & Stratton, 1978
93. Nylander I: Children of alcoholic fathers. Acta Paed 49:1–134, suppl 121, 1960
94. Stacey B, Davies J: Drinking behavior in children and adolescence: An evaluative review. Br J Addict 65:203–212, 1970
95. Wilson C, Orford J: Children of alcoholics: report of a preliminary study and comments on the literature. J Stud Alcohol 39:121–142, 1978
96. Olson RJ: Index of suspicion: Screening for child abusers. Am J Nurs 76:108–110, 1976
97. Bosma WG: Alcoholism and teenagers. Med Stud Med J 24:62–68, 1975
98. Kammeier ML: Adolescents from families with and without alcoholism. Q J Stud Alcohol 32:364–372, 1971
99. McLachlan JFC, Walderman RL, Thomas S: A study of teenagers with alcoholic parents. Toronto, Donwood Inst Mono no 3, 1973
100. Aronson H, Gilbert A: Preadolescent sons of male alchoholics: An experimental study of personality patterning. Arch Gen Psychiatry 3:235–241, 1963
101. Burk ED: Some contemporary issues in child development and the children of alcoholic parents. Ann NY Acad Sci 197:189–197, 1972
102. Mik G: Sons of alcoholic fathers. Br J Addict 65:305–315, 1970
103. Miller D, Jang M: Children of alcoholics: A 20-year longitudinal study. Social Work Res 13:23–29, 1977
104. Bromet E, Moos R: Environmental resources and the post-treatment functioning of alcoholic patients. J Health Soc Behav 18:326–338, 1977
105. Moos RH, Bromet E, TsuV, Moos B: Family characteristics and the outcome of treatment for alcoholics. J Stud Alcohol 40:78–88, 1979
106. Orford J, Oppenheimer E, Egert S, et al: The cohesiveness of alcoholism-complicated marriages, and its influence on treatment outcome. Br J Psychiatry 128:318–339, 1976
107. Rae JB: The influence of wives on the treatment outcome of alcoholics: A followup study at two years. Br J Psychiatry 120:601–613, 1972
108. Smith CG: Marital influences on treatment outcome in alcoholism. J Irish Med Ass 60:433–434, 1967
109. Webb NL, Pratt TC, Linn MW, Carmichael JS: Focus on the family as a factor in differential treatment outcomes. Int J Addict 13:783–796, 1978
110. Wright KD, Scott TB: The relationship of wives' treatment to the drinking status of alcoholics. J Stud Alcohol 39:1577–1581, 1978
111. Baldwin DS: Effectiveness of casework in marital discord with alcoholism. Smith Coll Stud Soc Work 18:69–122, 1947

112. Boggs MH: The role of social work in the treatment of inebriates. Quart J Stud Alcohol 4:557–567, 1944

113. Kalashian M: Working with the wives of alcoholics in an outpatient setting. J Marriage Fam 21:130–133, 1959

114. Lewis MS: Alcoholism and family casework. Family 18:39–44, 1937

115. Esser PH: Conjoint family therapy for alcoholics. Br J Addict 63:177–182, 1968

116. Esser PH. Cojoint family therapy with alcoholics—A new approach. Br J Addict 64:275–280, 1970

117. Esser PH: Evaluation of family therapy with alcoholics. Br J Addict 66:251–255, 1971

118. Smith CJ: Alcoholics: Their treatment and their wives. Br J Psychiatry 115:1039–1142, 1969

119. Paolina TJ Jr, BcCrady BS: Joint admission as a treatment modality for problem drinkers: A case report. Am J Psychiatry 137:222–224, 1976

120. Steinglass P, Davis DI, Berenson D: Observations on conjointly hospitalized alcoholic couples during sobriety and intoxication: Implications for theory and therapy. Fam Proc 16:146–170, 1977

121. Steinglass P: An experimental treatment program for alcoholic couples. J Stud Alcohol 40:159–182, 1979

122. Ewing JA, Long V, Wenzel GG: Concurrent group psychotherapy of alcoholic patients and their wives. Int J Group Psychother 11:329–340, 1961

123. Gleidman LH: Concurrent and combined group treatment of chronic alcoholics and their wives. Int J Group Psychother 7:414–424, 1957

124. Gleidman LH, Rosenthal P, Frank JD, Nash H: Group therapy of alcoholics with concurrent group meetings with their wives. Q J Stud Alcohol 17:655–666, 1956

125. MacDonald DE: Group psychotherapy with wives of alcoholics. Q J Stud Alcohol 19:125–130, 1958

126. Pattison EM, Courlas PG, Patti R, et al: Diagnostic-therapeutic intake groups for wives of alcoholics. Q J Stud Alcohol 26:605–616, 1965

127. Pixley JM, Stiefel JR: Group therapy designed to meet the needs of the alcoholic wife. Q J Stud Alcohol 24:304–313, 1963

128. Burton G: Group counseling with alcoholic husbands and their wives. Marr Fam Liv 24:56–60, 1962

129. Cadogan DA: Marital group therapy in the treatment of alcoholism. Q J Stud Alcohol 34:1187–1194, 1973

130. Corder BF, Corder RF, Laidlaw NL: An intesive treatment program for alcoholics and their wives. Q J Stud Alcohol 33:1144–1146, 1972

131. Gallant DM, Rich A, Bey E, Terranova L: Group psychotherapy with married couples: A successful technique in New Orleans alcoholism clinic patients. J La Stud Med Soc 122:41–44, 1970

132. Gliedman LH, Nash HT, Webb WL: Group psychotherapy of male alcoholics and their wives. Dis Nerv Syst 17:90–95, 1956

133. Loescher DA: Time limited group therapy for alcoholic marriages. Med Ecol Clin Res 3:30–32, 1970

134. Dulfano C: Alcoholism in the family system, in Buckley T (ed): New Directions in Family Therapy. Oceanside, New York, Tabor Sci Publ, 1977

135. Dulfano C: Family therapy of alcoholism, in Zimberg S et al (eds): Practical Approaches to Alcoholism Psychotherapy. New York, Plenum Press, 1978

136. Ewing JA, Fox R: Family therapy of alcoholism, in Masserman J (ed): Current Psychiatric Therapies (vol 8), New York, Grune & Stratton, 1968

137. Flanzer JP, O'Brian GM: Family focused treatment and management: A multi-discipline training approach, in Madden JS et al (eds): Alcoholism and Drug Dependence, New York, Plenum Press, 1977

138. Meeks DE, Kelly C: Family therapy with the families of recovered alcoholics. Q J Stud Alcohol 31:339–413, 1970

139. Pattison EM: Treatment of alcoholic families with nurse home visits. Fam Proc 4:75–94, 1965

140. Trotter AB, Gozali J, Cunningham LJ: Family participation in the treatment of alcoholism. Pers Guid J 48:140–143, 1969

141. Ablon J: Al-Anon family groups. Am J Psychother 28:30–45, 1974

142. Bailey M: Al-Anon family groups as an aid to wives of alcoholics. Soc Work 10:68–79, 1965

143. Kern JC, Tippman J, Fortgang J, Paul SR: A treatment approach for children of alcoholics. J Drug Educ 7:207–218, 1978

144. McElfresh O: Supportive groups for teenagers of the alcoholic parent: a preliminary report. Med Ecol Clin Res 3:26–29, 1970

145. Berman KK: Multiple conjoint family groups in the treatment of alcoholism. J Med Soc NJ 65:6–12, 1968

146. McKany LR: Multiple family therapy on an alcoholism treatment unit. Fam Ther 3:197–210, 1976

147. Catanzaro RJ, Pisani UD, Fox R, Kennedy ER: Familization therapy. Dis Nerv Syst 34:212–218, 1973

148. Finlay DG: Effect of role network pressures on an alcoholism approach to treatment. Soc Work 11:71–77, 1966

149. Howard DP, Howard NT: Treatment of the significant other, in Zimberg S et al (eds): Practical Approaches to Alcoholism Psychotherapy. New York, Plenum Press, 1978

150. Sands PM, Hanson PG: Psychotherapeutic groups for alcoholics and relatives in an outpatient setting. Int J Group Psychother 21:23–33, 1971

151. Ward RF, Faillace LA: The alcoholic and his helpers. Q J Stud Alcohol 31:684–691, 1970

152. Pattison EM, DeFrancisco D, Wood P, Frazier H, Crowder J: A psychosocial kinship model for family therapy. Am J Psychiatry 132: 1246–1251, 1975

153. Pattison EM: Psychosocial systems therapy, in Hirschowitz RG, Levy B

(eds): The Changing Mental Health Scene. New York, Spectrum Publ, 1976

154. Pattison EM: A theoretical-empirical base for social systems therapy, in Foulkes E et al (eds): Current Perspectives in Cultural Psychiatry. New York, Spectrum, 1977

155. Feldman DJ, Pattson EM, Sobell LC, et al: Outpatient alcohol detoxification: Initial findings on 564 patients. Am J Psychiatry 132:407–412, 1975

156. Pattison EM, Coe R, Rhodes RA: Evaluation of alcoholism treatment: Comparison of three facilities. Arch Gen Psychiatry 20:478–488, 1969

157. Pattison, EM, Coe, R, Doerr HO: Population variation among alcoholism treatment facilities. Int J Addict 8:199–229, 1973

Donald I. Davis

12

Special Problems in Family Therapy Posed by Alcohol Abuse

A CONSULTATION

In the middle of a therapy session, a woman joked about how her husband sometimes drinks in the morning. Nearly drowned out by the general laughter was her daughter's petulant reply that he drinks too much. Therapist and family returned to the previous topic, the timing of father's depressive moods. Soon the wife complained that in the evenings her husband can get into a mean mood and at those times has been known to hit her. The family therapist followed up with an exploration of links between depressed mood and conflicts between the spouses.

As they watched the videotape replay of this session, the therapist asked his consultant how to deal with the issue of drinking when it came up, as in this case, as a constant diversion whenever the family begins to talk about something conflictual. The family is bright and verbal, the consultant was told, and they ought to be getting somewhere in therapy, but the first few sessions seemed to have gotten bogged down. Previously, a month or so of hospitalization and a year of outpatient individual psychotherapy also had failed to make a sustained dent in the father's depression. It seemed now that if this family could overcome certain resistance to dealing with the core family issues, therapy would progress. Alcohol abuse, which had never been considered a major issue, seemed to be one of the more frequent vehicles for expressing resistance. The therapist reiterated that what he sought through consultation were ways to have done with the alcohol-related diversions.

The consultant told him, in effect, that he was asking the wrong question. He was told that like so many other therapists, he might be ignoring the horse (alcohol) while trying to budge the cart (the family). The therapist was assuming that the drinking resulted from marital conflicts, and that depression had led to more drinking; so, if drinking were really a primary problem, then someone either in the family or among previous therapists would have said so. Wrong, wrong, wrong, he was told; It usually is the other way around; or at least it is more useful to think of it that way. When one spouse is drinking frequently, marital conflicts don't go away; rather, they smolder and deepen. As for depression, alcohol is a depressant. Most alcoholics eventually become depressed. It may be impossible to tell if the depression has a life of its own without a period of abstinence. Finally, it is untrue that others would have made the diagnosis if it were there. Alcohol abuse frequently goes largely ignored. Family members and previous therapists may have missed the diagnosis, or failed to reinforce it. In fact, in this family we already know that the daughter thinks her father has a drinking problem, but her opinion has been ignored or overruled.

The therapist was asked to pose different questions, on the order of, "How can I assess how much alcohol abuse is a factor while doing family therapy?" and, "What do I do with that information once I have it?" The answers to these questions are the subject of this chapter.

In the case presented, some important information had already been elicited but not used. Based on the same videotaped session, the consultant reconstructed the family's story as follows. Some mornings, the father begins drinking shortly after arising. By evening, he is often intoxicated and capable of acting violent with his family. He misses work at times, ostensibly for depression and anxiety. His daughter thinks he has a drinking problem. This man is an alcoholic, but neither his family nor his therapist are acknowledging the fact.

In family therapy, it is likely that he will continue to show promise of improvement but never quite recover. That will happen for several reasons. One is that he continues to drink enough daily of the sedative drug, alcohol, to perpetuate a chemical basis for feeling depressed. Another is that, since nothing is being done to change his drinking habits, he will continue to miss work or perform poorly at work on occasional mornings, thereby generating covert or overt reprimands and lowered self-esteem. Also, under the sanction of intoxication, he may strike his wife again some evening, further scarring their already-wounded relationship. When they have problems to resolve, as all couples do, they will fail to work them through to a mutually acceptable conclusion. This failure may stem from either the expectation or the reality of his wrath or his fatigue, when drinking, or to her over-reaction when he has been drinking. When their teenage children are exposed to heavy peer pressure to be truant or to take drugs, their parents will have little moral clout with which to restrain them, because of the parent's hyprocrisy concerning alcohol misuse.

Of course, all of the above may become moot if father hurts or harms himself or someone else while driving under the influence of alcohol. But he may not have an accident; he may not even drink and drive. His work may suffer imperceptibly to others than himself. It may be years before an organ system of his body fails secondary to the effects of alcohol, and he may die of other causes before that occurs. It may be that only the relationship consequences of alcoholism will be in evidence. This is particularly true of the people who come to see a family therapist. Hence, the family therapist must know the more subtle cues to alcohol abuse. Fortunately, the family therapist has a tremendous advantage over other therapists of seeing and hearing first hand what role alcohol has come to play in the alcoholic's relationships to bring an end to the drinking problem. If he or she capitalizes on these aids, the odds are very good for successful outcomes in family therapy for families with an alcoholic member. If not—if the drinking continues—it is likely therapy will not progress to the desired end.

BACKGROUND

Alcoholism is a frequently occurring disorder in our society, with incidence figures generally ranging from 5 to 10 percent of the population.[1] If these were the percentages among a therapy population as well, it would be substantial. It appears, however, that alcoholism is found with much greater frequency among certain groups, groups that are also more likely to be seen in family therapy. For example, alcoholism has been identified in at least 20 to 40 percent of patients in some urban hospitals.[2]

If heavy drinking and job or social problems associated with drinking are considered, as opposed to only the confirmed diagnosis of alcoholism, the frequency with which alcohol abuse is found to be a potential complication in family therapy is very high. Heavy or problematic use of alcohol and/or some other substance of abuse has been found in nearly 40 percent of all patients in a largely middle class general psychiatric outpatient population.[3] Alcohol is the most frequent drug abused in these populations. Much of the other drug abuse involves various tranquilizers or sedative–hypnotics. While this chapter is about alcohol abuse, it should be understood that most of what is said here about the problems posed by alcohol abuse in family therapy is applicable to sedative–hypnotic abuse as well.

These surmises apply most to identified patients. They do not begin to take into account the number of identified patients who have alcohol-abusing spouses, parents, and children. Statistics are lacking in this area. It is known that there is a greater-than-normal frequency of alcoholism among parents of disturbed children who are patients in child psychiatric settings.[4] Beyond that, we can only say that it is not uncommon to find that a spouse's abuse of alcohol is a major factor in an individual's seeking therapy, or that parental abuse of alcohol figures prominently in a young adult's current mental conflicts. In short, if a family therapist does not deal with alcohol abuse frequently, it is not for want of opportunity.

A recent outpatient psychotherapy clinic study has revealed an increased rate of incorrect diagnosis on the part of therapists when dealing with substance abusing patients.[5] That is, therapists were more likely to mislabel patients, especially including them in major diagnostic categories such as depression or schizophrenia, if the patients misused drugs. These findings relate to other recent studies that predicted but failed to find higher-than-average rates of symptomatic depression in newly abstinent alcoholics.[6] Even though most alcoholics eventually appear clinically depressed, once they stop drinking the incidence of depression is not greater than that in the general population, perhaps 10 to 15 percent. Similarly, sexual problems that may not persist during periods of sobriety can arise from heavy drinking. These include impotence, diminished libido, decreased sensory pleasure, and partner distaste for sex. In general, the therapist's ability to accurately assess a situation will improve with a period of abstinence on the part of the heavy drinker. For this reason also the family therapist should learn to identify and to address alcohol abuse in a family member.

In the treatment literature, there is support for the application of family therapy techniques to the treatment of alcoholism. Although conclusive data are lacking, comparisons of familial and marital approaches to other approaches to the treatment of alcoholism have yielded either equal or favorable results for the family relationship approaches[7,8] and have indicated that, they can, at times, be a sufficient treatment in themselves.[9] However, family therapy can also become yet another means of forestalling treatment of alcohol abuse if the drinking is not adequately addressed. This fact will lead some family members to lack confidence in their therapist. These people will have seen or heard about individual, family, or marital therapy failures who finally got help through the self-help groups of Alcoholics Anonymous (AA), Al-Anon (for the alcoholic's mates or adult significant others), and Alateen (for the teenage children of alcoholics). They may test, indirectly or directly, the therapist's ability to address the fact that a drinking problem exists. If the therapist fails the test they will lose hope or confidence. The surest way to fail the test is to label alcohol abuse as a mere symptom of family conflict that will go away as faulty communication is removed from the family.[10]

The hope that the alcohol abuse will go away with effective family intervention that disregards drinking is an impractical strategy on pragmatic grounds. It also is squarely at odds with the disease concept of alcoholism espoused by AA and Al-Anon.[11] The disease concept holds that alcoholism is a primary illness, with typical symptoms and a predictable course, and requiring outside intervention. More than will power is needed for adequate treatment. And in family treatment, more is needed than changing others who are somehow to blame for the systems aspects of the problem. Therapists are ill-advised to take sides on the issue of cause versus effect when it comes to alcoholism, but in working with families, it cannot be assumed that emphasis on the system will be effective without some attention paid to alcoholism as a disease.[11]

Another useful conceptualization of alcoholism is as a final common pathway disorder; ie, one can get there from a multitude of origins—social, physiologic, psychological, etc.—but once a pattern of alcohol abuse develops, a family adapts to it. It is these self-reinforcing adaptive consequences that the family must substitute for, alter, or give up in successful therapy.[12] It is the need for treating the drinking problem and for treating the adaptations to it that create the special problems posed by alcohol abuse in family therapy.

There is extensive literature examining the premise that spouses of alcoholics, who invariably feel either like forlorn victims or frightful villains,[13] are in fact disturbed personalities themselves. Paolino and McCrady have reviewed this entire literature and in the process questioned the notion that there are characteristic pre-existing personality disturbances demonstrated that typifyspouses of alcoholics.[7] Similarly, little has been demonstrated to be characteristic of pre-existing personalities of alcoholics themselves. Paolino and McCrady conclude that the chaos, high disease rates, and higher-than-average rates of physical and emotional disturbances seen among alcoholics and their families are the consequence of years of disruption caused by heavy drinking. This is supported by the finding that marital interaction tends to improve when heavy drinking stops.[14] Overall, there is support in the literature for treatment approaches that do not stem from etiologic presuppositions and take advantage of multiple treatment resources, including self-help groups and family therapy. The latter is more effective if the therapist can comfortably reconcile the systems point of view with a disease model.[10]

There is much arising from clinical research, clinical experience, and concerns about prevention that supports taking a family therapy approach to the treatment of alcoholism.[15] An added task for the family therapist treating alcoholism is to become adept at identifying alcohol abuse in an individual and the adaptations to it on the part of the family.

SIGNALS AND CUES

If a person comes into a therapist's office with alcohol on his or her breath, the therapist should not shrug it off as a one-time event. The National Council on Alcoholism has even included such behavior in an inappropriate setting (such as a doctor's office) as presumptive evidence of alcoholism.[16] Many family therapists are not yet adept at creating some opportunity to "catch a whiff." Without the odor, one may have to watch for subtler cues of mild intoxication. (The chronic heavy drinker has a tolerance to alcohol and can hold a great deal without acting grossly drunk.) A little increased irritability, silliness, sleepiness, or accentuation of usual idiosyncratic behaviors may be all there is to clue the therapist. A hint of any such signs should lead to an inquiry about drinking in the previous few hours. If anyone in the family confirms that the person in question has been drinking, it should be taken as a signal of alcohol misuse until proven otherwise.

Among the other more blatant cues, there is concern raised by other family members about someone's drinking. In the case at the beginning of this chapter, a daughter's suspicions were ignored. They should have been taken seriously. Detailed questions about the extent and timing of drinking and immediate effects on the family should be asked post haste. To do so would serve two purposes: it would permit rapid identification of a drinking problem, and serve to model appropriate concern for the problem. In rare instances, it turns out that the concerned person has a very low threshold for seeing alcohol use as abuse. One or two drinks scares him or her. That ignorance can then be used as an opportunity for education, and move on. More often, unfortunately, therapists as well as family members have an unwarranted high threshold for identification of problematic alcohol use. Therapists are likely to lower their thresholds if they probe into what happens between family members when someone is drinking, and then compare that with what happens when no one is drinking.

Any symptom should be taken as a cue to look for alcohol abuse in the family. Psychosomatic disorders, low self-esteem, vague marital and life-stage complaints all indicate a careful look for alcoholism in the spouse as well as the identified patient. Of course, drug abuse by children requires alertness for alcoholism in parents or siblings, but so does under-achievement in school. Purely relationship symptoms should trigger questions about alcohol as well. Couples whose conflicts escalate to physical fighting or intense shouting are prime examples. Often it is easy to determine that the arguments only go out of control when one spouse has had something to drink, however small. Similarly, sexual imcompatibilities may relate to the use of alcohol by one spouse at times of lovemaking, though alcohol is less frequently the culprit with sexual complaints than with physical violence. Finally, the frequent statement, "My husband (or wife) drinks a lot, but he (or she) won't come in for therapy," should not be taken as a blithe endorsement to work only on the manifest problem. The presenting patient must be treated as a part of an alcoholic system. To make the point, he or she might at least be encouraged to seriously attend Al-Anon long enough to be exposed to others in similar situations, and thus learn something of how not to perpetuate the problem by overreacting in the presence of alcohol.

A TREATMENT DILEMMA

For many family therapists, there seems to be a dilemma inherent in treating alcoholism as a disease. It comes from the desire to treat family members equally, yet still keep a family systems perspective. Therapists often ask, "How can I tell them they are all part of the problem, and part of the solution, and then tell one person he or she is an alcoholic and has to stop drinking?" But the incompatibility is a false antithesis. Analogies are useful to allay these concerns. As an example: a couple is fighting at the top of the stairs. One pushes, the other falls downstairs and breaks a leg. If specific measures are not taken to treat the leg, it will heal poorly. There may be a chronic crippling effect. That effect in time will have its consequences, and the family will make adaptations to living with a crippled family member. The broken leg cannot be disregarded even though there are clearly relationship issues, in this case having to do at least with problem-solving, that precipitated this episode of physical injury. We must see to it that the broken leg is treated at the same time that we address both people for fighting; and so it should be with the treatment of alcoholism in family therapy.

It is not the tandem treatment of alcohol abuse and the family system that causes a dilemma, it is the approach that may create troublesome inconsistencies. If the couple who fought at the top of the stairs were in family therapy, the therapist could tell them that each member had the problem of living with somebody with an acute injury and with rapidly evolving subacute complications. It would be the responsibility of each person to do their part in overcoming the problem. The one with the broken leg must seek the best available medical care, follow treatment instructions to the letter, and take on rehabilitation vigorously. The partner must facilitate the healing process in several ways; eg, by helping with treatment-related transportation and with exercising procedures that call for assistance, and by practicing detachment to avoid overreactions of self-pity or irritibility. Both partners would be expected to take equal responsibility for attending therapy and doing assignments. Children might be called upon to be responsible for removing toys from tops of stairs or other hazardous zones, and also to practice detachment.

Leg-healing should be monitored frequently during our hypothetical family therapy. It would not take long, perhaps a few minutes out of each session if there are no problems. Is everyone doing their part well? How many fights were there in hazardous locations with toys underfoot last week? Last month? In what ways is the person with the healing leg still acting or being treated like a cripple? Poor healing or medical complications will perpetuate "cripple behavior," therefore it has to be stopped. Cripple behavior is incompatible with the new problem-solving behaviors between equals that the family is learning through therapy. If the cripple behavior persists and the therapist ignores it, progress with the family will be slow and erratic at best.

There are problems that reside in individuals, like broken legs and alcoholism, that can and must be addressed for family treatment to be fully effective. There need be no dilemma for the therapist if it is made clear to the family that each member will be held responsible for his or her efforts to deal with the problem and with the adaptation to it.

TREATMENT

Treatment of alcoholism within family therapy has three phases: (1) identification, (2) stopping, or severely curtailing (definitely second best), drinking, and (3) relinquishing the adaptations to alcohol misuse, and learning alternative behaviors. All these can be accomplished in family therapy. In fact, having other family members present often makes the first and second phases easier, and usually is essential to carry out the third phase.

Contrary to some opinion, identifying alcohol abuse is not difficult. A few detailed questions about quantity, frequency, timing, and consequences of alcohol use generally suffice. There are now some guidelines in the literature to make it easier. For example, there is the Michigan

Alcoholism Screening Test (MAST)[17] and its brief version[18] that include a number of useful questions about social consequences of drinking, such as "Have you ever neglected your family for two or more days in a row because you were drinking?" or, "Have friends or relatives ever raised any questions about your drinking?" or, "Have you ever lost friends or girlfriends/boyfriends because of drinking?" There is also the National Council on Alcoholism's Major and Minor Criteria for Alcoholism.[16] It is extremely powerful for a therapist to be able to say with confidence in front of several family members, for example, "From what you have told me about having blackouts and about drinking more than five or six drinks at a time, more than twice a week, I should tell you that by the Criteria of the National Council on Alcoholism you would be considered an alcoholic." The therapist can then add, "In addition, we have seen that there are several areas of your life—marital issues, driving habits, and on the job—where you have already experienced deleterious consequences to drinking, and yet you have been unable to change your drinking habits. Hence, by strictly social consequence measures, you also must be considered to have the problem of alcohol abuse." (Alcohol abuse and alcoholism are used interchangeably here. This is not the time to fight over the presence or absence of an "ism.") It is enough to establish that there is a serious problem that needs treatment. The drinker and family members can make up their own minds after some success with AA and family therapy as to whether they have been dealing with alcoholism.

The most productive time to ask questions about alcohol use and its consequences is in relation to an interpersonal issue. For example, "Sometimes we can't seem to talk without arguing," would be the ideal cue for "Is alcohol in the picture at those times?" If the answer is, "yes, always," or "usually," detailed questions can follow about how much wine, beer, and/or hard liquor both husband and wife have each had to drink on each day of the past week. (One drink of each is treated as equivalent in absolute alcohol content.) Other questions about job, driving, and social problems associated with alcohol can quickly follow.

Half the job of identification is thus readily completed. The other half, equally important, involves confirming the diagnosis to both drinker and family members. It is not enough to ask the questions. In fact, if all family members put themselves on the line and compelling answers are provided, yet the therapist still fails to explicitly state a diagnostic opinion, the experience may be worse than if no questions had been asked. Hearing the evidence and failing to commit to dealing with alcohol abuse as a first priority is tantamount to sanctioning the alcoholic behavior, or colluding with the idea that it is hopeless to discuss it, and thereby supporting whatever denial may be carried on by family members. Taking a position that alcoholism is present and that drinking must stop in order to achieve success with any other family therapy issues is, however, a powerful positive step with the system as well as the disease. It may be a sensitive step to negotiate, but it cannot be neglected without risk of failing at both systems and symptom treatment. Timing matters, but where alcohol is concerned the novice therapist will do better to err in the direction of addressing alcoholism too soon then to wait too long. Any risk of the former is balanced by the fact that the family will remember the therapist's diagnosis the next time they seek help; whereas, in the latter case, the family may continue to seek help that ignores the alcoholism and further postpone effective change.

Stopping alcohol-abusing behavior is the next phase of alcoholism treatment. It also is not enough to confirm that there is a drinking problem, even if this is done in front of the whole family. If the high volume and frequency of drinking persist, even the most creative and energetic work with couples and families will be thwarted.

The collusive interaction of one person abusing alcohol and other family members denying the fact or ineffectively complaining seems to be a central factor in obstructing change. For example, a family was seen in therapy for a period of months with some benefit but less than what might be expected. The oldest son was an underachiever in school, the younger son was quite shy, and the father was depressed and alcoholic. Early on, the father's drinking was seen as the paramount problem. He refused to go to AA or to stop drinking, but did enter into an agreement to greatly reduce his drinking "his own way" on a trial basis. The boys' mother attended Al-Anon and the boys attended Alateen. The father curbed his drinking substantially, and his depression lifted without medication. He continued to drink at times, though, and occasionally more than the two-drink limit he had set for himself. The father became an increasingly active participant in family therapy. He and his wife began to cooperate more around parenting issues, and it seemed that therapy would progress well. After a while it became apparent that the shy son had blossomed socially; but the underachieving son continued not to complete his homework. Eventually a parallel was drawn between that son's school behavior and his father's drinking. The son admitted that he felt his lying about whether he had completed his homework was no different from other lying that went on in the family. In the latter, he included both his father's lying about whether he was truly an alcoholic and needed to stop drinking altogether, and his mother's lying when she covered for her husband in many subtle ways.

The family treatment came to a stalemate. This stalemate persisted, until finally the son was helped to express his concerns for his father and offered to do his very best in school the coming year, provided father would accept his alcoholism and prove it by stopping drinking altogether. The father did not immediately agree; nor did his son expect him to, for he appeared to have some stake in his father's continued drinking as well, to keep the focus off the seriousness of his own difficulty with schoolwork. Hence, there remained much work to be done. Still, new lines had been drawn: it became clear that the drinking problem truly had to be stopped to adequately treat the family. It should be acknowledged that there is an alternative family approach to the son's problems, one that would focus on helping the older son more effectively disengage and individuate from his parents so that he could deal with his schoolwork problems independently from his parent's progress. An approach that bypasses drinking may be easier than one that successfully stops a family member's drinking, but results in treatment for the whole family are at risk of failure, as the above example demonstrates.

Stopping alcohol abuse by a family member requires the conviction that it is crucial; it requires perserverance on the part of the therapist. Those two qualities are more necessary than any specific technique. Assigning visits to AA for the drinker, Al-Anon for adult and young-adult family members and Alateen for teenage and preteen children is often a valuable starting point. In fact, *not* assigning them persistently may be experienced as showing less-than-total conviction, or timidity in insisting on necessary changes, even with reluctant clients. Each family member has a personal responsibility to attend a self-help group; this responsibility exists whether or not the drinker or another family member fails to go. Attendance serves multiple purposes that support and enhance family therapy. It provides a confirmatory experience, ie, that others who have experience say alcohol is a problem. It eventually provides 24-hour crisis support in the form of a sponsor. It helps teach family members how to detach themselves from the alcohol-abusing behavior and go on with their own lives, rather than contribute to perpetuating the problem. It also emphasizes that one is responsible, primarily to oneself.

I advise my clients to go to more than one meeting before deciding if they like it, and to shop around. There are hundreds of groups in most urban areas. People should find one that is socially compatible and geographically accessible. Check frequently to see if they have gone to the meetings and what they have learned from them, similar to drinking-behavior checks. Also, let people know that they may find others at the AA meetings who are bitterly opposed to any psychotherapy because of their own bad therapeutic experiences, which they feel delayed their alcoholism recovery progress. When prepared for these attacks, people usually are comfortable saying simply that their therapy and AA are compatible.

Predicting in front of the whole family what is likely to happen in therapy if drinking does not stop may also be helpful, at least in the long run. For example: I might say to a couple in therapy, "If the drinking does not stop, I would predict the following: You will seem to be working on the right things in therapy, but you will not resolve your differences. After a while you (the spouse) will get fed up and have an affair, or leave your marriage. You (the drinker), if you survive without a car accident or don't run over someone else or contract an alcohol-related illness, will gradually do less well in your job, and do less and less with other people except a few drinking companions. You will continue to lose the respect of your children." This is put forward in a matter-of-fact way, tailoring the details to the particular people. The couple is informed that it is their choice, but that the therapist has a responsibility as an expert to share with them evaluations and recommendations. The effect of this kind of approach is to foster a "no-lose" situation for the therapist and therapy. Hopefully, the family will be persuaded to commit to a plan for achieving abstinence as a first priority. If they have some members who are not ready to do that, however, it is then possible to proceed without hyprocisy. As the family is in therapy and the predictions come true, the therapist then has the leverage of an ongoing relationship and enhanced credibility. As with confirming the diagnosis, making such relevant predictions is more powerful because they have been made in front of other family members. Everyone knows what the authority has actually said first hand, and each person knows that the others know. This process also models alternatives to the usual subtle protective coverups of alcohol abuse within many families.

Resistance to working on overcoming alcohol abuse, then, is best handled by persistent open reassessment of the current family consequences of drinking, and by predictions of what will follow with and without stopping drinking. In addition, one can blatantly disregard the drinker in the family sessions when alcohol is in his or her system, and recognize the drinker atentively on a dry day. If someone cannot stop drinking or is in imminent danger because of the level of drinking or associated behavior, hospitalization for detoxification (essentially withdrawal from alcohol) should be recommended. Many alcohol abusers can stop drinking without hospitalization, and hospital detoxification in itself is often a stop-gap measure without lasting value; but when hospital detoxification is used as one component of an ongoing family treatment strategy, it can be invaluable.

Once abstinence is achieved, there are new alcoholism-related issues that must be addressed as part of family therapy. This third phase of treating alcoholism focuses on teaching the family how to substitute for the adaptations they have made to living with alcohol-abusing behavior. Families are inclined to have the same expectations of the newly-abstinent member as they had of that person drinking. For example, if the drinker is an adult, he or she may continue to be feared at the first hint of anger, yet disregarded in family decision-making and viewed contemptuously as a parent. To illustrate:

A family of five began therapy when the father was discharged from the medical service of a general hospital. He had been a daily heavy drinker for more than 10 years until the day he was hospitalized in a medical emergency for complications of his drinking. Having narrowly survived, he began attending AA from the hospital and remained abstinent after discharge. In he early stages of once-a-week therapy, he and his wife were frankly bewildered. They were encouraged to talk about family matters that previously had not been subject to joint discussion. He did not want to be bothered with thinking about such family matters as chores, home repair costs, vacation, or social plans, etc, while she openly resented even his reluctant contributions as intrusions into her affairs. They had no verbal mechanism for joint problem-solving, and she expected him to silently tolerate whatever she decided. When these roles were acknowledged and attributed benignly to a healthy adaptation to active alcoholism, the couple gradually came to try out more equal roles in decision making on everyday matters.

About that time, a 20-year-old prodigal returned home to live. He had been accustomed to getting his way in virtually all matters. He had done this through seeking a form of maternal protection from verbal lashings and other emotional wrongdoings on his father's part, and the pattern resumed immediately, even though his father was both abstinent and more approachable. If father objected to his son's drug use and noisy parties, the son would complain that his father was his old heartless self. Initially, the boy's mother would then automatically criticize her husband for his insensitivity toward his son; and the drugs and noise persisted. In therapy, much work was done with both mother and father in jointly setting limits with this son, and on supporting one another as parents. Through this process, the son was required to attend family therapy as a condition of living at home. Then it was possible to start the process of father and son talking with one another on a more open and respectful basis. This included giving the son a chance to vent his anger and dissappointment toward his father for his many drinking years marked by erratic and unapproachable behavior. That was followed by his father being helped to tell his son of his genuine concerns for his drug experimentation and lack of work discipline. He also shared his views of his own mistakes and what he now must do to change. As it became clear that the mother now supported the father's mandates, and that both consulted each other before committing themselves, there were fewer and fewer incidents caused by this son.

SUMMARY

It is important and often crucial to identify and treat alcoholism when it exists in a family in therapy. Relationship problems rarely go away while the drinking problem continues. Individual behavioral disturbances often do poorly as well. Disregarding alcohol abuse perpetuates a hopelessness in family members. Couples or parents and children fail to practice new problem-solving skills. Non-alcohol-related social activities continue to diminish, further reducing support systems, which should otherwise increase with effective family therapy. Furthermore, drinking problems are not likely to stop through treatment of other behavioral disorders in a family. The converse, however, is not so true. Marital relationships and symptoms, at least in the identified alcoholic, do tend to improve from the treatment of alcoholism. Still, there is much alcoholism treatment to do in families even after abstinence is achieved, in order to generate alternatives to some of the adaptations the family has made to alcohol abuse that are no longer appropriate.

There are a wide range of indirect cues that should trigger inquiries about patterns of alcohol use. They range from obvious statements, such as that a person only does a certain undesirable behavior when he or she drinks, to the presence of any inexplicably treatment-resistant symptom in any family member.

Effective intervention begins with gathering detailed information about quantity, frequency, timing, and setting of alcohol use. This must be followed by an explicit assertion of the presence and nature of an alcohol problem. Demonstrating an association between alcohol use and identified relationship issues can be useful in this process. Making treatment of the alcohol problem a first priority in the family therapy should then follow.

A treatment plan should require an equal commitment from all family members toward working on their family's alcoholism problem. Each member attending AA, Al-Anon, or Alateen (as appropriate) is an excellent way to reinforce this commitment. Frequent checks on the progress of each family member in carrying out his or her part of the alcoholism treatment facilitates this process. Once active drinking is no longer a problem, using family therapy techniques to foster changes in expectations of one another will complete the alcoholism treatment phase of family therapy.

REFERENCES

1. First Special Report To The US Congress on Alcohol and Health. US DHEW, Dec, 1971
2. Whitfield, CL, Williams K: The Patient with Alcoholism and Other Drug Problems. Southern Illinois University, 1976, pp 8–10
3. Davis D, Klagsbrun M: Substance Abuse in Psychiatric Versus general Medical Patients, unpublished manuscript
4. Habermen P: Childhood Symptoms in Children of Alcoholic and Comparison Group Patients. Journal of Marriage and the Family 28:152–154, 1966
5. Hall RCW, Popkin MK, DeVaul R, Stickney SK: The Effect of Unrecognized Drug Aguse on Diagnosis and Therapeutic Outcome. Am J Drug Alc Abuse 4:455, 1977
6. Schuckit MA: The Identification and Management of Alcoholic and Depressive Problems. Drug Abuse and Alcoholism Review 1:1–8, 1978
7. Paolino TJ, McCrady BS: The Alcoholic Marriage: Alternative Perspectives. New York, Grune & Stratton, 1977
8. Steinglass P: Experimenting with Family Treatment Approaches to Alcoholism, 1950–1975: A Review. Fam Proc 15:97–123, 1976
9. Janzen C: Families in the Treatment of Alcoholism. J Stud Alcohol 38:114–130, 1977
10. Davis D: Alcoholics Anonymous and Family therapy. J Marriage Fam Ther 6:65–73, 1980
11. King B, Bissell L, Holding E: The Usefulness of the Disease Concept of Alcoholism in Working with Wives of Alcoholics. Social Work in Health Care 3:443–455, 1978
12. Davis D, Berenson D, Steinglass P, Davis S: The Adaptive Consequences of Drinking. Psychiatry 37:209–215. 1974
13. Bailey M: Alcoholism and Family Casework: Theory and Practice. New York; Community Council of Greater New York, 1968
14. Burton G, Kaplan HM: Marriage Counseling with Alcoholics and Their Spouses, II, The Correlation of Excessive Drinking Behavior with Family Pathology and Social Deterioration. Br J Addict 63:161–170, 1968
15. Davis D: The Family in Alcoholism, in Fann E, Karacan I, Pokorny AD, Williams RL (eds): Phenomenology and Treatment of Alcoholism. New York, Spectrum, 1980
16. Criteria Committee, National Council on Alcoholism: Criteria for the Diagnosis of Alcoholism. Am J Psychiatry 129:127–135, 1972
17. Selzer M: The Michigan Alcoholism Screening Test (MAST): The Quest for a New Diagnostic Instrument. Am J Psychiatry 127:1653–1658, 1971
18. Pokorny AD, Miller BA, Kaplan HB: The Brief MAST: A Shortened Version of the Michigan Alcoholism Screening Test. Am J Psychiatry 129:342–345, 1972

PART V

Special Problems in Family Therapy

Joel Yager

13

Anorexia Nervosa and the Family

The earliest clinical descriptions of anorexia nervosa made note of the fact that families interacted with patients in peculiar ways often thought to be detrimental to the patients.[1,2] Over the years authorities have differed widely in their views about the role of the family in the pathogenesis of anorexia nervosa, and on how to include families in treatment. It should not surprise us to discover divergent opinions about this complicated syndrome. The fact that anorexia nervosa is currently being investigated and treated at virtually each level of bio–psycho–social organization (and that various experts intelligently argue for the primary importance of each level in pathogenesis and treatment), attests to our ignorance.[3,4] In order to put the role of the family in pathogenesis and treatment into perspective, this chapter will review available information on the transmission of anorexia nervosa in families, the known characteristics of parents, family stress response syndromes as they may relate to anorexia nervosa, frequently described parent–child interactions, and considerations of whole family systems. The prognostic importance of family characteristics are discussed, therapeutic strategies with respect to the family are described, and important research questions yet to be answered are enumerated.

DEFINING ANOREXIA NERVOSA

If one were to subscribe to currently prevalent views of "typical" family issues in anorexia nervosa, a clinical description would be as follows: The family is upper-middle-class, highly achievement-oriented, and values slimness and physical exercise. Although superficially a healthy family, certain unaddressed conflicts between the parents lurk below the surface. Because of lack of fulfillment as a couple (perhaps related to sexual hypocompatibility), the parents find themselves striving for fulfillment in other areas. The lines along which the family communicates are narrow, and concern is channeled toward the children so that the mother becomes excessively involved with them, perhaps overdirective, while simultaneously unable to acknowledge their individuality and somewhat fearful of their adolescent psychosexual development and impending separation. Parental overinvestment in and overdirectiveness of the children leads to high achievement orientation in which the vulnerable child becomes more concerned with external parental approval than with internal satisfaction; indeed, because of the parent's overdirectiveness and lack of acknowledgement, the child develops a very fragile self-image and feels that there are no real areas for self control. The child's poor sense of self and accompanying sense of being ineffective are ignored by the parents; parental approval fills the child's inner void in place of autonomy. At a point of disequilibrium in the family during the child's adolescence (perhaps due to increasing parental friction, the illness or death of a relative, the moving away of the child or a sibling to school, or an increased fearful awareness on the part of the mother that her daughter's adolescent moves toward independence and separation may produce an empty nest), the anorexia nervosa syndrome begins, often in the wake of an ordinary diet, where the patient "just wants to lose a few pounds" with the agreement and blessing of her family and friends.

REVIEWING THE STATUS QUO

The foregoing thumbnail sketch combines descriptions offered by Bruch,[5-7] Crisp et al,[8-13] Minuchin et al,[14-16] Russell et al,[17,18] and Selvini-Palazzoli,[19] among others. Although clinicians frequently encounter cases that contain elements of this typical situation, rarely are all the pieces neatly combined in any one case, and, as in most other clinical problems, many exceptions prove the rule. It will be the purpose of this chapter to dispel some of the stereotypes about anorectic families—or to at least put them into proper perspective—by critically evaluating the available studies and by considering them in a broad framework. We are well advised to reject premature "understanding" and to be skeptical about facile formulas that purport to explain anorexia nervosa; we are better off to retain a certain amount of confusion and ambiguity, waiting for additional information to support, modify, or refute current hypotheses.

Several factors limit our ability to accept the typical formulation described above. First, there is wide variation within the clinical syndromes. Although most authorities would agree that primary anorexia nervosa is characterized by a willful desire to be thin and by a loss of at least 15 to 25 percent of ideal body weight in the absence of other major psychopathology (such as delusional schizophrenia or depression), the diversity of the syndrome beyond this is great.[17,20] The age of onset is quite variable, so that some cases begin as early as 9 or 10 years of age, whereas others don't begin until their twenties or thirties, sometimes after the patient is married and has borne children. Ten to thirty percent of patients cease menstruating prior to a loss of weight, and others not until a good deal of weight has been lost. Some patients experience marked behavioral hyperactivity as one of the earliest symptoms, and others don't. A certain number develop a tendency toward binge eating, vomiting, and/or laxative abuse, whereas others don't. There is no uniformity of cognitive style so that obsessive, hysterical, and other patterns are encountered. Patients differ with respect to (1) their levels of ego development, (2) the nature and extent of features of borderline personality organization, (3) psychosexual development, (4) peer and heterosexual relationships and experience, (5) premorbid social competence, (6) academic striving, and a host of other areas. Recovered anorectics also vary widely: Some are exceptionally competent, industrious, purposeful, self-starting, and strong-willed, whereas others are timid and frightened. Some are perky and vivacious, whereas others are drab and colorless. Some are adaptive, resilient, and consistent, whereas others may demonstrate persistent and extreme borderline character disorganization in spite of some improvement in specific eating behavior disturbances, etc. A spectrum of anorexia nervosa syndromes may exist analagous to the schizophrenia syndromes, and anorexia nervosa may eventually best be considered as a symptom complex which is a final common pathway for several different pathogenetic processes. The extent to which differences in family characteristics are correlated with differences in the clinical subtypes remains unknown. Indeed, Crisp et al have suggested that the range of family psychopathology, too, is wide and in many respects may not be specific to the condition.[8,12]

METHODOLOGIC SHORTCOMINGS

Another set of problems relates to methodologic shortcomings that beset the family literature.[4] Just as with the early literature on the families of schizophrenics, much of the literature on anorexia nervosa and the family is speculative and impressionistic; the relationship of clinical observations to pathogenetic processes is unclear. Since no prospective studies exist, family processes are observed only subsequent to the onset of the condition, making it difficult to disentangle cause from effect; observer biases and retrospective distortion contaminate the data. There are few, if any, appropriate comparison samples, so that the relative significance of any presumed pathogenetic characteristic cannot be adequately evaluated. As is the case with many clinical syndromes in psychiatry, the initial "classic" descriptions of anorectic families were based on relatively small numbers, and findings were generalized as if to describe the entire lot. Each time this has happened in psychiatry's past (for example, with descriptions of the "typical" peptic ulcer personality or "typical" parental patterns for autistic children), the early formulae have proven inadequate and have had to be withdrawn and reconsidered. Also, psychiatry's history should teach us not to prematurely psychologize physiologic findings and to avoid glib statements (as have been made) to the effect that starving anorectics symbolize emotionally starving families;[21] such interpretations are risky at best. Finally, differences in sample selection, diagnostic criteria, socioeconomic status, etc., make it difficult to compare different series of patients reported in the literature.

In a problem as complicated and diverse as anorexia nervosa, we must appreciate that the clinical observer can rarely focus on all pertinent levels at the same time. Yet, symptoms are probably multi-determined (or at least multi-influenced), and may serve several simultaneous functions. In addition to expressing maladaptation and a breakdown in effective coping, symptoms are incorporated into the psychoeconomics of ongoing individual and family life to maximize their use. The clinical observer's perception and understanding of the symptoms will depend in part on the field of observation: a patient seen individually may appear to be helpless, dependent, timid, and victimized, whereas in a family context the same patient may appear to be exasperating and to have her parents intimidated, blackmailed, twisted around her finger, and bamboozled.

An adolescent anorectic's symptoms may be simultaneously considered from several points of views, and the symptoms may serve multiple purposes and convey several different but equally valid meanings. For example: (1) there is a biologic problem; and (2) the patient is conflicted about her wishes to separate from her family (and develops her symptoms in an effort to deal with this conflict); and (3) the patient develops her symptoms to create a diversion in the family, allowing her parents to shift their concern and attention away from their own problems and towards hers. Further, the "significance" of the symptoms may change over time: Early in her course a patient may view refusal to eat as a willful attempt to control her parents; later she may be helplessly and unwillingly controlled by the powerful autonomy of the symptom of refusing food, as if with the flow of time psychological superstructures were elaborated to maintain the symptom; that is, the behavior remains but its psychological meanings are altered.

With the foregoing introduction, let us address the following questions:

- What, if anything, is the role of the family in the pathogenesis of anorexia nervosa?
- What, if any, specific characteristics exist in a family that invite anorexia nervosa as opposed to any other mode of breakdown?
- What family characteristics may be nonspecific but permissive in promoting the appearance of anorexia nervosa in the vulnerable person?
- What family factors are conducive to maintaining an anorexic syndrome and affecting prognosis?
- How much of what we see in families represent stress reactions (*states*) in the wake of the impact of anorexia nervosa, rather than enduring family patterns (*traits*)?
- What is the incidence in the general population of various family patterns that have been described in relation to anorexia nervosa (eg, overcontrol, enmeshment, etc.)?
- What bearing does each of these issues have on rational family therapy?
- How much leverage can family therapy actually provide over and above that of nonspecific treatment and "spontaneous" remission to change the anorectic patient's psychological inner world and behavioral syndrome?
- How should family therapy be conducted to provide maximal benefit, and what specific pathology should be addressed?

Although satisfactory answers to these questions are not yet available, they focus on the major issues that demand consideration.

FAMILY TRANSMISSION OF ANOREXIA NERVOSA

Anorexia nervosa is a relatively uncommon disorder, but its incidence among members of afflicted families is much higher than in the general population. Although no suggestion of a genetic vulnerability can be made with confidence, the possibility cannot be ruled out. A number of reports have appeared of identical twins concordant for anorexia nervosa, but some discordant cases have also been reported (although the discordant twins have not all yet passed through the age of risk).[4,22–24] The estimated prevalence of anorexia nervosa among sisters of patients is between 3 and 10 percent, and a significant number of patients' mothers report that they experienced very low adolescent weight or outright anorexia nervosa.[18,25–27] Kalucy et al[12] studied 56 families and found an explicit history of significantly low adolescent weight, anorexia, or fears of weight phobia in 27 percent of mothers and 16 percent of fathers. In other series, 3 to 10 percent of mothers reported histories of anorexia nervosa or extreme thinness.[18,25,26,28] The incidence of anorexia nervosa in the children of women who were themselves anorectic is unknown. Among my own patients, many have older or younger sisters with full-blown or *forme fruste* anorectic syndromes. However, such findings cannot be simplistically attributed to genetic causation. Further research using adoptive and half-sibling studies is necessary to tease apart possible genetic contributions.

Biologic nongenetic vulnerability is also a strong possibility in at least some cases, since several series have reported problems with pregnancy and delivery in close to a third of patients, a higher-than-usual incidence.[25,29] The importance of determining whether there are genetic and biologic contributions to the syndrome is directly relevant to family therapy: guilt in parents is ubiquitous, and, as in schizophrenia, the absence of definitive etiology contributes to the manner in which parents blame themselves. The parents of diabetic children, too, feel guilty about the appearance of illness in their children, yet the guilt may be of a somewhat different nature and is dealt with differently. In a certain way biology "can't be helped," whereas psychogenesis still carries heavy negative moral implications.

Not surprisingly, weight pathology has been studied in the families of anorectics. However, largely because few include appropriate comparison groups, the reported incidence of overweight and underweight individuals in most of these studies cannot be adequately assessed. For example, Kalucy et al[12] found 23 percent of the mothers and 20 percent of the fathers in a 56-family study to be overweight; 16 percent of mothers and 9 percent of fathers to be underweight; 11 percent of mothers and 7 percent of fathers to have weight fluctuation; 27 percent of mothers and 16 percent of fathers to have dieting behavior; 25 percent of families to have an obese sibling; and 14 percent some other obese family member, almost always the maternal grandmother. Halmi et al found frank obesity in 18 percent of parents, 5 percent of siblings, and 16 percent of grandparents in a series of 44 patients.[25] Nevertheless, in a tightly controlled investigation in which parents of anorectics were matched very carefully with control parents for age, occupational levels, education, and height, parents of the anorectic patients did not differ from the controls with respect to either average weight or variations in weight.[30] The importance of proper control groups is emphasized.

FAMILY STRESS RESPONSE SYNDROMES

The phenomenon of stress response syndromes in the individual has been extensively studied; however, family patterns of stress responses have not been adequately addressed.[31,32] In the wake of major catastrophes, families evidence transient adjustment responses, and some of the observed phenomena may be very time-limited (states) rather than enduring patterns (traits). Under stress, exaggerated response patterns may reveal defensive operations of family members in bold relief; under less stressful situations, such families may not appear to be so pathologic.

What is the impact of the sick child on a family? According to one description:

Each day the parents feel worried, begin each day with fear and tension, and always wonder in what mood the child will wake up. Parents experience many levels of sorrow and it's critical not to remain at the deepest level too long... The tendency to be apprehensive of one's child forces the uncertain parent to do little, to live one's life around the child, not intruding or disrupting for fear of triggering a fit of temper. Parental attitudes and concerns about their child shift across the span of development reflecting changes and hopes and aspirations and diminution of energy... For some the drain of years of recalcitrant management problems takes its toll on family members whose resources and strengths have been depleted, and an alternative living situation may be required... A vulnerable area for parents, especially for mothers, is the adequacy of their self-concept. A mother's identity often is intimately tied to the child's condition. Parents are confronted with a terrible dilemma. Old discipline habits (verbal warnings, reasonings) are virtually worthless—they are unclear about why their child behaves as she does, what might work or what might be the emotional effect of a punishment."*

Although the foregoing remarks were written to describe the reactions of patients of autistic children, they could easily have been written to

---

*Reprinted from Marcus LM: Patterns of coping in families of psychotic children. American Journal of Orthopsychiatry 47:391, 395, 1977. With permission.

describe the parents of an anorectic or any child with a serious, baffling, and frightening disorder. This should reinforce the importance to family theorists of a coping-and-adaptation point of view, in which parental behavior is viewed as response to illness.[33]

With respect to anorexia, "there are few conditions that provoke so much concern, but also frustration, rage, and anger as the spectacle of a starving child refusing food."[6] In 1873, Lasegue observed that "the family has but two methods at its service which it always exhausts—entreaties and menaces—and which both serve as touchstone."[34] Parents of an anorectic are confronted with ambiguity, uncertainty, and a lack of knowing how to proceed. How should they decide what will work and what won't? When to force and when not to force? Threaten or not threaten? Be exceptionally vigilant or ignore? Parents are plagued by the threat of a potentially fatal situation, and by a starving child whose behavior and problem suggest at least the illusion of willfulness; they inevitably confront the problem at every family meal. Given the ambiguity of causation, parental guilt (or denial and projection of guilt) is virtually inescapable: parents entertain the possibility that they did something to cause it; they wonder if they did something dreadful to the child at an early age, if the other parent is to blame, and if they continue to act in a harmful way.

Individuals and families vary in their cognitive styles and stress-response patterns. Just as some individuals are predominantly minimizers, isolaters, or deniers, others hypervigilant and ruminative worriers, and still others typically-adaptive information-seekers and skill-learners,[35] families also vary in their coping styles. Crisp et al[8,12] have described how some parents appear exceedingly neurotic and disorganized at presentation, yet rapidly integrate and show unexpected ego resources with child's recovery; others are not so seriously disturbed at the time of admission, but then demonstrate serious adjustment problems as the child improves.[8,12] Dally reported five types of mother–daughter interactions likely to occur during the course of anorexia nervosa (and, transitively, in any other situation as well.[36] These basically describe in exaggerated fashion the usual adolescent conflicts, and they cover virtually all possible patterns of mother–daughter coping:

1. The mother will meet her daughter halfway; the two live amicably together, sharing household functions, somewhat like sisters.
2. The mother will not be able to withstand her daughter's competition, particularly if she and her husband are on bad terms. She may then break down, go to work, or leave the field in another way. Or, the

situation may be reversed and the patient may be pushed out of the home.

3. The mother withstands her daughter's attempts to take her place. Then the patient retreats and leaves the home, extruded.

4. The daughter's attacks are beaten off, but she is unable to bring herself to leave home and withdraws instead into virtual isolation and solitariness in the house. There is severe regression.

5. The daughter regresses to a baby-like state, and becomes utterly dependent on her mother or a mother-substitute, shows no initiative, acts delicately, and must be served hand and foot.

The differences, no doubt, result from the pairing of anorectics with variable ego strengths and personalities with mothers of variable ego strengths and personalities. The major point is that all such combinations and outcomes occur in anorexia nervosa.

Phenomena in stress responses change over time. Just as Kubler-Ross[37] described more-or-less sequential stages of denial, anger, depression, bargaining, and acceptance in response to gradual or sudden awareness of cancer, so may whole families' patterns of responses vary over time, acutely and chronically, in the aftermath of a crisis. While a family's own baseline pathology is of paramount importance in shaping its response, the extent of family disturbance may also be partly determined by the nature and severity of the child's anorectic syndrome. The amount of evident depression, enmeshment, or directiveness of parents, for example, may reflect how serious and out of control parents perceive the child's illness to be, and how frantic they feel. In somewhat caricaturized fashion, the mother and/or father may minimize or deny at first, then go through a period of high emotionality, perhaps followed by apathy after repeated chronic lack of success (a model of "learned helplessness"),[38] and perhaps ultimately become somewhat more realistic. Each family member's adaptive style and adjustment over time modifies the others, producing whole family patterns with different temporal phasic interaction characteristics. Thus, some commonly noted features of anorectic families (see below) may change over time. A family in acute crisis may appear to be exceptionally enmeshed (temporary enmeshment may reflect attempts to increase family cohesion), but after a while may "burn out" and disengage. Thus, enmeshment and disengagement may not just be traits, but may reflect state characteristics as well. Certainly such characteristics should be studied over time to see how enduring they are once an acute stress is alleviated. In this regard, reductions in family enmeshment attributed to family therapy may, in fact, represent the natural phasic resolution of a stress response.

CHARACTERISTICS OF PARENTS

What personality and psychopathology characteristics can one expect in the parents of anorectics? Considerable disturbance has been observed, but once again the lack of comparison groups prevents full assessment of the significance of these observations. This section and the following one describe research studies intended to convey the variety among families. The purpose is also to illustrate the considerable difficulty encountered in attempting to compare such basic concepts as anxiety or depression (to say nothing of borderline personality organization), in such studies. No doubt, many of our own pet notions would unravel considerably when subjected to the rigor of systematic study.

A variety of psychosomatic disturbances have been noted in the parents of anorectics, and gastrointestinal problems have undoubtedly been of interest. Halmi et al reported peptic ulcer in 16 percent, gastritis in 32 percent, and irritable colon in 23 percent of first-degree relatives of 44 patients,[25] and Dally found peptic ulcer in 11 percent of parents.[38] Kalucy et al reported migraine in 30 percent of mothers, and believed that to exceed the incidence in the general population.[12] Overall, Kaye and Leigh found a 16-percent incidence of psychosomatic disorders in their patients' parents.[39] Many studies report emotional disturbances in large numbers of the parents, but precise descriptions differ, no doubt due in part to diagnostic variation: the reported incidence of psychiatric illness among parents has ranged from about 25 to 65 percent.[12,18,26,28,36,39] However, whereas according to Kaye and Leigh about 34 percent of parents have anxiety neurosis, Cantwell et al reported that only 6 percent have anxiety, but that 33 percent merit a diagnosis of primary affective disorder.[28] Kalucy et al found manic-depressive psychosis in 14 percent among the fathers of patients, an unusually high incidence not reported in other series.[12] Morgan and Russell reported 20 percent of mothers to have mental illness, often resulting in prolonged separation during infancy from the child who developed anorexia nervosa.[18] Excessive use of alcohol in parents, especially fathers, is reported by several authors, but it is not always clear to what extent the heavy use of alcohol occurred in the wake of the family crisis.[12,26] Schizophrenia is rarely reported. Dally, who mentions a 33 percent incidence of emotional disturbances in parents in his large series, concluded that the incidence of neurosis or psychosis in first-degree relatives of patients with anorexia nervosa is similar to that found in other groups of neurotic patients.[36]

With respect to parental personality features, Kalucy et al reported that prior to the onset of the child's anorexia nervosa, marked phobic avoidance was said to be present in 33 percent of mothers and 11 percent of fathers, depression in 33 percent of mothers and 9 percent of fathers, marked obsessionality as a dominant lifestyle trait in 29 percent of fathers and 14 percent of mothers, and excessive alcohol use in 19 percent of fathers and 7 percent of mothers.[12]

"Typical" personalities of anorectic parents have been discussed for some time. Cobb described the typical home situation to consist of a "robust, nagging mother and passive father," but the personalities found by subsequent investigators have by no means been homogeneous.[40] Kay and Leigh found mothers who are often fussy and nervous, and fathers who are sometimes easy-going and sometimes quick-tempered.[39] Dally found great diversity: In 21 percent of families, he found mothers to be forceful and robust, while fathers were weak and remote; in 17 percent, he found a tense, neurotic, forceful mother and a passive father; in 3 percent a normal mother forced into a dominant role due to the early death of a husband; in 5 percent a domineering, aggressive, constantly-quarreling father; in 8 percent a domineering but not aggressive father; in 4 percent a psychopathic, unreliable, inconsistantly domineering father;[36] In other words, there is little consistency at this level of observation. Thus, if a common pattern is to be found in the families of anorectics, it would have to be at a more subtle level. We are reminded of Franz Alexander's reformulation of psychosomatic problems: He rejected Dunbar's suggestion that each psychosomatic illness was characterized by a specific personality profile. Instead, he focused on underlying "nuclear dynamic conflicts," each of which in Alexander's view could be manifest by many different superficial personality and defense characteristics.[41,42] Our own observations of large numbers of families would confirm that with respect to personality there is great diversity both among mothers and fathers. While in some families one or even both parents may evidence severe personality disturbance with borderline features, in many instances this is simply not the case.

PARENT–CHILD INTERACTIONS

Considerable variation similarly marks available descriptions of parent–child interactions in anorexia nervosa. The comments previously made in the discussion of family stress syndromes should be recalled, but in general the interactions to be described have been thought by the authors to exist pre-illness, on the basis of careful family interviews. Morgan and Russell felt that relations between family and patient were disturbed in 54 percent of their patients prior to the onset of illness.[18] Reports of oversolicitious mothers with "very" attached daughters (ie, excessive closeness in the family between mother and daughter) range from 31 to 39 percent;[12,36,39] ambivalent relationships between mother and daughter are reported in about a third of families[26,36] (excessive closeness and attachment in no way precludes ambivalence); some mothers are strict disciplinarians (11 to 12 percent);[26,39] and smaller percentages of mothers are seen as overtly rejecting (1 to 11 percent). Similarly, many types of father–daughter relationships are seen, with some fathers being lenient, kind, and affectionate, others cool and antagonistic, others overtly hostile, etc. In some families, both parents have similar attitudes toward the child, whereas in other families parents attitudes are opposite. Of note, satisfactory or "normal" relationships are also reported in the range of 11 to 25 percent.[36,39]

Overprotectivness is also manifest in some instances by the anorectic daughter toward one or another of the parents, often the mother. Overprotection of parents by children has been thought to represent projective identification as a component of the children's defenses.

Several experimental studies of parent–child interactions are of interest. Crisp and Kalucy and found some families in which parents revealed a desired body size for their daughters that was of anorectic proportion.[9] Sonne and Goldstein[43] studied 42 intact families with a variety of inpatient and outpatient adolescent females, 10 of whom were hospitalized anorectics. Using a structured test, they found mothers of anoretics to be generally highly directive of their childrens' behavior compared to the fathers and to mothers of the outpatient groups; but mothers were not more projective with respect to what they believed the children were thinking or intending. Fathers' responses varied: some were directive, whereas others were indirect and intrusive with high projection patterns. The authors suggest that differences in parental–child interactions such as those studied may correlate with differences in prognosis.

The findings that parents often invalidate statements of anorectics is clinically familiar. Among my own patients, for example, one explained, "people always ignore me, talk over me, and finish my sentences. It's as if I'm not there." Another described how she was explicitly prohibited from telling her mother how miserable she felt, since her mother did not want to become upset by hearing about such things. A third told how she would fancifully invent pleasant things to tell her father, since she feared that he would avoid all contact with her if she were to honestly tell him how she really felt and what she really did.

FAMILY SYSTEMS

A most interesting approach to the problem of anorexia nervosa has been proposed by family systems theorists, notably Minuchin et al.[14,15] Others, including Crisp et al[8,10,12] and Bruch[5-7] have also paid increasing attention to the family as a system and have offered formulations that relate family structure to anorexia. Such ideas have been widely influential throughout the United States and Europe.[18,44]

The symptoms of the anoretic patient can be considered from a new vantage when the family is viewed as a self-regulating system with characteristic transactions, redundancies in communication, and sub-systems composed of the members aligned by age, role, and other common qualities. Symptoms can be conceptualized as evoked, supported, and reinforced by certain transactions in the system, and can be seen to play a part in the system's entire economy and dynamics. Family systems can be characterized by their communicational rules, power structure, flexibility of roles, clarity and expressiveness of ideas and feelings, closeness and security of each individual's boundaries, and by the problem-solving efficacy of the family unit to accomplish the family's task of helping individuals to have a sense of belonging while developing their autonomy. Communications may be clear or diffuse, roles may be complimentary or incongruent, etc.[15,19,45] Lewis et al have described families at varying levels of competence, including the healthy family (*optimal*), the competent but pained family, the mid-range dysfunctional family, and the severely dysfunctional family.[45] In general, families of many anoretic patients would fall into the mid-range dysfunctional group. In Lewis' categorization, mid-range dysfunctional families are composed of two types: the family that is stable with respect to dominance and submission roles, and the chronically conflicted family, which always fights. (These bear some resemblance to the schizmatic families described by Lidz, but they are not as chaotic as those of some schizophrenic families.[46]) Such families are also characterized by powerful coalitions other than the one between the parents, for example, between a submissive parent with one of the children, or with a person outside of the nuclear family, such as a grandparent. This is often the maternal grandmother, and the "trailing grandmother sign," in which the grandmother accompanies the patient's mother to doctors and hospital visits, is not infrequent in these patients.

Systems concepts regarding anorectic families have been especially advanced by the work of Minuchin et al.[15] Employing standard clinical assessment measures, these researchers have identified a group of family system characteristics that in their view typify the psychosomatic families of diabetics, asthmatics, and anorectics that they studied, where family interactions appear to contribute to and sustain the appearance of symptoms in the child.

Minuchin's System

According to Minuchin et al, the anorectic system is characterized by the following features:

Enmeshment. This refers to an intense, close form of family interaction, where members are overinvolved, each person may answer for any other, and subsystem boundaries are poorly differentiated. There is excessive togetherness, and family members intrude on each others thoughts and feelings, which results in poorly-differentiated perceptions of each other and of themselves. Features of borderline personality organization may be evident in individual parents. In such a system, the child learns to subordinate the self and does not expect to develop internal competance, but rather seeks external approval. So, achievement and performance are not sought for the self but to obtain love from the rest of the system.

Overprotectiveness. In such child-oriented families, the family hypervigilantly focuses on the child, and the child focuses on the self and the parent, each extremely alert to the other's signals. Tight parental control over the children is exerted under the cloak of concern. the overprotectivness is a two-way street: the anorectic child may be highly protective of one or both parents and is often significantly involved in the parent's conflicts, supporting now one and then the other.

Rigidity. Such families are often inclined to maintain the status quo and have difficulty in allowing the individual development and autonomy of any of the members. Roles may be rigidly maintained, and while intrafamilial boundaries are diffuse, strong boundaries may separate the family from the rest of the world. The family sees itself as a little "odd." There is, though, a highly valued sense of family loyalty (and denial of self), and often the boundaries between the spouse pair and their own families of origin are diffuse, so that crossgenerational coalitions are common between parents and grandparents as well as between children and parents.

Low threshhold for overt conflict and lack of conflict resolution. These families characteristically avoid and put off conflicts rather than confront them. Three patterns of conflict avoidance are described: triangulation, parent–child coalitions, and detouring. Triangulation refers to a situation where the child is forced to side with one parent against the other, usually in a shifting pattern. Parent–child coalitions refer to a more stable alignment of a child with one parent against the other. In detouring, the parents submerge their own conflicts and focus on the child, often requiring the child to reassure them about their own parenting. Parental conflicts are common, and often include sexual dissatisfaction. (Perhaps more importantly, Kalucy et al reported that 34 percent of fathers and 19 percent of mothers explicitly threatened parental separation pre-illness.[12]) Therefore, being distracted by a sick child helps diffuse the conflict. This common concern serves both parents well. The child's symptoms are rewarded and sustained, and the symptoms become imbedded in the family organization.

OTHER CHARACTERISTCS

Also, the role of the child as protector of the parents is not unwelcome, and the child may demonstrate inappropriate protective behavior and protection-eliciting behavior. In Minuchin's terms,[15] the child's involvement in the parental conflict supports the particular system; the patient's symptom is significant as a "regulator" in the family system. The effectiveness of the symptom to handle the parental conflict and bind in this way reinforces the continuation of the symptoms and keeps the family together. Some experimental support for this formulation is offered by the findings of Crips et al,[8] who demonstrated that parents of anorectics, especially those with poor marriages, revealed more anxiety and depression on personality inventories when the anorectic child was improving and gaining weight as compared to when the child entered the hospital. This might be interpreted to mean that parental symptoms increase when the child can no longer serve as a focus for family conflict. (An alternative interpretation might be that such families become more anxious in the face of the patient's impending discharge from the hospital.)

Finally, within the anorectic family system, it is common to focus on bodily complaints, eating and its attendant behaviors, and food fads.

Other Family Systems

Similar family systems difficulties are described by Selvini-Palazzoli, based on work at the Milan Center of Family Studies.[19] She reports that in anorectic families, family members commonly reject messages sent by others; parents are reluctant to assume personal leadership or responsibility, and each parent blames decisions on the other; the actions of each member are never attributed to one's own personal preference but to the needs of another member, so that all decisions are "for the good" of someone else; there is a great deal of blame shifting, and while mothers may overblame themselves, they attribute their behavior to their devotion to the children. Each parent feels victimized and feels as if she or he is making great sacrifices for the family. In what Selvini-Palazzoli calls "three-way matrimony" (similar to triangulation) the child must serve as a go-between for the parents, and consequently uses up any energy she might have had to become autonomous and independent. Any attempt on the part of the child to escape is met by the concerted opposition of the parents.

Limitations of Family Systems Theory

Before going further, it is worth reviewing just how far family systems formulations such as those described above can take us toward understanding anorexia nervosa. Certain major limitations prevent us from generalizing any current systems formulation to all anorectic families. First, sample selection is biased in studies such as Minuchin's, where only intact families have been studied and where predominantly younger patients are seen. Second, the methods of participant-observation by clinician–researchers are plagued by observer rating biases—the initial formulations of the investigatores may heavily color what they subsequently see in families. Third, it is evident that the type of family described above is specific neither for anorexia nervosa nor for only psychosomatic families, one reason that so many clinicians who have little experience with anorexia nervosa find these concepts intuitively familiar. While the family system formulations may help to explain how symptoms can be sustained and reinforced once they appear, they so not account specifically for the occurence of anorexia nervosa, rather than any other breakdown syndrome (since one can imagine that even severe acne in an adolescent could serve a similar family system function by becoming the focus of parental overconcern). Nor do they explain the intermediate mechanisms whereby these family patterns translate into altered self-perceptions, desire for thinness, early amenorrhea, hyperactivity, and other features of the syndrome.

Together with Minuchin, Crisp et al[8] have postulated that anorexia nervosa is more likely to develop in families with "neurotic constellations" that prohibit adolescent maturation and where the child's symptoms can be viewed as protecting one or both parents. Where mothers have phobic avoidance, potential emancipation of the adolescent patient may provoke maternal anxiety, and the daughter's regression may be protective in a manner analogous to the dynamics of school phobia in a younger child. A wide variety of immediate pre-illness events that threaten family homeostasis can precipitate the illness. A further contribution by this group toward explaining specificity for anorexia nervosa in the family system is offered by Kalucy et al, who suggest several ways in which eating, body shape, and weight can be vehicles for family interaction and communication.[12] They reported that 23 percent of the families studied had very deviant eating patterns. Examples include one person always eating separately, restrictions against conversations at meals, etc, so that primary abnormalities in the family surrounding eating are evident. In weight-preoccupied families with narrow and inflexible ranges of coping mechanisms, food concern is one of the few channels of communication; food preoccupation helps emphasize oral and dependency aspects of development and defends against aggressive, sexual, and autonomous strivings. However, these writers clearly point out that such features are not shared by all anorectic families and that, within these formulations, much room exists for considering the intrapsychic capacities and vulnerabilities of the individual child.

In contrast to the intact families studied by Minuchin et al, a considerable number of anorectic families are broken, often before the onset of symptoms. In Kay and Leigh's group many patients were from broken homes, and in a quarter the fathers were lacking before the patient reached age 16.[39] In seven percent of Kalucy et al's families, actual parental separation occurred prior to the onset of symptoms.[12] Among our own patients (perhaps due to a bias of California culture) a considerable number come from homes where divorces occured years before the onset of anorexia nervosa. Such "fractured families" must be investigated before a comprehensive systems formulation for anorexia nervosa can be achieved. Anorectic symptoms remain long after patients leave their families, and years after the system's immediate reinforcers are no longer present and the secondary gains are no longer obvious.

Major questions remain regarding family systems described above in relation to anorexia nervosa: Are specific types of family systems a necessary prerequisite for the appearance of the syndrome in certain subtypes? Are they only permissive and facilitating for the appearance of the syndrome where vulnerability exists due to other, as yet unknown, factors? Are they unrelated? What other systems patterns can be found in anorectic families?

FAMILY PATHOLOGY AND PATIENT PROGNOSIS

In general, the sickest patients come from the sickest families. Several authors have found parental conflict and dominant, rejecting, or neurotic parents to be related to poor outcome.[8,18,36] For example, mothers of patients with poor outcome had significantly higher initial depression ratings on personality inventories (with a trend toward significantly elevated symptom ratings on other scales as well), than did mothers of patients with good outcome.[8] However, others have not found this relationship.[27,47] In Crisp's series, poor outcome was predicted by disturbed parental relationship and disturbed relationship of patients to parents prior to the illness.[11] Social class was another family characteristic related to outcome, and in one series, higher-social-class patients had a better apparent response to treatment.[12] The authors suggest that one factor at work is the relative ease with which higher-social-class patients and families could enter into psychotherapeutic work, but this notion requires a good deal of further study before it can be accepted. Finally, Beaumont et al reported that vomiters and purgers were far less likely than patients who were simply dieters to have histories of disturbances within the family as possible precipitating factors.[48]

FAMILY THERAPY AND THE TREATMENT
OF ANOREXIA NERVOSA

Family therapy must be considered as only one component of a total treatment plan for anorexia nervosa. The needs of the individual patient must be addressed through hospitalization when indicated (this need not be prolonged), modified supportive behavioral programs to help the patient gain weight in the initial phases, individual psychotherapy for the patient, medications when indicated, and family assessment and therapy. There is no evidence to support either the view that family therapy is the *only* mode of therapy to be employed, or the view that recovery is impossible without family therapy. However, there is general agreement that involvement of the whole family is of benefit and may increase chances for recovery (without any agreement on exactly what family therapy *is*). In this regard, Bruch appears to have modified her views over the last few years in the direction of family therapy. In 1973, she wrote, "I have not been able to convince myself that conjoint family therapy— which means seeing all of the family together for the full treatment period—offers any advantage or is even feasible with these serious disorders."[5] She felt that family therapy is but one component. Subsequently, in *The Golden Cage* (1978), she wrote, "there is no rule on how to handle this except for one generalization: clarification of the underlying family problems is a necessary part of treatment," and that family therapy is often an important and necessary adjunct.[7] Selvini-Palazzoli also began to work with anorectics with an individual psychoanalytic therapy orientation which over the years has given way to a family therapy/family systems approach.[19]

Many of the observations and formulations described above may provide a rationale for family therapy. To the extent that family operations such as enmeshment, overprotectiveness, rigidity, avoidance of conflict, weight preoccupation, etc, are thought to be pathogenic or even only sustaining of symptoms, then a determined attempt to alter these operations either directly or by working through their psychopathologic underpinnings might reasonably promise therapeutic benefit. Changing the family context should change the individual's responses and experiences.[15]

According to Selvini-Palazzoli, in organizations as complex as families, "transformations" can occur if rules of interaction are altered.[19] When internal organization is changed, family members are required, forced, allowed, or liberated to make use of other previously blocked communicational patterns. Viewed in another way, the impact of family therapy can alter the "ruts" in which a family system finds itself, and can have positive nonspecific effects as well as specific effects. A high-energy, high-valance family therapy intervention may serve to remoralize a family and reduce hopelessness (nonspecific effect), and at the same time may theoretically provide the energy of activation required to upset the pathologic family equilibrium and permit the establishment and testing of new patterns, ie, a specific effect—a transformation of organization.[49]

Viewed in yet another way, as a hydraulic model, the therapist may strive to reduce the pressure exerted by the family on the patient to sustain the symptoms, and in consequence symptoms may simply disappear. Here pressure is diverted away from the child toward the parent with a rechannelization of problems to be worked out between the parents.

As a critical reader of the available literature, I remain unconvinced about the demonstrated superiority of any one type of family therapy; moreover, I am unaware of any systematic study that has yet demonstrated to my satisfaction that *any* carefully described family therapy in and of itself or in combination with other therapies significantly altered the outcome in a series of cases of anorexia nervosa. Furthermore, I am sadly bewildered by the plethora of theoretical and metaphysical constructs, most of which lack adequate definition. Virtually all of them defy clear translation into the clinical setting such that two experienced clinicians can consistantly agree on what they see and what they are talking about (and in turn consistently demonstrate these "findings" and "tactics" to clinicians from various other institutions).

However, as a clinician working with anorectic patients, I find the notion of family therapy to be intuitively appealing and clinically useful.

The blend of tactics I employ reflects no one school and varies from case to case, depending on the specifics of patient and family. The remarks below reflect a personal synthesis of reading and experience. I pay particular attention to the nonspecific factors in therapy, and I attempt to be empirically pragmatic. Other family therapists employ strategies more closely married to particular theoretical notions about underlying family dynamics in anorexia nervosa, but since I remain skeptical about the universality of such formulations, my therapy varies with my assessment of the individual case. The following remarks on treatment focus exclusively on issues of the family and do not consider the necessary concurrent approaches to individual treatment of the patients that I have discussed elsewhere.[4]

Even if family factors play no role at all in etiology, family therapy may be of help in reducing the illness-sustaining factors, thereby facilitating natural remission. In a complex biosocial system, subsystems vary with respect to autonomy, permiability, malleability, the contributions each makes to pathogenesis, and how accessible each is to different therapeutic interventions. Rational therapy must be directed at the accessible therapeutic receptor sites where one can gain some leverage, even if these sites are far removed from the most potent levels of cause.

Goals of Family Therapy

Goals for family therapy have been implied in much of the previous discussion. With respect to individuals within the family, a first intention is to maintain each person's self-esteem and to help each person deal with issues of worry, panic, and shame that derive from the impact of the anorectic process on the family. In general, family therapy strives to help each family member, including the patient, become more autonomous and less enmeshed, to strengthen appropriate coalitions, and to enable family members to resolve conflicts at their proper locus, usually generation boundaries. Such therapy will attend to the concerns, anxieties, and depression in each family member, features that may have preceded or be consequent to the appearance of anorexia. Some family therapists attempt to treat and alter the borderline personality organization in the family. This is most often an ambitious and optimistic goal, at best exceedingly difficult to do, and in some cases an utter exercise in futility dedicated to an outcome that is theoretically possible but that has yet to be documented.

Therapeutic goals vary with the developmental status of the patient and with the family's stage of the life cycle. For preadolescents who will remain within the family, therapy should strive to increase parental effectiveness and control, to strengthen the parental coalition, and to resolve their conflicts. With adolescent patients, the family should be helped to allow the adolescent to develop autonomy, individuate, and become independent. With the young adult patient already out of the home, the family may be ambivalent or inconsistent about keeping the patient out of the parental home, and the issue of sustaining independence during periods of regression must be faced. It does not suffice to simply advise parents on how to ignore or instruct the child with regard to eating; the underlying ineffective family transactions and conflicts must be identified and dealt with.

The setting of goals also depends on the severity and chronicity of the syndrome. While a certain number of patients are virtually intractable, the majority are not. Careful assessment and reassessment over time are required, and generally, improvements of at least a modest sort are achievable in almost every case.

Roles of the Family Therapist

The family therapist serves multiple roles simultaneously, including those of questioner, listener, educator, clarifyer, focuser, confronter, identifier of process, modifier, reinforcer, introjective model, permission-giver, and suggestor or director. Working with anorectic families, the family therapist must be comfortable with flexibility, being able to join and separate from the family—to insert and to step back, to organize, control, conduct, and to become part of the system while maintaining distance. Because of the complexity of these events and the myriad of phenomena and levels of observation involved, it may be useful to work with a co-therapist, where one therapist may provide some balance, consolation, and perspective for the other. However, individual therapists can certainly function adequately in the absence of co-therapists.

Mechanics of Family Therapy

Since anorectic families and individual members within those families vary widely in their readiness and ability to enter into therapy and to deal with the family related aspects, great flexibility is required with respect to who in the family should be included and the frequency of visits. A complete family assessment, which often rapidly turns into therapy, should begin at the point of presentation. In my view, each member of the family should be seen alone as well as in a variety of combinations: the entire family including parents and children, parents alone, children alone, and grandparents included where germane. When family members are seen alone, each individual may appear at least somewhat different to the therapist than when family members are seen only in the whole family. To be seen alone invites each person to share sentiments, fears, and secrets that they may not be comfortable revealing in a whole family meeting where they might feel intimidated by other individuals or by coalitions. Meeting with individual family members may also allow the therapist to more accurately experience the characteristic transactions found among family members. Most importantly, these meetings afford each family member an opportunity to develop a trusting dyadic relationship with the therapist. In the individual assessments, I invite all family members to define their personal view of the problems, their views of the other family members, and their own needs, fears, concerns, and expectations. Part of the purpose of individual sessions with family members is to allow each of them to freely complain about the others, to "bitch and moan," to draw off the accumulated psychological "pus," resentments, and bad feelings; and to help each one deal with their impacted grief regarding disappointments about family members and their own lives. This preparation often enables the family sessions to be more fruitful and for communications in them to occur with less venom.

When the family is seen as a whole, I ordinarily try to set aside an extended period of time, 1½ to 2 hours for the initial meeting, to allow ample time for establishing sufficient rapport and ease to elicit a good sample of typical family interactions. Some of the time may be divided to see various subgroups, such as parents alone or children alone. Part of the therapist's task in the initial session is to determine the needs for family therapy, decide who in the family should be involved (not necessarily everyone), and set goals and priorities. With ongoing therapy, not every family member needs to be or will be seen all the time, and the spacing of sessions is variable from between once or twice a week (perhaps at the outset), to biweekly or monthly sessions later on, depending on the availability of the family. Many therapies are relatively time-limited, lasting months rather than years, with a waning of intensive family desire to be in therapy as the clinical syndrome subsides. In other cases, family therapy persists indefinitely; either on a regular basis or intermittantly, as "booster shots," or as therapist and/or family see fit. The use of tape is to be recommended, audio tape if videotape is not available. Taping permits the therapist to review family interactions out of the heat of battle, and also, when appropriate, to play illustrative interactions back to family members.

Assessing the whole family requires the therapist to identify the family "dances" and interactions—fast shuffles, sidewise feints, shielding of family members, diffusion of conflicts, etc. To do this, it is important that the therapist avoid being overly controlling or directive, allowing the family to interact naturally and spontaneously. To help the family feel sufficiently comfortable to reveal itself, the therapist should strive to create an atmosphere in which no blame is cast, where everyone feels that his or her own interests will be supported, and that the family's integrity and esteem will be preserved. In this regard, many families have found the analogy of the "non-zero-sum game" useful. As I explain this to them, zero-sum games require winners and losers. If one person wins (or improves) another one must suffer—the sum is always zero. Some family members, at least beneath the surface, fear that treatment or emancipation of one family member will be detrimental to another, ie, a zero-sum game. In a non-zero-sum (or cooperative) game, either everyone wins *or* everyone loses, and this type of situation should hold in family therapy, at least in theory. Of course, at a practical level many families play zero-sum games, where one individual may wilt and decline when left by another who is becoming autonomous.

When all family members are viewed sympathetically, heard out, and their plight and self-perceptions acknowledged, an arena of safety may be established that can permit the family to be itself with the alien therapist. The family members are told that it is necessary for them to clarify for the therapist and to help the therapist understand what the problems are. One easy route into the family is to ask them to describe, perhaps role play, some typical transaction that surrounds the symptomatic behavior, eg, to role play a threat, a coercion, some interaction around eating, etc. All family members are asked to "get into the act," as close to the way things operate at home as possible.

Minuchin et al advocate a "family lunch session" as part of the assessment, providing therapists with the opportunity to observe the family enact issues in vivo rather than report them.[15] One of the aims of such sessions is to change the focus from the patient to family patterns surrounding eating, and the therapist can try to alter the family's over- or under-focus on eating. The family therapist may shift figure and ground to bring submerged communications patterns and alternatives to the fore, as if moving the lens of the microscope to shift the focus so that new relationships appear. Several years ago, one resident conducted what appears to have been a highly successful family therapy of an adolescent male anorectic by means of weekly family therapy sessions during dinner at the patient's home. The resident, who was single, certainly didn't mind having dinner cooked for him, and the site of therapy enabled him to make many direct observations, model, and intervene in situ.

In the family sessions a here-and-now approach is taken, and the therapist needs to judiciously manage the interactions enough to make sure that fighting is fair, and that the scars and resentments that may erupt are not so grievous as to frighten the family away from further family sessions. In addition to being revealing, the family therapy must be set up to maximize the chance that each person experiences it as safe.

Within the family as a whole, the following therapeutic tactics are useful: To start, the therapist should not sidestep direct questions regarding information about the condition. Because of its ambiguity and the absence of clearly documented causal factors, it is cruel and counter-productive to simply allow the parents to believe that they created the situation. Each person simultaneously blames him- or herself, feels blamed by others, and blames others; the therapist should make this gently and compassionately explicit. One of the main tasks of the therapist is to help family members air the ambiguity of the situation. The family therapist must expect to be active, not impassive, to answer questions directly, not to reflect everything back on family members, and to share with the family what is and what is not known about the syndrome, its causes, treatment, and prognosis. The delicacy, timing, and nuances of therapist interpreta-tions are of considerable importance. Common themes include the follow-ing: The need of one or both parents to firmly believe that the problems are entirely physical and glandular (with the attendant risk of doctor- and procedure-shopping); the need of one or both parents to want the child hospitalized for long periods of time (until "she's *all* better so we don't have to worry about her at home"); the need of the parents to use the therapist as a threatening bogie man ("tell her that if she doesn't eat you'll do such and such"); the needs of one or both of the parents to blame the patient (for being "willful, spiteful, and wanting to kill me by how she behaves"). Very often the patient will be sullen, defiant, and intransigent with respect to her willingness to change her views or behavior, or to see anything wrong with herself early in the course of therapy. At times, she will be superficially cooperative and agree to adhere to a certain program but not be able to comply; she may undermine, sabotage, or simply give up on a treatment plan, thereby evoking parental responses that range from frank denial of difficulty to furious rage at the patient.

One important tactic that I emphasize for dealing with an enmeshed family is for the therapist to specifically instruct members that each one must speak *only* for himself or herself, saying what he or she wants from the other person(s). Each can speak only in the first person and cannot answer for another. This approach is designed to strengthen individual boundaries and to block the diffusion. Minuchin et al describe a number of tactics for challenging the enmeshment, overprotectiveness, and rigidity, and conflict avoidance in families.[15] Essentially, I insist that people assume responsibility for their own views and desires: overdirective patterns are pointed out and interrupted by the therapist; triangulations, detouring maneuvers, and coalitions are pointed out; individual autonomy and competence is underscored and provoked; children are kept out of parental arguments and are removed physically or temporally when parents need to deal with conflicts that they are avoiding. Additionally, the therapist points out discordance between words and body language messages, so that mixed messages are picked up, explored, and connotations identified and made explicit. These procedures must be repeated often, and the intensity of interpretations should increase until they seem to be actually received and integrated by the family members. When indicated by the course of therapy, the parents are offered couples therapy to deal with conflicts that have otherwise been avoided through detouring.

I often request that family members do certain homework. Here great ingenuity and inventiveness is required; the specific directions are designed to interrupt, block, or replace what are regarded as pathological family transactions. For example, a mother and father may be required to talk with each other for 15 minutes every day while holding hands; parents may be asked to go away with one another or with the patient alone; or the family asked to all eat together, or not to, depending on the individual situation. By prescribing parental behavior I take responsibility for the sequelae; sometimes old systems patterns are altered and sometimes not. In each instance one at least acquires new information about mechanisms that underly resistances to change. As described by Barcai, the parents may be co-opted as "paratherapists," to help the therapist engage in behavioral treatment of the "patient".[50] Many of the prescriptions include aspects of paradoxical intention, and they may become family rituals and "counter games" that can destroy the original ineffective family transactions.[19] Finally, multiple family therapy for anorectic patients may be useful. A number of self-help organizations have been established where parents and patients come together to share problems and coping strategies.

Pitfalls in Family Therapy

The tactics described above may work well with a cooperative and intact family under ideal circumstances. However, many real life situations do not occur in textbook fashion and they are often not predictable. Many problems arise in the application of family therapy; these may be therapist-, patient-, or family-generated.

Therapist-generated problems refer to countertransference problems and traps into which the unwary therapist may fall. The therapist may, by virtue of countertransference issues, be enticed into a coalition with one particular family member, seeing another one as "the bad guy," or be drawn into triangulations, etc. If the therapist dislikes *any* member of a family after the first few session there may be problems up ahead. The therapist may unwittingly play into becoming a paranoid object for the family (a generally unproductive situation that may drive the family away from therapy). Or the therapist may be provoked into taking an ineffective role vis a vis the patient, mimicking parental patterns that haven't worked. Supervision and co-therapy are useful.

Patient-generated problems are common. Just as laboratory rats in experimental psychology "do as they damn please" under the most controlled conditions, so do patients. Patients with marked ego deficits and borderline character structures are particularly difficult. Marked splitting, projection, and untempered emotionality may disrupt the best-intentioned family therapy. At times, if limits set in sessions don't suffice to contain the chaos at a workable level, it may be best to stop family therapy, and perhaps to reassess its practicability at a future date. Some anorectics verge on the psychotic, with hallucinations, primitive and powerful internalized objects, etc, and resemble chronically deteriorated patients. Very emaciated patients may suffer from some organic brain dysfunction, precluding effective work in individual or family psycho-therapy until those problems have been reversed.

For this chapter, family-generated problems merit particular attention. To list but a few: Some families refuse to participate in therapy, afraid to stir up old patterns; others have a "spare our mother" attitude and are willing to sacrifice the patient in this cause, afraid to upset a fragile mother at family sessions; divorced parents refuse to be in the same room with one another; some families have covert purposes for wishing to extrude the patient from the family by cutting off access to home and financial support, or sometimes, in the case of married patients, to ease the patient through a separation and divorce.

Where only parts of the family are available, the therapist must make do with what there is. Especially when family members refuse to partici-pate, the therapist may do "family" therapy with only the patient. The patient may have to be separated or free from parental enmeshment, overdirectiveness, rigidity, etc. through all the usual modes of individual psyhotherapy, often very active. Specific role plays are rehearsed that the patient can try to apply in real-life family interactions. Major psycho-pathology in another family member (eg, psychosis or family-therapy-limiting characterologic problems) should be treated separately.

ASSESSMENT OF FAMILY THERAPY

To properly assess the value of any therapeutic strategy in anorexia nervosa, we must heed Russell's caveat to first learn what the natural course of the illness is so that we have a basis for comparison.[17] It is only against a background of the natural course of nonspecific cures and spontaneous remissions that we can meaningfully determine whether any given therapeutic stategy indeed makes a difference. Such variables as age, the symptom types (eg, dieting alone versus binging and vomiting), the psychopathology of the patient (ie, ego deficits), the relative psychological health of the family, etc. must all be controlled in serious treatment studies. Long-term follow-up (at least five years) is also essential. Experienced clinicians are skeptical about quick and easy cure claims. Those who have worked with the anorectics, especially older patients with chronic problems, are aware of the tenacity of psychological and behavioral symptoms. Basically, the younger the patient and the healthier the family, the better the prognosis. I've met a number of women socially who've told me, after the fact, that they were anorectics as young adolescents and "got over it" with hardly any professional intervention, passing through a syndrome that may have lasted ½ year to a 1½ years as if it were a prolonged attack of mononucleosis.

Sometimes patients get better for reasons that remain extremely obscure. The family may not have changed much, but some internal psychological (and perhaps more fundamental physiologic) events take place in the patient; they become manifest as value changes, shifts in perspective, etc, so that the patient may one day decide to "give up" the symptoms. Such internal changes may or may not be related to changes in the family. In general, most studies have reported about 50 percent of patients to do well and up to two thirds to have reasonable recovery regardless of type of treatment.[5,11,17,18,36] In one follow-up study of 30 children whose age at onset ranged from 9½ to 16 years, Goetz et al reported that 5 to 20 years after initial treatment, outcome was poor in only 17 percent; treatment for that group was generally short-term, averaging six months, and included supportive therapy for parents and some individual therapy for patients.[51] Minuchin's claim of success in over 80 percent of his patients should be regarded with interest, but also with caution.[15] Selection bias exists in his patient sample; they are mostly younger in age and have intact families who are willing to come to therapy. These important factors may in themselves account in part for their better-than-average prognosis. It would also be interesting to see whether the family interventions that Minuchin et al employ yield demonstrable changes in family patterns consistent with their formulations. For example, family interviews and the structured tests should be repeated following recovery and observation made to ascertain whether these families indeed are less enmeshed, overprotective, rigid, and avoiding of conflict than they were to start. That is, did the therapy achieve its intended purposes? Bear in mind that control families (families of anorectics who did not receive this mode of intervention) should be observed as well, since, as discussed above, changes in these parameters may reflect the spontaneous resolution of a family stress response, not an effect of therapy.

Finally, the nonspecific effects of an active, multiple therapist intervention must be appreciated. A certain amount of power, charisma, or magic may be attributed to the energetic team approach that employs videotape, one-way mirrors, multiple consultations, etc. Self-assurance and intensity of the therapists may convince and win over the family, regardless of the ultimate validity of the scientific formulations. However, even with these limitations, if at this point in our knowledge a relative of mine were to develop anorexia nervosa, I would certainly suggest family assessment and therapy as indicated as one component of treatment.

IMPLICATIONS FOR FUTURE RESEARCH

The foregoing discussion is liberally sprinkled with unanswered questions. Here I will summarize some of the important directions that future research into anorexia nervosa and the family must take. Work is required to further elucidate the patterns and mechanisms of transmission of anorexia nervosa in families. Biologic vulnerability with a possible genetic component has not yet been adequately ruled out, and family pedigree studies, particularly adoption and half-sibling studies, would be valuable. Prospective studies on highly vulnerable but as yet unaffected children in a sibship where anorexia nervosa exists, and studies of children of previously anorectic mothers might be most revealing. Given that anorexia nervosa is an uncommon syndrome, pooled data from many series and central patient indexes would facilitate such research immeasurably. Standardization of instruments to assess families is necessary to characterize anorectic families and to gauge the incidence of typical family patterns in other psychopathologic conditions and in the population at large; leads suggested by previous systematic observations should be followed up. Minuchin's family-structured task should be validated by other researchers and applied to wider populations. In addition to the instruments developed by Minuchin et al[15] and by Goldstein,[43] other measures such as those of Lewis et al, Moos, and others might be profitably employed.[45,52,53] Finally, the contribution of specific approaches to family therapy must be assessed against firmer knowledge of the natural course of the various anorectic syndromes.

CONCLUSION

Anorexia nervosa remains a perplexing, serious, and challenging disorder for clinicians and researchers. Among the various approaches to its understanding, the study of the family and its interactions appears to be rewarding. However, major questions remain, regarding the role of the family in etiology and pathogenesis, the specificity or nonspecificity of characteristic family systems for the appearance of the syndrome, the role of the family in maintaining or alleviating the symptoms in the patient, and the value of family therapy in comprehensive treatment. Although an over-enthusiastic endorsement of a family approach as the major meaningful intervention is premature, experience and evidence support the value of family therapy as an important component of treatment.

REFERENCES

1. Lasegue EC: On hysterical anorexia. Archives Generales de Medecine, April, 1873
2. Gull WW: Anorexia nervosa. Lancet 1:516, 1888
3. Bemis KM: Current approaches to the etiology and treatment of anorexia nervosa. Psychol Bull 85:593–617, 1978
4. Yager J, Rudnick FD, Metzner RJ: Anorexia nervosa: A current perspective and some new directions, in Serafetinides E (ed): From Research to Practice: Biobehavioral Contributions. New York, Grune & Stratton, 1981
5. Bruch H: Eating Disorders. New York, Basic Books, 1973
6. Bruch H: Psychological antecedants of anorexia nervosa, in Vigersky RA (ed): Anorexia Nervosa. New York, Raven Press, 1977
7. Bruch H: The Golden Cage: The Enigma of Anorexia Nervosa. Cambridge, Mass, Harvard U Press, 1978
8. Crisp AH, Harding B, McGuinness B: Anorexia nervosa: Psychoneurotic characteristics of parents: Relationship to prognosis. J Psychosomatic Res 18:167–173, 1974
9. Crisp AH, Kaluchy RS: Aspects of the perceptual disorder in anorexia nervosa. Br J Med Psychol 47:349–361, 1974
10. Crisp AH, Kaluchy RS, Lacey JH, Harding B: The long-term prognosis in anorexia nervosa: Some factors predictive of outcome, in Vigersky RA (ed): Anorexia Nervosa. New York, Raven Press, 1977

11. Hsu LKG, Crisp AH, Harding B: Outcome of anorexia nervosa. Lancet 1:61–65, 1979

12. Kalucy RS, Crisp AH, Harding B: A study of 56 families with anorexia nervosa. Br J Med Psychol 50:381–395, 1977

13. Pillay M, Crisp AH: Some psychological characteristics of patients with anorexia nervosa whose weight has been newly restored. Br J Med Psychol 50:375–380, 1977

14. Liebman R, Minuchin S, Baker L: An integrated treatment program for anorexia nervosa. Am J Psychiatry 131:432–436, 1974

15. Minuchin S, Rosman BL, Baker L: Psychosomatic Families: Anorexia Nervosa in Context. Cambridge, Mass, Harvard University Press, 1978

16. Rosman BL, Minuchin S, Liebman R: Family lunch session: An introduction to family therapy in anorexia nervosa. Am J Orthopsychiatry 45:846–853, 1975

17. Russell GFM: General management of anorexia nervosa and difficulties in assessing the efficacy of treatment, in Vigersky RA (ed): Anorexia Nervosa. New York, Raven Press, 1977

18. Morgan HG, Russell GFM: Value of family background and clinical features as predictors of long-term outcome in anorexia nervosa: Four year follow-up study of 41 patients. Psychol Med 5:355–371, 1975

19. Selvini-Palazzoli M: Self-Starvation: From Individual to Family Therapy in the Treatment of Anorexia Nervosa. New York, Jason Aronson, 1978

20. Anderson AE: Atypical anorexia nervosa, in Vigersky RA (ed): Anorexia Nervosa. New York, Raven Press, 1977

21. Conrad DF: A starving family: An interactional view of anorexia nervosa. Bull Menninger Clin 41:487–495, 1977

22. Halmi KA, Brodland G: Monozygotic twins: Concordant and disconcordant for anorexia nervosa. Psychol Med 3:521–524, 1973

23. Shafi M, Salguero C, Finch SM: Anorexia à deux: Psychopathology and treatment of anorexia nervosa in latency age children. J Am Acad Child Psychiatry 14:617–632, 1975

24. Werman DS, Katz J: Anorexia nervosa in a pair of identical twins. J Am Acad Child Psychiatry 14:633–645, 1975

25. Halmi KA, Goldberg SC, Eckert E, et al: Pretreatment evaluation in anorexia nervosa, in Vigersky RA (ed): Anorexia Nervosa. New York, Raven Press, 1977

26. Beaumont DJV, Abraham SF, Argall WJ, et al: The onset of anorexia nervosa. Aust NZ J Psychiatry 12:145–149, 1978

27. Theander S: Anorexia nervosa: A psychiatric investigation of 94 female patients. Acta Psychiatr Scand (suppl) 214:38–51, 1970

28. Cantwell D, Sturnzenberger S, Burroughs J, et al: Anorexia nervosa: An affective disorder? Arch Gen Psychiatry 34:1087–1093, 1977

29. Kay DWK, Schapira K, Brandon S: Early factors in anorexia nervosa compared with non-anorexic groups: A preliminary report with a discussion of methodology. J Psychosom Res 11:133–139, 1967

30. Halmi KA, Struss A, Goldberg SC: An investigation of weights in the parents of anorexia nervosa patients. J Nerv Ment Dis 166:358–361, 1978

31. Parkes CM: Psychosocial transitions: A field of study. Soc Sci Med 5: 101–115, 1971

32. Horowitz MJ: Stress Response Syndromes. New York, Jason Aronson, 1976

33. Coelho GV, Hamburg DA, Adams JE (eds): Coping and Adaptation. New York, Basic Books, 1974

34. Kaufman MR, Heiman M (eds): Evolution of Psychosomatic Concepts: Anorexia Nervosa: A Paradigm. New York, International Universities Press, 1964

35. Lazarus RS, Averill JR, Opton EM Jr: The psychology of coping: Issues of research and assessment, in Coehlo GV, Hamburg DA, Adams JE (eds): Coping and Adaptation. New York, Basic Books, 1974

36. Dally P: Anorexia Nervosa. London, Heinemann Medical Books, 1969

37. Kubler-Ross E: On Death and Dying. New York, MacMillan, 1969

38. Seligman MEP: Helplessness. San Francisco, WH Freeman, 1975

39. Kay DWK, Leigh D: The natural history, treatment and prognosis of anorexia nervosa based on a study of 38 patients. J Ment Sci 100:411–431, 1954

40. Cobb S: Borderlands of Psychiatry. London, Oxford University Press, 1943

41. Alexander F, French TM, Pollack GH: Psychosomatic Specificity. Chicago, University of Chicago Press, 1968

42. Dunbar F: Emotions and Bodily Change. New York, Columbia U Press, 1947

43. Sonne JL, Goldstein MJ: A systematic study of parental intrusion in anorexia nervosa. Department of Psychology, University of California, Los Angeles, 1979, unpublished masters thesis

44. Caille P, Abrahamsen P, Girolami C, Sorbye B: A systems theory approach to a case of anorexia nervosa. Fam Proc 16:455–465, 1977

45. Lewis JM, Beavers WR, Gossett JT, Phillips VA: No Single Threat: Psychological Health in Family Systems. New York, Brunner Mazel, 1976

46. Lidz, T, Cornelison A, Fleck S, Terry D: The intrafamilial environment of schizophrenic patients: II. Marital schism and marital skew. Am J Psychiatry 114:241–248, 1957

47. Pierloot R, Wellens W, Houben M: Elements of resistance to a combined medical and psychotherapeutic program in anorexia nervosa, Psychother Psychosom 26:101–117, 1975

48. Beaumont PJV, George GCW, Smart DE: "Dieters" and "vomiters" and "purgers" in anorexia nervosa. Psychol Med 6:617–622, 1976

49. Frank JD: Psychotherapy: The restoration of morale. Am J Psychiatry 131:271–274, 1974

50. Barcai A: Family therapy in the treatment of anorexia nervosa. Am J Psychiatry 128:286–290, 1971

51. Goetz PL, Succop RA, Reinhart JB, Miller A: Anorexia nervosa in children: A follow-up study. Am J Orthopsychiatry 47:597–603, 1977
52. Moos RH: The Family Enviroment Scale. Palo Alto, California, Consulting Psychologists Press, 1974
53. Straus MA, Brown BW: Family Measurement Techniques (revised edition). Minneapolis, Minn, U of Minnesota Press, 1978

David K. Wellisch

14

On Stabilizing Families with an Unstable Illness: Helping Disturbed Families Cope with Cancer

My introduction to the experience of the family with a cancer patient first came during my adolescence, when my aunt was diagnosed with pancreatic cancer, which was terminal within two months of the diagnosis. During those two months, I was a participant–observer in a powerful drama that unfolded within my own nuclear and extended family system. This taught me lessons I remember well to this day. Almost a decade later, my mother was diagnosed with metastatic tumor of the small bowel, which was fatal within four months of the diagnosis. By this time, I was almost finished with my training as a clinical psychologist and by virtue of the passage of time, maturation, and professional training, I had a very different perspective on the experience of my family coping with cancer in a beloved member. I was also more able to assume an active, involved role in the management of the problems presented by the illness than previously. In retrospect, it is interesting and sad that the same family dealing with similar illnesses in two members had almost completely different emotional experiences, which was also true for the ill patients, my mother and my aunt. The deaths of my mother and aunt were very different, which I view as having been significantly shaped by the familial emotional environment which surrounded them during their illnesses. There were a few simple but significant differences in the family interactions in these two situations, separated by a decade. First, my aunt was never made a participant in her managment, especially in terms of decision-making about her care. My mother was always a participant in decision-making about her illness and its management. Second, my aunt asked for the truth but was never offered it, while my mother was consistently offered access to all facts about her condition. Finally, decisions about these two previous aspects of my aunt's condition were mainly made by one person, a sister who had always acted in a maternal role; decisions about my mother were made by a larger group in the family, which included my mother. There were major differences in how my aunt, my mother, and the family in general coped. My aunt was quite regressed, dysfunctional, and unresolved about her death, whereas my mother died a peaceful and majorly resolved death. My aunt was bedridden throughout her post-diagnosis period; my mother was bedridden only for the two final days of her illness. For my aunt, pain was a constant problem during her terminal period; for my mother, pain was almost a nonentity. The family showed signs of frustrated rage, which erupted into open conflict during my aunt's illness, directed both at hospital staff and at each other, but which was mostly absent during my mother's illness. The most interesting observation for me is that these two women, my aunt and my mother, were quite similar pre-illness, in terms of self-assertion and a ruggedly independent stance toward their own needs.

Thus, these two personal experiences combined with dozens of clinical experiences with families of cancer patients over the past five years have enabled me to construct a phenomenology of this painful but potentially growth-inducing family experience. I believe that the personal experience with my own family sharpened the phenomenology of the my experience far beyond what would have been possible only with clinical training and experience, and in doing so, required and enabled me to more completely deal with my own countertransference problems in these cases.

Perhaps one of the major lessons learned by my family's experience coping with cancer is the potential for avoidance by the health care deliverers. Most of the family interaction which took place was in the absence of physicians and nurses, with the family needing direction but being offered little. With the very disturbed family, this potential for avoidance often becomes extreme with the health care team minimizing or deflecting involvement. Paradoxically, a crisis such as cancer can become a good medium for change with very disturbed families, but only with proper direction. The underlying reason for this is that usually no other experience for such families has made them as dependent on outside people who are provided with continued access to their patterns of interaction. In addition, the homeostasis of such families, ordinarily extremely resistant to change, now becomes more stressed and vulnerable, thus providing some space for change. For the professional, contertransference is a major issue with these families from two perspectives. First, no one finds it easy to launch into work with the disturbed family in severe crisis. Second, terminal illness in a family often invokes significant, powerful, and unresolved feelings on the part of the professional. Taken together, these factors can result in avoidance or also in overinvolvement and lack of appropriate distance. On this basis, countertransference becomes an important section of this chapter.

This chapter will attempt to weave together the varied strands of my personal and clinical experiences with the general state of knowledge in the literature in terms of family therapy with these families carrying the dual burden of major psychopathology and cancer.

REVIEW OF THE LITERATURE

In assessing the literature on the emotional aspect of cancer, two issues are readily apparent. The bulk of the literature focuses on the nature and resolution of the crisis for the ill patient only, and minimizes focus on the family crisis of cancer. In addition, the literature largely sidesteps the interaction of major psychopathology and cancer. It is as if very disturbed individuals never are diagnosed with cancer and all family systems coping with cancer in a member start from a position of functional relating. This review will subdivide the family-oriented cancer literature into two sections, one on children as patients, and one on adults as patients, which follows the general pattern of literature in the field.

Child-Focused Literature

In a lengthy review of studies of family communication in relation to a child's fatal illness, Share observed two opposing models of communication to be described.[1] One is the "protective approach"; the child is shielded from knowledge of the disease, including diagnosis and prognosis; the other is the "open approach", which provides an environment for the child to express concerns and ask questions about his or her condition. The review generally concludes that the open approach is usually desired by the child, and that the "passively accepting and resigned child" may be a reflection of a closed environment where family and staff may be uncomfortable in communicating. For the disturbed family, the protective approach may be a translation of the usual state of interacting in such a family which exists long before the illness occurs. Although the open approach may be more desirable, disturbed families may cling tenaciously to their definition of their behavior as being protective for a time, but the unique pressure of the situation may ultimately force them into a different response pattern in spite of their characteristic, close-system, reality-skewing style. The following example illustrates this point:

A 16-year-old boy was diagnosed with a metastic osteosarcoma, with the treatment plan being pallation rather than any notion of cure. His divorced parents, never having been able to communicate well about most issues, both insisted that he be told only "good news" and not offered the truth, in spite of his requests. The mother maintained this position only for a few days; after talks with the psychological consultant, she relented from this position, stating that it felt, "too lonely and isolated" for her to bear. The staff was able to interact much more comfortably with her when she stopped insisting they join her in skewing information to her son. Although the mother was able to talk honestly with her son, the boy's father never was able to achieve this goal.

In a team approach with 50 families of leukemic children, Kaplan et al attempted to identify adaptive and maladaptive coping responses by the family as early as possible to facilitate rapid intervention.[2] This group observed 87 percent of their sample failing to cope with the consequences of childhood leukemia, according to well-defined criteria. The crucial aspect of parental coping involved how parental behavior either contributed to or interfered with meeting the needs of the ill child or other family members. The authors stressed the notion that denying reality prevented adaptive coping but rarely prevented appropriate medical treatment. Such parents usually prevented their child from knowing the diagnosis. Those parents who prevented the diagnosis from being told to the child feared emotional disaster or decompensation in the child, and were often unable to provide support to the ill child in later stages of the illness, due to their own emotional decompensation. The authors concluded that hypomanic family flights into activity and changes such as divorce, remarriage, pregnancy, or job changes overtax family emotional resources, and are to be discouraged during the long haul of childhood leukemia. The authors of this highly-regarded study did not discuss the family or marital unit which was not coping well prior to the onset of the illness.

A set of papers outline therapy for parents of leukemics. In one, Gilder et al detail a six-year group experience with such parents, but fail to give the total number of families (parental units) seen overall.[3] The group included hematologists, and parents frequently asked them medical questions. There is something of a debate in this area; some writers feel that having primary physicians in such a group dilutes the psychological direction of the group. Important functions of this group were to help parents feel more equipped to deal with their children's questions, and also to reflect to the parents that the denial/avoidance stance was not an optimal strategy for communication. The groups limitations included the inability to help families with children in final stages of illness, and the inability to go in depth into some problems, which illustrate that group discussion for these parents was not always sufficient in regard to emotional problems inherent to these situations. A very different strategy is presented by Heller and Schneider, working with parents of dying children.[4] Their strategy was to train groups of parents in techniques of counseling and then initiate a peer-counseling network which would not include professionals. Attendance was from one to six parents, a figure lower than that cited by Gilder et al for their group. They indicate failure in the peer-support network although modest success in bringing parents into the professionally-led training groups.

Spinetta et al, in an attempt to delineate optimal coping of 23 sets of parents post-death of a child, elicited three major factors.[5] Those who coped most optimally indicated (1) a consistent philosophy of life prior to diagnosis which could support the family and not damage their quest for meaning, (2) a viable, available, ongoing support system, and (3) communication abilities such that they gave the child needed information and emotional support. Unfortunately for the disturbed family, they often fall short in all three criteria described in the Spinetta study. The marital relationship may be heavily dependent on or "stuck together" by the glue of the child, and not only the quest for meaning but the means for relating are gone with the death of the child. The following example illustrates this:

The parents of a 9-year-old boy diagnosed with a brain stem glioma were referred to me for treatment during his radiation therapy. It was noted by the referring radiation therapist that they could not agree on anything, and were constantly fighting. In treatment they readily acknowledged that without their children they had little that bound them. Upon their son's death, they separated. The marital therapy facilitated their managing together during the course of the illness, but the marriage ultimately could not provide them the meaning for a life together offered by the child.

In addition, the disturbed family will often be isolated and alienated from a viable support system prior to the illness, which they then cannot call upon during the illness. However, as with the example of the 16-year-old's mother, the pressure of the child's illness may force the parent to open up the system. Finally, given the communications difficulties in such families, they will often be unable to communicate with their children during the illness, and hence carry major regrets and deeper scars into the post-death period.

An interesting absence in the cancer-oriented literature is the notion of the scapegoated child who has cancer. It is assumed that an ill child will always be a valued and positively viewed family member. It is well known in conventional family therapy literature that this is not always true, and some children may be negatively valued and perceived, as in Bell and Vogel's classic work on this subject.[6] For such families, although no literature exists, it has been my clinical experience that several directions may be taken. The family will often engage in a denial of their negative perception of the child and overinduldge and overvalue the child, with the child then tyranically dominating and punishing them. I have also observed families to quickly switch this function onto another child in order to fulfill this needed role. The marital tensions in these families, disguised by the scapegoating function, may become visible to all, including the marital partners. All of this may offer unique opportunities for intervention and change as the system is in high distress and flux.

Adult-Focused Literature

The adult-focused literature emphasizes the notion that advances of technology of cancer medicine are mixed blessings both for the patient and family. Both Sheldon et at and Cohen et al make the identical point that family life under circumstances of cancer treatment and fear of recurrance is a severe strain, at best.[7,8] In the program by Sheldon et al, continuity of care for 37 patients and families was achieved via a team approach, which included regular home visits by a Public Health Nurse. It was found that the two primary areas of patient concern were the effect of their illness on family emotional security, and the effect of their illness on family financial security. Interestingly, almost 30 percent of the families utilized massive denial in communication, while 32 percent were aware, but managed poorly in emotional areas. Only 11 percent were felt to be appropriately aware, open, and managing well with situation. Of the 30 percent who were viewed as massive deniers, level of family pathology was in no way assessed or evaluated.

CLINICAL OBSERVATIONS

Both the Sheldon group and my own writing focus on the problematic role reversals in families where adults have cancer and children are forced to become emotional parental figures to their parents.[7,9] Sheldon points out that this was often met in their project sample by counter-dependent stances, which for 25 percent of the patients, was a primary issue. My own work illustrates the developmental interference problems for adolescents in becoming pseudo-spouses or pseudo-parents.

Two examples follow to illustrate this point with adolescents who have a parent with cancer.

A 17-year-old boy with severely agitated depression was referred by his mother's oncologist for treatment. It became immediately evident that he had assumed the role of a caretaking spouse with her. She had metastatic breast cancer and required considerable home care. The boy was bathing his mother, giving her pain medication, and being her companion to the exclusion of his own social life. The father had left the family early in her illness, but had not divorced his wife. The boy became more frantically agitated as the time for graduating from high school and beginning college grew nearer. It seemed that he was at an impasse, whether to care for his mother and remain in his role, or whether to separate and go off to college. In a family session with the boy, his mother, and his father, the mother first told the boy, "All boys should go off to college" and a minute later, told him, "I don't know how I'm going to live without you." The boy's agitation rose to the point of suicidal thoughts until the father with urging from the therapist took a stand and agreed to take responsibility for his wife's care but not to live with her. She reluctantly agreed to enter a nursing home. This released the boy, and reduced but did not eliminate his agitation. He did go to college but remained only with concerted teamwork and support from the father and the therapist.

A 12-year-old boy began refusing to go to school or to cooperate around the house after the diagnosis of cancer in his young mother. His parents found this extremely stressful. His mother, diagnosed with a tumor of the kidney, received little support from her husband, who became acutely depressed and dysfunctional. The boy seemed to fill his father's shoes in regard to supporting the mother emotionally when she felt very distressed. Family therapy aimed at achieving functional support in the marriage by restoring appropriate generational boundaries which freed the boy both to go to school and from acting out defiantly, which served the maladaptive role of deflecting the attention of the family away from the mother's terminal illness and the father's inability to function onto himself.

For the less disturbed family, this parentification process may not have existed prior to caretaking needs required by the illness, but for both of these families, this process was evident for years before the cancer. The cancer in both of these cases accentuated an already problematic mode of family interaction to the point that it became unmanageable due to developmental mandates of the children's lives. The cancer, therefore, only served to speed up or highlight this problem.

In two papers on family therapy, my colleagues and I (Cohen et al, Wellisch et al) discuss single and multiple family therapy with adult-focused cancer problems.[8,10] In both papers, coordination with treating oncologists is emphasized. In the first, we emphasize three key points in terms of the families' ability to deal with cancer in a member and ability to utilize family therapy. These point include (1) family developmental level—a couple with two young children and one spouse having a cancer diagnosis being in a very different bind than the elderly couple where a spouse is ill, (2) usual style of interaction and communication, and (3) patterns of interaction and flexibility in terms of stress. My work dealing with multiple family therapy pointed up the advantages of having the patients attend the multiple family group with their family members, even if some families in attendence had recently lost a family member. No evidence of patient emotional decompensation was observed in such circumstances. The advantages of not having the primary oncologists attend the group was also discussed. A primary goal was the ability of the family to freely ventilate about the physicians, if need be, at any time. Interestingly, the only family that did not fit into the group was one with serious, long-standing psychotic pathology. In this family, the patient, a woman with breast cancer, coped well, but her husband became frankly manic.

The patient, a 55-year-old woman, had always been the mainstay and support, in both economic and emotional terms, in the marriage. With the advent of her breast cancer and subsequent mastectomy, she turned to her husband for support. He fell into a suicidal depression and then rebounded into clinical mania. In the group, he rambled and related in a manic state which disrupted the process completely and frightened the other families. It was decided that the couple would be asked to leave the group until he was stabilized on lithium. The man was referred to a noted authority on affective illness who attempted to treat the man with lithium and addressed the marital interaction. Success was not achieved on either front; the couple did not return to the group.

A final set of papers to complete this review are those of Grandstaff and my own in regard to the effect of breast cancer and mastectomy on the family of the patient, especially the spouse.[11,12] These papers are unique in that they address a different direction, mainly life-adjustment rather than adjustment to eventual or imminent terminality. They point up the reality that cancer is often a long-term illness with complicated adjustments besides loss of life. Grandstaff, in a study of 70 families, points up the need for joint husband–wife grieving over the loss of the breast. She further identifies specific time-related stages for the husband's coping process, whereby the husband can enter into an adaptive or maladaptive sequential track of coping. Our study of 31 couples identifies the notion that it can be the man rather than the woman who chooses not to view the surgical site of the mastectomy, contrary to what might be expected. Joint husband—wife grieving may be an admirable goal, but this must be thoughtfully considered with a highly dysfunctional and/or distant marriage (maladies extant prior to the diagnosis and mastectomy). The couple who does not talk together might not be able to grieve together without intensive intervention, which they might not tolerate. However, the spouses may reach out for individual help at this point, and can be seen separately before marital work is tried. An important step in couples therapy with the distant or unsupportive marriage and a mastectomy is to model concern and understanding of the woman's feelings for the male spouse, who may want to be supportive but not know how. The following case example illustrates this point:

A 49-year-old woman underwent a modified radical mastectomy with disasterous results to her self-image. Her husband, a highly successful business-man, was a good provider but never able, in her words, "to talk to me for more than five minutes about an emotional issue." In conjoint sessions, he reflected a task-oriented stance where he wanted to "get in, solve the problem, and get out." In short, he was treating this situation in his usual style, like a typical business problem. Needless to say, this style enhanced his wife's distress. He was encouraged, with modeling by the therapist, to simply listen to his wife with a passive, receptive stance. This was defined paradoxically to the husband's habitual style of active and decisive intervention. The crisis abated; the marriage remained stable and unsatisfactory in general.

With such marriages, basic change is a far-reaching and somewhat dubious goal, but the intensity of the crisis may promote interim changes. No literature exists on long-term outcome of such interventions.

The review points up certain differences and similarities of families coping with cancer in a child as opposed to an adult member. Of primary import is the fact that almost all families will find coping a fearsome, exhausting experience no matter who is sick. Communication makes a difference, but does not solve the most basic problems of the family with a member who has cancer. Pattison offers an observation why this may be so in stating, "The management of death in the family is rooted in the basic management of object relations, separation, and loss in the family."[13]

For some very disturbed, pathologically overinvolved, and over-dependent families, object loss becomes not simply a painful and natural development in the family life cycle, but a catastrophic assault on their integrity as a unit, especially if their involvement is really pseudo-involvement. Although such families often are far from achieving realistic satisfaction from each other, the ultimate separation due to death of a member assaults their collusive mythology that eventually family life will be different and satisfying.

Even this generalization is not universal, however, as some disturbed families will improve after experiencing such a loss, and may experience collective relief or a more-real sense of relatedness. The "coping vs non coping" prototype family has not yet been demonstrated in regard to cancer. It is evident in both the child- and adult-focused situations that the denying, reality-skewing family stance is grounds for current as well as future emotional maladaption. Given the difficulties with separation and frequently enmeshed interactional positions of highly distressed families, they more rigidly deny, skew the truth, and cope poorly in the process and in the aftermath of these events. However, in the absence of studies that confirm this impression, it is entirely possible that the shock of cancer in a family member may motivate them to change in ways that could not have been predicted. The clinician can never assume with any certainty that non-coping will be the outcome.

CLINICAL INTERVENTIONS

Family Phenomenology

As was evident with my own family and the vast majority of those seen in clinical practice, the major emotional problem for the family system confronting cancer is learning to live adrift in an uncharted sea with little concrete knowledge of where this situation will take them, but usually having brutal and punishing fantasies or images of what the future holds. The family must deal with two levels of major problems: unspoken fears and fantasies, and frustrations and emotional drain of real and known aspects of cancer. The real and known aspects become learned when the family attempts to live with the sequelae of chemotherapy, radiation, recurrance, and, finally, the reality of death.

General Issues for Intervention

Several issues are the same in conventional family therapy practice as with families facing cancer, but some are different, as specified below:

Families facing cancer will usually utilize family therapy on an "as needed" basis. I might see them when crises occur, such as recurrance of disease for several sessions, but not again for several months. As cancer is often a chronic remitting illness with a clinical course, the family therapist will usually not begin and work through to the ultimate resolution of a problem, as in conventional family therapy, but rather do family therapy as a series of discrete crisis interventions. Sometimes, this will not be so, as very dysfunctional families will need ongoing intervention. The very dysfunctional family will often find it difficult, if not impossible, to deal with the rigors of treatment, and hence will begin to employ mechanisms such as displacement of their intense conflicts onto the system around them, especially into the health care deliverers, who will not understand or long tolerate such behavior. This leads directly to the next point.[4]

It is very important to note who makes the referral and under what conditions. It is a very different situation to be called by a family just having been given a poor prognosis for a member, than to be called by an angry and frustrated oncologist who is "sentencing" a family to come to family therapy, partly as punishment, and partly a "last-ditch" attempt to salvage what remains of the doctor-family relationship. This is commonly the case with the highly pathological family unit. Such a unit is often isolated and counterdependent toward outsiders; However, the cancer situation has now placed the family in a hyperdependent position with the oncologist. The following case illustrates this process and its problems:

A 57-year-old man was diagnosed with metastatic colon cancer. He had a life-long history of irritable, suspicious, and isolative behavior with his co-workers. He had not worked for several years prior to his diagnosis, remaining at home with his wife. She wanted to socialize, but his demeanor limited this to a minimum for them. His relationship with the oncologist existed along the lines of his other relationships. He felt the oncologist cheated and "short-changed" him; the oncologist felt he was "paranoid" and impossible. Out of a sense of desperation, the couple were ordered to seek counseling. The therapy was successful and tensions abated in the marriage and in the oncologist-family relationship.

The therapist must create an effective relationship with the treating physician, medical team, and/or primary oncologist. In conventional family therapy, the family therapist usually does not interact with outside medical personnel; however, the case above above would never have been resolved if the therapist had not sought such a relationship with the oncologist. These relationships are pivotal in the family system, and interventions carried out in conjunction with them will be accepted by the family. For example, if the family therapist attempts to intervene into a family system which is anxiously trying to push food on a cancer patient, family members usually will not stop this maladaptive cycle. If, however, a coalition is formed with the oncologist, who also states it is not helpful to force food, this will usually reduce the pressure, and the patient may actually eat more. A strong coalition between medical and mental-health care providers in cancer work is crucial with the pathological family. These family units tend to be internally split into inflexible subgroups and will externalize this splitting, potentially creating havoc in the health care system. This can lead to a mirroring of the conflictual distrust existant within such families.

The location of family therapy is important. In conventional
family therapy, the family will always come to my office. In working with
families of cancer patients, this depends greatly on the stage of the illness
in the cancer patient. I will often do family therapy in the home, and have
done it both in the hospital room and also at the oncologist's office. Only
on very rare occasions, I have looked upon the families unwillingness to
come to my office as resistance. One case illustrates this point very well:

A 29-year-old man with widely-disseminated testicular carcinoma stubbornly
remained at home. His wife colluded in the fantasy that he could not leave. He was
told to come to the hospital by his oncologists for more diagnostic tests and he
resisted, remaining at home in a state of emotional paralysis, with mounting
anxiety. This therapist insisted his wife bring him to the office for a conjoint
session. She recited a litany of fears including, "What if he vomits in the car?
What if he vomits in your office?" It became readily evident that this was system
resistance to the separation, which was really resistance to acknowledge the
progress of the disease. The couple seemed to have the fantasy that staying home
would hold back the movement of the illness. The couple came to the session.
Shortly thereafter he entered the hospital, and death occurred in a few weeks. His
anxiety level had deescalated considerably once the emotional impasse was
resolved and his actual death was not as anxious as was the impasse itself.

Whenever possible, I go to the family home, which allows for very
easy entrance into the family emotional system. This also facilitates far
better evaluation of how the family interacts and communicates than is
possible in the office. The family responds to this move by the family
therapist as a statement of serious concern, which is met on their part by
added effort and heightened comfort in revealing issues. I have conducted
many such sessions in the bedrooms of patients, with the family literally
lying on the bed with the patient. The sense of intimacy and induction into
the family territory tends to make these sessions uniquely rewarding and
useful. The main point, therefore, is not to regard family hesitancy to come
to the office simply as resistance, but to see it as a predictable concom-
mitant of a physically and socially limiting illness.

*Evaluation by careful history-taking of pre-illness coping on the
part of the family is vital in treating cancer.* It is here that decisions can
start to be made about several aspects of treatment to follow and these
observations communicated to the oncologist. For example, the therapist
should evaluate whether family therapy can be merely supportive as an
avenue of ventilation, or whether real growth and increased intimacy will
be possible.

The family therapist must not undervalue the notion of supportive intervention without change as a goal with the highly disturbed family attempting to cope with cancer. Such intervention can delimit the potentiall destructive impact of displaced rage in these families. The end result may not seem substantial, but without such intervention, the family might easily have undermined or destroyed all their external supports, including medical, nursing, or social systems. Often therapy where nothing "changes" has actually altered the course of illness, in cases where deterioration and chaos might be expected.

Types of Clinical Interventions

All families are unique in their ways of interacting and functioning. Four general areas for clinical intervention with families facing cancer seem most noteworthy:

1. An educational and modeling stance on how to communicate
2. Management and attention to intimacy, and boundary keeping
3. The effect of cancer on the independence–dependence axis between patient and family
4. Attention to management of frustration

An educational and modeling stance on how to communicate. Families tend to project onto the patient a kind of exotic brittleness which is more a feature of their own projected anxiety than the patient's. However, it is true that the patient's defenses will ebb and flow in terms of ability to directly confront the meaning and potentiality of the illness. If the family is educated to understand and interact appropriately in relation to the ill member's defenses, they may begin to experience a type of communication that will create a working family alliance. The family therapist may model for the family how to do this with the patient, which can then enable the family to understand this process. As Kubler-Ross states: "The few people who have experienced the crisis of impending death have found that communication is only difficult the first time and becomes simpler with gained experience."[14]

This is true not only in regard to the terminal phase but also vital from the moment of diagnosis. This will also show the patient that he or she does not have to carefully censor thoughts to protect family members from distress. Thus, an educational stance around family communication facilitates the two ends of helping the family overtly talk more easily, and cutting down on their feelings that they are sure they know what other family members are saying or thinking without asking. Quite often, the truth is other than what is believed. This process carries directly into the cancer situation, with the family thinking they know exactly what the ill member is saying, feeling, or needing without ever validating their perceptions. This may have worked prior to the emergence of the cancer but now no longer works. The following case example illustrates this point:

A 55-year-old woman was diagnosed with metastatic liver cancer with a poor prognosis. The family decided it would be best for her not to know the prognosis or details of her situation, with the rationale that she would collapse emotionally if given such information. She had always been a dependent, passive woman prior to her illness. She sensed a strain in the family–doctor relationship which she could not understand. She pushed for the truth; the doctors told her and she did not collapse. Rather, she became openly angry, for the first time, with her family, stating, "You have no right to treat me like a child, I'm not helpless." Her family backed off and ceased further attempts at censorship under the guise of protective benevolence.

Such a process, when inability to cope is projected onto the ill member, may eventuate in a cycle, if left unchecked, where the ill member might confirm the families' projections and become an overdependent burden long before it is physically necessary. This the family resents and finds intolerable. The key questions are: Who cannot cope with the true facts? Where does the family have to place the sense of helplessness and dependency? Family therapy will enable the family to attain a more realistic, nonpathologically motivated view of just what is going on with the ill member psychologically. Less will then be assumed or projected and more reality and bonding can have a chance to take hold.

Management and attention to intimacy and boundary keeping. The impact of cancer is toward increased involvement within the family system. Some families can tolerate such increases in both amount and intensity of involvement; others cannot tolerate such shifts in involvement, although family members feel they should be vastly more involved, especially with the patient.

The key to this is actively giving permission to the family system to go on with "business as usual," with the full understanding that family interaction and life will never be totally as it was prior to the introduction of cancer into the family. The notion of reinforcing functional boundary keeping was particulary important with one very disturbed family:

A 58-year-old woman with late-stage metastatic breast cancer was referred for therapy. She was seen in her home throughout the remaining months of her life, along with her husband and, occasionally, their 17-year-old son. Her husband continued to work during this period, but did so with great guilt and conflict. She complained that he had never given her adequate time during their marriage. It was evident that he had significantly altered his work schedule, arriving home each day in the early afternoon. The nurses in the home reported that when he did spend time with her she was negative, and usually spent the time complaining of his inadequacies. She finally seized on an issue which had come up in their marriage 20 years previously which she revealed to the nurses. He reacted with a sense of mortified, angry humiliation but felt he must restrain himself as much as possible with his dying wife. Two interventions were emphasized: first, to reinforce his moves toward continued maintainence of individuation (through his separate identity as a valued executive), and second, to gently but firmly confront her, in his presence as a model for him, on how she was conditioning her husband to stay away in spite of his intentions to do otherwise. He seemed to feel any confrontation with her was either inappropriate or dangerous, given her condition. This stance on his part further depersonalized his ill wife who already felt herself to be a nonentity.

The wife was using the cancer as a powerful, guilt-inducing weapon to ask for that which she felt entitled to, but never felt she could ask for previously. The substance of her demands was legitimate in terms of the actual family history, but the vengeful way she was asking seemed doomed to failure, a re-enactment of the failure that historically had plagued the marriage. The goal of crisis intervention proved more realistic here than working toward a radical alteration of long-term intimacy and involvement patterns. To work toward basic change probably would have led to a sense of defeat for both spouses and an intensification of their basic problems. As illustrated by two earlier cases, it has been my repeated observation that families with an ill parent where there are adolescent children may need special attention in this regard. The primary task of adolescence is to shift primary involvements from inside the family to figures outside the family. Cancer in a parent can dramatically and negatively influence this developmental mandate, bringing parents and adolescents back into reintensified contact. Thus, the family therapist may have to strategically take sides to reinforce approriate boundary-keeping and levels of intimacy with the impact of the disease pushing in the other direction.

The effect of cancer on the independence–dependence axis between patient and family. This is an outgrowth of the boundary keeping–intimacy issue. Attention to dependence–independence issues becomes an important clinical focus. Cancer will lead, in its clinical course, toward an escalating shift in dependency-needs on the part of the patient. This escalation will be in large part physical, but also exists in psychological areas as well. As previously stated, the family can orchestrate an acceleration in the dependency-needs of the patient, which will plague and haunt them as time and illness progress. For example:

A 42-year-old woman with metastatic breast cancer in the very late stages of her illness was referred to us by her oncologist, who found her demands for time and attention intolerable. She always came to therapy with her husband, which was positive, but also negative, in that she would not tolerate coming alone. The wife entered her illness with a long-standing history of moderate to extreme overdependence on her husband, which he reinforced in both subtle and obvious ways. With the emergence of the cancer, this overdependence intensified and became absolute and stifling. The woman never permitted herself to be left alone, which the family accomodated completely, until they entered family treatment. Early in the family work it had become clear that the family members were overwhelmed with the her dependency needs and demands, and wished to leave. They never expressed such wishes to her, however, or even to themselves. She clearly sensed their wishes; her demands on them became even greater. As this interaction heightened, she became more and more somatically symptomatic in ways which were not disease-related, or vaguely related at best. The family was given permission, in the absence of the patient, to have such wishes, with the understanding that they would never act on them and that her demands were impossible for anyone to live with. Treatment with this family focused on how they reinforced the mother's demands, and explored the marriage further to the roots of her panic over being abandoned. Late in the treatment, the husband's past infidelity was revealed. The wife now elaborately punished him with the cancer, presenting him with even more endless tasks. This increased her great uncertainty about his reasons for staying with her. Treatment focused on the futility of such punishment and his needs for absorbing such behavior as his due for the past incident. The demanding–dependency reinforcing cycle was reduced by the treatment to a more bearable level for the patient and family.

Intervention into this cycle early in the illness process will obviously have greater effect than when this has already become a chronic problem as was evident for the family previously discussed.

Attention to management of frustration. This is a final "must" of family intervention. Family frustration without intervention often leads to selection and utilization of displaced targets for discharge of these feelings. Alternatively, in one family seen in treatment, the husband internalized these feelings which precipitated a psychotic depression. Generally, two steps need to be taken in dealing with cancer-generated frustration: (1) identifying and validating the legitimacy of these feelings in this circumstance, and (2) For the individual family members other than the patient, validating the legitimacy of their wishes that the illness was over and that they could go on with their lives. This can be done by saying, "Often family members have thoughts or feelings of wanting this crisis to be over. These are normal thoughts, but are ones that make people feel very guilty. I wonder if you have had such thoughts?" This may permit a kind of ventilation on the part of the family members that will allow them to feel normal, and will reduce their tendency to become overinvolved or to induce overdependency in the patient, due to reaction formation to such disturbing feelings as wishing the family member dead. Intervention here also facilitates help for the areas discussed previously. In situations involving overt conflict it can be very important to confront the family members in a supportive but firm fashion, and to facilitate refocusing on the source of frustration, namely the disease process. This can be particularly necessary for pathological families who cling to justified, extrafamilial targets of rage.

These four points are by no means exhaustive in regard to the myriad of clinical issues that arise, but they do address major and predictable conflicts for all families facing cancer.

Clinical Intervention Pitfalls

Several pitfalls are evident in family work with cancer. Perhaps the greatest danger, given the emotional intensity generated by cancer and the attendant catastrophic object loss is in therapist countertransference errors. These include:

1. *Overidentifying with the family.* This is a frequent problem in conventional family therapy, which can be easily mobilized in this area. In this situation, the therapist is often trying to recapture or re-experience object losses that have not been fully resolved. In addition, these unresolved feelings may prevent the therapist from addressing psychopathology in the patient or family members. The therapist, immersed in guilt, may identify on this basis with the family.
2. *Being rigid with the family.* This is an especially inappropriate style for families with a cancer patient. It can take the form of insisting that family therapy be done exactly as it is in conventional family therapy which, as previously discussed, is often impossible. This serves to protect the therapist from threatening overinvolvement with families in these circumstances.
3. *Pushing for more change than is possible.* The therapist can either induce or be swept up into a time urgency when death is the issue; this is counter productive in nature. Again, it can stem from the therapist's own unfinished business with dead family members. The need to

realistically assess how much families can give, do, or change with cancer as stimulus is of major importance.

4. *Overdoing.* The family therapist can become swept up into a *doing-defense* to guard against profound feelings of helplessness endemic to the situation. The task of learning to bow gracefully to such feelings is a primary therapeutic issue for such families. Overdoing may take the form of overinvolvement in medical aspects of the case, overinvolvement in legal issues in regard to family business, or in helping the family work out endless situational problems. All of these collusively avoid the emotional realities inherent in facing terminality. For the therapist, the setting of appropriate limits for availability are primary here, especially when the patient is in the hospital.

5. *Buying into the family projective process.* The therapist can become the official sanctioner of delimiting communication between family members. The therapist, in pronouncing the patient as brittle or unable to deal with issues of separation or death validates denial and avoidance as a family communicational style. Pattison reflects on this by stating:

> Our socio-cultural view of death may influence our view of life. If we cannot admit death as a part of life, it may be that we do not face the fundamental psychological issues of separation and individuation that contain the kernels of loss.[13]

6. *Taking the side of the family against the primary physician.* This is a serious pitfall which can result from therapist need for omnipotent control, as well as from family pressure on the therapist. A split between the therapist and medical team often works toward negating potential benefits of therapy for the family. Sometimes the difficult reality of real physician mismanagement occurs. It is vital to first establish that this is not the families' perception, as can so often be the case with highly pathological families. Communication should be at the level where mental and medical health care personnel should frankly discuss these differences. If physician emotional mismanagement occurs which troubles the patient and/or family and cannot be worked out, the family should then be supported in making the difficult break with the physician and establishing a new relationship with another doctor. Hopefully, this will be done during a non-crisis period, which is a far easier time to make such a switch. This will feel very fearful to the patient and family, no matter how bad the realtionship has been, given the dependency factors involved.

7. *Being utilized by physicians as crisis interventionist.* Allowing

referring physicians to send families only after crises have erupted does not teach them to use the family therapist to head off crises before they erupt. Referrals late in the course of the illness after families are emotionally worn out is a second-rate policy for all concerned. Many of the emotional crises secondary to cancer are preventable, given time and opportunity. All chronic problems are difficult to deal with, and those secondary to cancer are no exception.

8. *Last but not least is gross avoidance of these situations altogether.* This is easy to do, with a multitude of excuses by which the therapist avoids the basic dread of dealing with very primary emotional reactivity around issues of helplessness and loss.

The ultimate purpose of such family intervention is more far-reaching than the immediate resolution of problems, however severe. Ultimately, the therapist hopes to enable the family to achieve relatively comfortable closure to a major family developmental event, as well as to reduce the future negative effects of this event on the family.

REFERENCES

1. Share L: Family communication in the crisis of child's fatal illness: A literature review and analysis. Omega 3(3):187–201, 1972
2. Kaplan DM, Smith A, Grobstein R, Fischman SE: Family mediation of stress. Soc Work 18:60–69, 1973
3. Gilder R, Buschman PR, Sitarz AL, Wolff JA: Group therapy with parents of children with leukemia. Am J Psychother 32:276–286, 1978
4. Heller DB, Schneider CD: Interpersonal methods for coping with stress: Helping families of dying children. Omega 8(4):319–331, 1977
5. Spinetta J, Kard T, Sheposh JP: Effective parental coping following the death of a child from cancer. Paper presented at 58th Annual Convention of the Western Psycholoical Association, San Francisco, April 1978
6. Vogel EF, Bell NW: The emotionally disturbed child as the family scapegoat, in Bell, NW, Vogel EF (eds): A Modern Introduction to the Family. New York: The Free Press, 1960
7. Sheldon A, Ryser CP, Krant MG: An integrated family oriented cancer care program: The report of a pilot project in the socio-emotional management of chronic disease. J Chron Dis 22:743–755, 1970
8. Cohen MM, Wellisch DK: Living in limbo: Psychosocial intervention in families with cancer patient. Am J Psychother 32(4):561–571, 1978.
9. Wellisch DK: Adolescent acting out when a parent has cancer. Int J Fam Ther 1(3):230–241, 1979

10. Wellisch DK, Mosher MB, VanScoy C: Management of family stress: Family group therapy in a private oncology practice. Int J Group Psychother 28(6):225–231, 1978

11. Grandstaff NW: The impact of breast cancer on the family. Front Radiat Ther Onc 11:146–156, 1976

12. Wellisch DK, Jamison K, Pasnau RO: Psychosocial aspects of mastectomy: II. The man's perspective. Am J Psychiatry 135(5):543–546, 1978

13. Pattison EM: The fatal myth of death in the family. Presented in special symposium at American Psychiatric Association 128th Annual Meeting, Anaheim, Calif, 1975

14. Kubler-Ross E: On Death and Dying. New York; Macmillan, 1969

Robert O. Pasnau, Fawzy I. Fawzy,

and Melvin R. Lansky

15

Organic Brain Syndrome and the Family

In 1980 more United States hospital beds will be occupied by patients suffering from organic brain syndrome (OBS) than by patients belonging to any other medical or psychiatric diagnostic group. More people suffer from this condition at any one time than from any other major mental disorder. Yet the literature on organic brain syndrome is scanty, and almost no information is available regarding the role of family therapy for this condition.

The pathology of organic brain syndrome falls into three major categories. The first, acute brain syndrome or delirium, has multiple etiology. The second category, that of subacute brain syndrome, is a great mimic of psychiatric disorder, and may be confused with a variety of neurotic or psychotic conditions. The third major category, the chronic brain syndrome or dementia, is most frequently described in the literature. It is commonly believed that diagnosis of dementia implies irreversibility; yet many dementias are reversible and should be managed according to modern medical principles.

Family reactions to patients with organic brain syndrome run the gamut from disbelief to hopeless despair. They are determined not only by the severity of the pathology, but also by the place of the patient in the life cycle, in the collective assumptive world of the family, and in the relationships that exist between the family members. Children react differently to an elderly parent who cannot remember their names, than they do to siblings or to younger parents with acute disturbances. Occasionally, the patient's aggressive or abusive behavior causes the family to react with either distance or rejection. The problems are complicated by thee fact that the patient may be suffering from a serious physical condition in addition to the organic brain syndrome.

It is an error to assume that because an organic brain syndrome may be irreversible, the impact on the personality system or the family system is also irreversible. Even though reversal of cerebral pathology is obviously not a goal of psychotherapy, intervention that substantially ameliorates the expected morbidity of an illness justifies treatment. There is a great deal of evidence to suggest that family psychotherapy is especially effective with families of patients with organic brain disease.

In this chapter, the first section covers the pathology of organic brain syndromes, with particular emphasis on multiple etiology. The second section deals with the varied family responses to patients with OBS. The third section treats the principles of family therapy with such patients, and also explores the obstacles and resistances to the use of family psychotherapy in these situations.

PATHOLOGY

Organic brain syndrome encompasses a number of clinical entities that are multidetermined in nature, and frequently hazy enough to make categorization and diagnosis difficult. Primary-care physicians and health officers are usually the ones responsible for coping with this confusing area of psychiatry. This confusion is, in part, based on differing opinions as to what criteria should be used in the definition and diagnosis of organic brain syndrome. Psychologists generally use the concept of *organicity*. Organicity refers to the behavioral correlates of cerebral disease or damage. For purposes of diagnosis, psychological assessment of organicity includes tests of general intelligence, psychomotor functions, language and communications skills, learning, memory, attention, and aspects of perception and thinking. These abilities may be impaired in various patterns and degrees of severity. In general, detection of organicity is weighed strongly on signs of impaired higher-level cognitive function or impaired information processing.

Psychiatrists and neurologists are more likely to approach the diagnosis and classification of OBS by looking for changes in a patient's personality, affective state, and overall adaptive efficiency. The clinician first looks for psychopathologic signs and symptoms via the history, mental status examination, and observation of behavior. If there is evidence of subjective and objective changes in the patient's performance, then formal psychological and laboratory testing may be indicated. In attempts to diagnose organic brain syndromes, the physician will also look for changes in motivation, affect, impulse expression, and control, as well as cognition.

In an effort to clarify some of the confusion, Lipowski has offered a definition and a system of classification for the various organic brain syndromes (Table 1). He defines organic brain syndrome as "psychiatric syndromes resulting from cerebral damage (diffuse, focal, or both) and/or temporary metabolic derangement involving the brain as a whole, or some of its parts."[1] Lipowski's classification includes the following variables: (1) a relatively global versus selective psychological impairment or abnormality, (2) rate of onset and duration of syndromes, and (3) severity.

The global category of organic brain syndrome consists of three syndromes: delirium, subacute amnestic–confusional states, and dementia. These syndromes are characterized by acute, subacute, and chronic onsets and/or courses, respectively. The global syndromes are those in which the basic abnormality is a relatively uniform impairment of cognitive or intellectual functions. The term *global* connotes simultaneous or sequential impairment of cognitive functions, but does not imply that every patient displays equal impairment of every recognized higher mental function. These three syndromes will be discussed separately.

Delirium

Delirium is a transient syndrome caused by widespread impairment of cerebral metabolism and manifested clinically by a global impairment of cognitive function. The onset is acute, with the patient awake and verbally responsive. Attention, recent memory, thinking, and preception are impaired to varying degrees, fluctuating over time, with the most severe episodes usually occurring at night. The ability to process information and relate it meaningfully to past experience and knowledge is also impaired. The patient is usually somewhat disoriented. In most cases there is a concomitant slowing, sometimes mixed with fast activity, of the background electroencephalograph (EEG) frequencies. There is usually a disturbance of the normal sleep–wakefulness pattern. Hallucinations and illusions may present, but are not always diagnostic. Lipowski uses the term delirium as synonymous with "acute confusional states." The syndrome is self-limited, rarely lasting more than several weeks, and usually accompanies an acute intracranial or systemic illness. It may also accompany and complicate chronic cerebral disease, especially in the elderly. Of specific note to the mental health professional are deleria

Table 1
Etiology of Organic Brain Syndrome

Physiological abnormalities leading to brain dysfunction
    Oxygen, glucose, blood flow reduction
    Thiamine, nicotinic acid, B_{12}, folic acid deficiency
    Water, osmolality, sodium, calcium, magnesium imbalance
    Acidosis, carbon dioxide retention
    Internal toxins, including but not limited to ammonia, phenols, ketones,
        aromatic acids, toxins from infections
    External toxins (sedatives, organophosphates, anticholinergics, heavy metals)
    Convulsions (focal or general)
    Anatomical distortion, cerebral edema
    Acute of chronic infections of the nervous system, and immune reactions
    Neuronal or glial intrinsic metabolic or protein structural defect

Precipitating conditions leading to physiological abnormalities
    Organ failures (respiratory, cardiac, hepatic, renal)
    Intoxication with, and withdrawal from, sedative drugs and alcohol
    Systemic infections
    Head injury and its aftereffects
    Endocrine disorders
    Malnutrition
    Intracranial space-occupying lesions
    Sensory deprivation or overload

Common predisposing condition leading to organic brain syndromes
    Advancing age (aging and Alzheimer's disease changes)
    Brain injury (strokes and trauma)
    Alcoholism (toxic, nutritional, traumatic, and hepatic problems)
    Diabetes (metabolic, osmolar, and vascular changes)
    Hypertension (vascular, cardiac, and medication effects)
    Cardiac disease (cardiac failure, arrhythmia, medications)
    Cancer (metastases, endocrine, metabolic, and immune changes)
    Psychiatric illness (drug and overdose effects, poor ego integration)

Adapted with permission from Horvath TB: Organic brain syndromes, in Freeman et al (eds): Psychiatry for the Primary Care Physician. Baltimore, Williams and Wilkins, 1979

sometimes resulting from the use of disulfiram and anticholinergics such as aliphatic phenothiazines, certain tricyclic antidepressants, and antiparkinsonian agents, especially in combination.

There are two major clinical variations of delirium, hyperactivity and hypoactivity. *Hyperactivity* is characterized by marked psychomotor overactivity, excitability, a tendency to halluciations and persecutory delusions, and a high degree of behavioral and autonomic arousal. Such activity may be seen in alcohol or barbiturate withdrawal, but is not confined to these states. Hyperactive delirium may be seen as an expression of heightened cerebro-cortical excitability and arousal, associated with disorganization of cortical functions and corresponding clouding of consciousness. *Hypoactive delirium* is marked by reduced psychomotor activity to the point of stupor, apathy, and/or daytime somnolence. Arousal and exitability levels are greatly reduced, and there is generally a slowed, deficient thought process. Hallucinations are uncommon. Causes of delerium are listed in Table 2.

Subacute Amnesiac–Confusional States

This category includes amnestic syndrome, hallucinosis, personality and behavior disorders, and other circumscribed cognitive and psycho-motor disorders. These syndromes are labelled according to their predominant psychological impairment or abnormality. They are distinct clinically from the more extensive global syndromes. They also point towards focal rather than diffuse cerebral pathology. There is a narrow range of potential etiological factors. Patients with selective brain syndromes may require specific therapeutic measures designed to help them cope with their particular deficit. These states are characterized by a potentially reversible cognitive impairment, usually of insidious onset and/or protractive course. Clouding of consciousness is either absent or present to only a minor degree. The syndromes usually occur following an acute cerebral disorder, such as infection or trauma, or may develop insidiously in the presence of a chronic disorder, and are considered intermediate forms between delirium and dementia.

The amnestic syndrome. This is characterized predominantly by memory impairment. There are two types of memory pathology. The first is retrograde amnesia, in which there is impaired ability to recall what information has been acquired prior to the onset of illness. Retrograde amnesia may vary from patient to patient, and often from one occasion to another. The second type of amnesia is antrograde amnesia in which there is some degree of inability to form new memories. Amnestic syndrome may occur in the absence of any other cognitive impairment. Typically, the patient is alert, responsive, has no clouding of consciousness or impairment of grasp of the surroundings or of communications addressed to the patient. He or she is usually able to reason or problem-solve within the limits of immediate attention. Many patients, however, display other symptoms, including time disorientation, perception defects, impaired

Table 2
Causes of Delirium

Toxic
  Sedatives, alcohol, antipsychotics, antidepressants, anticholinergics, disulfiram, digitalis, corticosteroids

Withdrawal
  Alcohol, barbiturates, meprobamate

Organ failure
  Hepatic encephalopathy
  Renal: uremia, dialysis dysequilibrium
  Respiratory: chronic obstructive lung disease, status asthmaticus
  Cardiac: congestive cardiac failure, left ventricular failure, pulmonary edema, shock

Metabolic-endocrine
  Hypoglycemia, hypoxia; Wernicke's encephalopathy (thiamine deficiency); pellagra (nicotinic acid deficiency); thyrotoxicosis; Cushing's disease; Addison's disease; inappropriate antidiuretic hormone secretion; electrolyte imbalance (nutritional, postsurgical)

Trauma
  Postconcussion excitement; extradural, subdural, intracerebral hematomas

Systemic infections
  Pneumonia, rheumatic fever, septicemia (especially gram-negative sepsis)
  CNS infections: meningitis, encephalitis, brain abscess

Vascular
  Subarachnoid hemorrhage, transient ischemic attacks, hypertensive encephalopathy, systemic lupus encephalopathy

Neoplastic
  Rapidly growing primary or secondary tumors with cerebral edema or hemorrhage

---

Adapted with permission from Horvath TB: Organic brain syndromes, in Freeman et al (eds): Psychiatry for the Primary Care Physician. Baltimore, Williams and Wilkins, 1979

concept formation, lack of initiative, and emotional blandness. This syndrome may be either reversible or irreversible.

Hallucinosis. This is an organic brain syndrome in which the patient experiences hallucinations in one or more senses. The halucinations tend to be recurrent or constant. There is an absence of functional psychosis and a lack of clouding of consciousness in patients with hallucinosis. Hallucinosis may occur with either alcohol or drug intoxication. It can also be a manifestation of non-toxic conditions, including tumors, migraine, and diseases of the sense organs.

Personality and behavioral disorders. Some subacute organic brain syndromes resemble personality and behavioral *disorders*, in which affect, motivation, and/or behavior dominate the clinical picture. Impairment of cognitive functions is either absent or very minor. Such syndromes are caused by focal lesions in various areas of the brain. Features include loss of emotional control, impaired foresight, and loss of social skills. Frontal lobe lesions are associated with loss of planning ability, loss of emotional control, and loss of social judgment. Bilateral thalamic lesions result in reduced responsiveness and spontaneous emotional liability. Temporal lobe lesions seem to deepen emotional responses of all kinds and lead to strong mystical or religious feelings. (Patients may be unaware of these changes in their behavior.) Specific neurological signs as well as distinct psychiatric symptoms are usually absent. A careful history obtained from several reliable sources may be more revealing than a mental state examination.[2]

Other circumscribed cognitive, psychomotor, and/or perceptual disorders may involve relatively selective psychological impairment or abnormality in the absence of across-the-board intellectual deficits (Table 3). Depersonalization syndrome may occur in inflammatory, neoplastic, toxic, or other cerebral diseases. It may be accompanied by perceptual disturbances, body image disturbances, etc. Some patients may show relatively selective impairment of capacity for abstraction or psychomotor performance. Generalized intellectual deterioration or widespread derangement of information processing, which often categorizes organic brain syndrome, are absent.

Paranoia, schizophrenia, depressive and manic psychosis, as well as depresssive neuroses causally related to or precipitated by cerebral disorders may also be included in subacute brain syndrome. These may or may not be accompanied by some cognitive impairment. There is a generally held belief that cerebral disease can be ruled out in patients displaying one of these syndromes. This is not true; there appears to be a greater than random association with organic disorders. These syndromes are often referred to as *toxic psychoses* since they may be caused by drugs. However, they have also been observed in infectious, neoplastic, metabolic and endocrine disorders. The apparent precipitant is the presence of brain damage, cerebral metabolic derangement, or both. The

Table 3
Causes of Organic Brain Syndromes with Selective
Psychological Deficits

Amnestic syndrome
    Wernicke–Korsakoff syndrome
    Bilateral hippocampal infarction
    Trauma to the base of the brain
    Subarachnoid hemorrhage with basia organization
    Tuberculous meningitis
    Carbon-monoxide poisoning
    Herpes simplex encephalitis
    Tumors of the third ventricle
    Early Alzheimer's disease
    Transient global amnesia

Hallucinosis
    Psychedelic drug ingestion and "flashbacks"
    Chronic alcoholic auditory hallucinosis
    Brain turmor (especially in occipital and temporal
      areas)
    Epilepsy
    Sensory deprivation
    Deafness and/or blindness

Organic personality syndrome
    Early manifestation of a dementia (especially
      due to alcoholism, GPI, Pick's disease)
    Frontal lobe tumors or injury
    Closed head injury
    Temporal lobe epilepsy
    Pseudobulbar syndrome

Organic delusional syndrome
    Amphetamine psychosis
    Multiple drug abuse
    Temporal lobe epilepsy
      (especially in interictal period)
    Any of the causes of delirium or dementia

Organic affective syndrome
    Cushing's syndrome, excessive steroids
    Amphetamine and cocaine withdrawal
    Reserpine, alphamethyldopa
    Systemic viral illness, especially hepatitis
    Pancreatic carcinoma
    Any of the causes of delirium or dementia

Adapted with permission from Horvath TB: Organic brain
syndromes, in Freeman et al (eds): Psychiatry for the Primary Care
Physician. Baltimore, Williams and Wilkins, 1979

extent to which these potentially psychopathogenic mechanisms are operating in a given patient and whether or not they will give rise to a psychiatric disorder depends on the "complex interplay of multiple determinants inherent in the organic pathogenic factors, the patient, and his external environment."[2]

Dementia

Dementia is an organic brain syndrome due to cerebral cortical damage characterized by a global impairment of cognitive function. A list of causes of dementia is found in Table 4. There is a noticeable decrease in the patient's level of intellectual functioning. Cognitive deficits do not depend on any disorder of consciousness and there is usually some degree of personality change. The onset of dementia may be sudden or insidious. Its course is static or progressive, depending upon the nature of the underlying brain pathology. There may be some fluctuation in the level of impairment or different cognitive functions, especially in the early states. Recent memory is usually the first congitive function to be impaired. There is evidence of widespread or multifocal cerebral damage. The EEG may be normal or show diffuse slowing of background activity and/or focal abnormality, but it is less diagnostically reliable than in cases of delirium. It is important to remember that in dementia, like any other syndrome, there are degrees of severity. It is also helpful to remember that the patient's premorbid level of adjustment and intelligence, affective state, motivation, and access to environmental supports may help the patient to compensate for even severe degrees of cerebral damage. These observations are most relevent in diagnosing and managing the patient with dementia.

There are major host characteristics that play an important part in determing what psychopathological effects a particular organic etiological factor will have. One of the most important of these host characteristics is the age of the patient. In a yound child, adolescent, or young adult, infection, intoxication, head trauma, or brain tumor are likely to result in delirium or amnestic confusional states usually accompanied by irritability and somnolence. Mild to moderately severe and irreversible brain damage in this age group will probably lead to behavioral disorders and circumscribed cognitive deficits.

A changing personality is the usual result of chronic cerebral pathology in the 40-to 60-year-old age group; the personality change may or may not be accompanied by some cognitive impairment.

There appears to be a high incidence of some degree of cortical neuronal loss in people of 60 years or older. Such brain damage may not

Table 4
Causes of Dementia

Degenerative
    Alzheimer's disease (senile and presenile forms)
    Pick's disease
    Huntingon's chorea
    Parkinson's disease*
    Cerebrocerebellar degeneration

Vascular
    Multi-infarct dementia**
      Carotid distribution
      Vertebrobasilar distribution
      Lacunar syndrome (basal ganglia, white matter, pons)
    Strategically placed major stroke
    Vascular inflammatory disease*
      (systemic lupus erythematosus, polyarteritis)

Mechanical
    Traumatic cerebral atrophy
    Hydrocephalus* (obstruction, subarachnoid infection,
      hemorrhage)
    Normal pressure hydrocephalus*
    Chronic subdural hematoma*

Metabolic
    Hypothyroidism*
    Repeated hypoglycemia**
    B_{12} deficiency** (possible folic acid deficiency as well)
    Postanoxic encephalopathy
    Chronic hepatic or portosystemic shunt encephalopathy**
    Wilson's disease*
    Uremia**
    Nonmetastatic effects of carcinoma

Toxic
    Alcoholic cerebral atrophy**
    Chronic bromide or barbiturate intoxication*
    Metals (lead, mercury, manganese)*
    Organic compounds**: nitrobenzenes, organophosphates,
      carbon monoxide**

Infectious
    General paresis of neurosyphilis**
    Chronic meningitis**, fungal, tuberculosis
    Creutzfeldt–Jakob disease (and other "slow virus"
      diseases)
    Multifocal leukoencephalopathy
    Multiple sclerosis

Neoplastic
  Menigioma*
  Glioma
  Pituitary tumor*
  Metastatic tumor

Adapted with permission from Horvath TB: Organic brain syndromes, in Freeman et al (eds.): Psychiatry for the Primary Care Physician. Baltimore, Williams and Wilkins, 1979
  *Potentially reversible cause
  **Condition that can be arrested

affect their everyday functioning, but it may predispose them to cognitive decompensation in response to a number of noxious agents that would fail to negatively affect a person with an intact brain. Mild illnesses or psychological stresses such as bereavement can precipitate delirium or cognitive disorders in the elderly population.

THE FAMILY'S REACTION

Patients who are experiencing organic brain syndrome present a dilemma for both the physician and the family. The best place for the demented patient is in the home, where feels familiar to the patient and where he or she has the support of relatives and family members. Unfortunately, the medical illness which is usually associated with organic brain syndrome frequently requires that the patient remain in the hospital. Hospitalization is often prolonged. During this time, the family of the patient must remain with the patient for comfort and consolation. The family, therefore, must go through a complicated period of adaptation and adjustment to the seriousness of the medical problem and the complications of the organic brain syndrome.

A 67-year-old male, a professor of mathematics, presented with diffuse cerebral and cerebellar atrophy. He was becoming progressively unable to teach the graduate seminars at the university and was increasingly unsteady in gait and had great difficulty in interacting socially. His wife, who had previously been supportive and involved in his career, became increasingly harsh in her judgment. She believed that the problem was largely psychological, and that if he had more motivation, he could indeed perform better. She pointed to the fact that from time to time, when playing cards, he exhibited the same brilliance in execution of play that he had exhibited twenty years earlier. She was angry when, in the course of a dinner party, he forgot the topic of conversation, apparently he forgot where he was and launched into conversations that were non sequiturs. The patient was seen in psychiatric consultation, referred for hospitalization, and eventually died, following a prolonged hospitalization. Upon autopsy, he was found to have had carcinoma of the head and of the pancreas, with brain metastases.

The reaction of the family is also determined by the stage in the life cycle of the patient. Parents' reactions to a child's organic brain syndrome are quite different from the reaction of a spouse to an illness in an adult. Childrens' reactions to organic brain disease in their elderly parents pose a different kind of problem. The extended family will also be involved in reacting to the changes they perceive in the mental condition of the family member.

Imagine the horror and anxiety in children when the parent cannot even recall their names. When this occurs, children become frightened that the person they were dependent upon has become unable to meet their needs. Children often use a variety of rationalizations to account for their parents' deficit. Occasionally, they accuse the parent of abandonment. Sometimes, when the content of the parent's mentalia is of a religious nature, the child will excuse the parent, saying, for example, "Mother has always been religious. Now she is involved with a religious obsession. This will pass; she'll be back to normal again very soon. You don't need to worry about this, doctor." This example confirms our observation that individuals who develop organic brain syndrome often manifest an exaggeration of the preoccupations or pre-existing personality tendencies to an extreme degree. Therefore, the family members may not be aware when the onset of the brain syndrome occurs, because it occurs gradually and thus, also provides a rationalization to the family that the patient is not indeed as sick as the doctor has told them.

A 58-year-old dentist was diagnosed as hiving a brain metastasis from a primary gastrointestinal lesion. A major staff concern was his insistence in leaving against medical advice because he "had found a cure for cancer" and no longer needed medical care. The patient had long been an advocate of holistic medicine and had been involved in a number of food, drug, and exercise activities designed to promote health and prevent illness. His wife was unable to recognize the profound brain syndrome because she believed that the patient's statements about his cure and his having found the answer to his problem were consistent with his previous premorbid personality. The therapeutic task was to help the medical and nursing staff understand that care for patients can only go so far, and that after doing the best to help the patient and the family adjust to profound disability, they must accept the patient's right to refuse further treatment. In this case, the patient's delusion was joined by the family, and the medical team was unable to intervene further in the care of the patient. No follow-up information has been available.

The degree of stress experienced by the family also depends upon the position of the patient in the collective assumptive world of the family. Parkes has described the different reactions to the threat of cancer based upon the patient's concept of how the assumptive world would be disrupted. What this means is that the meaning of illness is not the same for each patient family.[3] This is particularly true when one observes parental reactions to organic brain syndrome in children.

An 18-year-old female premedical student presented with a metastatic brain syndrome. The course had been progressive, and her death was imminent. The patient was initially referred for psychiatric consultation because of the her father's reaction. He became increasingly angry with the staff, questioning their role, their knowledge, and their competence in treating his daughter. After an extensive evaluation of the situation, it become clear that the main problem was the father's feelings of inadequacy, helplessness, and sense of impending loss. Upon the death of the patient, the family was seen for continued psychotherapy, and a gradual resolution and acceptance of the illness and death occurred. Of particular interest was the brother's reaction: although he initially identified with the patient and was frightened that he might develop a similar illness, later he was able to express his anger at the patient for leaving the family and placing him in the responsibility of carrying the "family baton."

In the above case, the imminent death affected the family in a way that revealed the threat of the disruption of the family's assumptive world. For this family, the accomplishments of the young woman had been anticipated as the validation of the family's efforts toward education and social achievement. Both the father and mother had worked for many years to provide the necessary support for the patient in her accomplishments. Hence, the family reaction was not only a reflection of the intensity of the relationship between the parents, and their child, but also a reflection of the displaced helplessness and hopelessness experienced by a family when confronted with the frustration of their deeply-cherished ambitions for the patient. Interestingly, the earliest manifestation was the anger experienced by the family toward the medical staff treating the patient. It was only after several weeks of involvement with the family that the parents were able to reveal their frustration with the patient over her failure to achieve the family goals.

Siblings' reactions are also varied, and they depend upon the family dynamics as well as the sibling relationship. Sometimes, siblings experience extreme guilt over their relief that the illness has occurred to the sibling and not to themselves. At other times, they may exhibit a fear that the same situation may occur to them. Occasionally, when an OBS patient has a sibling, the family expectations of role or role assignments are shifted to the sibling, and he or she not only experiences the frustration of added responsibility but is also burdened with anger toward the ill sibling who is responsible for the new role assignment.

The spouse's reaction to the organic brain syndrome reflects the state of the relationship between the spouses. If the spouse has been dependent upon the patient, there is often a period of numbness and disbelief, followed by anger over the change in the relationship.

A 58-year-old male, professor of dental surgery had suffered a myocardial infarction while playing golf. He was on oxygen for approximately two minutes and was resuscitated. Upon recovery, he suffered from a severe dementia with permanent brain damage. The spouse's initial reaction was sympathy and understanding. This passed and was transfored into a rage and disbelief, when it became obvious that her husband was unable to regain his normal functions. This was complicated by the observation that he appeared to be in good health and was physically very robust and active. Nonetheless, his almost-total amnesia and inability to carry on his professional responsibilities led to her increasing frustration and rage. She was convinced that the dependency and his remaining home would only prolong his convalesence. Psychotherapy for the wife was directed at helping her understand his physical limitations and gradually accept the painful reality of his disability. Paradoxically, the patient was happy and unworried. This situation only made the tragedy for the family more poignant.

If the family has been withdrawn or rejecting, this may also be reflected in the reaction to the patient's illness.

The 45-year-old wife of a physician was admitted to the hospital for a minor repair of her bladder for stress incontinence. Shortly after the surgery, she developed symptoms of an acute brain syndrome. She experienced visual hallucinations of having telephone conservations with her husband, and believed that she was in a different hospital and was in a different geographical state. Psychiatric consultation revealed acute hallucinosis without any neurologic findings. Laboratory results were not helpful; the review of the operation revealed a nontraumatic surgery without significant blood loss. Vital signs were within normal limits. A consultation was requested because the physician believed that the patient was suffering from schizophrenia. Consultation with the patient's family revealed that the patient had been an alcoholic for many years, and had been daily ingesting a pint of vodka with her orange juice. The physician-husband, who was contemplating separation from his wife, was present neither during the operation nor during the hospitalization. Upon contact, he confided that he was involved in divorce proceedings with his wife. He had not thought to inform his wife's surgeon of her alcoholism. Upon return to the patient's beside, the impending signs of delirium tremens were observed. Corrective treatment was instituted, and the brain syndrome passed without difficulty. Interestingly, the patient's daughter and son gave no history of their mother's alcoholism. The family members appeared to be uninvolved in their mother's care and unconcerned about her physical and mental condition.

Sometimes pseudodementia secondary to profound depression may be confused with organic brain syndrome.

A 45-year-old woman presented with a history of "losing her mind." She had been well until a vacation with her husband, at which time she had been gradually unable to concentrate, had developed a rather severe memory loss, and was unable to perform her household activities. She was seen by a local psychiatrist who made a diagnosis of obsessive reaction and she was treated with psychoanalytic therapy four times a week for a two-year period. During this time, she did not respond and her dementia-like symptoms increased. At the time of consultation, the diagnosis of dementia was made, based upon the psychological testing. She was also begun on a regimen of tricyclic antidepressants, without response. She was eventually hospitalized and treated with electro-convulsive treatment. At that time, the depression cleared, and a diagnosis of pseudo-dementia was made, secondary to a primary affective disorder. The patient has remained clear of either dementia or depression for the past twelve months. Throughout the course of the illness the patient's family was supportive and helpful. The patient's husband, a successful professional, devoted much time to the care of his wife, although he spent long hours at work. During this time he became quite successful in his professional activities, and although the patient felt very guilty about the infliction of pain upon the family, she was greatly supported by his reaction as well as by her two grown daughters.

For the extended family, particularly if the illness is an acute one, the first reaction on arriving at the hospital is the feeling of relief that the patient has not died. Often there is a rationalization that often, "it could have been worse." The primary concern of the family is for recovery, no matter what the appearance of the patient. Indeed, even in moribund patients, the family is most concerned with the recovery of the patient and the return to a normal state.

However, for many relatives, the fear that the problem may ultimately prove fatal remains. During this period, the relatives may form feelings of trust or mistrust towards the medical staff. The relatives need to be reassured that everything is being done for the patient that can be done. Occasionally the relative questions the competence of the staff and feels that the patient is the subject of experimentation or is not being properly treated. Because the initial stage may be prolonged, there is sometimes a feeling that the patient may be abandoned or is being ignored. This intensifies the feelings of mistrust. At the same time, relatives are in a bind because they feel if they express these feelings, it may lead to poor treatment by the medical staff as a form of reprisal.

Occasionally, during an acute organic brain syndrome, the patient may become verbally abusive or quite confused and disoriented. Relatives have a difficult time in deciding whether the confusion is a result of mistreatment or actual occurrences in the hospital, or whether it is a result of delirium. Sometimes, relatives are very frightened by this "mental illness" and ask for a psychiatric consultation. We have also observed that physicians at this time will request a psychiatric consultation to rule out schizophrenia, even though the antecedent to brain trauma or brain syndrome is well documented.

A 28-year-old woman who was referred because of increasing signs of irritability and paranoid ideation. She believed that her husband was plotting against her, and she was convinced that many of the doctors who were involved in her care were incompetent and unable to care for her adequately. Her medical history was one of lupus erythematosis for many years, with a history of lupus cerebritis. She had experienced severe headaches in the past and was currently being treated with large doses of steroids. The physician was concerned over whether the syndrome which he was observing was a mainfestation of the lupus, a reaction to the steroid medication, or an indication that the patient was schizophrenic. It was the physician's belief that the patient was suffering primarily from schizophrenia. The husband was equally convinced that his wife was seriously mentally ill and needed institutional psychiatric treatment. The husband and wife were seen together and, with the cooperation of the internist, it was possible to reduce the steroid treatment and involve the husband in a supportive way so that the patient gradually regained her good premorbid adjustment. Upon termination, the patient returned to her work as a medical secretary, and the symptoms of the organic brain syndrome had cleared.

Another source of difficulty for the family is the regression of the patient. Previously healthy and mature adults become quite childlike and dependent. Patients who have been self-sufficient in conducting their daily lives become complaining, demanding, and dependent. Sometimes, they are unable to control their bodily functions. A family unaccustomed to this behavior becomes alternately confused and angry. Their motivation is to respond to the patient's wishes and demands, but they do not seem to understand that the patient is unable to give them credit for their wish to help them. This may mean that relatives who are spending long hours with the patient find very little reward for their activities, and their visits may decrease with time.

It is not uncommon, in our experience, to find that patients with longstanding organic brain syndrome are virtually abandoned by the relatives and family in the long term.

An 84-year-old man with senile dementia was concerned that he was no longer able to care for himself and that he was losing his memory. Psychiatric consultation was requested because the staff was concerned that the patient was depressed and giving up hope. No family members were observed to visit, even though the patient had been a wealthy and successful businessman. There was some concern that his daughter was hovering in the wings, waiting for the old man to die in order to collect her inheritance. With brief support, and allowing the patient to feel the right to rest and enjoy his old age, and with appropriate referral to a follow-up nursing home, he was able to permit himself to accept the help available to him. Here, clearly, the reaction of the family was one of abandonment and rejection.

In summary, the reactions of the family are determined and affected by many factors. The fact that many patients must remain in the hospital because of the impairment and cannot be home causes problems for the family in relating to the patient. In addition, the family must not only adapt to the altered mental state, but often also to a serious physical illness. The reaction is also be determined by stage of the patient in the life cycle. Parents will react differently to the illness in a child, spouses to their beloved spouse, and children to their parents. All the families will be subject to the problems of anger at the staff, with the regression or abusive behavior of the patient, and with the mental illness of the patient. All of this is affected by the degree to which the illness of the patient affects the dynamics of the family interactions and goals.

THE PSYCHOTHERAPY OF OBS PATIENTS AND THEIR FAMILIES

Obstacles to Family Psychotherapy

The psychotherapy of the organic brain syndrome (OBS) patient in the family context is often avoided. This reluctance may be shared by the patient, the family and the therapist. The avoidance is often rationalized by assuming that the patient's condition is irreversible; a deficit situation, not a conflictual one. The difficulties in the family are felt by both patients and family to be the result of the predicament and are presumed to be more or less appropriate. The undue pessimism can be seen as coming from a combination of ignorance of the psychopathology involved, reactions of the therapist to specific features in the emotional field of the family system, and specific countertransference difficulties in the therapist.

Ignorance of the psychopathology tends to come from the notion that cognitive deficits explain the whole psychopathologic picture; that emotional responses are simply a consequence of those deficits, of the resulting change in family circumstances, or of the emotional reaction of the patient and the family to basically objective realities.

Actually, the impact of the cognitive deficit can be understood only in terms of role expectations and fantasies within the family. These have evolved with the family and have, in turn, been influenced by the family of origin of each of the family members. Fantasy systems may coincide with the actual role performance of the affected person, eg, caretaker, bread-winner, provider of status. When actual role performance does change as the result of OBS, fantasies (and wishes based on them) emerge that may be more evident from behavior reactive to them than from the direct expression of them. In the patient's relatives, common fantasies are that the patient will demand all of the family resources; that others will get more than their due share of property, or do less than their due share of care-taking; that caretaking obligations will close off other options in life; and that no responsibility can be expected of the person with OBS. These fantasies may be accompanied by wishes on the part of the family members to be rid of the patient, to have him die, to grab up all his belongings, to relegate his care to others, etc. The patient may have dovetailing fantasies that people would like to get rid of him, to inherit his possessions, or to see him die. The reason for calling these anxiety-based beliefs "fantasies" is not that they are without truth, but rather that they are not available to the family members' or patient's awareness under circumstances where they can be examined and modified by experience.

Because of anxiety, guilt, or shame that would accompany awareness of these thoughts, there is often prominent behavior that can be understood as reactive to such thoughts and which serves to conceal them, including overinvolvement with the patient, failure to set limits, and/or failure to discuss the deficits. It is this reactive behavior that seals off implicit, shared assumptions from the influence of experience and tends to prevent learning from experience by negotiation or discussion. Since most of these fantasies have some substance, they are felt to be entirely validated in the most fearful way if they do become sealed off from reality. If that happens, a fear with some substance to it becomes a fantasy that is powerfully operative from outside awareness. The reactive behavior that ensues—visiting too much, not setting limits, constricting the family's other involvements, not planning realistically—these in themselves breed increased futility and resentment and generate more desire to be done with the patient, and further intensify reactive behavior.

The net result of this process is an intensification of a kind of intrafamilial split that interacts with caretaking institutions—hospitals or rest homes—in a predictable way. The family will often amplify demands on the hospital and minimize the effect of treatment efforts that might return the OBS patient to the home. It is not uncommon for relatives of such patients to be demanding, irritating, and outright saboteurs of treatment efforts. The same behavior may be seen in an acute hospital ward that faces the same difficulties as the family.

A psychiatric consultant was called in to evaluate a 68-year-old man convalescing from cataract surgery, and to arrange for a transfer to a psychiatric service, because of recurrent psychotic episodes and fear of violence. Examination in the daytime revealed a calm man with mild to moderate organic brain syndrome, but capable of grooming and comporting himself reasonably. The psychiatrist met with the family and ward staff and suggested that some changes be made in management: substitution of a mild hourly neuroleptic for the sedative given at night; keeping lights on in the evening; moving the patient nearer the nurses' station and having family members present. Staff reported much improvement the next morning. A few days later, he was discharged home. However, despite careful instructions by the psychiatrist, the family kept kept the patient in a dark lonely part of the house on the weekend and gave him sedatives. A psychotic episode ensued, and the patient was returned to hospital. He was placed away from the nurses' station and given sedatives. A third psychotic episode occured and the family complained to the hospital director about his poor care.

The primary gain of these maneuvers was to replace the awareness of the family's wish to be rid of the patient with a self-righteous conviction that the problems reflectged shortcomings on the part of the caretakers. The secondary gain included actual financial interests, and freedom from caretaking responsibilities.

There is often pressure to triangle the therapist and/or the hospital in these cases and to move away from patient improvement and toward placement of the patient. At these times when the family feels exposed, resentful, ineffective, and exhausted, they are unusally sensitive to being blamed or having demands made on them. This is the case even for people who have previously shouldered responsibility, scrutiny, and criticism well. When there is an intrafamilial split, the sensitivity to blame and demands is such that even straightforward inquiries by the therapist may be experienced by the family as blaming, demanding, or humiliating.[4]

It is to these emotional burdens that the therapist may respond with hopelessness, anger, or anxiety. If the family is undercutting, cold, demanding, or blaming, or if they set caretakers in opposition to each other, the therapist's anger and anxiety are expectable. If actual impingements, say, of financial circumstances are added, the therapist may despair even more, and attempt extrication by attributing the hopelessness to the organic brain syndrome.

The situation is further complicated if there are in the therapist unresolved issues that resonate with those in the family. If the therapist has not come to terms with his own struggle about demands and obligations with elderly parents, wishes to be rid of them, or if issues dovetail with those that are poorly tolerated by the family, that therapist will be unable to help the family see more clearly, deal with overwhelming affects, and go on to learn from the experience and minimize the losses by direct dealing with each other. If the therapist cannot deal with the depression at the awareness that he or she may be a caretaker of someone who does not improve, there is the risk that therapy will incline toward hypomanic maneuvers with increasing resentment and guilt, rather than uncovering and working through anxieties behind fantasies that are preapratory to negotiating new family roles and minimizing the impact of the deficit for all concerned. In general, hypomanic rescue fantasies and corresponding incapacity to bear depression together with the need to be gratified by either praise or improvement on the part of the patient are powerful impediments to the treatment. Such traits often result in maneuvers that stalemate treatment of otherwise treatable families.

If the organic brain syndrome deficit impinges on the family in a way that unmasks, precipitates, or aggravates tendencies towqard psychopathology in other family members, the situation is more complicated. If, for example, the patient had previously overfunctioned in the family, had been an object of unresolved ambivalence in another member with depressive tendencies, or pivotal in establishing limits for a child or adolescent, the newly unstable situation can be expected to result in overt symptomatology in other family members.

PRINCIPLES OF FAMILY PSYCHOTHERAPY WITH OBS PATIENTS

Although the ultimate goal of family psychotherapy is the minimization of effects of the deficit through renegotiating family roles and learning from experience, it is rarely the case that this can be done at the outset. Untimely attempts at negotiation risk defeat due to the impingement from pathological preoccupations (fantasies), behavior that keeps those from awareness, or pathologic affects (shame, guilt, catastrophic reactions) that ensue when such awareness is forced on the family.[4] Since the family usually gets psychotherapeutic attention because psychological and material resources are near exhaustion, they are more likely than not to see therapist interventions as blaming them or making demands on them, neither of which can be tolerated when they feel that they have failed to contain the difficulties within the family. The usual sequence of effective family psychotherapy with the organic brain syndrome patient follows.

Empathic Sharing of Failed Containment

The first step in work with the family, one that precedes the formal work-up, is the empathetic sharing by the therapist of the experience both of the organic brain syndrome patient and of the family when the deficit cannot be contained. In the patient, the experiene of humiliation at being exposed as defective (Goldstein's catastrophic reaction[3]) can be overwhelming to the point where global defenses such as denial or confabulation may be seen.[4] These only subside in a sustained empathic atmosphere.

Guilt, reactive blaming, and demandingness are often found in family members, together with marked anxiety discussing the difficulties directly. These reactions tend to support an intrafamilial split (ie, the more to extrude the patient from the family), when a helping institution is seen to be available. The family may bombard the caretakers (somatic and psychotherapeutic) with demands, reproaches, and complaints of inadequate care and/or financial distress. The result may be doctors fighting with each other, wards fighting to avoid the patient, or the therapists feeling that the case is hopeless because of "reality" issues.[5]

In the earliest stages of contact with the family, it is important to be aware that the work-up process itself may be experienced by the family as humiliating, blaming, or making demands.[4] That is why the empathic contact with *each* family member as one dealing with a situation of uncontained chaos is crucial. If this is not done, the inquiry itself is likely to be experienced as wounding and will likely intensify defensiveness and intrafamilial splitting.

In making such contact, the therapist must be able to empathize nonjudgmentally and to avoid what had been very fearful fantasies. To the organic brain syndrome patient: "You think, perhaps, they'd rather be rid of you," or "You're concerned that they're secretly thinking about your money or property." To family members: "You blame yourself for resenting him," or "You perhaps feel that what's required of you will use up all the family's resources and exhaust you," or "You must have strong feelings about not being able to rely on the patient the way you used to." The therapist, by empathizing with such disowned fantasies without discrediting some basis for the fears behind them, enables the family to work toward the time when the strong anxieties may be approached. Then what were *fantasies* become *anxieties* to be explored openly and have a chance of being minimized.

Family History

After the vulnerability to blame and demands has begun to subside, it is important to get a history of the family evolution and construct a multigenerational history, involving at least three generations. It is especially important to note whether a complementary set of family role assignments prior to the onset of the organic brain syndrome has been disturbed in a manner that requires working through.

A retired officer of high rank was admitted for a work-up that led to a diagnosis of presenile dementia. In addition to his military success, this man was forceful and decisive in financial and political matters. His wife, an attractive woman some years his junior, had hosted many social functions required of his position, and did so with great poise and enjoyment. Both enjoyed the role assignments, and the marriage was satisfactory to both. After the decline of her husband's cognitive capacities, his wife became overwhelmed, attacked staff members verbally, sought unnecessary redundant consultation, made demands on the hospital staff, and bombarded their superiors with complaints. It was many months before she could face the depression stemming from her own sense of inadequacy and traceable to her family of origin. This had been satisfactorily covered over in the marriage before her husband's illness by his dominance and overfunctioning. She attempted to cover over the same issues since hospitalization by complaining, blaming, and demanding.

Reassessment

After empathic contact has been made with the family in their experience of failed containment, fantasies voiced by the therapist nonjudgmentally, affect dealt with, and the significance of the change in the patient viewed in the light of the history of the family's evolution, the more businesslike work of negotiation and problem-solving can begin.

The actual status of the patient, both medically and psychiatrically, needs to be assessed. Often working hypotheses framed in an atmosphere of defensiveness need to be revised. Cognitive deficits can be explored within the family with great accuracy—a spouse's observations about tasks requiring foresight and planning may be much more sensitive than psychometric measurement. Results of psychometrics should be explained within the family seting and realistic plans for financial matters, caretaking, living arrangements, etc, worked out among family members. There is an advantage if the patient's primary physicians can be included in family sessions at this point.

Medication and Management

Psychotropic medication needs to be carefully considered and reviewed. Sedatives and minor tranquilizers often have an adverse effect, especially if they are used for a long time. Often very small doses of a neuroleptic given hourly beginning at dusk will avoid a 'sundown' syndrome of night psychosis exacerbated by social isolation and sedatives. Antidepressant medication may be necessary, and may even help with cognitive slowing due to depression that had been attributed to organic brain syndrome. It is important that the issues of management and containment that form the indication for mediction not be split off and handled outside the family session. If they do, the risk is that some overwhelming management issue will be be avoided, only to re-emerge and jeopardize the whole therapy.

Negotiation

Realistic assessment of the family's involvement with the patient is a major area of negotiation. Requirements of family members should be made explicit and should be questioned if they constrict activities of family members unduly, or if they are in response to uncontrolled upsets in the patient. The patient's capacity and motivation to take responsibility for his or her actions must be explored. If too much regression occurs when the patient goes home on a weekend pass or when the family comes to the hospital, short visits with the family at some other place may be indicated. A short pass for dinner out may be surprisingly more manageable that a full weekend's vigil at the hospital or nursing home, and is much less likely to create circumstances feeding resentment and ultimate rejection of the patient.

Once very labile issues of blaming and demanding have been dealt with, more reasonable negotiations of who is responsible for what, and who is entitled to what, can take place.

CONCLUSION

In this chapter, an attempt has been made to avoid foreclosure of the family treatment of the patient with organic brain disease. Treatment is often avoided with the rationalization, implicit or explicit, that it is simply supportive therapy of an irreversible condition in an older person. The organic brain syndrome population is quite heterogeneous in age distribution, and many such disorders are reversible. Definitive psychotherapy is indicated if the deficit alters the patient's ability to meet role expectations that are nonetheless maintained by the family rather than modified in the light of correct assessment of the deficit, ie, when learning from experience is blocked by rigidified role models in the family. In such cases, working through may be in the family system. Even with an irreversible cognitive deficit, intervention is justified if the overall course of the disorder changes for the better or, in some cases, stays the same when deterioration is probable. The overall course of the disorder includes much more than the status of the patient's neural tissue; it includes his or her personality, and those of family members, and the impact of that family system on systems that provide health care.

The patient may react to organic impairment with depression that may give the deficit a sense of being more encompassing that it is. He or she may show a reactive self-sufficiency denial, and rageful attempts to maintain a position in the family that is no longer tenable. The family may be unable to give up role expectations made impossible by the deficit. Over-involvement with the patient or overwhelming pressure on care-taking institutions to take the patient are common reactions. Both serve to make actual assessment of the deficit and its effect on responsibilities in the family very difficult.

The physician may be faced with an intrafamilial split. This often surfaces as disagreeable pressure put on medical facilities to take the patient. Combined with unresolved issues in the makeup of the physician, this pressure may color the response to the patient with more pessimism than is warranted.

Family intervention faciliates more accurate assessment and deals with overreactivity and despair by altering distorted views of any of the obstacles, as long as the family therapist does not collude with forces that obstruct the treatment by intensifying splitting. Family intervention may drastically alter the overall morbidity resulting from the impact of the organic deficit even if the actual deficit is not reversed. Family therapy sets the stage for learning from experience, and for that reason it forms a vital part of the treatment situation.

REFERENCES

1. Horvath TB: organic brain syndromes, in Freeman AM, Sack RI, Berger PA (eds): Psychiatry for the Primary Care Physician. Baltimore, Williams and Wilkins, 1979
2. Lipowski ZJ: Organic brain syndromes: Overview and classification, in Benson DF, Blumer D (eds): Psychiatric Aspects of Neurologic Disease. New York, Grune & Stratton, 1975
3. Parkes CM Psychosocial transitions; Comparisons between reactions to loss of a limb and loss of a spouse. Br J Psychiatry 127:204–210, 1975
4. Goldstein K: Functional disturbance in brain damage, in Arieti S (ed): The American Handbook of Psychiatry (ed 1), vol I. New York, Basic Books, 1959
5. Lansky MR: The initial stage of family therapy in the hospital. Int J Fam Psychiatry (in press)

PART VI

Assessment and Treatment

Kathryn L. West

16

The Assessment and Treatment of Disturbed Adolescents and Their Families: A Clinical Research Perspective

Mental health professionals have long recognized the importance of the family to the psychological well-being of the individual, and, since 1955, there has been a significant increase in the examination of family factors in relationship to individual psychopathology. The result of this heightened interest has been a considerable literature in which theoretical concepts about families as social systems have been introduced, research studies of family variables have been reported, and techniques of intervention known collectively as family therapy have been described.

For those who are interested in the role of environmental factors in the genesis of psychopathology, this focus on the family is particularly relevant. To be a family-oriented clinician is to regard the health of one's patient as, in part, a reflection of his or her relationships within the family, and to examine interactional family phenomena in concert with data about the individual's psychological status. This orientation also implies a therapeutic commitment to intervene, when necessary, in terms of the family situation. In this context, family therapy becomes one part of the large armamentarium of treatment available for a modern clinician to employ on his or her patient's behalf.

There are some advocates of family therapy who go beyond the view expressed above, to the extent of suggesting that family therapy is the

The research from which material included in this chapter was drawn was supported by grants MH-08744 and MH-14584 from the National Institute of Mental Health (NIMH).

treatment of choice in almost every clinical situation. One can understand their enthusiasm without accepting their claims for what family therapy can accomplish. It stands to reason, however, that such enthusiasm would be questioned by other professionals who doubt the applicability of family therapy to many situations. The questions asked by such skeptics should be welcomed, for they are questions that family-oriented clinicians must address in order to understand more fully the degree to which psychopathology is a function of group processes.

This chapter describes a family-oriented approach to the assessment and treatment of disturbed adolescents and their families, specifically, five families from which cases are presented in some detail. In evaluating the problems that were presented by these families, attention was paid to the psychological strengths and weaknesses of the family members and also to the nature of the relationships and communications among individuals and subgroups within each family. In the course of providing treatment, a variety of therapeutic modalities were pursued and selected for their value in dealing with specific types of personal and interpersonal pathologies.

Underlying all of the clinical considerations was the recognition that change was required. It was necessary to evaluate the ability of individual family *members* to change, but it was equally essential to consider the capacity of the family *system* to change, for change it must if it were to support the personal growth and development of the designated patient.

The requirement for change is usually notable in the family with a disturbed adolescent child. One of a teenager's primary developmental tasks is to move from the role of child within the family of origin to the role of young adult with a potential for establishing a procreational family. The move from one role to another necessitates changes in the attitudes and behaviors of the adolescent, and change on the part of parents and siblings as well. Even in families that are free of psychopathology, this period of adolescent growth, with its redefinition of roles and relationships within the family, can be experienced as a time of stressful flux.

The flexibility of an individual or of a family structure is a function of numerous factors that deserve the early attention of the therapist. The cases presented in this chapter emphasize assessment of the nature and severity of the adolescent's disturbance, the psychological functioning of the parents as individuals, the parents' relationship to each other, and the parents' interactions with their teenager. In our experience, each area of assessment proved to be valuable in discovering how individual and family factors contributed to or delineated the adolescent's psychopathology, and thus relevant to the decision-making in treatment.

The assessment techniques employed in these cases were, for the most part, standard clinical procedures, but also included a few that were devised for research purposes. The five families described below were participants (along with many others) in the UCLA Family Project, a longitudinal clinical research study.[1] The study was directed towards identifying factors related to the psychiatric prognosis of the disturbed adolescent in the family. To this end, it involved a thorough assessment of each family at the time the disturbed member was a teenager, and a careful reassessment of the index patient five years later. The initial assessment served both clinical and research purposes, because the families participating in the study were troubled families seeking help for a disturbed adolescent.

To meet the needs of these families, the investigators functioned as clinicians as well as researchers. Clinical data obtained during the assessment were then utilized to make decisions about disposition and treatment. Such decisions were made without knowing (at that time) which family attributes would later prove to be related to outcome. These correlations could be determined only after the teenagers were reassessed as young adults. Now, some years later, these reassessments have been completed. This paper undertakes to bridge the gap between the research findings and clinical evaluations of the families that were studied, treated, and followed.

From the growing body of published family research, which has been reviewed recently, it is clear that one goal of family research is to define clinical applications of theoretical concepts as they develop.[2-4] Another is to identify additional factors in family structure and function that may prove to have both scientific and clinical relevance. This chapter therefore undertakes to provide a look at both sides of the clinical research coin.

INITIAL ASSESSMENT AREAS

The Nature and Severity of the Adolescent's Disturbance

The patients were teenage children brought by their parents to the UCLA Psychology Clinic. None of them were psychotic on evaluation, but all were disturbed, although they differed in the severity of their symptoms. The problems they presented were essentially of three sorts: conflicts with their parents over issues of autonomy and independence; impulsive acting-out and antisocial behavior; and marked adjustment problems manifested by poor peer relationships, immaturity, overdependency, or bizarre behaviors.

Each adolescent's problems were evaluated from information

received from both the parent and the teenager at intake and subsequently through structured clinical interviews, behavioral observations, and psychological testing of the adolescent. The test battery included subtests from the WISC and WAIS, selected TAT cards, the Zulliger Test (a three-card inkblot test), the UCLA Word Association Test, and the Bender-Gestalt Test.

The Psychological Functioning of the Parents

An assessment of both parents was made, since these families had intact marital dyads. As with the adolescent, the parents' psychological functioning was evaluated on the basis of information from intake and clinical interviews, behavioral observations, and psychological test data. Each parent was examined by instruments comparable to those used with their adolescent child. The parents varied in the degree to which they showed problems of personal adjustment. Some appeared to be essentially free of psychopathology; others showed evidence of considerable emotional disturbance.

The Parents' Relationship as a Marital Pair

The assessment of marital relationships was also based on intake, interview information, and on behavioral observations. Of particular value were the parents' responses to sections of the standardized interview that focused on their relationship with each other. When disagreement between couples exceeded what could be considered minimal or superficial, the conflict was classified into one of three general patterns, described below.

One conflict pattern was that of situational or patient-centered discord. Disagreement was directly related to the problems the couple were having with their son or daughter, usually centering on how to control or respond to the adolescent, and sometimes arising from their different views about the consequences of his or her behavior. On other family matters, however, including those that involved other children, the parents were not in conflict. Furthermore, they were able to function collaboratively as a marital pair, and they appeared to have a genuine positive regard for each other.

A second pattern was one of overt disagreement that transcended the problems presented by the adolescent and extended into basic aspects of the marriage. In these cases, the adolescent was caught in the cross fire of the parental warfare; the marital conflict either contributed directly to the adolescent's difficulties or interfered markedly with the task of diminishing them. It was not uncommon in such a pattern to find one parent relying heavily upon the child to fill needs unmet by the spouse. There were also cases in which one or both of the parents maintained separate and relatively positive individual relationships with the adolescent in spite of a discordant relationship with the other spouse.

The third pattern was one of covert discord in which marital conflict was denied or suppressed by the parents. Conflict of this sort was usually inferred by the clinical staff during the initial assessment, but often its full nature and extent was revealed only after continued contact in therapy. In these families, the adolescent was almost invariably affected by the parental relationship, usually in the sense that the child's problems served to divert attention from the troubled marriage. In most such cases it was clear that the parental conflict operated to intensify the adolescent's difficulties.

Parent–Adolescent Interations

The assessment procedures provided opportunities for observing the parents and their teenager relating to one another in a variety of settings. During the intake and disposition sessions, the three family members met with the clinical staff. There were also structured interactional sessions designed as research procedures for studying direct interactions between the parents and the adolescent. For these, each parent initially met alone with the adolescent; subsequently, the three met together. In every structured interaction the assigned task was to discuss the family problems that they had earlier identified as personally relevant to them. These confrontations were videotaped and then shown to them. Their responses to the taped materials provided additional samples of their interactions.

CASE HISTORIES

Family A

Alan A, 15 years old, was referred by a school psychologist who had counseled him after he had been truant several times and subsequently placed on probation. Alan's parents cooperated in the referral, because they were alarmed not only by Alan's truancy but also by their discovery that he had engaged in a number of thefts with other boys during his school absences. Psychological testing indicated that Alan was depressed and preoccupied with aggressive and self-destructive fantasies.

Alan's troublesome behavior was recent in origin, dating from the time of his family's move from another city the year before. He had resented the move, which separated him from lifelong friends, and from extended family members with whom he had enjoyed close relationships. Once a relatively conscientious student, he now resisted learning and was sullen and negative toward his teachers. He had previously been an agreeable older brother to two younger sisters, but now he was irritable and agressive toward them, and complained vociferously that they were receiving privileges that were denied him. In contrast to his preteen behavior, he had become uncooperative at home, slovenly in his personal habits, hostile toward his mother, and adamant in refusing to participate in family activities.

Mr. and Mrs. A were conservative, religious, middle-class people who were frightened and distressed by their son's behavior. Their initial response had been to take disciplinary action. They restricted Alan's activities and tried to supervise him more carefully. They themselves informed the police of Alan's involvement in the thefts. Their only explanation for his behavior was that he had come under the bad influence of undesirable peers in the new school and neighborhood.

Neither parent had a history of emotional illness. Their individual psychological testing gave no evidence of psychopathology, their marital history was uneventful, and they voiced no complaints about their current relationship. However, the family's recent move had drained their economic resources, and Mrs. A now worked full time in order to supplement her husband's salary. At first, both parents denied that this put any serious strain on their marriage. In basic matters such as standards of behavior for their children and themselves, or methods and degrees of parental discipline, they appeared to be in agreement. They both expected Alan, as the oldest child, to assume a large number of household responsibilities, especially now that his mother was obliged to work. It was characteristic of them to spend their leisure time with their children, engaging in inexpensive family-oriented activities such as picnics or church-sponsored family parties.

Neither of Alan's parents was a particularly verbal person. Mr. A was soft-spoken in manner and tended to be matter-of-fact in his observations. His wife was more expressive, but she, too, found it difficult to articulate her ideas and feelings. Both parents expressed their dissatisfaction with Alan's behavior and their perplexity over his problems, but they emphasized their concern for his welfare.

The staff recommended family therapy as the treatment modality of choice because the problems appeared to be interactional and resolvable at that level and were not complicated by individual psychopathology in the parents. Alan and his parents agreed to participate. Therapy sessions were scheduled weekly, and continued for a period of eight months. Alan's younger sisters participated in a few sessions early in treatment, which provided the therapists with the opportunity to observe the girls' roles in the family and their relationships with their parents and brother. Subsequent therapy sessions involved only Alan and his parents.

The therapists steadily reinforced the parents' expressions of positive feelings for Alan and worked with them on specific communication skills, such as listening to Alan more patiently and attentively, and learning new ways of responding to what he said. Mr. and Mrs. A were guided toward considering alternative forms of interacting with Alan at home, and encouraged to explore their own adolescent years for experiences that would foster their empathy with him. The therapists communicated to Mr. and Mrs. A their observations that the two parents behaved with exceptional tolerance toward their daughters and with relative intolerance toward their son.

Alan, in turn, was encouraged to give voice to his feelings. He still grieved over being separated from former friends. He especially missed a young uncle with whom he had a close, brotherly relationship. He longed for expressions of affection and reassurance from his parents, but was ashamed of such desires. He resented the fact that his sisters still received favored treatment (as children), while he was expected to act more like an adult. His involvement in the acts of theft with other boys had frightened him, but had also made him feel manly. The therapists helped Alan to realize that his continued need for expressions of love and affection from his parents was nothing to be ashamed of, and that his delinquent behavior was an understandable but maladaptive way of getting their attention. The therapists also supported Alan's observations that his sisters received preferential treatment.

Six months into therapy, the clinicians elected to meet alone with Mr. and Mrs. A for several additional sessions. This provided the parents with an opportunity to examine their own relationship and how it had been affected by recent events. Both of them had become aware of the stresses under which they, also, had labored since their move. They had grown more at ease about expressing their own feelings of anxiety and deprivation, and less obliged to deny them for each other's sake. One result of this interlude of marital therapy was that Mr. and Mrs. A started to budget time and money for themselves without feeling guilty. When the parents began occasionally going out to dinner by themselves, all three children were at first outraged, but they quickly adapted to their parents' decision. Mr. and Mrs. A also discovered the extent to which their joint punitive stance toward Alan had been taken largely because each thought the other expected it. Both had stifled urges to be more nurturant and supportive toward him. Each knowing how the other really felt made it easier for them both to change their relationship with their son. Subsequent family sessions were particularly productive because of what the parents learned during their period of conjoint therapy.

When family therapy was terminated, Alan was offered the opportunity to have individual therapy if he wished. After three sessions he decided that it was a waste of time, and the therapist agreed with him.

Five years later, when he was 20, Alan was seen in follow-up and showed no psychiatric symptomatology. After completing high school he had enlisted in the military, and been promoted twice. He regularly sent money home to his mother and was building up a personal savings account so that when he met "the right girl" he'd be able to marry her without being in any way dependent upon his parents for support. His sisters were by then adolescents and doing well. Mr. and Mrs. A were under less financial pressure, but Mrs. A continued working so that she and her husband would have the money to take a vacation trip by themselves the following year, their first such excursion since their honeymoon. Mr. and Mrs. A were extremely proud of their son.

Family B

Brad B, 16 years old, was referred by the counselor of a drug-abuse program in which Brad had participated voluntarily for several months. Brad's parents welcomed the referral because they had been in constant conflict with Brad for two years, and his behavior, as they saw it, was getting worse instead of better. Brad was their youngest child. His older brother and sister were college students, living away from home. With neither of these children had the parents experienced the problems they now faced with Brad.

In spite of the counseling he had received, Brad still used marijuana. His parents were certain that it would be only a matter of time until he was apprehended by the police. Brad insisted on letting his hair grow long. He played his guitar late into the night, and was chronically late getting to school in the mornings. He was failing all of his classes and persisted in associating with friends who behaved very much like himself. His parents had tried everything from exhortations to prohibiting his use of a family automobile, but nothing that they said or did seemed to affect his behavior. Rather, he became hostile whenever his parents tried to interact with him. Life in their home was one constant battle.

Brad was a picture of bitterness, tension, and guilt. He felt utterly worthless as a person, and admitted smoking marijuana several times a week as a means of escape from his unhappiness and anxiety. He despaired of ever pleasing his parents, particularly in the area of academic achievement, for he had long held the conviction that he was intellectually handicapped in some way. This view of himself had been formed when he was nine years old, during a year spent in a special school for youngsters with learning disabilities. His school performance did not improve during that year or subsequently. Instead, his self-esteem was significantly lowered by the experience. As he put it, "I even flunked the school for dummies."

Except for being a poor student, Brad had given his parents no cause for concern until he entered high school. He had been an attractive, compliant child, clearly favored over his siblings by their mother. Now it was with his mother that his conflicts were particularly virulent.

Mr. and Mrs. B were sophisticated, upper-class people who were astonished and outraged by their son's behavior. Mrs. B, an attractive, youthful-looking woman, took pride in her performance as a homemaker, and she had witnessed the conventional successes of her other children with great satisfaction. She was utterly unprepared for the problems that Brad presented when he entered adolescence. As raising the children had been primarily her responsibility, she felt very much to blame for what was happening, but could not comprehend why or where things had suddenly gone worng. She looked to the staff for solutions to Brad's problems and for exoneration of herself as a mother.

Mrs. B had no history of psychiatric illness and showed no symptoms of severe psychopathology. Her psychological testing confirmed the clinical evidence that she was extremely anxious and had a strong need to appear effective and in control. Her ego strength was tenuous at best and her self-esteem had clearly been shaken by Brad's adolescent turmoil. She maintained her self-confidence by confining her activities to areas in which she felt competent. The quality of her appeal for help from the staff was infantile, desperate, and demanding.

Mr. B was a poised, self-confident man who was openly and intensely angry about what was happening to his family. He found the constant conflict enormously stressful. He was an attorney who routinely worked ten hours a day, but recently he had reached the point where he dreaded returning home and now frequently remained in his office until late in the evening. He avoided directly blaming his wife for Brad's behavior, but it was clear that he held her responsible. He saw her as overly indulgent and inconsistent in her discipline, and felt that she should change her way of relating to their son. He resented being drawn into family conflicts with or about Brad, and avoided interacting with him as much as he could. If provoked into action, he was excessively punitive toward the boy, albeit to no avail.

At the suggestion of his internist, Mr. B had reluctantly attended a few sessions of individual psychotherapy three years before, following a peptic ulcer attack. In his opinion, the sessions had been worthless. Given this orientation, his participation in the family assessment and in the treatment that was recommended was reluctant at best. His psychological testing showed no evidence of severe psychopathology, but he was a rigidly self-disciplined man, perfectionistic, demanding of himself, and intolerant of others. Although guarded in his expression of feelings, he was not emotionally cold or devoid of affect.

Mr. and Mrs. B both had difficulties in the way they entered into verbal exchanges. His took the form of not listening carefully to what people said. She spoke in a flighty manner, and her remarks were full of repetitions. When they spoke to Brad they were incessantly critical; their messages to him were primarily ones of reproach. His father pointed to Brad's older brother and sister as exemplars of how he was expected to behave. His mother reminded him that his activities were sure to cause a recurrence of his father's ulcer. Both parents made it clear that in their opinion he was capable of behaving properly but preferred to make them miserable.

In making treatment recommendations, the staff dealt with a number of clinical considerations. In spite of Mr. and Mrs. B's assertions that their marriage was nonconflictual except with regard to Brad, the staff felt certain that the parents' personalities and relationship to each other were contributing significantly to their problems with their son. However, it was evident that Mr. and Mrs. B would not be receptive toward the staff's clinical impression, because they viewed the situation otherwise. It was decided that family therapy would be offered because it was a way of engaging the parents initially, at least, and it would provide the therapists with an opportunity to observe them further and acquire additional clinical information on which to make a fuller appraisal of the total family situation.

The staff decided that Brad required individual psychotherapy as well. Of primary concern was that he should receive treatment for his low self-esteem and drug dependence. It was also recognized that he would require the support of an individual therapeutic relationship during the period of family therapy with his parents, because their joint negative posture toward him, particularly their proclivity to be guiltinducing, was enormously stressful for him.

Weekly family sessions and individual therapy sessions for Brad were begun. A major focus of the family therapy was on examining the parents' negative attitudes toward Brad, modifying their expressions of those feelings, and teaching them alternative forms of relating to him. Work was also done on specific communication skills with all three of them. Mr. B's problems in attending to others were particularly marked when he was required to deal with the sort of psychological and interpersonal information that arose in his interactions with his wife and son. Mrs. B's disruptive speech appeared to be intensified when she was in anxiety-provoking situations, such as those relating to family or marital problems. The therapists worked to help them become aware of and correct their communication difficulties. Brad improved in his ability to talk more coherently and less provocatively with his parents. This resulted in part from his experiences in family therapy, but also from his individual treatment sessions and the increased self-respect he acquired through his relationship with an individual therapist.

In the course of treatment the therapists confirmed their clinical hypotheses about covert turmoil within the parents' marriage and the extent of their personal problems as individuals. Mr. and Mrs. B eventually grew to recognize the degree to which their conflicts with and about Brad were secondary to their conflict with each other. They became aware of their need not only for marital therapy but for supplemental individual sessions as well. For example, it developed that Mr. B was secretly apprehensive because for several years he had experienced a diminished sexual potency and was concerned about his wife's fidelity. Mrs. B, while not guilty of what her husband suspected, felt rejected and insecure and had turned to her son for the affection she craved. At that time Brad was entering puberty. An increased closeness with his attractive mother was intolerable to him. His intense conflicts with her helped to create distance between them. However, the same behavior alienated him from his father, with whom he longed for a closer relationship.

Family therapy was terminated after ten months and replaced by marital therapy which continued for the better part of a year. On a number of occasions, Mr. and Mrs. B were seen individually rather than conjointly. Brad's personal treatment was terminated a few months after his parents completed their course of psychotherapy.

Five years later, when he was twenty-one, Brad was seen in follow-up and found to be moderately neurotic. He had graduated from high school and then enrolled in college, but his record there was poor, and he discontinued his schooling after one semester. However, he had at last become financially independent of his parents and was living with two other young men whom he had met on his job. His work involved both manual and artistic ability, and he was proud to discover that he had talent in both areas. He continued to experience episodes of moderate depression, but his anxiety was diminished. He no longer used any drug to excess.

Mr. and Mrs. B were finding gratification in their relationship with each other and new pleasure in the role of grandparents to their elder son's first child. They remained apprehensive about Brad's future, but had come to accept the lifestyle he had chosen. Brad's contacts with his parents were infrequent by choice, but these rare interactions were cordial.

Family C

Carol C, 15 years old, was referred by a community agency that had provided a few sessions of counseling for her and her parents the previous year. Carol, in ninth grade at that time, had begun to refuse to go to school, and on two occasions had run away from home for periods of several days. After the family was counseled, Carol managed to maintain regular school attendance for the rest of the term and gave her parents no difficulties during the following summer months. However, when she resumed school activities in the fall, she started cutting classes and ran away from home on two consecutive weekends. The following week she was apprehended for shoplifting. At the suggestion of the juvenile court authorities, Mr. and Mrs. C recontacted the agency which, in turn, sought an independent assessment and consultation about strategies for intervention.

Mr. and Mrs. C were a middle-class couple with two daughters. Mr. C held a middle-management position with a small, successful business firm. He was a strong-willed, domineering man who was accustomed to exercising complete control over his family. He was openly critical of everyone else's behavior, particularly Carol's. Although he denied being an alcoholic, Mr. C was a heavy drinker. On a few occasions he had become physically abusive when drunk, but only once had he struck anyone in his family. His psychological testing showed no signs of psychosis, but did indicate a rigid, authoritarian personality structure, poor impulse control, antisocial attitudes, and a tendency to externalize blame. In his speech he was articulate, fluent, and forceful.

Mrs. C was a physically frail woman whose manner was timid and conciliatory. She was a housewife with no interests or activities outside the home. She admitted being indulgent as a mother but rationalized her behavior as a way of making up to the children for their father's stern manner. When Carol first refused to attend school she had been able to persuade her mother to provide her with false excuses, but this was done without her father's knowledge. Mrs. C's psychological testing showed her to be anxious and depressed. Her style of speaking was hesitant, but she expressed herself clearly. When speaking with or about Carol, she was neither critical nor supportive of the girl.

Mr. C denied that his marriage was a source of problems for either him or his wife. Rather, he directly blamed Carol and her older sister, Connie, for the troubles experienced by the family. He reported that their difficulties began with their first child, Connie, who was four years older than Carol. Until her senior year in high school, Connie had been a model child, but then she began to date a boy to whom her father took an instant dislike. He ordered her to stop seeing the young man, which she refused to do. Their relationship from then on was one of constant bitter quarreling. As soon as Connie graduated, she found a job and moved out of the home. Since then she occasionally saw her mother and sister but avoided having any contact with her father.

Carol, though less successful as a student than her sister, had been a tractable, obedient child prior to adolescence. She began to misbehave shortly after her sister left home. Mr. C attributed her unacceptable behavior to her older sister's bad influence. Since he did not at first hold Carol responsible, Mr. C was willing to paticipate in the counseling offered by the agency. He viewed it as a way of "getting her straightened out again, once and for all." However, when she resumed her misconduct he concluded that the counseling had been useless and that Carol, like her older sister, had turned out to be a "bad apple." He had agreed to recontact the agency only because the juvenile court authorities insisted that he do so.

Carol was an attractive, well-developed girl, who was sullen and unresponsive in the presence of her parents, but vocal and expressive when alone. She was full of rage at both of her parents. She hated her father for his dominating behavior and his double standards. She decribed him as insisting on perfect behavior from everybody else while he himself was a liar and a miser. As an example, she cited his pattern of promising things as rewards for good behavior and then reneging with the excuse that what he had promised would cost too much. She admitted having been frightened of him when she was younger but claimed that she no longer feared him even though he had struck her in an outburst of anger when he learned of the shoplifting charge.

Carol reported that she had once felt very close to her mother, but had grown to despise her for constantly yielding to her tyrannical husband, and refusing to get a divorce. All Carol now wanted was to get away from both of her parents. Psychological tests indicated that in addition to being angry she was also markedly depressed.

The staff felt that intervention was strongly indicated and consulted with the referring agency about forms of treatment that might be effective and that the family would accept. The professionals at both UCLA and the agency recognized that it would be difficult to enlist the family's cooperation, given the father's pattern of hostility and externalization of blame, the mother's ineffectiveness, and the daughter's eagerness to disengage from her parents.

The first recommendation was of individual treatment for Carol, the focus of which would be to help her better understand her mixed feelings of anger and depression and to find ways of becoming independent of her parents that were neither self-destructive nor antisocial. Secondly, it was recommended that Mr. and Mrs. C participate as a couple in a series of training sessions designed to teach them alternative behaviors in their interactions with Carol. It was hoped that Mr. C would be willing to learn less critical ways of relating to his daughter and that Mrs. C could be encouraged to take a more actively supportive role.

The family refused further help of any sort. On follow-up five years later it was learned that a year after the assessment, Carol was arrested for selling marijuana and sent to a county residential facility for delinquent girls for two years. During that time, she made a serious suicide attempt. Within one year of her discharge from the facility, Carol was arrested for prostitution and possession of heroin. She spent several months in jail. While she was there her mother and sister visited her regularly, but her father refused to have any contact with her. As of this writing, she was on parole and living with her sister.

Family D

Donald D, 16 years old, was referred with his parents by juvenile court authorities following his arrest along with three other boys for stealing coins from food dispensers. Donald was a listless, uncommunicative boy whose attitude about his problems, himself, and his parents was one of indifference. For several years he had been an underachiever in school. In the past year he had become a behavior problem as well. He cut classes, forged his father's signature on a report card, and was caught along with several other boys smoking cigarettes on one occasion, and sniffing glue on another.

Mr. and Mrs. D were an upper-middle-class couple that owned and operated a successful family business in partnership with Mr. D's older brother. Their work had for many years totally engaged their time and attention. Donald and his sister, four years younger, had been raised primarily by their aunt, Mr. D's sister-in-law. The two families lived within a few blocks of each other, and the arragement had been convenient. The aunt, childless herself, was happy to assume responsibility for her nephew and niece and took care of them from the time they came home from school until their parents finished work in the evenings.

Mr. D was cooperative throughout the assessment, but his manner was pretentious and condescending. He was a person of above-average intelligence who made an effort to appear more erudite than he was. For example, he claimed to be familiar with the psychological tests that were administered, and talked about them at length, using a vocabulary filled with incorrect terms and malapropisms. Aloof and detached in interactions with his wife and son, he admitted being surprised that Donald had turned out to be a problem, but expressed neither criticism of the boy nor concern about him. He admitted that they had never had a close relationship, but explained this on the basis of his heavy business responsibilities. His psychological testing showed no signs of psychoses but indicated shallow affect and a tendency to externalize responsibility.

Mrs. D was a much more emotionally expressive person. She was highly critical of Donald, but also supportive of him. Her psychological testing showed no severe psychopathology but revealed marked aggressive feelings and sadistic fantasies.

Mr. and Mrs. D openly agreed that their marital relationship was one of emotional estrangement and had been so for many years. Neither had sought to dissolve the marriage, however, because they had grown accustomed to each other, and because divorce would have complicated their business affairs. They did not argue in front of their children, so they saw no reason why their relationship should be a source of any stress or concern for the children. Both of them spoke fondly of the children's aunt and expressed appreciation of the care she had given their son and daughter. They described her as devoted, somewhat overindulgent, and at times inconsistent in her discipline, but they did not blame her for Donald's difficulties. Neither did they show any insight into how the childcare arrangement might have contributed to his problems.

When alone, each parent expressed strong hostility toward the other. Mr. D. confided that there was something definitely "unnatural" about his wife that accounted for her having decided to work rather than stay home to raise her children. He complained that having her in business with him had been "a tribulation from the genesis of the arrangement," because of her bossy nature and sour disposition. Mrs. D directly blamed her husband for Donald's problems, declaring that he had never been willing to take the role of father seriously and used his work as an excuse to neglect his children. She also made it clear that she considered him to be totally inept as a businessman, and she attributed the success of the family enterprise entirely to her own efforts and those of her brother-in-law.

Although it was difficult at first to elicit any response from Donald other than, "I don't know," or "I don't care," he was willing finally to talk about some of his experiences, particularly those demonstrating his cleverness in manipulating his aunt. She was a gullible woman who had readily accepted his explanations for where he was and what he was doing after school, and she could be persuaded to cover up for him whenever he was late coming home for supper or left the house in the evenings. His aunt was a generous person who gave him pocket money over and above the allowance provided by his parents, but he expressed no gratitude.

During the past two years he had become actively involved in the exploits of a group of boys, most of whom were a year or two older than he. They had engaged in a variety of antisocial activities, primarily thefts and vandalism. Donald was proud of the numerous crimes they had committed without being caught, and he looked upon their arrest as a matter of bad luck, which was just one of those things that couldn't always be avoided. He expressed no remorse for his behavior or concern for his future. He was contemptuous of his parents and his aunt, and he volunteered that he "could care less" what his family thought or did. There was little beyond the companionship of his peers that Donald valued. His psychological testing revealed shallow affect, impulsivity, inability to judge consequences, and sadistic fantasies.

Donald's case was discussed with a representative of the juvenile court. Several alternative forms of intervention, either through the clinic or the probation service, were offered for the family's consideration. The parents rejected any program that required their participation because they could not afford to be absent from their business. They finally decided to send Donald to a military school in a nearby state, which satisfied the court's requirements. This alternative had not been included in the recommendations of the professional staff.

On follow-up five yers later it was learned that Donald had run away from the school four months after he was sent there. He did not return home, and attempts to locate him were unsuccessful. For 18 months, his parents had no idea where he was. Finally they were contacted by the police in an eastern state and notified that Donald had been arrested and charged with breaking and entering. Because he was not yet 18 years old, Donald received a suspended sentence and was released to the custody of his parents.

Two years later, at the time of his follow-up assessment, Donald was living on the fringe of society. He claimed to be working on a deal that would soon net him considerable money, but he was unwilling to reveal any details. He denied being involved in the sale of illegal drugs, but admitted being a heavy drug user himself. Mrs. D was aware of Donald's use of drugs, and she was convinced that he was dealing in them as well. He had never been steadily employed or self-supporting. His mother regularly gave him money without her husband's knowledge. Shortly after the follow-up, Mrs. D contacted our staff to let them know that Donald was being treated for heroin addiction.

Family E

Ellen E, on her second birthday, was spanked until her buttocks bled. Her mother, who wielded the metal-edged ruler that lacerated Ellen's flesh, had been similarly beaten by her own mother when she was even younger.

Ellen was brought to the clinic by her parents shortly before her seventeenth birthday. She sat, mute and wide-eyed, as her mother recounted the history of her problems. Ellen had been a cranky baby, an overactive toddler, a timid preschooler, a slow learner in elementary school, a friendless 10-year-old, an obese preadolescent, a clumsy and unhygienic 13-year-old. She had failed tenth grade. Now Ellen was a social isolate, she refused to wash her hair when it was dirty, she was again failing most of her classes, and she was a chronic liar. The crisis that brought her and her parents to the clinic was that she had grabbed a pair of scissors from her mother and locked herself into the bathroom, screaming that she was going to kill herself.

Mrs. E was an attractive, bright, articulate woman who was familiar with the language of psychotherapy and was disarmingly frank about the problems in her family. She admitted having physically abused Ellen and described the episode in detail. She made no attempt to minimize the event, but she explained it on the basis of having been abused herself, and she detailed the many steps she had taken subsequently to compensate for what she had done. Among other things, she had provided Ellen with one therapist after another for most of the girl's life; now she was once again seeking treatment for her at the UCLA Psychology Clinic. She was clearly not optimistic about how much Ellen would profit from further psychotherapy. However, she would never let anyone have a reason for saying that she had failed to be a good mother who provided whatever was needed for her only child.

Beneath the surface, Mrs. E was a severely disturbed woman. Psychological testing and clinical observations during the project assessment and throughout an extended period of psychotherapy reflected a borderline personality disorder. The charm and restraint that she could display in social situations quickly evaporated under other conditions. With members of her immediate and extended families she constantly tried to control what everyone said or did. Much of the time she succeeded in getting her way, because whenever she encountered disagreement she interpreted it as evidence that the person was unappreciative of her interest or unworthy of her devotion. She would then either take to her bed in a profound state of depression, threaten suicide, or fly into an intense rage during which she behaved irrationally and often destructively. Over the years, this pattern of manipulative behavior had served to alienate most of her relatives, but her husband and daughter remained hopelessly dependent on her.

Mr. E was an anxious, uncertain man with an almost childlike quality about him. He was as bright as his wife, but unlike her he was socially ill at ease and hesitant in his speech. His expressions of concern for his daughter were sincere, but he voiced them, literally as well as figuratively, with one eye on his wife. As long as he phrased his views about Ellen in terms that were consonant with his wife's, he was safe; but if he misjudged or dared to conceptualize what was going on in his family in terms that implied either incompetence or negative motives on Mrs. E's part, the full force of her fury would be directed toward him. He wanted to help his daughter, but he didn't know how to do so, just as he had never known how to help himself in his relationship to the woman he had married.

Mr. E's ineffectualness was as much a measure of the family dynamics as it was a statement about his personal resources. In his first year of marriage he had learned where his loyalties must lie. His wife provoked one confrontation after another with the significant persons in their lives, each time demanding his support of her as a test of his devotion. When Ellen was born, she became the new target. If he had failed to recognize this at first, Mr. E was forced to do so on her second birthday. His wife had carefully planned the child's party and decided on the gifts she would receive. On his way home from work, Mr. E impulsively picked up an extra trinket for his daughter. The little girl displayed far more delight with his toy than with any of the gifts her mother had chosen for her. Unfortunately, Ellen's pleasure was experienced by Mrs. E as evidence that she had failed in her maternal role. This was intolerable. Enraged, she attacked her child.

Both Mr. and Mrs. E communicated in peculiar ways. Mr. E was long-winded and often unintelligible; he tended to use idiosyncratic words and phrases, and his speech was marked with uncertainty. Mrs. E's style of speaking was bombastic, over-personalized, and full of statements that attributed negative qualities or intent to those of whom she spoke. When talking to her daughter, Mrs. E was harshly critical. Mr. E was not critical of Ellen, but neither was he supportive.

Ellen's psychological testing and her behavior during the project assessment showed her to be a severely disturbed adolescent. Her cognitive functioning was markedly impaired. Her performance on structured tests was poor, mirroring the way in which she functioned in school. At least in part this was due to her intense anxiety. It also reflected her emotional immaturity and her history of constricted opportunities for learning, both of which were the result of her excessive dependence upon her mother.

Ellen was, indeed, a graceless, ignorant, inarticulate 17-year-old, but she was not stupid. She was intelligent enough to know that her welfare depended upon learning to judge her mother's moods, decipher her messages, and avoid precipitating her rages. For Ellen these were far more meaningful skills than the three Rs or the social graces that her peers were acquiring in the process of growing up. Unfortunately for Ellen, her efforts to cope with her mother were seldom successful, and over the years she became a guarded, suspicious, devious person. By the time she was assessed by our staff, her behavior pattern was that of an inadequate personality characterized by ineffectual responses to the demands made of her, inability to adapt, ineptness, and poor judgment.

One of the episodes that unfolded during the course of therapy illustrated the chronic pattern of Ellen's interactions with her parents. When she turned 16, Ellen was faced with the task of learning to drive an automobile. The prospect terrified her, because she was certain that she would fail to master the skills required by law, and equally certain that she would never meet the additional standards that would be imposed by her mother. For over a year she managed to postpone the problem, first by forgetting to register for the driver training course, and then by forgetting to attend once she was registered. Each maneuver angered her mother and provided additional proof to her that Ellen was hopelessly careless and incompetent. The issue was raised again shortly after the family entered treatment. Ellen, in desperation, claimed that the current course was already filled. Mrs. E soon discovered that this was not the case and cited Ellen's behavior as further evidence that her daughter was deliberately oppositional and had become a chronic liar. Ellen felt cornered. When her mother demanded an explanation, the girl froze in fear, for she knew that to say she was afraid of her mother would only enrage the woman further. Ellen's appraisal of the situation was absolutely accurate, for when Mrs. E saw her daugher's ill-concealed expression of terror she screamed at her: "Don't look at me like that! You have no reason to be afraid of me! I'm trying to help you! I can't stand it when you look at me as though I were a monster!" Mr. E sat to one side in an agony of silence.

It was a similar situation, but one involving another area of conflict, that had driven Ellen to the desperate act of threatening to kill herseif, therefore bringing her and her parents to the psychology clinic. More and more, as she was faced with the increasing demands of adolescence, Ellen was finding herself in such situations, unable to cope with them or escape from them.

Three therapists collaborated in an intensive, multifaceted program of treatment for the E family. Ellen was seen individually twice a week by Dr. X, who first focused solely on developing her trust and providing her with emotional support. For a while Ellen resisted establishing a relationship with Dr. X. This was in part due to a loyalty conflict, since in the past her mother had always stopped her therapy as soon as it showed signs of being effective, and on each occasion the girl was left feeling bereft. However, her previous therapists were the only sympathetic adults she had ever encountered, and her need for such a relationship was so profound that she did not long resist the opportunity for another.

Family sessions were scheduled weekly, and for these Dr. X was joined by Drs. Y and Z. Without the support of individual therapy from the outset, Ellen could hardly have tolerated a family treatment modality. In the family sessions she was continually subjected to harsh, critical attacks by her mother, and her vulnerability to blame was evident from her history. Episodes such as the one described above occurred regularly, in spite of the therapists' efforts to prevent or modify them. In fact, during the first few weeks of family therapy, Dr X often functioned as Ellen's voice, because the mere presence of Mrs. E rendered her daugher virtually mute with fear.

Painful as they were for Ellen, the early family sessions were invaluable, because they provided an opportunity for the clinicians to assess more fully the individual and interactional pathologies that characterized the E family, and to devise specific strategies of intervention. The therapists' long-range goal for Ellen was to help her separate from her parents, but until her limited assets could be strengthened enough to make autonomy possible, she would be obliged to remain a part of the family. Therefore, every possible effort was required to penetrate the family system and modify its pathology. It seemed likely that Ellen's individual therapy in the past had been doomed to failure because no simultaneous intervention on a family level had ever been undertaken.

Mrs. E's hostile, critical manner of interacting was not restricted to her relationship with Ellen. Mr. E received his share of criticism and irrational attacks. He responded with characteristic passivity, which was what his wife seemed to require of him but which only infuriated her more. As the conflict in their marital relationship became overt, the therapists were able to deal directly with it as an area of pathology. Drs. Y and Z met with Mr. and Mrs. E as a couple, substituting marital treatment for family sessions. Meetings with all three family members were rescheduled as needed.

The clinicians were also aware of Mr. and Mrs. E's additional needs for individual treatment. Mrs. E had never received direct therapy for her own emotional problems. The defenses typical of one with borderline personality organization intensified as she encountered pressures to change in family and marital therapy. Dr. Y provided her with individual therapy through which she could deal with her own lifelong problems that had stemmed, essentially, from her relationship with her own abusing mother.

Dr. Z engaged Mr. E in sessions of assertion training, first alone, and then in a group setting. Eventually, Ellen joined her father in the assertion training course. Her behaviors changed very little as a result, but this mutual endeavor served an important psychological purpose: it justified her development of an attachment to still another person other than her mother, and fostered the development of a relationship with her father that had always been denied her.

The treatment program for the E family extended over a period of 2½ years, and individual therapy for Ellen continued beyond that. Gradually, as her own ego strengthened, Ellen was able to comprehend the role that her mother's emotional disabilities had played in their relationship. Her treatment was terminated approximately one year before she was scheduled to be seen in follow-up. At that time her psychiatric status was assessed by members of the staff who had not been involved in the family's treatment. They found Ellen to be a handicapped young woman, but not as severely disabled as she had been as an adolescent. She continued to show some of the features of an inadequate personality, but considerable progress was observed. She had moved out of her parents' home and was living in a supportive communal setting with a group of benignly religious people her own age and older. Her cognitive skills remained limited, but she had completed high school. In the commune she had quickly learned to work productively in the food service. Her self-esteem remained modest, but she took genuine pride in being able to make a contribution to the group's welfare through her work. She had made a few close female friends among the members of the group, although it had been difficult at first for her to tolerate or trust any close relationship. She had had no sexual experiences.

Ellen regularly saw her parents for brief visits. Her anxiety still mounted whenever she was around her mother, but Mrs. E had profited from treatment enough to be able to contain most of her critical feelings about her daughter, and to restrain herself when they were together. Mr. E now took an active role in structuring and controlling their activities when they were together as a family; he saw to it that Ellen's visits were never longer than she could tolerate.

Ellen had occasionally thought about resuming individual therapy, but, living as she was in a somewhat sheltered environment, she was relatively content. Furthermore, she was not sure that additional therapy would ever provide her with what she really wanted and needed. "You see," she said, "I'll always wish that Mom had loved me in the right way from the beginning, but that's past history. At least now I understand why she couldn't."

CLINICAL CONSIDERATIONS

These clinical histories reflect the range of pathology that can be found within each assessment area, and the significance of specific pathologies for planning effective programs of intervention.

Both Alan and Brad were seriously troubled adolescents, depressed because they felt that their parents were unsympathetic and uncaring, and frustrated in their attempts to achieve an autonomy that was acceptable to the family. However, both also had psychological strengths that were developed during the relatively trouble-free years of childhood, a period when they enjoyed healthy, role-appropriate relationships with their parents. Perhaps this investment in maintaining a positive relationship helped motivate them to cooperate in treatment, for a major aspect of the conflict that each of these boys encountered as an adolescent was the desire to be independent without becoming alienated from his mother and father.

Brad was additionally handicapped as an individual because of his poor self-image with regard to academic achievement, and also because he had begun to abuse drugs as a way of allieviating his tensions. These factors were clear indications for individual treatment in addition to the family therapy involving him and his mother and father.

The psychological functioning of the parents in these two families was a basis for further differentiation in their treatment. Mr. and Mrs. A were essentially free of individual pathology and required no psychotherapy for themselves. Their marital relationship was basically nonconflictual, and a brief interlude of sessions with the two of them alone sufficed to help them focus constructively on the their needs as a couple. Since Alan was their eldest child, it was with him that they first faced the task of being parents to a teenage offspring. They were both willing and able, however, to take on these altered roles and to learn new dialogues through which they could effectively communicate the basic positive regard they had for their son. This combination of factors meant that the A family could effectively utilize therapy that focused primarily on system factors operating among the three of them as a family group.

In contrast, Mr. and Mrs. B were emotionally disturbed, both as individuals and as a marital pair, and it was necessary to intervene therapeutically in each area. The decision to treat them and their son initially as a unit was made largely because the parents were resistant to alternative forms of therapy. The decision proved to be of clinical value, however, because working with the family in that treatment mode provided the therapists with the opportunity to assess more fully interactions among the three of them and to gain a better understanding of the ways in which the couple's problems interfered with their effectiveness as parents. It became clear that their critical, guilt-inducing posture toward Brad served to help them avoid dealing with their personal and relational problems, which had intensified for them as Brad entered adolescence. There was no evidence that they had responded to him in this manner when he was younger.

The cases of Connie and Donald illustrate the problems confronting a therapist who attempts to provide treatment for severely antisocial adolescents and their families. In each instance the degree of alienation between family members was profound, making it virtually impossible to elicit cooperation from them as individuals or as a family unit. By the time they came for assessment, the adolescents were already estranged from their parents and were generally negativistic toward all authority figures. Each was entrenched, though to different degrees, in antisocial or self-destructive behaviors. They manifested personality patterns consistent with those of delinquent youth described by Robins, including impulsivity, inability to delay gratification, aggression, manipulation, poor judgment, and little (if any) regard for others or guilt over their own actions.[5]

Connie's father and both of Donald's parents were self-centered persons who, though not overtly antisocial, were themselves aggressive or antagonistic in interpersonal relations and unable to tolerate frustration. They lacked the ability to assess realistically the consequences of their own behavior, and they appeared to feel little sense of responsibility for their actions. None of the four parents was able to assume appropriately nurturant yet firm parental roles, or to serve as adequate models for mature growth. They negated personal responsibility for controlling or monitoring the behaviors of their teenagers and were themselves inclined to be erratic or uncooperative in their interactions with probationary, school, or clinic personnel. They showed the qualities of antisocial attitude and emotional remoteness from their children that Robins and Alexander observed in the parents of antisocially deviant children.[5,6]

Members of the C and D families did not see themselves as emotionally disturbed, nor did they conceptualize their difficulties in psychological terms. For example, neither couple viewed their loveless marriages as relationships that they might want to change, let alone sever. Mrs. C's passivity and resignation was such that she could not even articulate her discontent, while Mr. C was characteristically insensitive to the impact of his behavior on his wife. As for Mr. and Mrs. D, they had become thoroughly accustomed to their state of mutual disregard. It is not surprising that neither set of parents was willing to engage in any form of treatment.

Families such as these oblige a clinician to be realistic about the difficulties faced in attempting to provide effective intervention for severely antisocial adolescents. It is more than likely, because of the characteristic absence of affiliational bonds or affectional ties in these families, that neither the parents nor the teenager will cooperate in any treatment program that is offered. Even if the parents were willing to participate in therapy, their character deficits would make it difficult for them to provide their child with the mature, nurturant, adult relationships the child needs, or to serve as models from whom the adolescent could learn alternative modes of relating to society.

Ellen's case illustrates the need for extensive use of multiple forms of intervention when severe pathology is found in all major areas of assessed functioning. Ellen was psychosocially retarded when she entered adolescence, already handicapped by a childhood of emotional and physical trauma. Her deficits were so numerous and profound that, even with treatment, her prognosis was guarded. The staff recognized that individual therapy for her was essential. Initially, it served to establish a supportive relationship that would meet her acute needs and prevent further regression. Subsequently, it helped her develop survival skills that would permit her to separate from the psychopathogenic relationship she had with her mother.

Had circumstances permitted Ellen to live apart from her parents, the staff would have supported such a move as soon as it could be arranged. Her parents would not tolerate such an alternative, however, so reality dictated that Ellen's therapy be pursued while she remained in a noxious family environment. Under such circumstances it was essential to address the parents' dysfunctional states in order to modify their behavior toward their daughter. Dr. Y's individual therapy with Mrs. E was critical in this regard, for she provided a therapeutic object for this woman who, herself, had never known a proper mother. Without a relationship of this nature, Mrs. E would not have allowed her daughter to establish an alliance with Dr. X. Mr. E was less dysfunctional than his wife, but he required individual therapy to help him alter his relationships with both his daughter and his spouse. Although Ellen, as the identified patient, was the primary responsibility of the clinical staff, little if any therapeutic work would have been accomplished had the psychological needs of her parents not been appropriately addressed.

Any patient's dependence upon the family must be evaluated; this is a particularly critical consideration for therapists who work with adolescents. Few teenagers are equipped with the skills required to survive independent of their parents, and desirable alternative environments are seldom available. Under such circumstances, the clinician must base treatment plans on an assessment of the resources and potential for change in both the adolescent and the family. In the E family there were few positive features on which to build. Change in the family environment occurred very slowly and was minimal at best. Ellen was so ill-equipped to care for herself that she was obliged to remain in close contact with her parents.

In the B family, the balance of assets and liabilities was different. Mr. and Mrs. B's personalities required an object for their projections, and the therapists initially were not optimistic about either parent's ability to modify a pattern of psychological defenses that engulfed their son. However, Mr. and Mrs. B proved capable of change, and the emotional climate of the home improved significantly as a consequence. This made it feasible for Brad to continue living with them until he could become properly prepared to live independently, and his personal assets were such that he learned the required skills quickly.

DISCUSSION

In a series of publications, Rodnick, Goldstein, and their associates reported on the methodology of the UCLA Family Project, and described differences found among families of four types of disturbed adolescents.[1,7-12] In other publications, this group of investigators has reported on the relationship of family factors to risk for schizophrenia and to the outcome of the index patient.[13-20] Parental attributes that the Family Project has identified as significant predictors of outcome in the index patient are worthy of discussion here, because of their special relevance for issues of assessment and treatment. These parental attributes are *communication deviance* and *affective style*.

Communication Deviance

Communication deviance is an index of communication disorder. It was identified by Singer and Wynne as characteristic of the parents of schizophrenics.[21-24] The essence of this communication disorder is an inability of the parent to establish and maintain a shared focus of attention during transactions with another family member. The clinical relevance of parental communication deviance lies in the extent to which it handicaps the parent in communicating effectively with the child, with the result that the child is left in a confused or distressed state, and is thus more vulnerable to psychological breakdown.[21]

Jones adapted the Singer–Wynne index[21,22] to parental Thematic Apperception Test data from the UCLA Family Project assessment, thus providing a measure of the degree to which that group of parents exhibited disordered styles of communication.[17] The factors he identified included the following qualities of speech: the use of unintelligible, fragmented, contorted, or peculiar language; faulty overintellectualization, flightiness or anxiousness of manner; and indecisiveness in formulating or concluding a story. Another factor was the clear misperception of a major visual element in one of the TAT pictures.

Fragmented speech and closure problems are illustrated in the following story told by a parent in response to TAT Card 13MF, which shows a female figure on a bed and a male figure to one side: "Uh, well, this reminds me of...I don't think that's...well, she could be dead or only sick, I don't...well, and maybe he's, uh, grief-stricken, or maybe he killed...well, either that or..but I couldn't say, because I don't know how it turns out." An example of gross perceptual distortion is demonstrated in the following response to TAT Card 1, which shows a boy looking at a violin lying on a surface in front of him: "Well, it looks like a young boy, and I don't know what this is, but it looks something like deep-sea diving equipment."

The presence of communication deviance in a parent would clearly indicate to the therapist the need to intervene directly at the level of communication skills in order to minimize the negative impact upon the child or adolescent. In the cases described above, one of the techniques employed was auditory feedback, using audio tape cassettes. More frequently, however, the therapists intervened by requesting clarification of what was said, or by rephrasing the communication in order to model and teach a clearer way of expressing what was intended. Focused intervention of this sort can be undertaken within the framework of virtually any therapy modality.

Affective Style

Affective style is an index of the positive or negative emotional quality of verbal interactions. It was identified by Doane in the speech of parents who were talking to their disturbed adolescent about mutual problems,[13] and it indicates components of parental speech that convey either positive or negative messages to the youngster. The clinical relevance of parental affective style lies in what it indicates about emotional dimensions of the family environment in which the child or adolescent lives. Its crucial positive components are expressions of caring or concern that convey the parents' genuine support of or regard for their son or daughter as a person. Its crucial negative components are expressions of harsh criticism, excessive intrusiveness, and guilt inducement that reflect the parents' pathological attitudes and feelings toward the child.

Positive feelings in the parent's affective style are those expressed to the teenager in terms of genuine regard, support, or concern for his or her problems. Examples include the following: "I want you to know I care about you," or "I want you to feel wanted in the family," or "I respect your ideas. It's just that I want the best for you." Statements of this sort reassure the child that the parents value him or her as a human being, and they convey the parents' willingness to be empathic and nurturant.

Negative feelings are conveyed in three distinct ways. One is through general and excessive criticism by the parent of the adolescent as a person, such as: "Your are never responsible," or "You don't contribute anything to the family," or "You will fail, sure enough." The second way is through attributing negative thoughts, feelings, or motives to the child: "Isn't it true that you really don't care about us?" or "You enjoy your problems," or "I know you don't want to grow up." The third way is through guilt-inducement, defined as statements indicating that a parent feels distress, and that the adolescent is responsible: "Your father works hard to keep you in style and when do you ever thank him?" or "You keep on about it even when you can see that your mother is upset," or "The house is in constant chaos because of the way you lose things." Expressions of this nature serve to lower the child's self-esteem, increase the child's sense of isolation, and reinforce his or her oppositional stance toward the parents.

It is worth noting that the qualities conveyed by the affective-style measure resemble some of those incorporated in the components of expressed emotion (EE) described by Brown, Birley, and Wing, and by Vaughn and Leff.[25,26] These investigators showed that the likelihood of relapse in psychiatric patients was increased when they returned to high EE environments, ie, ones which were characterized by harsh criticism, hostility, and overinvolvement directed toward the target patient. The concepts of affective style and EE have both preventive and remedial implications for the therapist working with disturbed adolescents. They underscore the importance of intervention directed toward altering the emotional climate of the home from negative to positive.

As indicated above, both parental communication deviance and parental affective style were related to the psychiatric outcome of the adolescent. In addition, Doane et al found that when these two parental attributes were considered together, the relationship to outcome was even stronger.[13] A high degree of parental communication deviance combined with negative parental affective style significantly predicted relatively poor outcome; a low degree or absence of parental communication deviance combined with positive parental affective style significantly predicted relatively good outcome. In reporting their results, these investigators discuss ways in which the two parental factors might operate together in their impact on a child. One explanatory model considers parental communication deviance as a direct contributor to the etiology of schizophrenia-like disorders, with parental affective style an interactive or potentiating variable. A second explanation is to regard both attributes as directly contributory to the development of psychopathology. In the latter alternative, an adolescent could be seen as doubly handicapped, should the parents be not only highly deviant in their styles of communicating but also critical, intrusive, or guilt-inducing in their interactions. Such a child would have little verbal recourse for exploring or clarifying, with the parents, the feelings of unworthiness or rejection that they engender. For the teenager whose parents manifest only one of the negative factors, there would be compensation of sorts in the absence of the other. That is, the parents might be poorly focused in the way they communicate yet serve as a source of emotional support for their child. Or, if the parents were hostile but clear-thinking, there would remain the opportunity for the adolescent to cope with the parents' negative feelings through verbal channels. The authors go on to describe as "relatively fortunate...the adolescent who, though disturbed, experiences his parents as basically supportive of him and persons with whom he can communicate effectively."[13]

The attributes of communication deviance and affective style were identified as significant predictors of outcome only after the adolescents were assessed on follow-up, and the data analyses were completed. The initial assessments and subsequent interventions, such as those described above for five of the families, were conducted without preconceived ideas or knowledge of which clinical or research factors would ultimately emerge as significant. What the research findings provide is a scientific rationale for attending to these two parental attributes in clinical assessment and treatment procedures.

As others have observed, family theoreticians are prone to introduce constructs that are attractive, but often prove difficult to render operational.[27,28] Fortunately, the constructs of communication deviance and affective style derive from observable behavior patterns of people actually engaging in direct interactions. Thus, they refer to processes that are recognizable and experientially valid for a clinician. The close relationship of these two interactional research measures to the clinical data is particularly well-illustrated in three of the previously-described cases.

Alan's parents were relatively nonverbal, but they were nevertheless able to express themselves clearly (low communication deviance). They were distressed by their son's behavior, but their affection and concern for him as a person was genuine (positive affective style). Both of these parental qualities were recognized clinically to be assets. Subsequently, Family Project researchers (who were blind to any clinical information about the A family) independently coded the parents' speech as free of communication deviance and their affective styles as positive. This combination of attributes predicted the good outcome that Alan achieved. Alan would be an example of the "relatively fortunate" adolescent described by Doane et al above.

In Brad's case, the clinicians' concern was not his parents' ability to express themselves but the hostility that they communicated all too clearly. The picture presented by the research coding was consistent, in that neither parent showed an elevated level of communication deviance, but both had severely negative affective styles. This combination of one positive and one negative parental attribute predicted a poorer outcome for Brad than for Alan, which was found to be the case when his psychiatric status on follow-up was independently assessed.

In the E family, the clinically pathologic features are well reflected in the research data. The consuming hostility that Mrs. E expressed toward her daughter, and the convoluted rationalizations she used to justify her feelings and behaviors, were mirrored by affective style components of criticism and negative attribution. Mrs. E showed communication deviance factors of idiosyncratic language, overpersonalization, and faulty intellectualization. Mr. E also showed communication deviance in his fragmented and circumstantial speech, his bumbling attempts to express himself, and his inability to convey his affection for his daughter. The combination of two negative indices confirms the relevance of clinical data on which Ellen's poor prognosis was based.

In families A, B, and E, the family members were involved in close emotional relationships with each other. The *quality of their interactions* was central to the psychological functioning of the family. Communication deviance and affective style were understandably relevant indices, because they were based on directly observed interactional behavior, and thus provided meaningful dimensions along which the families could be seen to differ from one another.

The C and D families, on the other hand, were remarkable for their interpersonal distance, not closeness. Communication and emotion have less impact, one way or another, in situations characterized by alienation and disregard. True, Mr. C's negative affective style was blatant, and Mr. D's verbal pretentiousness earned him a moderately elevated degree of communication deviance. But in these two families the predicitive implications of these variables were of minor significance alongside the clear evidence that the child was already grossly alienated from the family and from society, and that major antisocial behavior patterns were already well-developed.

Data from two preliminary studies suggest a number of attributes that may prove useful in developing an index that will have particular relevance in the assessment of antisocial adolescents. These factors include a paucity of meaningful communication, and parental characteristics of poor impluse management, externalization of responsibility, and problems of integration and organization.[29,30] These criteria would certainly seem to have applied in the C and D families, and would have added weight to the clinical judgement of a guarded or even grave prognosis.

CONCLUSIONS

The histories of five disturbed adolescents and their families have been presented in detail. The clinical information was collected within the framework of a family-oriented research project. The clinicians, who served also as research investigators, were interested in examining family factors. Their procedures provided for a thorough assessment of the personalities of the parents as well as the teenager, and employed standardized methods of examining interactions among family members. Each case was followed, and an evaluation made of the adolescent's psychiatric status as a young adult five years later.

The clinical research context permits a comparison of these five families with each other, and offers an opportunity to examine meaningful parallels between clinical dimensions and research factors. I believe that research on families will prove to be exceedingly relevant to clinicians whose approach to psychopathology is family-oriented, and who must deal with the challenging complexities that this approach involves.

REFERENCES

1.   Goldstein MJ, Judd LL, Rodnick EH, et al: A method for studying social influence and coping patterns within families of disturbed adolescents. J Nerv Ment Dis 147:233–251, 1968

2. Doane JA: Family interaction and communication deviance in disturbed and normal families; A review of research. Fam Proc 17:357–376, 1978
3. Goldstein MJ, Rodnick EH: The family's contribution to the etiology of schizophrenia: Current status. Schiz Bull 1:48–63, 1975
4. Jacob T: Family interaction in disturbed and normal families: A methodological and substantive review. Psych Bull 82:33–65, 1975
5. Robins LN: Deviant Children Grown Up. Baltimore, Williams & Wilkins, 1966
6. Alexander JF: Defensive and supportive communication in normal and deviant families. J Cons Clin Psychol 40:223–231, 1973
7. Alkire AA, Goldstein MJ, Rodnick EH, et al: Social influence and counterinfluence within families of four types of disturbed adolescents. J Abn Psychol 77:32–41, 1971
8. Goldstein MJ, Gould E, Alkire A, et al: Interpersonal themes in the Thematic Apperception Test stories of families of disturbed adolescents. J. Nerv Ment Dis 150:354–365, 1970
9. Goldstein MJ, Rodnick EH, Judd LL, et al: Galvanic skin reactivity among family groups containing disturbed adolescents. J Abn Psychol 75:57–67, 1970
10. McPherson SR: Communication of intents among parents and their disturbed adolescent child. J Abn Psychol 76:98–105, 1970
11. McPherson SR: Parental interactions at various levels. J Nerv Ment Dis 158:424–431, 1974
12. McPherson SR, Goldstein MJ, Bodnick EH: Who listens? Who communicates? How?: Styles of interactions among parents and their disturbed adolescent children. Arch Gen Psychiatry 28:393–399, 1973
13. Doane JA, West KL, Goldstein MJ, et al: Parental communication deviance and affective style as predictors of subsequent schizophrenia spectrum disorders in vulnerable adolescents. Arch Gen Psychiatry (in press)
14. Goldstein MJ, Jones JE: Adolescent and familial precursors of borderline and schizophrenic conditions, in Hartocollis P (ed): Borderline Personality Disorders: The Concept, the Syndrome, the Patient. New York, International Universities Press, 1977
15. Goldstein MJ, Rodnick EH, Jones JE, et al: Familial precursors of schizophrenia spectrum disorders, in Wynne LD, Cromwell RL, Matthysse S (eds): The Nature of Schizophrenia. New York, Wiley, 1978
16. Herman BF, Jones JE: Lack of acknowledgment in the family Rorschachs of families with a child at risk for schizophrenia. Fam Proc 15:289–302, 1976
17. Jones JE: Patterns of transactional style deviance in the TAT's of parents of schizophrenics. Fam Proc 16:327–337, 1977
18. Jones JE, Rodnick EH, Goldstein MJ, et al: Parental transactional style deviance as a possible indicator of risk for schizophrenia. Arch Gen Psychiatry 34:71–74, 1977
19. Lieber DJ: Parental focus of attention in a videotaped feedback task as a

function of hypothesized risk for offspring schizophrenia. Fam Proc 16:467–475, 1977

20. Rodnick EH, Goldstein MJ: A research strategy for studying risk for schizophrenia during adolescence and early adulthood, in Anthony EJ, Koupernik C (eds): The Child in his Family: Children at Psychiatric Risk. New York, Wiley, 1974

21. Singer M: Family transactions and schizophrenia, I, Recent research findings, in Romano J (ed): The Origins of Schizophrenia. New York, Excerpta Medica Foundation, 1967

22. Singer M, Wynne, L: Thought disorder and family relations of schizophrenics: IV. Results and implications. Arch Gen Psychiatry 12:201–212, 1965

23. Wild C, Singer M, Rosman B, et al: Measuring disordered styles of thinking. Arch Gen Psychiatry 13:471–476, 1965

24. Wynne L, Ryckoff I, Day J, et al: Pseudomutuality in the family relations of schizophrenics. Psychiatry 21:205–220, 1958

25. Brown GW, Birley JLT, Wing JF: Influence of family life on the course of schizophrenic disorders: A replication. Br J Psychiatry 121:241–258, 1972

26. Vaughn CE, Leff JP: The influence of family and social factors on the course of psychiatric illness. Br J Psychiatry 129:125–137, 1976

27. Gurman A, Kniskern D: Research on marital and family therapy: Progress, perspective and prospect, in Garfield SL, Bergin AE (eds): Handbook of Psychotherapy and Behavior Change: An Empirical Analysis (ed 2). New York, Wiley, 1978

28. Lewis JM, Goldstein MJ: A review of the family interaction research literature in regard to its applicability to analysis of family therapy process. NIMH Professional Services (in press)

29. West KL, Rodnick EH, Armstrong JR: Parental attributes and the differentiated behavior of disturbed adolescents. Annual meeting, Western Psychological Assn, Portland, Oregon, 1972

30. Echeandia DM: A study of hypothesized antisocial attitude styles in parents of antisocial children. Unpublished masters thesis, University of California, Los Angeles, 1976

Stephen R. Marder

17

Combining Family Therapy and Pharmacotherapy: Literature Review and Methodologic Issues

Contemporary views of mental illness acknowledge that both psychological and biologic factors may influence the course of the major psychiatric disorders. With this in mind, clinicians commonly combine treatments in the hope that this will have the greatest possible therapeutic impact. Unfortunately, in the case of family therapy and pharmacotherapy there is neither an established conceptual framework for combining treatments, nor a firm scientific basis. Whether acting on faith, clinical experience, or on a pragmatic trial-and-error basis, clinicians increasingly mix the two treatments with what Klerman calls "weak and vague" justifications.[1]

ESTABLISHING GROUNDS FOR COMBINATION THERAPY

A clinician usually combines different treatments when it is felt that the two together are somehow superior to either treatment alone. The advantage for the combination may stem from one of several reasons: It may be that the two treatments are additive. Each may appropriately treat a different aspect of the patient's illness. As an example, drug treatment for schizophrenia may alleviate psychotic symptoms, while a psychosocial treatment, such as family therapy, is necessary for maximum improvement of social deficits. Alternatively, two treatments may conceivably interact in a more complex manner. In some cases, neither treatment may be effective unless the two are combined. For example, the patient's

359

perception of medication as a family member's controlling device may result in nonadherence to treatment plans. Until this perception is dealt with in therapy, medication refusal may prevent adequate symptomatic improvement. Still another model suggests that treatments may be appropriate at different stages of a patient's illness. In this model, family treatment may be seen as appropriate only after a patient's most acute symptoms have been modified by drugs.

Negative interactions of drugs and family treatment are also conceivable and need consideration. Proponents of drug treatment have suggested that psychological therapies, such as family therapy, may uncover areas of conflict which would be best left alone during certain stages of illness. On the other hand, certain psychotherapists have suggested that drugs may be detrimental to psychological intervention—either by decreasing a patient's anxiety to the degree that therapeutic work becomes impossible, or by altering the transference such that the prescriber becomes more authoritarian or assumes pseudo-magical powers. In the context of family treatment, drug treatment could conceivably reinforce the view that the chief family problem is a biological illness residing totally in the patient.

REVIEW OF THE LITERATURE

For a number of reasons, the clinical practice of combining drugs with family therapy is not supported by well designed empirical studies. This is not surprising, since clinical practices are commonly adapted before the results of systematic clinical trials are available. It is obviously important that clinical treatment be based on firm scientific evidence. Nevertheless, it is also important to acknowledge that, at times, the results of controlled studies will be of limited use to the clinician. Research trials usually focus on the responses of groups of patients to particular interventions. The determination of efficacy is based on the overall response of one group compared to another. Within groups, individuals may vary widely in their responses to treatment. Few studies have the necessary samples sizes to identify subgroups who may respond dramatically to a particular treatment which fails to elicit a response from the majority of patients.

Another reason why available controlled studies may be of limited usefulness for clinicians is that treatments in a clinical setting are administered differently from treatments in a research setting. Controlled studies of either family or drug treatment would, by necessity, attempt to administer approximately the same treatment to a number of patients. The clinician–researcher may select the treatment technique most likely to help the largest number of patients, and then (hopefully) administers it in an almost-identical manner to all individuals. Neither drug nor family treatment is usually administered in this way by clinicians. An expert in pharmacotherapy will, whenever possible, individualize drug treatment based on a large number of factors. An individual's prior responses to drugs, his or her subjective experience on medication, the severity of his or her symptoms, as well as the person's attitude towards drug treatment, should influence the selection of drug, the route of administration, and the dose. Pharmacokinetic evidence also suggests that even when groups of patients are given an identical dose of medication, there is marked individual variation in blood levels.

Perhaps even more than drug treatment, family treatment is difficult to control. For one thing, family therapy means different things to different therapists. Some reject the illness model outright, and instead see themselves as improving the individuation of family members, or as improving family communication. Among those who acknowledge the importance of signs and symptoms of illness, treatment models can vary considerably. Treatment may focus on single families or multiple family groups, conjoint or individual marital therapy. It is impossible to discuss family therapy meaningfully without being more specific about the goals of treatment, the techniques of family therapy being used and, of course, the skill of the therapist.

Lacking a scientific basis for combining treatments, one would hope that at least a reasonable theoretical framework would exist. Unfortunately, conceptual problems also exist. The approach to clinical problems of the pharmacotherapist and the family psychotherapist differs substantially. The former tends to espouse a medical model in which the patient is viewed as having a diseased organ, while the latter may perceive a disturbed person in an ill family. Combining treatments requires that the clinician adopt two rather different modes of conceptualizing a clinical problem. Docherty et al have previously pointed out certain resistances that prevent therapists from arriving at a smooth integration.[2]

Diagnosis

Differences in approach to clinical problems may be most obvious in the area of diagnosis. Clinical psychiatrists have recently become increasingly aware of the importance of accurate diagnosis. In the rather recent past, a psychiatric diagnosis conveyed relatively little meaning, since the classification system used by an individual tended to depend on the professional's theoretical bias, the country one lived in, or on other variables not residing in the patient. The discovery that specific pharmacological agents are appropriate for different illnesses certainly revealed that serious problems could be associated with incorrect diagnosis. Furthermore, clinical genetic and biologic studies have also emphasized that the careful classification of patients can not only lead to better communication, but also to an improved ability to predict outcome.

It is fair to state that many family therapists have a rather different view of diagnosis. This is certainly understandable in light of the treatment bias of the therapist. That is, the family therapist may take the stance that psychopathology resides within the family system, rather than in individual family members, and treat the patient with this in mind. Evaluations of this sort may be adequate for communications among individuals involved in family therapy, but for obvious reasons are inadequate for conveying information to others. For example, pharmacotherapists and family therapists may associate different meanings with the term *schizophrenia*. The resultant confusion could lead to a mutual mistrust of the respective advances in each area.

For the above reasons, it is important that professionals with different biases about etiology and treatment utilize the same systems for describing and classifying patients. The Diagnostic and Statistical Manual, third edition (DSM III), would seem like a reasonable starting point, since it does not appear to be wedded to a particular bias.[3] This should not be a serious problem for family therapists, since an expanding literature points to particular family difficulties which appear to be characteristic of the major mental illnesses. A rational approach has been suggested by Lansky, who believes that family therapy research should focus on linking particular technical treatments to specific psychopathology.[4] This review will critically report the evidence which suggests that such an approach may improve upon the results of drug treatment alone.

ANTIPSYCHOTIC DRUGS

Whereas drug treatment in schizophrenia has time and again been tested by controlled studies, most family therapists have not involved themselves in controlled research. Early studies of the families of schizophrenic patients suggested to researchers that family processes might lead to the development of schizophrenia. Observations were made on very small patient samples; scientific methods were largely ignored. According to a review by Lansky, these early investigations provide little evidence that family processes can either cause schizophrenia or alter its course.[4]

At the same time that these studies were being reported, a rather dramatic revolution was taking place in treatment and research in schizophrenia. The discovery of specific antipsychotic agents not only had profound effects on the course of schizophrenia but also supported the notion that biologic defects underly the development of schizophrenia. In addition, the need to study these agents has led to important improvements in research techniques, including the development of objective diagnostic criteria and instruments for measuring the outcome of treatment. Unfortunately, many of these advances have not been utilized by most family researchers. As a result, while drug treatment has clearly been demonstrated effective in schizophrenia, the efficacy of family treatment remains unclear. Nevertheless, evidence from different sources suggests that combining the two treatments may be useful.

A study by Goldstein et al provides the only empirical evidence to support combining drugs with family therapy.[5] In their study, 104 acute patients were discharged from the hospital on either a conventional or a very low dose of depot fluphenazine. In addition, one-half of the patients were treated for six weeks with a type of crisis-oriented family therapy focusing on stresses which may have precipitated the patient's psychosis. Since both drug doses are probably active for some patients, their study is probably most useful for testing whether family therapy contributes to the effectiveness of drug therapy. Since there was not a placebo group in this study, it is not possible to test whether improvement in patients receiving the combination is due to the effects of family therapy alone.

At the end of six months, patients who received family therapy demonstrated less residual psychopathology than those who did not. Schizophrenic withdrawal in particular improved with family therapy, with patients showing less flattening of affect. This is interesting, since this symptom is commonly refractory to drug treatment. The ability of the family therapy to maintain improvement over a period of six months suggests that the treatment has specific effects on the social adjustment of patients. Their results suggest that crisis-oriented family therapy added significantly to the effectiveness of drug treatment.

Other evidence, although not resulting from controlled empirical studies, suggests that there are rational justifications for combining treatments. Brown, Birley and Wing found that patients who lived in an environment which was high in expressed emotion (EE) tended to have higher relapse rates.[6] High EE relatives tended to be highly critical, hostile, and emotionally overinvolved. Relapse rates were lower with family members who were more accepting and emotionally neutral. A later study by Vaughn and Leff confirmed these findings and included information on drug maintenance.[7] Patients who lived in protected, emotionally-neutral home environments had low relapse rates whether or not they were treated with drugs. Patients who lived with families which were high in expressed emotion had very high relapse rates, both on and off drugs. Medications in these patients certainly made a difference, in that 92 percent of patients relapsed off-drug and 53 percent on-drug. Nevertheless, these rates emphasize that a toxic, overstimulating family environment can overwhelm the effects of drugs.

Other evidence from the same group suggests that an impoverished social environment can also lead to poor psychosocial outcome. According to Wing, both psychiatric institutions and homes can provide understimulating environments, which may worsen negative impairments of schizophrenia, such as social withdrawal, flatness of affect, poverty of speech, slowness, and underactivity.[8] Wing and Freudenburg found that these symptoms—at least in a hospital—can be improved when patients are given extra social activities.[9] Other studies also demonstrate that enriching the environment in which a schizophrenic patient resides can improve negative impairments.

Wing summarized the findings on social environment and schizophrenia as follows: Too much social stimulation, which is experienced by the patient as intrusive, may lead to relapse. Too little social stimulation can exacerbate a patient's tendency towards social withdrawal and a lack of motivation.[8] Since drugs may act by reducing physiological arousal, they may be most effective in patients who are being overstimulated. The psychiatrist, therefore, has two methods which can conceivably assist patients to adapt to their environment: (1) modification of the amount of social stimulation a patient will be exposed to, and (2) adjustment of the patient's stimulus barrier with antipsychotic drugs. The former method provides a rationale for family interventions by a therapist who can "diagnose" the circumstances which lead to poor outcome in particular patients and treat them. Combining family treatment with drugs in this model should maximize the therapist's impact.

Combination Strategies

Other strategies have also been suggested for combining treatments. Perhaps the most important reason for poor outcome in schizophrenia is the failure of many schizophrenic patients to comply with treatment regimens. Involving family members in the treatment process has the potential for improving adherence. Lansky believes that schizophrenic patients are reluctant to take their medication when drugs are identified as a means by which the patient is controlled by family members.[4] Drug refusal may then be seen as a means of regaining the power which psychotic behavior gives to the patient. Klein and Davis confirm that patients may view medications as an external dominating agent—one to which they refuse to succumb.[10] In Lansky's experience, drug reluctance resulting from such feelings may be reduced if domination issues can be resolved by open discussion.

Other evidence suggests that families who are supportive of drug treatment can significantly aid compliance. Parkes et al found that patients who had their medications supervised by a family member had a greater likelihood of compliance.[11] In reviewing the literature on treatment adherence, Blackwell emphasizes the important role of the physician in ensuring that drug-taking is adequately supervised.[12] Treating patients in a family setting certainly has the potential for increasing the physician's ability to evaluate any family-related issues which might jeopardize medication compliance.

ANTIDEPRESSANTS AND FAMILY TREATMENT

Depressed patients are commonly plagued by problems in their families. Paykel et al found that events, such as arguments with a spouse, or marital separation, were reported by patients suffering from depression more often than by control patients.[13] Other evidence suggests that issues relating to the family are often very much on the minds of depressed women. Weissman and Klerman studied the problems which were most commonly brought up during treatment sessions.[14] They found that family-related issues, such as children, interpersonal relationships, and the spouse were more often discussed than mental or physical symptoms, early life experiences, or sex.

Depression is also commonly associated with serious impairments in the functioning of women within their families. These impairments commonly involve relationships with the woman's spouse and children, as well as her work within the home, and the role of homemaker. These problems do not necessarily resolve when women recover. Women who had been depressed and demonstrated symptomatic improvement were still impaired in their marital relationships four years after the initial episode.[15]

Impairments in the parenting role of depressed women has been the focus of some attention. Weissman and Siegal found that depressed mothers showed more impaired communication, resentment, and hostility when relating with their adolescent children than a control group of mothers[16] In addition, they tended to over- or undercontrol their children. As a likely result, their children tended to demonstrate more school and legal problems, as well as more drug abuse and sexual acting out. Cohler et al found that impaired intellectual ability and decreased ability to attend to tasks were more characteristic of children of depressed (as opposed to schizophrenic) mothers.[17] They hypothesized that a depressed mother's lack of involvement in childcare and resentment about child-rearing may seriously impair the cognitive development of her children.

The evidence when put together certainly suggests that family issues are uppermost in the minds of depressed patients. Furthermore, the family functioning of depressed patients is severely impaired. From here it is something of a leap to conclude that family or marital therapy is the treatment of choice, or that it should be combined with antidepressant drug therapy. Nevertheless, studies suggest that psychological treatments, such as marital or family therapy and drug treatment, effect different outcome measures. The pattern which emerges from these and other well-controlled studies is that both treatments lead to improvement of depression. However, whereas drug therapy affects symptoms of depression such as vegetative signs, psychological treatments affect the social functioning of patients. The clinical implication is that combining therapies is likely to be more effective than either treatment alone.

A study by Friedman fulfills research design requirements for comparing marital therapy, drug therapy, and the combination.[18] In this particularly well-done investigation, 196 depressed patients were assigned to one of four treatment groups: drug (amitriptyline) and marital therapy, drug and minimal contact (a type of supportive physician contact), placebo and marital therapy, and placebo and minimal contact. Both drug and marital therapy alone were substantially better than their corresponding controls. Drug was both better and faster with regard to improving the patients' clinical condition. However, marital treatment also led to some symptom relief when it was compared to minimal contact with a physician. Marital therapy was more effective than drug therapy in improving a patient's role in his or her family.

Combining drug and marital therapy for depression is supported by the Friedman study. Items reflecting both symptoms and family-role task were improved more on combined treatment than on either drug or marital therapy alone. Marital therapy appeared to be most helpful for those patients who were being treated with drug as opposed to placebo, suggesting that drugs may make depressive patients more able to benefit from marital treatment. This is important, since one of the hypotheses of combined treatment proponents is that drug-treated individuals are more likely to do well with a psychological treatment. Of similar importance, Friedman found no evidence to suggest that drug treatment interferes with marital therapy.

In summary, there are several lines of evidence which suggest that marital or family treatment might be a useful addition to drug therapy. Only a single study—that of Friedman—has addressed this issue using scientific methods.

LITHIUM AND FAMILY TREATMENT

A rather substantial literature suggests that manic–depressive patients are particularly vulnerable to marital problems. Brodie and Leff found that 57 percent of their bipolar patients had experienced marital failure, as opposed to only eight percent of unipolars.[19] They found that episodes of mania were particularly destructive to marriages, although mania is by no means the only marital difficulty. Others have noted that bipolar patients tend to select spouses who may be characterized as overcontrolling.[20] In this manner, the patient may be seeking a degree of protection from his or her mood swings. The spouse in turn may be attracted to the patient's spontaneity and emotional expressiveness.

For many reasons, this system fails to give the family the stability it seeks. Davenport and her coworkers found that spouses of bipolar patients often have severe problems and may be clinically depressed.[21] They often suffer humiliation, financial disaster, insults, and abuse during manic periods, as well as other problems during depressed periods. The result is that certain themes appear to haunt the marriages of bipolar patients and their spouses. These include: (1) a family fear that mania or depression will recur; (2) a sense of helplessness and dependency on the part of the patient; (3) a need to avoid expression of all affect and to defend against closeness; (4) the use of massive denial to manage feelings of hostility, anxiety, loss, and grief; and (5) themes related to earlier parental loss.

Lithium carbonate has had a powerful impact on the course of bipolar illness. In appropriately diagnosed patients, manic and depressive episodes can be treated, and future episodes can either be prevented or attenuated. Unfortunately, patients on lithium still have a relatively poor outcome when compared with controls. Carlson et al found that one third of manic–depressive patients, most of whom had been treated with lithium, were functionally impaired with moderate-to-severe affective symptoms which interfered with work, social, and family life.[22] Although lithium patients were found by Demers and Davis to be more reasonable, easier to talk to, and improved in family participation, many were less enthusiastic and less sexually responsive than non-lithium-treated patients.[23] In addition, lithium did not increase the spouse's ratings of the patient's desirable attributes. Many spouses, failing to understand the biology of bipolar illness, encourage patients to stop their medications.

These findings convinced Davenport that family treatment is useful when combined with lithium. Patients and their spouses are treated in groups consisting of three to five couples. The primary focus of the homogeneous couples groups is on interaction within the marital dyad, rather than on group process. Discussion of the details of lithium treatment is viewed as digressive, and is saved for a period prior to each group. Involving spouses in treatment appears to counteract a patient's tendency to flee treatment, a commonly observed clinical problem with bipolar patients. In addition, members of the group appear to be sensitive to early signs of deterioration, and may assist in insuring earlier drug or psychotherapeutic intervention. Davenport and her co-workers compared the outcome of patients who received both psychotherapy in couples groups and lithium and patients who failed to cooperate with group treatment. The patients who received the combination did well, as demonstrated by their lower rate of rehospitalization and their benign course, which included minimal marital disruption. The patients who did not take part in the couples group had both a rather high relapse rate and a significant number of divorces (one third). Although their study has methodologic problems, such as patients not being randomized to the combined treatment and the lack of control groups), it certainly suggests that this is a fruitful area for future research.

METHODOLOGIC ISSUES

Although clinicians often combine drugs and family treatment, systematic study of this combination is quite another thing. Psychopharmacology and family psychotherapy have vastly different theoretical backgrounds. Very few individuals possess both the research skills and the professional expertise necessary for researching both treatments. In addition, systematically studying two treatment variables and utilizing controls is significantly more expensive, requires much larger study populations, and is more complicated than studying a single variable. With all of these problems in mind, studies by Goldstein et al and Friedman clearly demonstrate that the problems are solvable.[5,18] Nevertheless, particular problems are inherent in this sort of research.

Subject Selection

Even the most vigorous advocates of drug or family therapy would probably admit that no particular treatment is indicated for all patients with a given illness. For example, in depression, drugs should probably be withheld from patients with rather mild depressions, if psychotherapy has a chance of working. In schizophrenia, some patients may have family systems which are working well and require no intervention. If family therapy and drug treatment are to be studied, it is important that subjects be selected who seem appropriate for either treatment. Randomly assigning a group of schizophrenic patients to family therapy is probably an unfair test of the treatment if the patients have well-functioning family systems.

An important goal of future studies would be to provide information which would allow a clinician to predict which patients are most likely to respond to a particular treatment or a combination of treatments. It is therefore important for investigators to categorize patients in a manner which permits reasonable attempts at subtyping. It is obviously important that patients be classified in a manner acceptable to family therapists and pharmacotherapists. In addition, it is important to understand which manifestations of family psychopathology are treatable in family psychotherapy. This requires that instruments be developed to characterize families, using particular theories of how family dynamics interact with a patient's psychopathology. A good example of such an instrument is the Camberwell Family Interview, which allows the investigator to quantify family interactions by utilizing measures, such as hostility and expressed warmth.[6] The availability of such an instrument permits a researcher or clinician to prescribe family treatment for the purpose of modifying a particular family trait, and to measure the outcome of treatment.

Study Design

Design issues, such as the use of proper controls and elimination of sources of bias, need to be addressed in designing all systematic clinical trials. These problems become much more difficult when more than one type of active treatment is involved. It is rather simple to design controls for drug treatment: either a placebo pill can be administered, or the drug can be compared to another agent of documented effectiveness. The problem is much more difficult in controlling for family treatment. Patients and staff are, for good reasons, frequently intolerant of a condition in which psychological treatment is not provided. Some studies have utilized a minimal-contact condition, in which patients see a therapist, but the interaction is severely limited. Friedman has reported that well-meaning therapists find it difficult to operate within such limits, leading to a situation in which patients receive more treatment than is provided for in the study protocol.[18] In addition, double-blind methodology—perhaps the best means of eliminating both subject and observer bias—becomes nearly impossible with regard to family therapy controls.

The number of groups to be studied depends on the questions which are to be addressed. A recent report by the Group for the Advancement of

Psychiatry described some of the issues that need to be addressed before a design is decided upon.[24] It is fair to state that, in most studies, a treatment of proven effectiveness, namely a drug, has been combined with a treatment that may add to the effectiveness of drug treatment, namely, family therapy. The simplest effective design would compare drug alone (or drug with minimal contact), and drug combined with family treatment. This design has the advantage of simplicity. However, a design in which psychotherapy alone is included will provide considerably more information. In particular, such a design will indicate whether family therapy alone is as beneficial as family therapy plus drug therapy.

Defining the nature of the treatment to be tested also becomes a problem when two treatments are studied. This is a rather trivial problem with drug therapy in that variables, such as dose, frequency, and duration, are not hard to describe. In the case of family therapy, the issue becomes far more complex: Psychological treatment can not be administered by doses. Instead, variables (such as the therapist's skill and experience, theoretical orientation, the cooperativeness of family members, the cultural background of the patient, etc.), all confound the description of the treatment provided. Moreover, the frequency and duration of a psychological treatment commonly depend upon the quality and degree of the problem which is being treated. Many of these problems are, at least to the point of avoiding research nihilism, solvable. For example, once a patient is randomized to the family therapy condition, the treatment could be provided in the manner the therapist believes to be appropriate.

Empirical studies of combined treatment have generally been directed toward resolving the issue of efficacy: which treatment or combination works and for whom? This is altogether reasonable since this brief review reflects the poverty of such evidence. Appropriate attention should also be given to the technical aspects of family treatment. The early literature on drug treatment focused largely on which signs and symptoms of the major illnesses were affected by drugs. In a similar manner, it would be helpful to increase our understanding of the mechanism by which psychopathology is altered by family treatment. This would require considerably more precision in the description of how various treatment techniques affect treatment outcome. The goal of such an endeavor would be to make family treatment more specific; to tailor the treatment to the individual's pathology.

Measurement of Outcome

Some studies of drug and psychoptherapy in schizophrenia and depression indicate that the two treatments effect different outcome measures.[26] Whereas drugs seem to be most effective in relieving signs and symptoms, psychological treatments are most effective in treating social adjustment and interpersonal relations. It would obviously be unfair to test a treatment using an inappropriate outcome measure. Valid and reliable methods for measuring signs and symptoms are available for all of the major psychiatric disorders. Recent advances in monitoring the social adjustment of patients with major psychopathology certainly make it more likely that family-related effects can be monitored. If, however, an investigator wishes to measure psychopathology in the family system, considerable work needs to be done to develop instruments which will tell therapists whether or not they are having an effect on such a system.

CONCLUSION

The widespread clinical practice of combining drugs with family therapy has received only meager support from controlled clinical trials. This lack of support is not likely to discourage the many clinicians who are convinced of the effectiveness of combined treatment. Nevertheless, new systematic studies are likely to answer a number of important clinical questions. It would be particularly useful for clinicians to be able to predict which patients are most likely to benefit from the two treatments. In addition, many technical questions in combining treatments would be best answered by empirical studies, including the best time for initiating each therapy, the indications for individual family treatment versus multiple family groups, the appropriateness of treating severely disturbed individuals in families, and the specificity of various family techniques for specific illnesses.

The lack of supporting evidence is understandable, given the technical complexities inherent in studying two different modalities. These difficulties are, unfortunately, compounded by various conceptual problems, which have made communication between pharmacotherapists and family therapists more difficult than it should be. It would certainly be helpful to have common methods for describing patients, particularly their diagnoses and clinical states, that are not dependent on biases related to treatment. Alternatively, training programs might focus on developing professionals who feel comfortable in being associated with both biologic and psychosocial treatments.

REFERENCES

1. Klerman GL: Combining drugs and psychotherapy in the treatment of depression, in Cole JO, Schatzberg AE, Frazier SM, (eds): Depression: Biology, Psychodynamics and Treatment. New York, Plenum Press, 1978

2. Docherty JP, Marder SR, VanKammen DP, et al: Psychotherapy and pharmacotherapy: Conceptual issues. Am J Psychiatry 134:529–533, 1977
3. American Psychiatric Association: Diagnostic and Statistical Manual of Mental Disorders (ed 3). Washington, DC, American Psychiatric Association, 1980
4. Lansky MR: Research in family therapy, in Serafetidines, EA (ed): Methods of Biobehavioral Research. New York, Grune & Stratton, 1979
5. Goldstein MS, Rodnick EM, Evans JR, et al: Drugs and family therapy in the aftercare of acute schizophrenics. Arch Gen Psychiatry 35:1169–1177, 1978
6. Brown GS, Birley JLT, Wing JK: Influence of family life on the course of schizophrenic disorders. Br J Psychiatry 121:241–258, 1972
7. Vaughn CE, Leff JP: The influence of family and social factors on the course of psychiatric illness. Br J Psychiatry 129:125–37, 1976
8. Wing JK: Social context of schizophrenia. Am J Psychiatry 135: 1333–1339, 1978
9. Wing JK, Freudenberg RK: The response of severely ill chronic schizophrenic patients to social stimulation. Am J Psychiatry 118:311–322, 1961
10. Klein DF, Davis JM: Diagnosis and Drug Treatment of Psychiatric Disorders. Baltimore, Williams and Wilkins, 1969, p 17
11. Parkes CM, Brown GW, Monck EM: The general practitioner and the schizophrenic patient. Br Med J 2:972–876, 1962
12. Blackwell B: Treatment adherence. Br J Psychiatry 129:513–531, 1976
13. Paykel ES, Myers JK, Dienelt M, et al: Life events and depression: A controlled study. Arch Gen Psychiatry 21:753–760, 1969
14. Weissman MM, Klerman GL: Psychotherapy with depressed women: Empirical study of content themes and reflection. Br J Psychiatry 123: 55–61, 1973
15. Bothwell S, Weissman MM: Social impairments four years after an acute depressive episode. Am J Orthopsychiatry 47:231–237, 1977
16. Weissman MM, Siegal R: The depressed woman and her rebellious adolescent. Social Casework 53:563–570, 1972
17. Cohler BJ, Gruenbaum H, Weiss JL, et al: Disturbances of attention among schizophrenic, depressed, and well mothers and their young children. J Child Psychol Psychiatr 18:115–135, 1977
18. Friedman AS: Interaction of drug therapy with marital therapy in depressed patients. Arch Gen Psychiatry 32:619–637, 1975
19. Brodie HKH, Leff MJ: Bipolar depression—a cooperative study of patient characteristics. Am J Psychiatry 127:1086–1090, 1971
20. Greene B, Lustig N, Lee R: Marital therapy when one spouse has a primary affective disorder. Am J Psychiatry 133:827–830, 1976
21. Davenport YB, Evert MH, Adland ML, et al: Couples group therapy as adjunct to lithium maintenance of the manic patient. Am J Psychiatry 47:495–502, 1977
22. Carlson F, Davenport Y, Jamison K: Followup of 53 bipolar manic-depressive patients. Br J Psychiatry 124:134–139, 1974

23. Demers R, Davis L: The influence of prophylactic lithium treatment on the marital adjustment of manic-depressives and their spouses. Compr Psychiatry 21 348–353, 1971

24. Group for the Advancement of Psychiatry, Pharmacotherapy, and Psychotherapy: Paradoxes, Problems and Progress. New York, Brunner Mazel, 1975

25. Hogarty GE, Ulrich RF, Mussore F, et al: Drug and sociotherapy in the after care of schizophrenic patients: II. One-year relapse rates. Arch Gen Psychiatry 31:603–608, 1974

26. DiMascio A, Weissman MM, Prusoff BA, et al: Differential symptom reduction by drugs and psychotherapy in acute depression. Arch Gen Psychiatry 36:1450–1456, 1979

Melvin R. Lansky

18

Medication and Family Process

Remarkably little attention, either systematic or anecdotal, has been paid to the problems and advantages of combining medication and family therapy.[1] In part, this inattention may emanate from the justifiable concerns of pharmacologists and family therapists to avoid development of a premature eclecticism before the understanding of either field is advanced to its fullest extent. The requirements for competence in psychopharmacology and in family therapy, as they are commonly practiced, are so different that they overlap very little. When it comes to reliance on systematic research assessment and to adherence to the disease model, the divergence is even greater.

For the dedicated clinician, there are many difficulties in the path of really useful clinical judgments concerning the use of medication and family therapy together. They will be considered here from three points of view: First, the fact that the therapist has responsibility for the decision to medicate or refrain from medicating presents the possibility that factors other than knowledge of the specific indications for the drug, and recognition of those factors in the patient, may impinge on the therapist's decision to give or withhold medication. Such difficulties are homologous to countertransference problems in psychoanalysis. Second, the act of medication, as well as some of the primary and side effects of medication, can be seen to make statements about family process that may collude with or oppose family phantasies or myths; the psychotherapeutic aspects of treatment may be aided or opposed by realization of this, especially if a major effect of the drugs or the process of giving them correspond to a major, unexamined myth. A case in point is the impotence in men so prevalent with neuroleptic usage, which may be felt to confirm the family's view that the patient's sexuality and feelings of manliness do not matter. The therapist's interest in the problem, and resolution to try various alternative medications (to avoid potency difficulties), may be tantamount to a major interpretive effort with lasting ameliorative changes, whereas failure to do so would be felt as collusion with the family's view. Such implicit meanings attached to features of the medication situation may be made explicit by interpretation in ways that are advantageous and, not uncommonly, decisive for the course of treatment. The attention in family therapy to meanings attached to the process and effects of medication is homologous to the interpretation of transference in psychoanalysis, and may be as definitive. The third point of view to be discussed is the effect, (usually negative) that unexamined family process may have on the psychopharmacologic enterprise. While much drug reluctance or drug resistance may be attributed to subtle side effects, it is also true that failure to follow a pharmacologic regimen may be opposed by factors only intelligible in the light of family process. From the point of view of pharmacotherapy, these may be seen as resistances, and quite transplantable to the psychoanalytic concept of forces that consciously or unconsciously oppose the treatment.

Consideration of the homologues to psychoanalytic notions of countertransference, transference, and resistance are made mindful of the fact that neither family therapy nor pharmacotherapy make use of the frequency of sessions or associative method so essential to psychoanalytic work. Conclusive verification is not to be had by observing complexes of associations within sessions, as is the case with psychoanalysis. This makes the source of information less systematic than it is in psychoanalysis, and the risk greater that treatment stalemates and outright failures can persist and recur not only not understood, but unrecognized as such.

Clinically common difficulties will be considered from the point of view of the therapist's decisions, the effect of medication on family process, and the effect of family process on pharmacotherapy. Some guidelines for the combination of family therapy and psychopharmacology will be put forward with special emphasis on clinical situations that may be indicative of the need for more understanding of the prevailing process. Finally, some problems in evaluation will be discussed.

THE DECISION PROCESS

It is difficult to incorporate factors that affect the therapist's decisions into systematic understanding of medication and family therapy. Most research that attempts to scrutinize the combination of drug and psychotherapy will build into the design all decisions that need to be made. Simple designs of combinations of two treatment factors include four groups: drug and therapy, drug alone, therapy alone, and neither. But in these circumstances, the decision to employ or not to employ a modality is taken away from the therapist. In the absence of such decision-making, it is not possible to behave optimally as a pharmacotherapist, in cases where timing of medication and changing of drug and dose to minimize side effects is crucial. In the case of psychotherapy—of any kind—the situation is even more critical. This is because, with any type of psychotherapy, the assignation of responsibility is of crucial importance, and the introduction or withholding of medication makes a powerful statement about that responsibility. The stimulus for decisions to withhold or prescribe are not measureable in research protocols that measure the combination of drug and therapy, nor are the meanings of the decisions within the therapeutic situation. It is important to discern whether the stimulus is a justifiable change in the clinical situation, or something within the therapist that is drawn out of the therapeutic role by invitation or provocation from the family.

If statements made by the act of medicating are not discussed, particularly if they are at variance with the verbal thrust of the therapy, the result may be as confusing as situations that have been referred to as double binds.

Case 1

A man in his late twenties was admitted to a psychiatric ward and evaluated without a conclusive diagnosis. He showed some clinical features suggestive of schizophrenia, but lacked conclusive signs. He was begun on a neuroleptic and transferred to an inpatient unit specializing in family treatment. Diagnosis remained enigmatic. He had a petulant, demanding attitude in sessions with his mother, a depressed woman who had tried to raise him conscientiously after the death of her husband, but went through long intervals when she left his care to others. The resident physician kept him on the neuroleptic, and treated him as though he had personality difficulties emanating from the erratic and deficient nurturance. In the course of dealing with his demandingness, guilt induction, and general display of incompetence, the resident did not set as a clearly-defined task of the treatment the determination of what the patient could actually be responsible for, and what he could not. Accordingly, the expectation that he be self-sufficient was never realigned with an agreed-upon view of his capacities. These difficulties found their way into a split set of expectations toward the patient: medicating him like a psychotic, and treating him in psychotherapy as an immature, demanding man who eluded responsibilities that he could actually be expected to handle. The patient remained a diagnostic enigma for some time, but the resident was able to integrate into his own thinking a need to work on responsibilities in the light of capacities that could be explored in the therapy. After considerable agony on the part of patient and family, consistent expectations about responsibility were reached and progress was made.

There is a tendency on the part of psychotherapeutic purists to emphasize irrational elements in introducing medication, and to ignore equally powerful statements made by the failure to give medication. Assuming that in many cases medication will decisively enable the psychotherapeutic process to be of benefit, the issue of withholding a medication is as much an object for scrutiny as is prescribing it.

Either giving or withholding medication may emanate from irrational anxieties or professional shortcomings in the therapist, or from genuine dictates of the clinical situation. Appropriate prescription and withholding may both be supportive. The former may give the message that the therapist hears and assesses the patient's needs, and responds to them skillfully and humanely, while still preserving the psychotherapeutic situation. The latter may be a tremendous vote of confidence for the patient's ability to work through his or her difficulties with only psycho-therapeutic support.

Prescribing may serve sadistic purposes if it colludes with a process that needs to locate defectiveness or chaos in the medicated patient only, and to humiliate and control by the act of medicating. Likewise, with-holding when the patient has actual confusional or affective states that interfere with his or her negotiating therapy may be a cruel reminder that the patient has again relied on someone who could have helped, but didn't. There are inevitable attributions of such meanings to inaction or action on the therapist's part that are distorted; but any therapist must be mindful that he or she may be responding to some provocation in the therapeutic process which invites sadistic control or withholding. If this escapes scrutiny, the process of psychotherapy is confounded, if not sabotaged altogether.

The decision to prescribe may be tantamount to a decision to be done with the family's problems, simply confirming the status of the "identified patient" by medication. Likewise, withholding medication may indicate a reluctance to be involved with a real assessment of or response to the patient's difficulties.

Unscrutinized identification with the patient may cause the therapist, swept up in feelings of anxiety, futility, emptiness, and despair, to medicate for the unwitting purpose of dealing with these feelings in him- or herself. The act of medicating may serve the therapist by dissolving the frightening identification with the patient and establishing boundaries between the therapist and the patient by the giving of medication, or by engaging in a hypomanic attempt to deal with painful affects in ways that transcend demonstrable pharmacologic indications.[2] In general, physi-cians' incapacity to bear the patient's depression accounts for an enor-mous number of poorly rationalized decisions to medicate in psycho-therapeutic situations and elsewhere. For those opting to work psychotherapeutically with severely disturbed patients, the capacity to engage in hypomanic maneuvers to avoid such depression is a constant risk.

In those who do not elect to work psychotherapeutically with disturbed patients, there is the danger of the development of a rhetoric of psychopharmacology—one that frames every problem as a drug problem, because the physician finds it difficult to step outside of a pharmacologic framework. In an era where it can no longer be presumed that psychiatrists have basically dynamic orientation, such a rhetorical justification of an entirely pharmacological approach is increasingly prevalent.

When patients, with or without collusion from other family members, provoke the therapist, and invite control, the therapist may be drawn into medicating nonspecific chaos. Anger at the patient, anxiety about control, and the irrational notion that any chaos must be stopped immediately, are clues that the therapist may be swept up in emotional entanglements at a great risk to the clearness of clinical judgement. The family therapist has the advantage of observing whether he or she has been caught up in such a reaction *with* the family (ie, has fallen into scapegoating the patient), or whether the patient's and family's failure to express concern over the chaos collude in inviting the therapist to control the whole family, and to feel responsible for containing all the chaos within it. In psychotherapy in general, it is easier to tell with families than with individuals when one ought to resist the provocation to medicate, and re-examine the clinical indications. Frequently, the curious therapist finds that the patient has generated similar actions in others, emanating from the feeling that the patient induces in the therapist(s) that only they can restore order to the patient's chaotic life. Such response may lead to overcontrolling the patient, or to finding the patient burdensome and therefore rejecting him or her. The unreflective therapist risks either extreme, and loses the opportunity for psychotherapeutic attention within the family. Often, explorations of the provocation to medicate will complete the history, by explaining some connection between what happens to the patient and the hitherto-unscrutinized effect the patient has on people (see case 2).

The therapist, by medicating someone, may be engaging in some competitive display of prowess or caretaking. This competition is usually with an adult of the same sex, and may indicate seductiveness of the opposite-sex person, or competition with the same-sex adult.

A disastrous stalemate may occur if conflicting attitudes on the part of the therapist find expression in pharmacotherapeutic and psychotherapeutic decisions that are not integrated (See case 1). The mixed messages in unintegrated form, like any other pathological split, impede an integrated view of the difficulty, and preclude a working definition of responsibility so crucial for therapy really to progress.

Needless to say, the symbolic or phantasied meaning of any of these situations is greatly embellished by the actual pharmacologic effects of the medication, be they sedation, compliance, impotence, obesity, or others. Frequent or precipitous decision-making is more suspect of inappropriate emotional involvement than one decision to medicate, with occasional adjustments.

EFFECTS OF MEDICATION ON FAMILY THERAPY

The therapist's decision to medicate an identified patient, and the actual effects of that medication may seem to confirm explicit or implicit family myths or shared phantasies about the patient. This may undermine the psychotherapeutic aspect of the treatment altogether, and magnify factors that subsequently appear as drug refusal. If these considerations are in the therapist's awareness, and their meaning understood, the very act of medicating may often be turned to decisive therapeutic advantage. The addition of psychopharmacologic decisions into the therapeutic field, far from opposing the treatment, may enhance it by forming a supportive confrontation of the patient's family-derived phantasies about the meaning and motives for the therapist's action, with the more benign realities behind the therapist's intent. The therapist's decisions, the effects of medication, and their secondary elaboration provide a useful focus for the interpretive comparison that may have the full effect of a definitive transference interpretation. Some examples will make this clear.

Medication can have an effect (even if it is central and primary in reducing pathology that the patient complains about) that confirms family myths.

Case 2

A 45-year-old woman was in couples psychotherapy for marital dysharmony of many years duration. In the course of treatment she admitted yelling, blaming, and provoking situations in which quarrels would be inevitable. There were also neurovegetative manifestions of depression. The patient was started on a moderate dose of a tricyclic antidepressant, with remarkably good results for all symptoms and freedom from side effects. She was able to negotiate marital disagreements without blaming. Her husband overcame his difficulties and was able to make some agreements in the marriage. He kept them, but she decided to go off the medication anyway because "he was domineering," and she was defenseless in the marriage. In her family and his, women had always been peacemakers, and her only protection had been to be quarrelsome and blaming. She also felt he could not stand the chaotic side of her, and as soon as she would voice any report of turbulence, he would say, "Take your pills."

With this patient, interpretation of the significance of being calmed and therefore dominated at the cost of being unable to resist had to be interpreted in the family of origin, in the marriage, and in relation to the therapist, before the quite useful effects of the medication could be experienced as helpful. The medication situation brought to the fore central issues in her dynamics that went beyond what could have been handled by interpretation alone.

Side effects of medications may have a similar significance.

Case 3

A 29-year-old single male reported in a family therapy session that he was unable to have an erection, and wondered if this could be due to his neuroleptic medication. His mother burst forth, "Have you been to Tijuana again, going to prostitutes?" The therapist wondered if the implication was that the only thing she thought the patient would need his potency for was relationships with prostitutes. The mother looked disgusted, and the son became furious for the first time in therapy. The mother's control of her schizophrenic son and her contempt of his sexuality became a major therapeutic issue and one with which the therapist had unwittingly been colluding by medicating the patient with a drug adversely affecting potency. The difference between the therapist's response and the mother's served not only to reaffirm the patient's right to his sexuality, but also raised the question of how much of his dignity the caretaking relationship had cost him.

In this case, the family's debunking of the patient's sexuality stood in sharp contrast to the therapist's concern to minimize side effects. The comparison of that attitude with the parents' opened the way to continued successful steps toward individuation. Potency disorders are extremely common with neuroleptic drugs, as are motor disturbances. The latter are difficult to distinguish from psychosis, even by the patient who may be unable to discuss them coherently.

Case 4

A 30-year-old woman was placed on moderate-dose neuroleptics for persistent psychotic episodes. The hallucinations, referential thinking, and thought disorganization cleared rapidly, but even minimal dosages of medication failed to reduce her considerable clumsiness in fine movements. She did not discuss this at first, and in fact did not notice it until she was fired from a new job as a typist—her first foray into the working world after many years of intermittent psychosis. Her mother had helped her to get the job through a friend of the family, then found out secretly that her typing performance was substandard. The mother began to berate the patient to try harder, neglecting to mention that she had information that the patient didn't about the clumsiness; the patient's supervisor had told the mother about her clumsiness but had not spoken with the patient. The patient's clumsiness, of which she was only barely aware, played into a family theme that she, the patient, was constantly messing things up and in need of intervention from her parents. The recognition of the side effect came to the awareness of the patient too late for this episode to contribute to her steps as competent and free from family needs that she be designated defective. In the light of her subsequent successful efforts, the notion that she exploited the side effect and used it only to fulfill a regressive wish appeared doubtful.

The clumsiness may be seen as part of the general ineptitude, or as bungling that invites parental intrusion. In families organized around scapegoating, such clumsiness can become the stimulus for scapegoating the patient once more.

A particularly insidious collusion on the part of the therapist—or whole treatment team—is to recapitulate the family's split attitude toward the patient. This happens commonly when the focus of pharmacotherapy and of psychotherapy give different messages about the patient's capacity to behave responsibly (see case 1).

This type of split attitude registers the equivalent of conflicting injunctions about responsibility. The therapist was unable to conclude whether or not the patient was psychotic. As a result, the family therapy with this hospitalized man could not deepen into an exploration of mutual expectations and responsibility.

A similar situation arises with the problem of destructiveness.

Case 5

A schizophrenic man in his early thirties went into severe rages, and in one such attack put out both of his eyes. His enucleation and subsequent blindness so filled the family with horror that their attempts to deal with him were even more futile than before. He had numerous hospitalizations. On one of these admissions he was started on Dilantin (Parke-Davis) for presumptive episodic dyscontrol. In the course of his workup, electroencephalography failed to show more than drug effects. Nothing in the history suggested seizures. The inability of previous psychiatrists and neurologists to deal with what part of his behavior was "neurologic" and what part "psychiatric" mirrored the difficulty in the family, and of the staff on all of the wards he had been on, in deciding what he had to be made responsible for and what was assumed to be beyond his control. Even a neurologic consultant mindful of the absent indications recommended continuing Dilantin. The decision to stop anticonvulsants coincided with a decision to deal with the issue of responsibility in this man's life, and in family sessions. After many difficult months, the man was discharged to a community placement center and remained out of the hospital.

The physician's revulsion at the thought of enucleation quite likely influenced the physician to respond with insufficient and even conflicting evidence, as though the patient had a paroxysmal disorder rather than a psychosis.

The success of pharmacotherapy may require that early and vigorous interpretation take place, so that a readjustment problem can be identified. If this is not done, the improved patient runs the risk of being forced into a rapid remission in the absence of negotiating skills appropriate to the new level of functioning. The result of a failure to appreciate the effect of remission itself on individual and familial homeostasis is often to invite sabotage of the pharmacotherapy, and to restore dysfunctional but powerful methods of control within the family system.

Case 6

A 43-year-old man was persuaded to come to the hospital for evaluation after erratic behavior. He lived with his parents, both in their mid-sixties. A divorced sister and invalid uncle suffering from chronic lung disease lived with the family. The uncle had lived there for about six weeks. The patient was on a phenothiazine, and had been hospitalized many times for psychotic exacerbations. He arrived with his parents and admitted hallucinating, staying up all night, and not taking medication. He claimed that his mother plotted to drive him crazy by making him share a room with the uncle whose condition kept him up all night. This was a crisis situation that the patient could not handle, except by drug refusal and reversion to his psychotic symptoms.

At times medication may be of use in family therapy for extra-pharmacologic reasons.

Case 7

In the course of treatment of a 47-year-old alcoholic husband and his wife, it became clear that she had a need to see herself as the rescuer and savior of her husband by constant admonitions to stop drinking. The blaming humiliated him to the point where he claimed they intensified his need to drink and drove him to it. Lengthy exploration of the motivations of the couple did not lead to behavior change. Finally, the husband agreed with the staff's recommendation to begin Antabuse. He insisted on keeping the medication himself, but left his wife with the clear message that he often forgot to take the medication. He did stop drinking, but there were constant arguments, similar to those over drinking on the subject of his negligence taking Antabuse. The symptom of alcoholism improved in the face of a totally stalemated family therapy and a refusal to take medication. In both cases a chemical agent provided the excuse for blaming transactions which had enormous restitutive significance for this very disturbed couple.

Here, the medication refusal served to provoke blaming behavior in the wife the same way that drinking had done formerly. The symptom of excessive drinking improved in the absence of any improvement in the marriage, and in the absence of taking prescribed medication. The themes of transgression and blame continued inexorably. In other cases, medication may enable blaming and demanding behavior that nobody has ever tolerated enough to let the patient confront and resolve.

Case 8

A man in his fifties who had had postoperative cerebellar damage had a serious depression unresponsive to tricyclics, monoamine oxidase inhibitors, or electro-convulsive therapy. He refused lithium carbonate until many months of persuasion by his wife and family succeeded in convincing him to follow the therapist's recommendation. The mood amelioration was dramatic, but the patient complained constantly of tremor, which was compounded by his cerebellar damage. The tremor was indeed present and very troublesome, but for some time the patient could only acknowledge the tremor and the failure of the therapist (and the neurological consultants) to help. In the midst of a family session, he flew into a rage at the therapist. The wife stopped him. He turned to her and said, "Shut up, damn it, you always interrupt." The therapist asked, "What happens to the anger when she always interrupted?" She said, "Yes, I don't know what's come over him. He never used to be so angry." The raging continued, first with the therapist, later with his smothering wife and sons who could not tolerate anger in him, any more than could his psychotic mother. The mood stabilization from lithium carbonate, together with an opportunity to blame a therapist who could tolerate it, helped this patient to express the chaotic part of his personality that nobody in his past could tolerate before.

One serendipitous effect of drug discontinuance may be the value of observing tension states that can be identified through the use of medications even when they are stopped.

Case 9

A 45-year-old woman who had been in a blaming marriage for twenty years complained of anorexia, weight loss, irritability, sleep disturbance, and constant interpersonal friction. She was begun on tricyclic antidepressants with rapid amelioration of all neurovegetative signs, together with an improvement in mood and a marked decrease in blaming behavior. (This is the same woman discussed in case 2). She discontinued the medication on the grounds that she was unduly vulnerable to domination unless she fought all the time. Many of the symptoms returned, but decreased when she again resumed the medication. Finally, she refused all medication, but continued to make note of the tense, depressive states that triggered her blaming attacks. The brief time on medication had allowed her to compare these blaming attacks to calmer states where she did not feel the need to blame. The medication, even though it was discontinued, enabled her to have some awareness of the effect of her mood states on the behavior that her husband disliked so intensely. The trial on medication had a interpretive effect similar to that of clarification of feeling in psychotherapy. Since her defenses were projective and her affect quite labile, it is doubtful that such clarification could have been accomplished without the medication.

A type of tension was distinguished that was hitherto unrecognized because it failed to contrast with a calmer state. The patient continued to refuse medication but was able to recognize and deal therapeutically with the mood states that presaged her blaming behavior and that so upset her husband.

It has been emphasized in this section that the process of medicating, as well as the pharmacologic effects of medication, are experienced on levels that make statements. Such statements may be explicit or inexplicit, or in ways, collude with phantasies held by the family. Under the best of conditions, the statements are useful and signify without comment that benign, compassionate help is available. But in families where collusive and inexplicit phantasies have a malignant influence on the process, the cost of failing to interpret the meaning of giving the drug (or its effects) may be tantamount to a nonverbal destructive statement, supporting family processes that work to the detriment of treatment. Homologous to interpretation of transference, bringing the meaning to light by exploration, may turn these processes into the greatest allies of the treatment.

THE EFFECTS OF FAMILY DYNAMICS
ON MEDICATION

Family process enters into the overall scheme of pharmacotherapy in ways other than those that are analogous to countertransference and transference. The family may be used to enhance compliance with treatment. They may be used as auxiliary therapists, they may be involved in didactic sessions, and they may be used psychotherapeutically.

The use of the family as auxiliary therapists and dispensers of medication has been advocated in many circumstances.[3] It is a valuable technique, particularly during the transition from hospital to outpatient status. There is the risk of adding to forces that make the family dominate the patient, of setting as their task to get rid of the patient's chaos or to control him, or of validating the feeling that all defectiveness comes from him. Nonetheless, dismissal of family members as assistants is not justified on these grounds alone. The labile, suicidal, unreliable, or demented patient who is out of the hospital rarely has better supports for treatment than the family.

The involvement of the family for didactic purposes to better understand and cope with manifestations of the patient's condition is underutilized, not just in psychiatric situations, but in the treatment of many somatic illnesses. It is incorrectly overgeneralized from the psychoanalytic situation that instruction aids the forces of resistance by substitution of intellectualizing for therapeutic work and that patients seek instruction as a regressive avoidance of self-reliance. Instruction should be avoided only if it is certain that the patient is not really suffering from ignorance. There are conditions in which neither the patient nor the family can be presumed to understand crucial features of the illness. This is especially true of manic–depressive psychosis.

Case 10

The family of a 42-year-old manic–depressive man gained great relief from a discussion of the condition that first became evident in a pathological querulousness and domineering, and later progressed to the point of spending sprees, constant telephoning, and uncontrolled sexual exploits. To them it was incomprehensible at first that he was sickest when he appeared strongest, that when he was most inclined to be argumentative was the time he needed to be managed without argument in return, and when he was most energetic and active was the time he needed to be constrained against his will. Planning sessions, which later included the patient, included rapid hospitalization upon recognition of hypomanic or manic behavior and exploration of circumstances stimulating such episodes— sometimes these were very small rejections or brief absences. The tendency for manic–depressive psychosis to exacerbate was not worked through in this successful family therapy, but the mangement of the overall course of the condition was smoother and the impingement on the family's life was dramatically reduced.

In general, instruction is valuable when the vulnerability to the illness can be expected to remain. Psychotic conditions and alcoholism are cases in point. There is, in current practice, more agreement on this point with manic–depressive psychosis and substance abuse than with schizophrenia. The prevailing sentiment, that schizophrenia should not be identified for the patient and family and discussed as such, may be in need of revision.

The therapeutic use of the family to enhance drug compliance may involve the use of interpretation to clarify collusion and uncover anxieties. Multiple family group therapy is very effective in dealing with drug discontinuance.

Case 11

Several months into multiple family group therapy (MFGT), one patient mentioned casually that he had felt nervous and had had to resume full time medication. Another said, "Yes, I had stopped mine, and then I began to hear voices." A third mentioned ideas of reference, transient paranoid episodes, and intermittent drug reluctance, together with a host of somatic and perceptual distortions that were well recognized by other schizophrenics in the group. This is a common experience in MFGT: patients will get the courage to talk about residual symptoms and subtle side effects of the medication that they do not otherwise mention, because they do not dare for fear of domination by family or therapist, because other people lack the vocabulary to understand what they're talking about, or because they themselves are frightened to acknowledge that all is not as well as they would like. In such a group, the patients' ego strength becomes additive; the families get to explore the significance of residual pathology and what it means to be medicated; and the therapist learns to understand what the patient is talking about with respect to subtle residual effects of illness and of the drugs. Patient, family, and therapist all change. An unexpected finding in MFGT is that the incidence of drug discontinuance is extremely low.[4]

From the point of view of the pharmacotherapist, any of the situations in the previous two sections may escalate to the point where unrecognized and unresolved familial tensions result in discontinuance of medication. A very common cause of failure to comply with medication are presence of side effects: motoric (see case 4), weight gain, impotence (see case 3), and anticholinergic effects, including hypotension, sedation, and tremor. Also of major importance is the unwitting collusion of the pharmacologic enterprise with family processes which serve to dominate the patient, calm the patient to subservience, label as crazy his or her dysharmonious or inconsistent parts, castrate him by chemical impotence, and deprive him of the adaptive advantages of his symptomatology (see cases 2, 6, and 9). A great deal of noncompliance with medication, including that attributable to side effects, can be understood best in terms of the family process.

Assuming that a decision to medicate was made for rational indications and not under the sway of unrecognized phantasies, anything opposing the pharmacologic treatment may be considered dynamically as unconscious resistance. Accordingly, even in presumably biologic treatment, it is crucial to understand family processes that overtly or covertly erupt and sabotage drug treatment. Any of the homologues to unrecognized countertransference or transference difficulties may lead to such drug resistance, and failure of the patient to comply with presumably-rational drug treatment.

Foremost among the attitudes that invite drug discontinuance is a view of the patient's problems as symptoms only.

Case 12

A 47-year-old man was brought by his mother for hospitalization because of his repeated hallucinations and inability to work. He would not reveal the nature of the hallucinations, but acknowledged their presence and other front-rank psychotic symptoms. The mother was told that her son would be evaluated; his medication was readjusted; and a family interview was suggested. She became irate and took him to another doctor. Later the patient returned to tell the therapist that the voices he had heard were telling him to kill his mother.

Overemphasis on symptoms per se may stem from the pharmacologist's inability to tolerate feelings of depression and helplessness attendant to comprehending the limitations of drug treatment in most psychiatric disorders.

Case 13

In the course of supervision, a young resident, gifted in internal medicine and eager to advance his knowledge of biologic aspects of psychiatry, had come on the ward at the same time that a schizophrenic patient in his care had been contemplating discharge. The patient was the same age and of similar social background as the resident. He was no longer delusional, and most of the florid signs of decompensation had yielded to several months of moderate dose of a neuroleptic. A postpsychotic depression had been medicated with a tricyclic antidepressant, but the resident reported that it was effective for only a few weeks. In subsequent supervisory hours, the resident suggested taking serum levels, test dosages of ritalin, and different antidepressants. The supervisor pointed out that exclusive attention was devoted to pharmacotherapeutic issues that could be dealt with by a simple plan involving less discussion. The resident persisted in pursuing a totally pharmacologic approach to the patient for some weeks, neglecting to deal psychotherapeutically with the family's announcement that they would no longer attend sessions, and the patient's request to get his prescriptions filled elsewhere. A few months later, the patient's condition deteriorated and he was rehospitalized.

Conceptualizing every problem as a drug problem results in errors, such as attempts to medicate emptiness as opposed to depression that has neurovegetative accompaniments. Similar vain attempts may be made to prescribe drugs for primarily characterologic difficulties such as panic or diffuse tension.

A major transactional factor increasing the risk of drug refusal, even in the face of success, is the pharmcotherapist's failure to recognize the significance of blame in relationships including that with the therapist (see case 8).

Case 14

A 26-year-old woman came in, depressed after the birth of her baby girl. She had originally come in for marital counseling, but on examination she was found to be depressed and suicidally inclined, with sleep loss, decreased libido, violent feelings toward the baby, and perpetual quarreling with her husband. The latter was her complaint on examination. She had a tendency to blame him for any shortcoming, and to be humiliated by any sort of criticism, so much so that she would provoke fights and blame when she felt criticized by others or herself. She was started on moderate doses of a tricyclic antidepressant with very beneficial effects. In a few weeks, however, she stopped the medication. Further discussion revealed her tendency to take the fact of being medicated as blame itself and thereby intolerable.

CLINICAL GUIDELINES

Sabotage or stalemate in family therapy in combination with psychopharmacologic agents can often be attributed to unrecognized factors entering into the therapist's decisions or collusion with personal or familial phantasy to the point where drug discontinuance or therapeutic impasse result. These considerations, homologous to countertransference and transference stalemates in psychoanalysis, and culminating in resistance that sabotages the treatment, are not distinct from each other. Countertransferences may be in response to the personal or familial transference and, insofar as the treatment is opposed, all constitute resistance from unrecognized sources. Most of the examples of one kind of difficulty can be seen as examples of the other two, with little or no amplification. Insofar as transference is unrecognized, there is a countertransference problem and increased likelihood that resistances will proceed to jeopardize the treatment.

A major consideration in the evaluation of research on psychotherapy–pharmacotherapy combinations of any kind is that these considerations are not measurable by the designs of most studies that evaluate combinations of drugs and psychotherapy. It might be possible to design research that would, in principle, study these difficulties, but agreement on criteria would be staggering far beyond the already-overwhelming requirements posed by research using the comparison design for two treatments together: drug alone; therapy alone; drug plus therapy; neither. That model becomes generalizable only insofar as it may be presumed that family therapy may be conceptualized as a finished intervention procedure, like a dose. Such a presumption systematically omits the type of considerations emphasized above.

These comments on our present ability to measure do not detract in the least from the necessity for the skilled family psychotherapist to use medications, and for the pharmacotherapist to be aware of family process so that therapeutic success may be enhanced. The combination is crucial and, as is often the case, today's clinical exigencies cannot await tomorrow's research data. In the face of this uncertainty, some of the following may serve as warnings to the clinician to carefully look at the prevailing interpersonal process.

1. Frequent changes in medication that do not follow a rational flow scheme of alteration in dose, duration of trial, and type of drug, particularly if attention to the drug changes occupies most of the therapist's attention.

2. The therapist's temptation to act either in a way similar to responses by the family that have been inappropriately fearful, dominating, or controlling, or in a way making the history of the patient's difficulty more understandable, eg, if the patient's provocations make the therapist feel the need to either control or reject the patient when other options are possible; or if the patient represents himself or herself as uncontrollable except by regulation from someone else in a way that would be unthinkable in a job, a marriage, or a friendship.

3. The therapist acting in discord with the usual indications for the drug or falling prey to feelings of extreme helplessness (unwarranted by the clinical situation), futility, guilt, anxiety, panic, or feeling of inadequacy.

4. The therapist feeling that the responsibility for the case belongs entirely to him or her, and not to the family. This familial indifference should be dealt with in the therapy, no matter what medication decisions are made.

5. If all defectiveness in the family is felt to emanate from the patient (who thereby becomes the scapegoat with the sanction of the pharmacotherapist). Scrutiny of the family process is strongly indicated if the patient's difficulties are episodic, and appear temporally in situations that take the focus away from the difficulties of other family members

or relationships, ie, if the patient becomes symptomatic in a way that repeatedly takes the pressure off of others in the family.

6. If the therapist discharges strong feelings outside of the treatment setting or if an unwarranted lack of feeling is present. Laughter in staff conferences, relief at missed sessions, indifference to the patient's request to stop treatment, or to change doctors are examples.

7. If the patient claims persistently to be misunderstood or unheard. The risk here may be either on the side of medicating too much or refusing too quickly. The therapist, depending on his or her particular strengths or weaknesses, may miss drug side effects, especially movement disorders; disabling affect that precludes engagement in meaningful psychotherapy; outright psychosis that is understood as ordinary anxiety; fragmentation experiences that are neglected because of overattention to the adaptive or manipulative features of the behavior; and a host of other possibilities. In general, recognition of such phenomena increases when the therapist is open to hearing them, and sees complications as opportunities to take the work further. The risks increase if there is any attitude on the part of the therapist prior to seeing the patient that problems must be formulated only as problems for medication or, at the other extreme, that the demand for medication is itself a resistance and the enactment of a regressive wish that ought to be given up.

THE PROBLEM OF EVALUATION

The need for evaluation of drug and family therapy does not require justification beyond the obvious, especially in research where two very different types of treatment are compared. Such research almost always falls short of being generalizable as much as pharmacologic research, but treatment combinations must be scrutinized nonetheless.

Systematic research on psychotherapy and medication requires making an assumption that is never quite accurate; that should be borne in mind when the results of such studies come to scrutiny. The assumption (or phantasy, if it is not explicit), is that a psychotherapeutic intervention can be usefully conceptualized in a standardized way, somewhat in the manner of a *dose* of medication. To measure, one needs to assume that psychotherapy (1) took place; (2) under circumstances comparable to its use in nonresearch settings; (3) in a way such that differences in therapists and circumstances would randomize with a sufficiently large sample; (4) so that the therapy could be considered a complete intervention; and (5) that no meaningful relationship effects operate in the research field that might modify the generalizability of the results beyond the research situation.

The assumption that a period of family therapy can be treated like a dose risks improper generalization of results of studies that are available. The issues: Who does it? Of what does the therapy consist? What is it aimed at? Who is selected for treatment and on what indication? These issues become more sensitive when medication is being considered, because it is the more disturbed patient who requires medication, and the matters of therapist experience and specific type of family therapy are more essential.

Furthermore, it is only certain families that find their way into studies that randomize cases for research. The results of such research do not, in principle, distinguish the kind of cases that become available for randomization from that which does not. The treating source, whether individual or institutional, has loyalties to the research design that take precedence over the needs of the patient or family. The divided loyalties of the therapist cannot be presumed to be of negligible impact on the selection of patients for randomization and the actual experience of family psychotherapy.

A central methodologic shortcoming that must be carefully considered when generalizations are drawn from any study of drugs and family psychotherapy is the impingement of the research design on the decisions available to the therapist. Psychotherapeutic treatment, any time it responds other than to the dictates of the clinical situation, is at considerable risk. Impingements may be based on preoccupations from the therapist's past, provocations from the family in the here-and-now of the session, or impingements by research design. Whatever they are, if they stimulate therapeutic action for less-than-disciplined indications, the therapy (psychotherapy and pharmacotherapy) is at risk. Previously, I have touched on the significance of decisions that are impinged upon by the therapist's response to provocation from the patient or family, or by the therapist's inability to tolerate his or her own feelings of helplessness, anger, or futility. When research design is considered, it must be realized that the pharmcotherapy and psychotherapy are both limited, insofar as the therapist has decision-making powers about them. A family whose psychotherapeutic 'dose' has been predecided by protocol cannot be scrutinized at all in terms of questions such as: Why was family therapy prescribed at the point it was? Why was the particular drug chosen? Have other major interventions (hospital, individual therapy) been considered? What has the family been told about the rationale for family therapy, drug, combination, or neither options? Are the stimuli for the therapist's decisions at the time they were made entirely understandable in terms of clinical indications? What is the meaning of the process of case selection and randomization in the context of psychotherapy? How does it affect the therapist's credibility?

These are a few of the considerations that apply to even the best of the fairly scanty research studies available at this writing. Hopefully, these criteria can be borne in mind for interpretation of research results in the present, and research hypotheses in the future.

REFERENCES

1. Lansky MR: Research in family therapy, in Serafetinides EA (ed): Methods of Biobehavioral Research. New York, Grune & Stratton, 1979
2. Levy ST: Countertransference aspects of pharmacotherapy in the treatment of schizphrenia. Int J Psychoanal Psychother 6:15–30, 1977
3. Green B, Lustig N, Lee R: Marital therapy where one spouse has a primary affective disorder. Am J Psychiatry 133:827–830, 1976
4. Lansky MR, Bley CR, McVey GG, et al: Multiple family groups as aftercare. Int J Group Psychotherapy 28:211–224, 1978

Melvin R. Lansky

19

Family Psychotherapy in the Hospital

Failure to distinguish hospital-based family psychotherapy from out-patient family therapy risks abortive, ineffectual, or even harmful attempts at involving the family of the hospitalized patient. Although hospital family therapy makes use of the same basic concepts familiar to all family therapists, the two types of therapy differ significantly: Family therapy evolves from family work-up in different ways, family therapy in the hospital is never the only intervention made, data in hospital family therapy do not arise in the confines of the sessions alone, and hospital family therapy makes specific assumptions about the nature and significance of major psychopathology, which results in the need for hospitalization.

It can be said that some family contact is indicated on the admission of any patient to a psychiatric hospital.[1] Nonetheless, the progression from family involvement in the assessment of the patient to involvement in hospital family psychotherapy can never be an offhand matter. The assumption that family therapy is taking place should never emanate from countertransference scapegoating of either patient or family or from therapeutic grandiosity. The latter may assume that the need for family therapy is a procedure that does not require explanation and consent. Therapy evolves from initial contact with the family in a way that should shape the course of the entire hospital treatment and make a statement about the tasks of aftercare. These issues are preparatory to the patient's and family's settling into the tasks of family psychotherapy in the hospital, and will be discussed as features of the initial stage of family therapy in the hospital.[2]

The fact that other interventions accompany family therapy in the hospital present both difficulties and opportunities for the therapist. Difficulties arise especially if the family therapist cannot assume the family therapy to be a major format for decisions about medication, discharge, and ward management—that is to say, if hospitalization and other treatment modalities are not handled within the confines of family psychotherapy. Hospitalization can be thought of as providing a temporary system for containment of pathology when neither the personality system nor the family system suffices, but consistent hospital treatment based on this conceptualization is rare. Family involvement should be the central and primary organizer of hospital treatment, but it is often neglected. The reasons for this neglect include an exclusively biologic outlook on the part of many hospital psychiatrists—who actually make most hospital-based decisions—and a dislike of the notion of illness or major psychopathology on the part of many family therapists. Insofar as hospitalization is conceptualized from the point of view of a system containing chaos that the patient's personality system or the family system could not contain, data from outside the family therapy sessions can be brought to bear on the family psychotherapy itself. Psychotherapy that is oblivious to such data—management issues in particular—risks disastrous splitting in the therapy, and failure to address issues of containment that distinguish situations where major psychopathology is present from those where it is not. If serious management issues arise and are dealt with elsewhere, or if the patient's provocations result in responses by the ward staff that are similar to those of the family, the definitive handling of major pathology is bypassed in favor of attention to more superficial, conflictual issues that do not reflect the actual, initial reasons for hospitalization. These considerations come to bear on the midphase of hospital family psychotherapy, where issues of deep and disowned symbiotic attachments and split-off management issues must be recognized and brought into the treatment if the results are not to be imperiled.

The central notion of major psychopathology as necessitating hospital containment may be overlooked without apparent risk until discharge becomes imminent.[3] At that point, unrecognized or disowned needs for containment present themselves precipitously, shortly before or after discharge, in the form of decompensations, self-destructive acts, sabotage of carefully planned after-hospital commitments, medication refusal, and the like. The work not connected with the needs of the patient for containment is often totally undone, unless deeper issues involving disowned symbiotic needs have been addressed. This danger serves to emphasize the centrality of separations for those with major psychopathology—separations from nurturant sources, individual, familial or to the hospital—that hold the patient together. The avoidance of disaster when hospitalization stops is minimized by conceptualization and proper handling of a termination phase of family psychotherapy in the hospital.

INITIAL PHASE

If the initial phase of family psychotherapy in the hospital is that period of time until the patient settles into an acceptance of hospital containment to do work that he or she could not do without the hospital, then it becomes clear that many such therapies never get beyond the initial stage, ie, they never settle into productive use of the support of the hospital. Since it is my conviction that many treatment failures of this type could be prevented by proper understanding and handling of the initial phase, I shall discuss some common pitfalls in this stage. These include (1) failure to handle the prehospital situation properly, (2) failure to adequately define the field of work for the family, (3) failure to anticipate specific resistances to the work, and (4) failure to handle the acute crisis situation leading to hospitalization within the context of the family. There is considerable overlap in these tasks.

Framing the Treatment

The predicament of the family prior to hospitalization must be understood in order for the therapist to be aware of what intense affect is aroused by the family's inability to contain the difficulties of a family member within the family, and to help with the handling of that affect. Empathic response to the family in their time of need is often decisive in securing the treatment alliance. Frequently, the patient's disturbance was treated as a variant of normal emotional turbulence, and the family tried to cheer up or motivate a depressed member, reason with a paranoid or manic one, or otherwise handle a basically pathological situation as though normal responsibilities could be expected of the patient, and normal encouragement or sanctions could restore equilibrium to the family. When this attempt at containment by normal familial support and sanction fails, the result is some combination of anger at the patient or others; shame at having the family seen as uncontrolled, aberrant, crazy, or chaotic; humiliation within the family, seeing itself as impotent to deal with its own problems; and guilt toward the patient once it is realized that some of the anger was for failure to fulfill responsibilities beyond the patient's capacities. Combined with bewilderment about the nature of mental illness in the first place and how to handle it, these factors incline the family away from involvement with the patient in psychotherapy, and toward certifying their dismay as legitimate by making it entirely the problem of the hospital that the patient needs containment.

Reluctance on the part of staff to encounter the family, and fear on the part of the hospitalized patient to deal with members of the family, may complete *triangulation* of the hospital to stabilize an unstable situation between patient and family.[4] This stabilization is at the cost of growth, since all of these factors conspire to oppose the family's involvement with the patient.[1] Proper understanding and vigorous interpretive anticipation of these as major obstacles to be overcome convey not only a sense of mastery on the part of the staff, but also an empathic acceptance of the family in the midst of their worst turmoil. Addressing the feelings of shame, guilt, and humiliation that foster the family's withdrawal from active involvement in treatment immediately buttresses the treatment alliance.

It is likewise crucial in the early stages of family psychotherapy in the hospital to anticipate the family's sensitivity to subtle nuances of blaming and demanding on the part of the staff. These are extraordinarily hurtful issues in the family system that, more likely than not, regards itself as having failed, feels culpable, has exhausted its resources, and feels that more demands are not possible. The sensitivity of the family to blame may manifest itself in the form of questions that have etiologic implications: "Can megavitamins help?" or, "Could his smoking marijuana have caused this?" or, "How about diet or jogging?" The experienced clinician will be wise to consider *any* etiologic query at this stage as though it were a plea for exculpation, and to respond by noting that the cause of most psychiatric difficulties isn't known, and that what can be done is to meet, get everyone's view of the situation, and try to minimize the difficulties and plan realistically for the future. The therapist is likewise best to indicate in advance that participation in the family sessions does not presume the family's continued involvement with the patient. They agree only to planning sessions, to estimate what might be required and what is or isn't available.

The issues of blame of the family and demands on them should be addressed early, whether or not the patient or family brings them up directly. Anticipation of blame and demands are major factors in the early reluctance of family to participate. Needless to say, any countertransference difficulty (often unresolved in the therapist's family of origin), manifested by the therapist actually blaming family or making demands on them *eo ipso* scapegoat the family, and jettisons effective treatment.

Proper technique in asking the family's participation is often of great importance. Too much flexibility about appointments tends to devalue the treatment. Family participation within days of admission should be mandatory, and not sacrificed to usual demands of their busy schedules. The reason given by the therapist should never presume that psychotherapy has been prescribed or agreed upon, or even that the family is seen as part of the problem. Any agreement to continue family meetings should evolve from work that begins by examining what the difficulties are that led to hospitalization and whether or not they are understood in the same way by the patient and by those closest to him or her. It should be emphasized that all significant family members should be present, because it can never be presumed that there is agreement on the events and significance of what happened or on what steps remain to be taken. The therapist who fails to state this explicitly, even when the family does not ask, risks pushing the family's fears underground at the expense of the alliance.

In the event that only part of the pertinent family agrees to come in, the therapist should consider direct contact with the reluctant members. It is quite common for fathers, in particular, to fail to come in, either because their importance is not stressed, or because they are told that their presence is unimportant. Direct calls from therapist to father are astoundingly effective in most cases, and often serve to unearth anxiety-producing coalitions in the family that excludes the father.

When there is a choice about who to include, it is usually more revealing to include everyone available, including small infants and animals. More may be revealed about the family process by seeing who responds to an infant's needs than by confining the interview to the strictly articulate members of the family, and skewing assessment toward this part of the family.

Sessions should also include a newly admitted acute patient, even if that person is psychotic. This is not the prevailing attitude.[5,6] It is usually assumed that acutely-explosive crisis situations, and psychosis in particular, contraindicate family therapy. This view is based on a failure to conceptualize a stage at which the therapist enters the family system and experiences uncontained chaos in that system, making contact with parts of the system that are uncontained, and with the parts of the system that feel that it is up to them do the containing.

This empathic contact is crucial and often decisive in imparting to the family relief from overwhelming anxiety about their responsibilities and capacities. This can only happen when they feel understood by someone capable of entering the system at its most chaotic time, and emerging from the chaos with the family. The most powerful support to the treatment alliance with the family comes from this sense of the therapist's having shared the experience of lost containment with the family.

If this line of reasoning is accepted, it follows not only that acutely disruptive states do not contraindicate family therapy but, rather, that such states provide a strong indication for family sessions at the earliest possible time—before hospital commitment or medication provide containment that seals off the experience.

Even in cases of schizophrenia, drug or alcohol intoxication, or mania, when the patient may be refractory to ameliorative influence and have to leave the room, the family can usefully be put in touch with their depression, futility, anxiety, and rage in ways that may be utilized for comparison with other, less chaotic situations later in treatment.

Conducting the Sessions

Modification of the disturbance is not the immediate goal of hospital family therapy in its earliest stages with a volatile or psychotic member. Elucidation of the cognitive and emotional field is something that can best be done when patient and family are at their greatest disruption. Several types of interventions are useful when the therapist makes empathic entry into the family system.

Process comments about containment. "When he's like this (manic) you can't rely on reasoning with him," or (intoxicated), "You can't judge whether you can stop her without getting hit." "You feel you're responsible for controlling him (schizophrenic), yet he won't listen to reason as he did before he stopped the medication."

Questions to either the person needing containment or to those providing it. "Is there agreement on what's going on now?" "Is this typical of what has been happening these last few days?" "How would you like them to treat you (the psychotic person) when you're like this?" "What do you (family member) feel is required of you when he is this way?"

Modeling of containment functions. "I know you think we're exploiting you and controlling you, but for the time you have to stay here and take medication." "I know you need to go to work, but I'm too worried about suicide to go along with a pass." "You have to go to the hospital when you are high (manic patient), no matter how much you argue or how convincing your arguments sound." "I feel as though you make me feel responsible for whether you live or die (suicidal patient) and that you act as though it's not your worry at all. That gives me no choice but to do things that you call demeaning and dominating."

Sharing emotional reactions. "I feel frightened when she does this, and I suppose you must." "I feel irritation at your interrupting with more demands just when we're trying to decide who has to be responsible for you." "You act as though you can't take any responsibility for the way you act. Is that so?"

These very early types of intervention have as their aim the sharing of the experience of failed containment in the family with an empathic and skilled therapist who can identify within himself and all others what is transpiring in the here-and-now, including feelings the family may not feel free to own: fear, anger, shame, guilt, confusion, inadequacy. There is also a chance to empathically question each family member about what he feels he is responsible for, entitled to, and actually needs, for present use and later comparison.

Even if the session becomes unmanageable, it does not follow that the intervention is not useful. If the patient has to leave, or if others have untoward reactions to the patient, these events can be explored and compared to the situation immediately preceding hospitalization. Even if the session results in more disruption, it is worthwhile if the therapist has the family's attention when he finally says from his own experience "So this is what we're dealing with."

The formal work-up of the family should follow after the shared experience of the crisis and explications of the failure of containment. If formal work-up is done before empathic contact has been made and worked with, the therapist risks the implications that the work-up has etiologic significance—that the family caused the disturbance—or that the family's resources may not have been fully deployed for the patient's benefit. That is to say, premature emphasis on the work-up may be seen as blaming the family, or as making demands on them, when they are not likely to be able to tolerate either.

The formal work-up, including a genogram of at least three generations, is the starting point for inquiring what the family is like apart from the immediate disruption.[4] Each member of the family should emerge as a center of hopes, aspirations, and struggles, inside the family and out. This sets the stage for widening the scope of family work in the middle phase, or for individual referrals if they are indicated.

It should not be presumed that the family is available for, or interested in, dealing with matters other than those which necessitated hospitalization, or those containment issues to be faced during or after the hospital. The formal work-up heralds the end of the initial phase of family psychotherapy in the hospital. After the work-up, a formal prescription should be made by the therapist to clarify the nature of the proposed future meetings which, if all agree, can then proceed as middle-phase hospital family therapy using hospital containment for work not heretofore possible.

MIDDLE PHASE

Middle-phase hospital family therapy is that part of the treatment concerned with using the containment provided by the hospital and not with establishing that containment or giving it up. To the extent that the family is involved in work at a level not possible when absence of containment precludes all else, middle-phase work may resemble the type of outpatient family psychotherapy that is done in less-disturbed cases, where major psychopathology and its containment are not salient issues.

The middle phase may proceed smoothly, with the hospital supplying support and stability in a way that has not been provided before, but this is not always the case. It is a common circumstance where containment and the need for it are disowned, as are the needs being supplied by the hospital. The failure to deal with those issues presages a precipitous discharge or posthospital period where the very issues necessitating hospitalization re-emerge and must be faced again.

Manifestations of Splitting in the Hospital

For the therapist unmindful of defensive operations in cases of major psychopathology, and insensitive to manifestations of splitting, it is common to have a family therapy that stresses conflict resolution progress with apparent gains that later become undone or irrelevant at the end of hospitalization.

Some clues that issues that should be in the family therapy are split off and dealt with elsewhere are:

1. If relationships with family are cast in entirely negative, disowning tones with no mention of the patient's need for the family, or other needs of the patient that are being met by the hospital. The situation may be similar to a chronically conflictual blaming marriage with overt conflict on the surface and collusive disowning of deep ties to the relationship. Such marriages often give the impression of imminent breakup, but endure for decades with homeostasis often re-established by some sort of flamboyant aggressive or self-sabotaging maneuver that prevents a final separation. There is disowning of the underlying need for the blamed spouse to hold the other together, and to serve as a

target for projections that evacuate the awareness of defectiveness or inadequacy. The hospital family therapist must be alert to the prevalence of such collusive disowning with self-defeating maneuvers that re-establish the relationship, or hold it in place by some sort of intimidation. If splitting takes place so that conflictual surface issues that keep the family apart occur in the family therapy, and maneuvers such as sabotage of discharge plans or self-destructive acts which work against separation appear elsewhere, then split-off parts of the same problem appear in different settings and cannot be integrated. There may be talk within a therapy session of marital breakup, or of an adolescent living separately and concern with management issues dealt with elsewhere. Such issues include drunkenness, drugs, job losses, suicidality, or threat of violence—matters that invite a containing or controlling relationship. If the split is not addressed by the family therapist, truly useful learning from the therapeutic experience cannot happen.

2. If major management issues occur in the hospital. These include substance abuse, suicidality, self-sabotage or threats of violence. If anxiety is felt by the ward staff and not put back into the family system, particularly if the patient shows no concern about controlling them, there is probably evidence of pathologic projective identification that must be handled before therapy can take a decisive turn.[8] If, say, a suicidal patient provokes intense anxiety about his safety in the ward staff, but feels no anxiety himself, and if family meetings proceed without integrating the management of suicidality into the therapy, the patient probably sustains the phantasy that if others worry about containment, he will not have to worry about controlling himself and will also be able to control *them*. It is this sort of unintegrated split in the personality handled in this way that invites eventual rejection, failure, or other disasters. Often something like this leads to hospitalization in the first place. Proper handling of the issue psychotherapeutically occurs only when management is dealt with in the psychotherapy and not split off.

3. A history of early trauma in the patient's life that reflects change in nurturance due to character pathology of the parents; intrusiveness by parents by parentification, scapegoating, or blame of the child; or abusiveness, sexual or physical, that is sustained despite the knowledge of one or both parents. The results of such tenuous nurturance is the patient's failure to have sufficient security in nurturant attachments with resulting tendencies toward clinginess and fear of abandonment. The patient's awareness of his or her own need to attach for security is usually not present without intense resentment that may be expressed as blame or in hostile actions such as financial irresponsibility,

drunkenness, infidelity, recklessness, violence, or self-destructiveness.

4. Evidence of patterns of response to the patient on the ward that underscore pathologic character traits alluded to or evident in the family sessions. The following are some examples, among many:

● The patient lounges around ward without making constructive efforts to help himself yet patients and staff are too intimidated to bring this up.

● The patient becomes an outcast by perpetual borrowing, demanding, requiring assistance.

● The patient pairs off with a dominant person who cares for him, but impinges to the point where the patient resents it.

● The patient is high-handed, debunking, contemptuous of caretaking staff, and demands to talk to higher-ranking authorities.

● The patient becomes a *cause celebré* on the ward, with one faction seeing him as unfairly treated, and another faction seeing him as manipulative. Often, staff members take sides and oppose each other when such patients exploit pre-existing staff conflicts.

● The patient will identify with staff and be helpful to other patients at cost of dealing with her own problems. This is especially important if this person was parentified in the family of origin, or was a placator or pacifier.

● The patient manifests an obvious disturbance that can be seen to divert attention away from the difficulties of others—especially when there is a history of some deviant or underfunctioning behavior in the family of origin that served to take attention away from parental depression, drinking, or marital dysharmony.

● The patient plans to organize his life outside of the hospital in ways that keep the treatment staff in perpetual turmoil by cancellations of meetings and requests that rules and procedures be changed.

● The patient interacts with patients or staff with constant feelings of entitlement, somatizations, or guilt inducing attitudes.

These manifestations of pathologic character traits are more meaningful if they can be added to the history of the family's difficulties with some increased clarity; that is, if they complete the history by showing some connection between what the patient characteristically does and what the patient reports as mysterious rejections, estrangements, punishment from authority, job losses, lack of support from relatives to whom he or she has done nothing, etc.

5. The above factors tend to emphasize the hospitalized patient's contribution to the family system, rather than the dovetailing of pathologic needs. The role of the rest of the family may, at times, be elucidated by specific countertransference constellations among staff, involving the

patient, and bearing resemblance to similar constellations in the family. It is, unfortunately, no rarity for hospital staff to attract those with needs to focus on, and thereby encourage the defectiveness of others. If this is the case and countertransference problems result in pathologic and pathogenic coalitions between patients and staff, it is usually along lines established by previous collusions. Obviously, inferences about what is taking place are more convincing if they show up in more than one system: the family of origin, current family, ward system, job. Some of these patterns resemble those described in pathologic families.

● Socialization outside of the system is felt to be imbued with danger. It is a common countertransference constellation on hospital wards to treat some patients as though extra-hospital activities are dangerous, and must be justified as therapeutic before they can be sanctioned. This parallels descriptions in extremely pathologic families where such prohibitions have been noticed as limitations of extrafamilial socialization, the "rubber fence," and the tertiary injunction of the double bind, prohibiting the victim from leaving the field.[9,10,11] When this happens on the ward, the patient undergoes not only a paranoid distortion of reality that causes him to overestimate the danger without and the need of protection within the system, but also the humiliation of having to account for everything he does to someone who presumes to know what is good for the patient. In effective hospital family therapy, the high cost and low yield of these operations, and the patient's feeling that he or she has to invite them, must be interpreted vigorously.

● Mythology within a system may preserve a malignant homeostasis by rigidifying roles of people actually living together.[12] The patient may invite the same sort of rigidified scapegoating by all-too-eager staff who are willing to act as though all the tensions on the ward emanated from, say, the patient's drug abuse or drinking. Such scapegoating myths serve to exculpate all others in the system. Redemption myths extolling the virtures of the program at the expense of those in it may mirror family myths that sustain the beneficence of a family member at others' expense.

● Patient behavior is often understandable when seen in relation to conflict between others on whom the patient depends. Staff conflict, even if it is not openly acknowledged, is usually detected by some patients who consciously or unconsciously exploit the conflict by some behavior that will organize the disputants' attention around the patient. The dysfunction must be understood as an attempt not only to exploit the conflict for gain and attention, but also to control the conflict and to attack the combatants. Wards are often polarized into those who feel the patient is manipulative and those who feel the patient is damaged or ill-treated. There is usually truth on both sides, but the split itself is inimical to dealing with it. The therapist should explore the possibility that the patient had similarly exploited two embattled parents for the purpose not only of getting sympathy and attention, but also of avoiding divorce. The same constellation may appear in family of procreation, or in extended family or job systems.

● Disturbances of communication, usually disguising the needs of the staff so that they are voiced as what is good for the patient, may be similar to those in the family. These may justify intensive control, humiliation, and other indignities that the patient feels too insecure to label as such. This 'adaptation to the stronger person's reality', or inability to metacommunicate, is indicative of impaired self-esteem and weak ego strength.[13]

Dealing productively with ward countertransference runs the risk of introducing another split—between the therapist and the ward staff engaged in the countertransference recapitulation of pathologic family transactions. This presents potential problems if the therapist proceeds with antagonism to the staff, or is felt to do so by others. There are no simple solutions to the risks entailed by dealing with ward counter-transference problems. Needless to say, a disintegrated ward system with the family therapist not integrated with the rest of the ward staff risks recapitulating splits in the family, and having the same divisive effect on the integration of the patient's personality.

Handling Manifestations of Splitting

To avoid a therapy that is stalemated or fails to deal with this loss of containment, middle-phase family therapy must respond to these splits. Techniques for doing this include using family therapy sessions for management involving containment, utilization of data out of the sessions to deal with split off-manifestations of the need for containment or scapegoating maneuvers, special use of intergenerational explorations and constructions, and the introduction of a demarcated termination phase.

The bringing of management issues into the family therapy has a rationale that arises from an understanding of splitting. The split works against the integration of issues that appear disparately as conflictual issues in the therapy, and containment issues elsewhere. Frequently, the family may show great exhilaration at the progress made in sessions dealing with the overt conflict, whereas deeper issues are split off and handled elsewhere. The therapist may be loath to introduce the turbulence of management into the family therapy session. When these issues are introduced, the difficulty managing usually becomes much more straight-forward. The entire issue is often of major importance in understanding why resolution of other issues could not take place in the first place: A husband who is drunk and abusive cannot really negotiate the fact that he feels his authority as a father is undermined; the substance-abusing adolescent cannot really negotiate more independence when his behavior invites intrusiveness and control; the wife who is threatening divorce and suicide cannot negotiate more affection and foreplay in the bedroom. The person who acts in ways that are labile, explosive, and unreliable is better off considering how these factors result in rejections, exclusions, job failures, and widespread distrust. For example, such an individual may correctly identify rejection from other people but not see this as a response to the chaos emanating from his actions. There is little likelihood that the patient can negotiate within the family to get what he wants and needs if he does not come to grips with the undermining effect of his own chaotic behavior.

When turbulent management issues are brought into the family therapy, one of two outcomes is likely. The family may show confidence in handling, say, the pass of a suicidal or psychotic family member. In this case, the ward staff has probably overestimated the risk. It is rare for such management issues to explode where there is discussion of the problem with appropriate anxiety and direct communication. If, on the other hand, the patient generates anxiety in others without showing anxiety himself and if this situation is dealt with directly in the family meetings, there may be overwhelming anxiety unmasked in the family when their terror of uncontrollable chaos is laid bare. For example, a family may be asked to be custodians for the weekend pass of a patient who broadcasts suicidality but does not seem worried about it. The usual response of such a family when the ward staff hands over responsibility for the patient is stark panic. It is this type of controlling through chaotic symptoms that must be seen as impinging on more explicit issues in the therapy.

It is clear that considerable material for such handling of management problems must come from sources outside of the therapy session. This applies also to the exploration of manifestations of pathologic character traits and patient's collusion with staff countertransference tendencies. To be effective at doing this, the therapist must be in a position to monitor, in broad outline at least, the full thrust of what is transpiring on the ward. Family therapy relegated to the sidelines of the caseworker's office, and out of touch with the issues of concern to the nursing staff, cannot deal effectively with the splitting. The result is that the family therapist cannot effectively do therapy and that management has to be done elsewhere. The latter situation usually results in overcontrol of patients, because the finer innuendos of the patient's containment needs cannot be assessed in the natural unit of containment, the family. The ward staff perforce becomes overcontrolling, intrusive, restrictive, and humiliating as a result, often to the overall detriment of the treatment.

A few words must be said here about the significance of inter-generational reconstructions in family psychotherapy. I refer here not to the confluence of three or more generations in the consulting room but to the attempt to understand pathologic phenomena in terms of their develop-mental or historical significance to the patient and the family. When specific pathologic patterns can be seen in more than one interpersonal system, the advantage to the understanding is greater. When the patient repeatedly gravitates towards relationships that are disastrous, that tendency is usually more understandable if a similar situation has been found to occur in the family. Likewise, it is important to trace inter-generationally specifics of what has come to be pathologic: the parentified child, grown into a person who is mistrustful in her marriage; the son of an alcoholic who drinks, or the alcoholic's daughter, who marries an alco-holic; the child of several divorces for whom the awareness that his well-being depends on the presence of another is mortifying; the beaten child who beats, and many more. What is studied is never the past! It is an historical embryologic view of a pathologic preoccupation and the way that preoccupation has come to be handled. But the purpose is not simply to enhance understanding. When the patient and the family accept pathologic manifestations more as the result of an understandable *process* than as defectiveness in the *product*, there is more of a likelihood that they can understand the significance of major themes, without overwhelming affects of shame, fear, and guilt, and the defenses against them that so impede the work of family therapy. This is not an historic alibi justifying the patient's irresponsibility, but rather an appreciation of what the patient is preoccupied with—abandonment, caretaking, unfairness of one sex or the other, self control—and how the patient handles it. Intergenerational reconstruction is particularly useful in understanding problems of contain-ment and the humiliation that has accompanied the failure of containment early in life.

If containment issues cannot be brought into focus during the midphase of hospital family therapy, it is necessary to consider a distinctly demarcated termination phase.

TERMINATION PHASE

Family therapy in the hospital may proceed in oblivion to split-off issues of containment so long as containment—acknowledged or not—is provided by the hospital. As discharge approaches or arrives, the impact of the withdrawn support becomes a reality. If issues of containment have escaped the therapeutic task, maneuvers to reestablish the symbiotic homeostasis may occur abruptly or explosively. Often, these mirror those that take place to avoid the fragmentation of a family: drunken bouts, job losses, direct or indirect threats, or attempts at suicide or violence, to name only a few. Not every case of family therapy in the hospital runs such a risk, but it is extremely important to recognize those that do. In those cases, especially, a well-demarcated termination phase of at least several weeks may be decisive in addressing the central issue of separation and the patient's reaction to it.

For purposes of the discussion of hospital family psychotherapy, it must be realized that termination refers to termination with the hospital, not with the therapist. Aftercare is here presumed to continue with the same therapist for at least six months with some frequency, and with some contact for at least the next year. Maintaining the same therapist for the transition to aftercare and for providing aftercare is so essential that the same set of considerations cannot be presumed if the patient is let loose from hospital, therapist (and, perhaps, family) on the same day. The presence of the same therapist to handle the problem of giving up the hospital presents a different situation also from the termination of intensive psychotherapy where the termination phase deals with the giving up of the relation with the therapist altogether. From the point of view of the overall family therapy begun in the hospital, I am discussing the transition to aftercare. It is only a termination phase in relation to the hospital.

Some hospitalizations may be seen as terminating by remission of the acute pathological disruption so that further containment is not required by the hospital. Acute schizophrenic exacerbations (ie, acute episodes in essentially process schizophrenia), may be seen to remit. So do many unipolar depressions. In such cases, what the patient needs for containment may be discussed along with the rest of the therapeutic issues. The containment problem is dealt with all along and recedes by simple exhaustion when the illness remits. In most such cases, the patient's early history will not come to bear in a clearcut way, and intergenerational exploration gives less-distinct results than it does when preoccupation with past traumata is primary and central. Anticipation of discharge is always important, but a special phase where other material is interpreted only in relation to termination is not necessary. Containment interpretations can be made in the here-and-now, comparing one system and another: "We notice that we have to get you out of bed in the morning; will they have to do that at home?" or, "You felt you couldn't be alone because you'd be suicidal; is that something the family is willing to deal with?" or, "You argued with the nurse about medication; will you be able to be responsible for yourself at home?" Reassuring comparisons may be made between the current situation and the initial phase: "We notice a world of difference now from when you came in; was that the impression when you went home last weekend?" This kind of gradual handling of termination is common in cases of unipolar depression and schizophrenia. In such cases there may be more planning based on the recent precipitants of disruption than on early life experiences that form the characterological preoccupation.

In other cases, it is necessary to conceptualize, demarcate, and label a distinct termination phase, because major issues of containment have been split off or denied and have not come into the therapy. Any of the features that reinforce a splitting off of containment issues from the therapeutic process favor a discrete termination phase. These include (1) use of hospital containment for support in times of family conflict with apparent oblivion to deeper collusively disowned needs in both family and hospital; (2) the prominence of management issues on the ward or a history of explosive, labile, or self-sabotaging acts that serve to hold the family together; (3) instability, intensiveness, or abuse from the parental dyad early in life; (4) characterologic patterns inviting rejection; and (5) colluding with malignant ward countertransference configurations. To this list must be added (6) mania because of the intense vulnerability of manic patients to separation and because of the pervasiveness of denial during a manic or hypomanic attack.

In a hospitalization of, say, three to six months duration—long enough for useful midphase work to have been done, but too short for deep reorganization—identifying a distinct termination phase of several weeks to several months may serve important functions. In demarcating such a stage, the therapist steps out of a collusive role in denying nurturant needs by identifying deep ties to the hospital as basic. The demarcation anticipates difficulties; it thereby becomes less easy for the patient and the family to get lost in the reality of the drunken binge or the job loss, in the service of denying the significance of the disruption for the family and hospital systems. Demarcation sets up circumstances whereby the only method of spiting the therapist is to have a smooth termination, and it identifies the focus of the work. Interpretation in a demarcated termination phase differs from that in the middle phase. From the point of view of the significance of the withdrawal of hospital containment, there is a definite change away from taking middle-phase issues (negotiating life with containment in place), at face value, and more toward seeing issues not connected with containment as deflections from more basic issues. This does not imply that everything new in the patient's life is regarded with suspicion, but only that containment issues are seen as primary. In the termination phase there is often the therapeutic dilemma of wanting to respect the patient's plans—no matter how tenuous they are—and the opposite pull to question unlikely prospects for success, such as business alliances with family, temporary living situations with extended family, unrealistic job situations, and the like.

The therapist and the entire treatment team are at risk for making impulsive decisions during termination crises. Any request to change plans, particularly cautionary ones, of medications based on feelings of desperation must be carefully scrutinized in the treatment setting.

Especially with manic patients, detailed explanations of the illness and the significance of terminations is of value, not so much in instilling insight into the psychotic patient, but in mobilizing resources without delay and in avoiding or minimizing the effect of separations. It is unwise to discharge a remitted manic patient when other separations are imminent.

Intergenerational interpretation aimed at reconstructing the unfolding of the patient's pathological preoccupations (with abandonment and humiliating attachments in particular), go a long way in helping the patient accept the existence of preoccupations and enduring vulnerabilities, and in dealing with anxieties that lead to attempts to avoid humiliation by chaotic action.

This proneness to humiliation makes separations particularly explosive stimuli to self-sabotage. In part, this can be mitigated by the actual work of the therapy, which may make family ties less tenuous. The fact that the termination from the hospital is not accompanied by termination of the therapy (even if the patient doesn't return to live with the family), makes for continued support as the transition to aftercare occurs. For this reason, any break in the alliance with the hospital therapist, whether due to altered geographic location, hospital policy, or financial realities, must be treated with great importance; maneuvers on the part of patient or family that threaten discharge must be viewed as though they serve to maintain ties to the therapist. Assuming that the therapy continues, the termination from the hospital is actually a transition to aftercare.

A modality of major magnitude in hospital treatment is multiple family group therapy.[14] Its full significance has not been fully appreciated by either the mainstream of family therapists or of hospital psychiatrists. Multiple family groups are powerful. The shaping of aftercare and major support during the post-hospital period is provided. Groups should contain a number of whole families selected on the basis of predicaments similar enough so that the families can be felt to be facing the same situation. Ideally, families enter them in the middle or termination phase of the hospitalization, and continue indefinitely so that the groups at any one time consist of families in varying stages of dealing with somewhat similar disruptions.

Multiple family groups, by utilizing identifications constructively, create a supportive atmosphere whereby family members in the same constellation may provide both empathic confrontation and support. A comment that a mother is overinvolved with her psychotic child is experienced differently if it comes from another mother, with yet other mothers there to react to both. A psychotic adolescent may argue about matters of rights and responsibilities with another father before risking the same negotiations with his or her own father. The therapist may either mobilize any of what Laqueur[15] has called *identification constellations* to buttress ego strength and provide empathetic support, or interpret collusive activity as scapegoating, as the situation warrants. The potential of identification constellations to provide more support, constructive confrontation, learning via similar experiences in others, overcoming the ubiquitous isolation found in disturbed families, learning by safe negotiating circumstances, and learning by actual collaboration make multiple family group therapy a major modality of hospital treatment and aftercare.

No matter in what form the family psychotherapy continues, it should be intensive for the first six months after hospitalization, and should continue for at least a year after that. This may be at decreasing frequency unless actual therapeutic work indicates more contact.

SUMMARY

The method of conceptualizing hospital family therapy presented here lays deliberate emphasis on the handling of chaotic parts of the personality that may become split off and manifest themselves outside of the family therapy situation. Integration of states that become split off at great risk to ultimate integration is of principal concern in the treatment of major psychopathology. Splitting manifests in different ways when the family seeks containment for one of its members, when the containment is utilized, and when it is given up. These are dealt with in discussing the initial, middle, and termination phases of family therapy respectively.

In the initial stage, splits may arise if perceived blame and demands from the hospital staff combine with the family's humiliation, guilt, and sense of inadequacy. These incline the family away from family involvement. The result is that the patient, as the carrier of emotional turbulence, becomes split off from the family. It is important that work with the family emanate from experience with the family system in its most disrupted state. The therapist's presence, even in the midst of an acute psychosis, is crucial and the therapeutic experience is useful, albeit of a different kind than therapy taking place when patient and family are less disturbed.

Midphase work utilizes hospital containment to make gains not possible in the absence of such containment. This work may come closest to resembling outpatient family therapy; nonetheless, considerable monitoring of data from outside of the therapy sessions is necessary to deal with containment issues that have become split off from the sessions. Splitting is suspect if negotiating of family conflict takes place oblivious to deeper needs for contact from family and hospital; if management issues, such as suicidality, intimidation, violence, substance abuse, or self-sabotage, are dealt with elsewhere; if past family history reflects frequent change of nurturance, intrusiveness by parents who blame, scapegoat, or parentify, or sexual or physical abuse continued with knowledge of parents; if there are manifestations of character traits that would make heretofore unexplained rejections more understandable; and collusion with ward countertransference constellations that shed light on similar patterns in the family. Splitting may be handled by negotiating management issues in family therapy so that anxiety is brought back to the family system; by intergenerational interpretations to help the patient and family appreciate disturbed behaviors as manifestations of longstanding preoccupations; and the introduction of a termination phase.

Termination phase refers to termination of hospitalization, not to stopping family therapy. If containment is central and primary in the therapeutic work, termination is completed *pari passu* with the remission of the acute disorder; no discrete phase need be demarcated. Containment issues can be elucidated by comparing various systems (ward, family, job) in the here-and-now. If containment issues have become split off from the family therapy, there is the distinct risk of their precipitous coming to the fore in the termination phase or after discharge. Indications that such splitting is taking place should result in attempts to bring the containment issues back into the therapy. The use of intergenerational interpretations and reconstructions are aimed at elucidation of lifelong preoccupations, and at mitigating the humiliation that the patient experiences when unintegrated chaotic personality facets manifest in disrupted behavior. A well-demarcated termination phase of several weeks to several months focuses on such issues, predicts turbulence, and differentiates the therapist's activities from the kind of collusive relationship that serves to disown deep attachments.

Well-handled termination of family therapy in the hospital serves as a transition to aftercare. Often, multiple family group therapy provides the most empathic method of support and confrontation for isolated families sharing similar predicaments. Its use as a central and primary focus of intervention has been neglected.

REFERENCES

1. Lansky MR: Establishing a family-oriented inpatient unit. J Operational Psychiatry 8:66–74, 1977
2. Lansky MR: The initial phase of family therapy in the hospital. Int J Fam Psychiatry (in press)
3. Lansky MR: On the idea of a termination phase for family therapy in the hospital. Group and Family Therapy 1980—An overview. New York: Brunner Mazel, 1980, pp. 323–334
4. Bowen M: The use of family theory in clinical practice. Compr Psychiatry 7:345–374, 1966
5. Guttman H: A contraindication to family therapy. Arch Gen Psychiatry 29:352–355, 1973
6. Glick I, Kessler D: Family and Marital Therapy. New York: Grune & Stratton, 1974
7. Lansky MR: On blame. Int J Psychoanal Psychother 8:429–456, 1980
8. Bion WR: Seven Servants. New York, Jason Aronson, 1977
9. Lidz T: The limitation of extrafamilial socialization, in Lidz T, Fleck S (eds): Schizophrenia and the Family. New York, International Universities Press, 1965
10. Wynne L, et al: Pseudomutuality in the family relations of schizophrenics. Psychiatry 21:205–220, 1958
11. Bateson G, Jackson D, Weakland J, et al: Toward a theory of schizophrenia. Behav Sci 1:251–264, 1956
12. Stierlin H: Group fantasies and family myths. Fam Proc 12:111–127, 1973
13. Stierlin H: The adaptation to the stronger person's reality. Psychiatry 22:143–152, 1959
14. Lansky MR, Bley CR, McVey GG, et al: Multiple family groups as aftercare. Int J Group Psychother 28:211–224, 1978
15. Laqueur HP: Mechanisms of change in multiple family therapy, in Sager C, Kaplan H (eds): Progress in: Group and Family Therapy. New York, Brunner Mazel, 1972

Index

Abandonment anxiety. *See* Separation anxiety
Absent family system, alcoholism in, 206, 216–217
Abuse
of child
in alcoholism, 206, 211, 338, 339
and disturbed adolescence, 338, 339, 343, 344
intergenerational view of, 343, 347
and maternal depression, 95, 343, 344
of drugs
alcohol in. *See* Alcoholism
by disturbed adolescents, 334–338, 340, 342–343, 348
of wife, in narcissistically vulnerable marriage, 172, 174
Academic achievement
and disturbed adolescence, 334–335, 338, 340, 343, 348
and self-image, 334–335, 348
Adolescents. *See* Children and adolescents
Affective disorders, 12, 91–160, 308
bipolar, and group therapy for married couples, 123–143
in borderline personality, 183
and maternal depression, 95–118
and suicide, 147–154
Affective style of family, 352–356
with communication deviance, 353–356
and expressed emotions concept, 353
guilt-inducing, 353, 354
and self-image of members, 353, 354

Aftercare treatment programs
for bipolar patients, 134, 140
for depressed mothers and their children, 91–121
for schizophrenics
communication training in, 35–56
drug therapy in, 21–33
duration of, 52–53
extrafamilial socialization in, 36
family therapy in, 21–34
vocational training in, 36, 37
transition to, from hospital, 409, 411, 413
Age
of anorexia nervosa patients, 251, 269
and generation gap in disturbed families, 60
of organic brain syndrome patients, 301, 309, 311, 312, 317
of suicidal patient, and treatment plan, 154
Aggressive behavior
in borderline personality, 184, 192
of suicidal persons, 147–148, 152
Al-Anon, 205, 209, 217, 234, 237
disease concept of alcoholism in, 235
enmeshed families aided by, 214–215, 216
reinforcing family therapy, 241, 244
Alateen, 234, 240, 241, 244
Alcoholics Anonymous, 150, 205, 206, 216, 234
attendance as therapy goal in, 217, 240, 241–242, 244

Alcoholics Anonymous *(continued)*
  disease concept of alcoholism in, 235
  treatment approach of, 213, 214
Alcoholism, 13, 203–245
  in absent family system, 206, 216–217
  of anorectic's parent, 258, 259
  Antabuse therapy in, 204, 214, 383, 384
  children in family with, 204–206, 208–
      209, 211–213, 233, 240–241, 243–
      244, 338, 339
  and co-alcoholism, 212
  collusive family interactions maintaining,
      240–241
  contracts in family therapy for, 217
  countertransference in family therapy for,
      220–221
  diagnosis of, 232, 234, 236–237, 238–
      240
  disease concept of, 235
  in disintegrated family system, 205, 216
  dry drunk phase in, 212
  dry treatment system in, 213–214, 243–
      244
  education of family about, 215–216, 220
  employment in, 204–205, 206, 211, 232
  in enmeshed family system, 150, 204–
      205, 214–215, 216, 219–220
  family dynamics in typical, 206, 207,
      210–213, 232, 235, 244
  frequency of, 233–234
  in functional family system, 204, 215
  hallucinosis in, 307, 308
  hospitalization for, 242–243
    family therapy during, 400
  learning alternative behaviors to, 243–
      244
  in narcissistically vulnerable marriages,
      168, 169, 177, 179
  paradoxical directives in family therapy
      for, 218–219
  pre-existing personality in, 235
  re-enactment in family therapy for, 219
  rehabilitation in, family as determinant of,
      209
  resistance to therapy in, 242
  in suicidal patients, 150
  as system problem, 207–208
  task assignments in therapy for, 218
  total family network in therapy for, 220
  violent behavior in, 206, 210, 211, 232,
      237, 338, 339

  wet treatment systems for, 214–215,
      240–241
  withdrawal from, 240–243
    delirium in, 305, 314–315
Amitryptiline therapy
  in depression, 164
    family therapy with, 366
  in narcissistically vulnerable marriages,
      164, 178
Amnesia, 305–309
Anorexia nervosa, 13–14, 249–280
  age at onset of, 251, 269
  assessment procedures in
    of effectiveness of therapy, 275–276
    of family, 269–271
  and communication in families, 261, 265,
      267, 273
  diversity of, 251
  and enmeshment of families, 257, 262,
      272
  family-generated problems in, 274
  family therapy in treatment of, 266–276
    effectiveness of, 275–276
    goals of, 268–269
    mechanics of, 269–272
    problems in, 273–274
    role of therapist in, 269, 273–274
  family transmission of, 253–255, 276
  literature on, 251–252, 266–267
  parental characteristics in, 254–260, 262
    alcoholism in, 258, 259
    overprotectiveness in, 260, 262, 264,
      272
  patient-generated problems in, 274
  prognosis in, 265–266, 275–276
  and roles in family, 261, 262, 271, 274
  and stress response patterns of family,
      255–257
  systems theory of, 261–265
    limitations of, 264–265
  typical family situation in, 249–250,
      265–266
Antabuse therapy, in alcoholism, 204, 214,
      383–384
Antidepressant therapy
  discontinuance of, 384–385, 389
  family therapy combined with, 365–367,
      380–381, 384–385, 388–389
  in narcissistically vulnerable marriages,
      164, 177–178, 180
  in organic brain syndrome, 323

Antipsychotic drug therapy, family therapy
    with, 362–364
Antisocial behavior
    in adolescents, 349–350
    in parents, 349
Anxiety
    of schizophrenics, 26, 33
    in separation. *See* Separation anxiety
    and suicide, 147, 148, 149–150, 156
Assessment procedures
    in alcoholism, 238–239
    in anorexia nervosa
        effectiveness of therapy, 275–276
        family assessment, 269–271
    in bipolar illness, 131–132
    in communication disorders, 42, 352
    for disturbed adolescents and their
        families, 327–358
    in drug therapy combined with family
        therapy, 359–393
    in hospital-based family therapy, 395–
        414
    in maternal depression, 109
    in multiple family therapy, 68
    in organic brain syndrome, 322
    for parent–adolescent interactions, 331,
        337, 339, 345
    in schizophrenia, 26–33, 53
    for suicidal patients, 154–155
    in Thresholds Mothers' Project, 99, 103,
        109, 114
Attendance rules, in multiple family
    therapy, 82, 83
Autonomy/control conflicts, in mother–child
    relationships, 114–115

Back-to-back exercise, in multiple family
    therapy, 63–64
Behavioral approach to schizophrenia
    management, 12, 48–52, 54
Bender-Gestalt Test, in assessment of
    disturbed adolescent, 330
Biologic vulnerability, to anorexia nervosa,
    254, 276
Bipolar illness, 9, 12
    assessment of attitudes in, 131–132
    children of patients with, 141
    cognitive functioning in, 136–137
    conflict resolution in, 137–138
    co-therapist model in, 135
    definition of, 124–126

denial of, 129, 132, 133
dependency in, 133
detection of mood change in, 125–126
drug therapy for, 123, 124, 125, 127–129
    development of, 127–129
    lithium carbonate in, 123, 128, 129,
        134–135, 136, 140–141, 288, 367–
        368
    psychotherapy with, 129, 134–135,
        140–141, 367–368, 384
    side effects of, 136–137
education of family about, 386
extrafamilial socialization in, 133
genetic factors in, 124, 140, 141
group therapy for, 123–143
    advantages of, 140
    multiple families in, 368
    outcome of, 140
    patients and spouses in, 134–141
hospitalization for, 123, 124, 125, 134,
    140
intergenerational view of, 133
literature on, review of, 126–130
married patients with, 123–143, 367
    communication between patient and
        spouse, 133
    mate selection of, 129–130, 131, 367
    and mother–child relationships, 126, 127
    repression of grief in, 133
    self-image in, 133
    spouse syndrome in, 136
Blaming behavior, 402
    in anorectic's familiy, 263–264, 272
    and borderline personality, 191, 196
    in cancer, 285–286
    in drug therapy, 383–385, 389
    in hospitalization of family member, 398,
        401, 412
    in multiple family therapy, 85, 86
    in narcissistically vulnerable marriage,
        164–166, 167, 168, 169, 170, 171,
        172
    and suicide, 147
Blunted affect, in schizophrenia, 27, 33
Body language
    in multiple family therapy, 63–64
    of schizophrenic's family, 43
    and suicidal behavior, 157
Borderline personality
    of adolescents, 13, 183–201
    case studies of, 192–193

Borderline personality *(continued)*
    and narcissistic vulnerability in parents,
        187–188, 189, 191, 195, 196
    treatment of, 193–197
    in anorectic's family, 268
    characteristics of, 183–185, 192
    developmental process in, 184–190
    diagnosis of, 183
    of disturbed adolescent's parent, 343, 347
    family regression in, 189, 190, 191–192
    separation anxiety in, 184–186, 187,
        189, 190–191, 196–197, 198
    suicidal behavior in, 148, 192, 193
Boundaries within families, enmeshed. *See*
    Enmeshed family system
Breast cancer, family coping with, 288–289,
    294–295, 296
Brief Psychiatric Rating Scale (BPRS), 26–
    27, 29, 30, 31

Camberwell Family Interview, 369
Cancer, 14
    in adults, 286–289, 290
        with adolescent children, 286–287,
            295
        literature on, 286
        multiple family therapy in, 287–288
    of breast, effect on family, 288–289,
        294–295, 296
    in children
        family responses to, 283–286, 289–
            290
        literature on, 283–286
    and communication in patient's family,
        283–284, 289, 293–294, 298, 299
    dependency of patient in, 295–296
    disturbed families of patients with, 281–
        300
        interventions in, 290–299
        observations on, 286–290
    and educational intervention with
        patient's family, 293–294
    and enmeshed family system of patient,
        289–290, 294–296
    as guilt-inducing weapon, 295, 296
    and home-based therapy for patients and
        families, 292
    management of frustration in, 296–297
    oncologist–family relationship in, 291,
        294, 298–299
    and role reversals in family, 286–287

and therapist's role in family approach,
    282–283, 297–299
Case studies
    of borderline adolescents, 192–193
    of disturbed adolescents, 331–348
    of drug and family therapy combined,
        377, 380–385, 386–389
    of maternal depression, 108–117
    of narcissistically vulnerable marriages,
        164–166, 172–175, 177, 178
Catastrophic reaction, to organic brain
    syndrome, 320, 321
Central processing unit (CPU), in systems
    theory of families, 61
Children and adolescents, 13
    abuse of
        and alcoholism in families, 206, 211,
            338, 339
        and disturbed adolescence, 338, 339,
            343, 344
        intergenerational view of, 343, 347
        and maternal depression, 95, 343, 344
    academic achievement of, 334–335, 338,
        340, 343, 348
    and affective styles of families of, 352–
        356
    alcoholism in families of, 204–206, 208–
        209, 211–213, 233, 240–241, 243–
        244, 338, 339
    anorexia nervosa in, 13–14, 249–280
    antisocial behavior in, 349–350
    bipolar illness in parents of, 141
    borderline personality of, 13, 183–201
    cancer in, 283–286, 289–290
    cancer in parents of, 286–287, 295
    case studies of, 108–117, 192–193, 331–
        348
    communication within families of, 333,
        336–337, 340, 344, 347, 351–355
    of depressed mothers, 91–121, 365–366
    depression in, 96
    developmental processes in adolescence,
        186–190
    disturbed adolescence of, 327–358
    drug abuse by, 334–338, 340, 342–343,
        348
    holding environment for, 187, 188
    individual therapy for, 336–337, 340,
        346, 348, 350
    individuation of, 186, 187, 189–190, 191
    marital relationship of parents affecting,
        330–331

moving to new community, behavior
    problems related to, 331–334
nature and severity of disturbances in,
    329–330, 344–345
parent interactions with. *See* Parent-child
    interactions
problems in therapy with, 186–187
psychological functioning of parents
    affecting, 330
resistance of family to therapy with, 340,
    342, 349
roles of, stress due to, 328, 332, 333, 348
running away by, 338, 342
of schizophrenic mothers, 95
self-image of, 335–337, 348
stealing by, 331, 332, 333, 338, 340, 342
suicidal behavior of adolescents, 192,
    193, 343
Clarification of feelings
    in communication intervention, 352
    in drug therapy, 384–385
Cognitive functioning
    in bipolar illness, 136–137
    in depression, 95
    genetic and environmental factors
        affecting, 94
    mother–child relationship affecting, 92,
        96, 109, 113, 115
    in organic brain syndrome, 303, 305, 307,
        309, 311, 317–318, 323–324
Collusion
    by borderline adolescent, 191
    in hospital-based family therapy, 402–
        403, 410
    in maintaining parent's alcoholism, 240–
        241
    in narcissistically vulnerable marriage,
        164–166, 167, 168, 169, 170, 171,
        172
Communication within families, 60, 65
    affective style of, 353–356
    and alcoholism, 211, 219
    amplification and modulation of signals
        in, 66
    and anorexia nervosa, 261, 265, 267,
        273
    assessment of, 42, 352
    of bipolar patients, 133
    of cancer patients, 283–284, 285, 289,
        293–294, 298, 299
    with depressed mothers, 101, 102, 109,
        110, 113

of disturbed adolescents, 333, 336–337,
    340, 344, 347, 351–352, 354, 355
intrafamilial code in, 65, 68
in multiple family therapy, 58, 63–64,
    65, 68
in narcissistically vulnerable marriages,
    166, 167, 169, 172–173
in problem solving, 45–48
of schizophrenics, 4–5, 72–73, 351,
    354
    expressed emotion in, 11, 32, 36–39,
        53, 363–364
    training for, 35–56
and secrets in, 68, 80, 84, 166
of suicidal patient, 147, 148–149, 152,
    155, 157–158
Community setting, for aftercare treatment
    of acute schizophrenia, 21–34
Competition, between and within family
    systems, 66
Complaining, by narcissistically vulnerable
    person, 171, 176
Conflict resolution. *See* Problem-solving
Confusional states
    acute, 301, 303–305, 316
    subacute, 303, 305–309
Conjoint family therapy, 62
Containment failure of families
    with hospitalized member, 396, 397, 399,
        400–401, 402, 408–409, 410,
        413
    with organic brain syndrome in member,
        321–322
Contracts in therapy
    for alcoholism, 217
    for schizophrenia, 48–50
Coping response(s)
    alcoholism as, 207
    to cancer, 284–285, 288–290, 292–293,
        294
    in managing schizophrenic's behavior,
        48–51
    of schizophrenics, 38, 44–48
Countertransference, 7
    in alcoholism family therapy, 220–221
    in anorexia nervosa family therapy, 273–
        274
    of cancer patient in family therapy, 282–
        283, 297
Crisis-oriented family therapy
    with cancer patient, 290–291, 295, 298–
        299

Crisis-oriented family therapy *(continued)*
   in schizophrenia, 24, 27–32, 33, 363

Death of child, family responses to, 285
Defensive mechanisms, of borderline
   personality, 184, 186, 191
Delirium, 301, 303–305, 316
   causes of, 306
   hyperactivity and hypoactivity in, 304–
     305
Delusional syndromes, organic, 308
Dementia, 301, 309–311
   causes of, 310–311
   presenile, 322
   and pseudodementia, 315
   senile, family reactions to, 317
Denial of illness
   in bipolar marriage, 129, 132, 133
   in borderline personality, 191
Dependency of patients
   in bipolar illness, 133
   in cancer, 295–296
   in organic brain syndrome, 314, 316
Depersonalization syndrome, in cerebral
   disease, 307
Depression
   in alcoholism, 231, 232, 234, 240
   bipolar, 9, 12, 123–143, 367. *See also*
     Bipolar illness
   in children, 96
   cognitive and affective disturbances in, 95
   drug therapy in, 129, 164, 177–178, 180,
     323
     family therapy combined with, 365–
       367, 380–381, 384–385, 388–389
   family atmosphere of, and suicides, 147,
     152–153
   hospitalization for, 124
   and posthospital treatment, 91–121
   mania alternating with. *See* Bipolar illness
   maternal, 91–121, 365–366. *See also*
     Maternal depression
   normal feelings of, 124
   in organic brain syndrome, 307, 324
   pseudodementia secondary to, 315
   about roles in family, 365, 366
   in schizophrenia, 26, 33
   signs and symptoms of, 124
Despair and suicides, 153–154
Detoxification, hospitalization for, 242–243
Developmental processes

   in adolescence, 186–190
   and borderline personality, 184–190
   education of depressed mothers about,
     97, 99, 100, 111
   interaction of genetic and environmental
     factors in, 94, 110
   mother–child relationship affecting, 91–
     93, 94, 95
   motherhood as stage in, 93–94
   nursery program stimulating, 103, 113
   role changes in, 328
Diabetic children, guilt in parents of, 254
Diagnosis, psychiatric
   approaches to, 361–362
   DSM III as system of, 362
Diagnostic and Statistical Manual, third
     edition (DSM III), 362
Disintegrated family system, alcoholism in,
     205, 216
Double-bind theory of schizophrenia, 4–5
Drug(s)
   borderline personality dependent on, 183,
     192
   delirium in withdrawal from, 305
   disturbed adolescent abusing, 334–338,
     340, 342–343, 348
   hallucinosis from, 307, 308
   sexual functioning affected by, 14, 376,
     381, 387
   toxic psychoses from, 307
Drug therapy, 6, 10, 14
   in alcoholism, 204, 214
     family therapy with, 383–384
   antidepressants in, 164, 177–178, 180,
     323
     family therapy with, 365–367, 380–
       381, 384–385, 388–389
   antipsychotic drugs in, 362–364
   in bipolar illness, 123, 124, 125, 127–
     129
     development of, 127–129
     lithium carbonate in, 123, 128, 129,
       134–135, 136, 140–141, 288, 367–
       368
     psychotherapy with, 129, 134–135,
       140–141, 367–368
     side effects of, 136–137
   and blaming behavior, 383–385, 389
   case studies on, 377, 380–385, 386–389
   clarification of feelings in, 384–385
   clinical guidelines for, 389–391

collusion with family in, 379, 382, 385
compliance with, 76–77, 123, 364–365,
    376, 383–384, 387, 389
confirming family myths about patient,
    380, 381–382, 385
deliria from, 303–304
in depression, 129, 164, 177–178, 180,
    323
    family therapy with, 365–367, 380–
    381, 384–385, 388–389
    maternal, 389
discontinuance of, 14, 384–385, 389
dispensing medication in, 385
evaluation of, 359–393
    design of study on, 369–370
    measurement of outcome in, 370–371
    subject selection in, 360–369, 392
and effects of family dynamics on
    medication, 385–389
and effects of medication on family
    therapy, 380–385
family as auxiliary therapists in, 385
family therapy combined with, 11–12,
    359–393
    establishing grounds for, 359–360
    multiple family approach to, 76–77,
    387
    negative interactions in, 360
    review of literature on, 360–362
for hallucinations, 388
introduction and withholding of, 14, 377–
    378, 382–383, 384–385, 388–389
movement disorders due to, 381–382,
    387, 391
in narcissistically vulnerable marriages,
    164, 177–178, 179, 180
in organic brain syndrome, 319, 322–323
responsibilities of patient in, 377, 382–
    383
in schizophrenia, 21–33, 41
    family therapy with, 359, 362–364,
    381, 382–383, 387, 388
    relapse rates in, 36, 38, 41, 54, 364,
    388
split attitudes toward patient in, 382–
    383
therapist's role in, 376–380, 382–383,
    388–389, 390–391
    guidelines for, 390–391
Dysfunctional family systems, anorexia
    nervosa in, 261

Eating disturbances
    in anorexia nervosa, 249–280
    lunchtime intervention for
    in anorexia nervosa, 271
    with depressed mothers and their
    children, 104–105
Educational interventions in family therapy,
    11, 15
    in alcoholism, 215–216, 220
    in anorexia nervosa, 272
    in bipolar illness, 386
    with cancer patients, 293–294
    in maternal depression, 97, 98, 99, 100,
    102, 111, 116
    in schizophrenia, 11, 38, 39–42, 54
Ego development
    in adolescence, 187
    in children of depressed mothers, 109
    mother–child relationship affecting, 92,
    93
    in narcissistically vulnerable marriages,
    167, 169, 170, 174
Emotional blunting, in schizophrenia, 27,
    33
Empathic sharing in family therapy
    with hospitalized patient, 397–398, 401
    with organic brain syndrome patient,
    321
Employment
    of alcoholics, 204–205, 206, 211, 232
    of depressed mothers, 97–98, 111
    of married couple in same office, 164–
    165
    problem-solving skills needed for, 47, 49
    of schizophrenics, 36, 37
Enmeshed family system
    alcoholism in, 150, 204–205, 214–215,
    216, 219–220
    anorexia nervosa in, 257, 262, 268
    of cancer patient, 289–290, 294–296
    multiple family therapy for, 77–78
Environmental factors in developmental
    process, interaction with genetic
    factors, 94, 110
Ethnic groups, in multiple family therapy,
    76–77
Evaluation procedures. See Assessment
    procedures
Evocative memory, in borderline
    personality, 185
Expressed emotions within families

Expressed emotions *(continued)*
  affective style compared to, 353
  of schizophrenics, 11, 32, 36–39, 53,
    363–364
  and suicides, 147, 148–149, 152, 157–
    158
  See also Communication within families
Extrafamilial socialization. *See*
    Socialization, extrafamilial
Extramarital affairs, and mistrust in
    marriage, 165

Family Attitudes Questionaire, in
    assessment of bipolar patients, 131–
    132
Fantasies, of family of brain syndrome
    patient, 318, 321
Feedback loop, in systems theory of families,
    61
Fluphenazine therapy, in schizophrenia, 22,
    23–33, 36, 38, 363
Frontal lobe lesions, 307
Frustration tolerance
  in borderline personality, 183, 184, 187,
    192
  of cancer patients and their families, 296–
    297
  or organic brain syndrome patients and
    their families, 314
Functional family system, alcoholism in,
    204, 215

Generation gap, in disturbed families, 60
Genetic factors
  in alcoholism, 208
  in anorexia nervosa, 253–254, 276
  in bipolar illness, 124, 140, 141
  in developmental process, interaction
    with environmental factors, 94, 110
Giving up, and suicide, 153–154
Global Assessment Scale (GAS), 29–31
Grief, repression of, in bipolar illness, 133
Group therapy
  in bipolar illness, 123–143
    advantages of, 140
    co-therapists in, 135
    drug therapy with, 134–135, 140–141
    modeling in, 135, 138
    multiple families in, 368
    outcome of, 140
    process of change in, 138–139
    support of patient's spouse in, 135–136

depressed mothers in, 97, 99, 106, 112
multiple families in, 12, 15, 57–88. *See
  also* Multiple family therapy
Guilt
  affective style inducing, 353, 354
  of anorectic's parents, 254, 256
  cancer inducing, 295, 296
  of diabetic's parents, 254
  with hospitalization of family member,
    397–398, 401, 412
  of schizophrenic's family, 40–41, 76, 82
  about sexual behavior, suicide in, 150–
    152

Hallucinations, drug and family therapy in,
    388
Hallucinosis, 306–307, 308
Heroin use, after disturbed adolescence,
    340, 343
Hierarchy within family, 60, 64
Historical background of family therapy, 3–
    8
Holding environment, during adolescence,
    187, 188
Holding introjects, in borderline personality,
    185
Home-based therapy
  in anorexia nervosa, 271
  with cancer patients and their families,
    292
  in schizophrenia, 51–52
Homeostasis of family
  borderline adolescent maintaining, 191–
    192, 194
  humiliation and shame maintaining, 148
  and need for dysfunctional member, 9
Homework task assignments
  in alcoholism, 218
  in anorexia nervosa, 273
  in schizophrenia, 44, 48, 51
Hopelessness and suicide, 153–154, 155
Hospitalization
  for alcoholism, 213, 242–243, 400
  for anorexia nervosa, 266, 272
  for bipolar illness, 123, 124, 125
    group therapy after, 134, 140
  of borderline adolescent, 192, 193, 194,
    195, 197
  to contain chaos of family, 396, 397, 399,
    400–401, 402, 408–409, 410, 413
  for depression, 124

maternal, and posthospital treatment for, 91–121
and extra-hospital socialization, 405
and family's sensitivity to blame and guilt, 397–398, 401, 412
family therapy during, 15, 179, 395–414
  initial phase of, 395, 397–402, 412
  intergenerational reconstructions in, 401, 408, 411, 413
  middle phase of, 396, 403–408, 413
  multiple families in, 411–412, 413
  patient management issues in, 403, 406–407, 413
  patient's responsibilities in, 403
  resistance to, 399
  splitting in, 396, 402–408, 412–413
  termination of, 396–397, 408–412, 413
maintaining family myths about patient, 405
for mania, 125, 400, 409, 410, 411
for narcissistic vulnerability, 178–179, 180
for organic brain syndrome, 311, 315, 317, 318–319
and patient's behavior reflecting family pathology, 404–406, 413
patient–staff interactions in, 404–406, 413
and prehospital situation, 397–398, 401, 403–404
for psychosis, 399, 400
for schizophrenia, 58, 62, 74, 75, 400, 409, 410
  and aftercare treatment programs, 21–56
  and rehospitalization for, 9, 11, 22, 25–26, 78
for suicidal behavior, 400, 403, 407
termination of, 396–397, 408–412, 413
  and transition to aftercare treatment programs, 409, 411, 413
Hostility, in schizophrenia, 26, 29, 30
Humiliation proneness
  drug therapy in, 164, 177
  in hospitalization termination, 411, 413
  intergenerational view of, 172, 174, 411
  in narcissistically vulnerable marriages, 13, 165–166, 167, 169, 170, 171, 172, 173, 174
  of schizophrenic's family, 71–72, 87
Hyperactive delirium, 304–305

Hypoactive delirium, 305

Idealization, in borderline personality, 184
Identification constellations in multiple family therapy, 66–67
  for hospitalized patients, 412
  for narcissistic vulnerability, 177
  for schizophrenia, 74, 80, 82, 86
Immaturity, and schizophrenia in offspring, 5
Impotence
  drug-induced, 376, 381, 387
  and suicide, 151
Impulsive behavior, in borderline personality, 183, 187, 192, 193
Incestuous sexual contact, and suicide, 151
Individual therapy
  for borderline adolescent, 194–195
  for depressed mother, 97, 101
  for disturbed adolescent, 336–337, 340, 346, 348, 350
  group therapy combined with, 80
  multiple family therapy compared to, 62, 72
  for narcissistic vulnerability, 175–176, 180
Individuation
  in adolescence, 186, 187, 189, 190
  in borderline personality, 184–185, 186, 189–190, 191, 194, 196, 198
  of cancer patient's family, 294–296
  and pseudo-individuation of alcoholic, 216
Infantile rage, in narcissistically vulnerable marriages, 166, 172
Inkblot test, in assessment of disturbed adolescent, 330
Input, in systems theory of families, 61, 62
Insulin coma therapy, for schizophrenia, 58
Intergenerational view
  of alcoholism, 208, 211, 217
  of bipolar illness, 133
  of borderline adolescent, 191, 195, 196–197
  of child abuse, 343, 347
  of hospitalized patient, 401, 408, 411, 413
  of humiliation proneness, 172, 174, 411
  of narcissistically vulnerable marriages, 172, 173–174, 177
  of organic brain syndrome patient, 322

Intimacy
  of cancer patient's family, 294–296
  in narcissistically vulnerable marriages,
    167, 170, 171, 172, 174–175

Language development, mother–child
    relationship affecting, 91–92, 101,
    102, 109, 113
Learning
  mother–child relationship affecting, 92,
    96, 103, 113
  in multiple family therapy, 66–67, 74
    by analogy, 63, 66, 74
    by identification, 66–67, 74
    by trial and error, 66, 74
  self-image related to, 334–335, 348
Leukemia, in child, family responses to, 284
Limit setting, in behavior management, 50
Lithium carbonate, for bipolar illness, 123,
    128, 136, 288
  psychotherapy with, 129, 134–135, 140–
    141, 367–368, 384
  side effects of, 136–137
Loyalty conflicts
  in narcissistically vulnerable marriages,
    167–168
  in schizophrenia, 4–5
Lunchtime intervention
  in anorexia nervosa, 271
  with depressed mothers and their children,
    104–105

Mania
  and cancer in family, 288
  depression alternating with, 123–143. See
    also Bipolar illness
  hospitalization for, 125
    family therapy during, 400, 410, 411
    termination of, 409, 410
  lithium therapy in, 288
  in organic brain syndrome, 307
  signs and symptoms of, 124–125
Marijuana, disturbed adolescents using,
    334–338, 340
Marriage(s)
  of alcoholics, 207, 208, 210, 211
  of bipolar patients, 123–143, 367
    mate selection in, 129–130, 131, 367
  chronic conflictual behavior in, 402
  collusion and blame in, 164–166, 169,
    170, 171

  of disturbed adolescent's parents, 330–
    331, 333–334, 336, 337–339, 341,
    344, 346–347, 350
  and extramarital affairs affecting trust in,
    165
  narcissistic vulnerability in, 163–182
    case studies of, 172–175, 177, 178
    clinical difficulties in treatment of,
      168–70
    features of, 166–168
    problem solving in, 166–167
    research needed on, 181–182
  of schizophrenic's parents, 5
  sexual functioning and stress in, 337
Mastectomy, in breast cancer, family
    response to, 288–289
Masturbation guilt, and suicide, 150
Mate selection
  by alcoholics, 207, 208, 210, 211
  by bipolar patient, 129–130, 131, 367
Maternal depression, 91–121, 365–366
  assessment of, 109
  case study on, 108–117
  child abuse in, 95, 343, 344
  child's therapy in, 97, 101–103, 113
  clinical program for, 97–118
  communication skills of mother in, 110
  and depression in child, 96
  drug therapy in, 389
  educational intervention in, 98, 99, 100,
    102, 111, 116
  goals of therapy in, 97, 106–108, 117
  group therapy in, 97, 99, 106, 112
  husband in, 98, 101, 108, 115–117
  individual therapy in, 97, 101
  mother–child relationship in, 95–97, 101,
    103–106, 109–110, 112, 113–115
  mother's history in, 108
  nursery program in, 97, 102–106, 109,
    111, 112
  posthospital treatment of, 91–121
  rehabilitation in, 97–101, 110–113
  self-image in, 98, 111–112, 118
  social development of child in, 110
  suicide attempts in, 108
  Thresholds Mothers' Project for, 97–118
  videotape intervention in, 105–106, 112,
    115
Medications. See Drug(s); Drug therapy
Memory
  in amnesia, 305–309

in borderline personality, 185
Merger-hunger personality, 189–190
Metacommunication
  in narcissistically vulnerable marriages,
    169, 173, 175
  in schizophrenia, 4–5
Michigan Alcoholism Screening Test
    (MAST), 238–239
Modeling, in therapy process
  for bipolar patients, 135, 138
  for cancer patients and their families, 293
  for disturbed adolescents, 352
  for hospitalized patient, 400
  with multiple families, 67, 74
  for narcissistically vulnerable marriages,
    172
Mood changes, of bipolar patient, detection
    of, 125–126
Mother(s)
  –child relationships. See Parent–child
    interactions
  posthospital treatment of depression in,
    91–121. See also Maternal
    depression
Mothers' Project of Thresholds agency, 97–
    118
Movement disorders, drug-induced, 381–
    382, 387, 391
Moving to new community, and adolescent
    behavior problems related to, 331–
    334
Multiple family therapy, 12, 15, 57–88
  for anorexia nervosa, 273
  attendance in, 82, 83
  back-to-back exercise in, 63–64
  bipolar patients in, 368
  body language in, 63–64
  cancer patients in, 287–288
  communication training in, 58, 65, 72–73
  compared with other forms of
    psychotherapy, 62, 72
  competition and cooperation in, 66, 74
  conduct of, 85–86
  co-therapists in, 67, 74, 83
  contraindications for, 68, 80
  description of, 58–59
  drug therapy with, 76–77, 387
  for enmeshed families, 77–78
  ethnic diversity in, 76–77
  frequency of meetings in, 84
  goals and results of, 67–68

history of, 58, 62–64, 74
  for hospitalized patients, 411–412, 413
  identification constellations in, 66–67,
    74, 80, 82, 86, 177, 412
  individual family therapy with, 80
  intrafamilial communication code in, 65,
    68
  learning in, 63, 66–67, 74
  mechanisms of change in, 65–67, 74, 86–
    88
  model families in, 67, 74
  for narcissistically vulnerable marriages,
    175, 176–177, 180
  open-ended, 59, 67, 81
  phases in process of, 64–65
  for predicament-specific information, 78
  preparation of families for, 82–83
  psychodrama technique in, 64
  for psychosis, 72, 80
  rationale for, 75
  reality testing in, 78–79, 86
  resistance to, 64–65, 67, 79
  rules of, 82, 83–84
  scapegoating in, 85, 86
  for schizophrenia, 12, 52, 58, 62, 71–88,
    387
  sculpting family in, 64
  secrets of family in, 68, 80, 84
  selecting families for, 59, 81–82
  self-image of families in, 71–72, 76
  setting for, 59, 75, 85
  shortening process of, 62–63
  for socially isolated families, 76–77
  structures of families in, 59–60, 63, 67
  systems theory in, 60–62, 65, 67–68
  termination of, 84–85, 87
  therapist's role in, 66, 83, 85–86
  videotape recording of, 59, 64, 67
  yes–no exercise in, 63

Narcissistic vulnerability, 7, 13, 185, 186
  and alcoholism 168, 169, 177, 179
  blame and collusion in, 164–166, 167,
    168, 169, 170, 171, 172
  of borderline adolescent's parents, 187–
    188, 189, 191, 195, 196
  case studies of, 164–166, 172–175, 177,
    178
  clinical difficulties in treatment of, 168–
    170
  drug therapy in, 164, 177–178, 179, 180

Narcissistic vulnerability *(continued)*
    features of, 166–168
    hospitalization for, 178–179, 180
    individual therapy for, 175–176, 180
    intergenerational view of, 172, 173–174,
        177
    in marriage, 163–182
        trauma preceding, 166, 167, 169–170,
            173–174
        violent behavior in, 172, 174
    multiple family therapy for, 175, 176–
        177, 180
    research needed on, 181–182
    therapist's role in treatment of, 170–171,
        172, 178
National Council on Alcoholism, criteria for
    alcoholism, 239
Negotiation
    with organic brain syndrome patient's
        family, 323
    in multiple family therapy, 412
Neuroleptic therapy
    in organic brain syndrome, 319, 323
    for psychotic episodes, 381–382
    in schizophrenia, 38, 41, 54, 388
    side effects of, 41, 376, 381–382
Nonverbal communication
    in multiple family therapy, 63–64
    in schizophrenic's family, 43
    and suicide, 157
Non-zero-sum game, in anorexia nervosa
    family therapy, 271
Nursery program, for children of depressed
    mothers, 97, 102–106, 109, 111,
        112
    curriculum of, 102–103
    lunchtime in, 104–105
    mothers in, 103–106, 111, 112
    videotaping of, 105–106, 112

Object relations therapy, 6–7
Oncologist–family relationships, 291, 294,
    298–299
Organic brain syndrome, 14, 301–324
    age at onset of, 301, 309, 311, 312, 317
    amnestic, 305–306, 308
    delirium as, 301, 303–305, 316
    dementia as, 301, 309–311
    diagnosis and classification of, 302–303
    drug therapy in, 319, 322–323

etiology of, 304
    family–medical staff relationship in, 313,
        315–316, 317, 319, 321, 322, 324
    family reactions to, 301–302, 311–320
    family therapy for
        empathic sharing in, 321
        negotiation in, 323
        obstacles to, 317–320
        principles of, 320–323
        reassessment in, 322
        therapist's role in, 319–320, 321
    global category of, 303
    hallucinosis as, 306–307, 308
    intergenerational view of, 322
    pathology of, 301, 302–311
    personality and behavioral disorders due
        to, 307
    roles in family affected by, 313–314, 318,
        320, 322, 323–324
    subacute, 301, 305–309
Osteosarcoma, in child, family response to,
    284
Output, in systems theory of families, 61
Overidentification, of therapist with family
    facing cancer, 297
Overlearning of behavior, in therapy, 51
Overprotectiveness of parents, and anorexia
    nervosa, 260, 262, 264

Paradoxical directives in family therapy
    for alcoholism, 218–219
    for anorexia nervosa, 273
Paranoia
    multiple family therapy for, 76–77
    in organic brain syndrome, 307, 316
Parent–child interactions
    affective style of, 352–356
    in anorexia nervosa, 256–257, 259–
        260, 262, 264
    assessment of, 331, 337, 339, 345
    autonomy/control conflicts in, 114–115
    and borderline personality, 184–185,
        187–190, 192–193
    cancer affecting, 286–287
    and cognitive development, 92, 109, 115
    communication deviance in, 352
    in disturbed adolescence, 331, 337, 339,
        345
    and ego development, 92, 93
    guilt-inducing, 353, 354

and language development, 91–92
and manic-depressive illness, 126, 127
in maternal depression, 95–97, 101, 103–
    106, 109–110, 112, 113–115
at mealtime, 104–105, 271
and personality development, 91–93
physical abuse in, 95, 206, 211, 338,
    339, 343, 344, 347
and schizophrenia, 77–78, 78–79, 87
and self-image of child, 92–93
and social development, 91–92, 110
in toilet training, 114, 115, 116
videotaping of, 105–106, 112, 115, 331
Peer support groups
for families with fatally ill children, 285
multiple family therapy compared to, 62
Personality, 9, 12–13
of anorectic's parents, 258–259
mother–child relationship affecting, 91–
    93
in organic brain syndrome, 307, 308
Pharmacotherapy. See Drug therapy
Phenothiazine therapy
for psychotic symptoms, 383
for schizophrenia, 22, 23–33, 363
    dose levels in, 23–24, 25–26, 27, 29,
        33
    relapse rate in, 36
Posthospital treatment programs. See
    Aftercare treatment programs
Preschool program, for children of
    depressed mothers, 97, 102–106,
    109, 111, 112
Problem solving
in anorexia nervosa, 262–263
of bipolar patients, 137–138
in community, 47
in family, 47, 48, 49
interpersonal, 47
in job seeking, 47, 49
in narcissistically vulnerable marriages,
    166–167
in schizophrenia, 38, 39, 44–48, 53, 54
steps in, 45–47
Projective mechanisms, 6, 7
in borderline personality, 184, 191
in narcissistically vulnerable marriages,
    167–168, 169, 175–176
Prostitution, after disturbed adolescence,
    340

Pseudodementia, 315
Pseudohostility, 5
Pseudomutuality, 5
Psychiatric treatment, divergence from
    family therapy, 3–8
Psychoanalysis
for patients previously thought
    untreatable, 6, 7
in narcissistically vulnerable marriages,
    175–176
Psychodrama, in multiple family therapy,
    64
Psychosis
drug therapy for, 362–364, 383
hospital-based family therapy for, 399,
    400
multiple family therapy for, 72, 80
Psychosomatic disturbances, of anorectic's
    parents, 258

Reality testing, in multiple family therapy,
    78–79, 86
Reciprocity of communication
family training for, 43
and suicide, 152
Re-enactment, in family therapy for
    alcoholism, 219
Regression, of family with borderline
    adolescent, 189, 190, 191–192
Reinforcement of behavior
shaping in, 50
token economies in, 50
Relapse in schizophrenia, 37
in aftercare program, 22, 25–26, 32, 33–
    34
communication training affecting, 35–56
in drug therapy, 36, 38, 41, 54, 364, 388
and expressed emotion in family, 32, 36–
    39, 363–364
in multiple family therapy, 78
time of risk for, 52
warning signals for, 50–51
Resistance to therapy
in alcoholism, 242
in anorectic's family, 274
in borderline adolescent and family, 193–
    194
in cancer patient and family, 292
in disturbed adolescent's family, 340,
    342, 349

Resistance to therapy *(continued)*
  in hospitalized patient's family, 399
  in husband of depressed mother, 116
  in multiple family therapy, 64–65, 67, 79
Roles in family
  in adolescence, stress due to, 328, 332, 333, 348
  in alcoholism, 211, 215
    and learning of new roles, 243
  and anorexia nervosa, 261, 262, 271, 274
  cancer in family affecting, 286–287
  in communication training, 42–43, 44
  depression about, 91–121, 365, 366. *See also* Maternal depression
  in multiple family therapy, 66
  organic brain syndrome affecting, 313–314, 318, 320, 322, 323–324
  sex differences in, 60, 332, 333
  and suicide, 146, 156–157
Role of therapist. *See* Therapist's role in treatment
Rubber fence family system, 5, 76, 405
Running away, by disturbed adolescents, 338, 342

Sadomasochistic sexual relationships, and suicide, 151
Scapegoating. *See* Blaming behavior
Schizophrenia, 21–88
  assessment of treatment outcome in, 28–32, 33, 53
  behavior management in, 12, 48–52, 54
  blunted affect in, 27, 33
  communication of families with, 4–5, 72–73, 351–354
    expressed emotion in, 11, 32, 36–39, 53, 363–364
    training for, 35–56
  coping mechanisms in, 38, 44–48
  crisis-oriented family therapy in, 24, 27–32, 33, 363
  double-bind theory of, 4–5
  drug therapy for, 21–33, 41
    family therapy with, 359, 362–364, 381, 382–383, 387, 388
    phenothiazine in, 22, 23–33, 36, 363
    relapse rates in, 36, 38, 41, 54, 364, 388
  duration of treatment in, 52–53
  education of family about, 11, 38, 39–42, 54

emotional withdrawal in, 26–27, 33, 72–73
extrafamilial socialization in, 5, 36, 76–77, 364
family risk factors for, 351, 354
  in females, 5
historical background of family therapy for, 4–6
home-based therapy for, 51–52
hospitalization for
  and aftercare treatment programs for, 21–56
  family therapy during, 400, 409, 410
  multiple family therapy during, 58, 62, 74, 75
  and rehospitalization, 9, 11, 22, 25–26, 78
  termination of, 409, 410
and immaturity of parents, 5
insulin coma therapy in, 58
in males, 5
and marriage of parents, 5
maternal, 95
mother–son relationships in, 77–78, 78–79, 87
multiple family therapy for, 12, 52, 58, 62, 71–88, 387
  enhancing drug compliance, 387
  individual family therapy combined with, 80
  relapse rate in, 78
objectives of family therapy for, 24, 27–28
in organic brain syndrome, 307, 316
problem-solving skills in, 38, 39, 44–48, 53, 54
structure of family in, 77–78, 79, 87
warning signals for relapse in, 50–51
Sculpting family
  in alcoholism treatment, 219
  in multiple family therapy, 64
Secrecy in therapy
  avoidance of, 166
  with multiple families, 68, 80, 84
Self-image
  academic achievement affecting, 334–335, 348
  and affective style of family, 353, 354
  in alcoholism, 210
  of anorectic's parents, 254, 255
  in anorexia nervosa, 268

of bipolar patients, 133
of borderline adolescent's parents, 191
of disturbed adolescent, 335–337, 348
of disturbed adolescent's parents, 335, 344
mastectomy affecting, 289
in maternal depression, 98, 111–112, 118
mother–child relationship affecting, 92–93
multiple family therapy affecting, 71–72, 76
in narcissistically vulnerable marriages, 167, 168
of schizophrenic's family, 71–72, 87
Separation anxiety
in borderline personality, 184–186, 187, 189, 190–191, 196–197, 198
in narcissistically vulnerable marriages, 166, 168, 169, 170, 171, 174–175
and suicide, 149–150, 156, 157
in termination of hospitalization, 396–397, 411
Severely disturbed families, structure of, 60
Sexual behavior
in alcoholism, 206, 211, 234, 237
in borderline personality, 183, 184, 193
after disturbed adolescence, 340
drugs affecting, 14, 376, 381, 387
and marital stress, 165, 337
in narcissistically vulnerable marriages, 165, 173, 175, 177, 178
and suicide, 147, 148, 150–152
Shaping, in reinforcement of behavior, 50
Social class, and anorexia nervosa outcome, 266
Social development
genetic and environmental factors in, 94, 110
mother–child relationship affecting, 91–92, 110
Social rehabilitation programs, for depressed mothers, 97–98
Socialization, extrafamilial
of bipolar patients, 133
and borderline personality, 190
in development process, 91
and extra-hospital activities, 405
multiple family therapy for, 76–77
in schizophrenia, 5, 36, 76–77, 364
and suicide, 147, 157
Splitting, 6, 7, 13

in borderline personality, 184
in countertransference phenomena, 15–16
in hosital-based family therapy, 396, 402–408, 412–413
handling of, 406–408, 413
on management of patient, 403, 406–407, 413
signs of, 402–406, 412–413
Stealing by disturbed adolescents, 331, 332, 333, 338, 340, 342
Stress response syndromes and anorexia nervosa, 255–257
Structures of families
disturbed and healthy compared, 59–60
enmeshed. See Enmeshed family system
in multiple family therapy, 59–60, 63, 67, 77–78
and schizophrenia, 77–78, 78–79, 87
and suicide, 146–147, 156–157
Subsystems, in systems theory of families, 61, 65
Suicidal behavior, 12, 145–160
of adolescents, 192, 193, 343
and affective disturbances, 147–154
age-dependent treatment of, 154
and aggression, 147–148, 152
alcoholism in, 150
anxiety in, 146, 147, 148, 149–150, 156, 157
assessment of, 154–155
in borderline personality, 148, 192, 193
and cancer in family, 287, 288
and communication disturbances, 147, 148–149, 152, 155, 157–158
and depressed family atmosphere, 147, 152–153
family approach to treatment of, 155–159
hospital-based, 400, 403, 407
family characteristics common in, 146–147
hopelessness, despair, and giving up in, 153–154, 155
in maternal depresion, 108
in narcissistically vulnerable marriages, 166, 168, 179, 180
and sexual disturbances, 147, 148, 150–152
and social role, 156–157
Suprasystem, in systems theory of families, 61, 62, 65

Suspiciousness
  in narcissistically vulnerable marriages,
    165, 168
  of schizophrenics, 29
Systems theory of families, 7–8, 60–62
  alcoholism in, 204–206, 207–208, 215
  anorexia nervosa in, 261–265
  competition in, 66
  mother–child relationship in, 91–92
  in multiple family therapy, 60–62, 65,
    67–68
  in narcissistically vulnerable marriages,
    168, 180–181
  personality disorders in, 12–13
  rubber fence families in, 5, 76, 405
  system malfunctions in, 61–62

Task assignments in therapy
  in alcoholism, 218
  in anorexia nervosa, 273
  in schizophrenia, 44, 48, 51
Temporal lobe lesions, 307
Terminal illness, and helping family cope,
    281–300
Termination
  of drug therapy, 384–385, 389
  of hospitalization, 396–397, 408–412,
    413
  of multiple family therapy, 84–85, 87
Thalamic lesions, bilateral, 307
Thematic Apperception Test, 330, 352
Therapist's role in treatment
  in alcoholism, 219, 220–221, 234–235,
    240
  in anorexia nervosa, 269, 273–274
  in bipolar illness, 135
  in borderline adolescence, 194–197
  with cancer patient and family, 282–283,
    297–299
  in drug therapy, 376–380, 382–383,
    388–389, 390–391
  as model for effective communication, 44
  in multiple family therapy, 66, 67, 74, 83,
    85–86
  in narcissistically vulnerable marriages,
    170–171, 172, 178
  in organic brain syndrome, 319–320,
    321
  in schizophrenia, 32
Thought disorders, in schizophrenia, 26,
    30–32, 33

Thresholds Mothers' Project, 12, 97–118
  assessment procedures of, 99, 103, 109,
    114
  case study of, 108–117
  children in, 101–103, 109–110
  goals of, 97, 106–108, 117
  husbands in, 98, 101, 108, 115–117
  lunchtime in, 104–105
  mother–child dyad in, 101, 103–106,
    109–110, 113–115
  mothers in, 99–101, 108, 110–112
  programs of, 97–99
  staff for, 98
  videotape intervention in, 105–106, 112,
    115
Time-out, in coping with stressful
    situations, 50
Toilet training, parent–child conflicts in,
    114, 115, 116
Token economies, for behavior
    reinforcement, 50
Toxic psychoses, 307
Transfer of behavior, from therapy setting to
    home environment, 51–52
Transference phenomena, narcissistic, 176
Treatment site
  in anorexia nervosa, 266, 271, 272
  for cancer patient and family, 292
  in hospitals. See Hospitalization
  in multiple family therapy, 59, 75, 85,
    411–412, 413
  in schizophrenia, 51–52
  and transfer of behavior to home
    environment, 51–52
Trial-and-error learning, in multiple family
    therapy, 66, 74
Trust
  in borderline personality, 184, 187, 194,
    195, 197
  extramarital affairs affecting, 165

UCLA Family Project, disturbed
    adolescents in, 329–356
UCLA Word Association Test, 330
Uncooperativeness, of schizophrenics, 29

Verbal content of communication, in family
    communication training, 43, 44
Veterans, in multiple family therapy, 72, 75,
    87

Videotaping of therapy
  in alcoholism, 231, 232
  in anorexia nervosa, 270
  disturbed adolescents in, 331
  in maternal depression, 105–106, 112, 115
  multiple families in, 59, 64, 67
Violent behavior
  in alcoholism, 206, 210, 211, 232, 237, 338, 339
  in narcissistically vulnerable marriage, 172, 174
Vocational rehabilitation
  in alcoholism, 205, 206
  in maternal depression, 97–98, 111
  in schizophrenia, 36, 37
Vulnerability, narcissistic, in marriage, 163–182

WAIS test, 330
Warning signals
  of alcoholism, 236–237

of mood changes in bipolar illness, 125–126
  in schizophrenia relapse, 50–51
Weissman Dysfunctional Attitude Scale, 132
WISC tests, 330
Withdrawal
  from drugs
    in alcoholism, 240–243, 305, 314–315
    delirium in, 305, 314–315
  emotional
    in alcoholism, 211
    in schizophrenia, 26–27, 33, 72–73

Yes–no exercise, in multiple family therapy, 63

Zero-sum game, 271
Zulliger Test, 330